Special Education for Adolescents

Issues and Perspectives

Douglas Cullinan

Michael H. Epstein

Northern Illinois University

Charles E. Merrill Publishing Co.
A Bell & Howell Company
Columbus   Toronto   London   Sydney

The Merrill Personal Perspectives in Special Education Series
James M. Kauffman, editor

Published by Charles E. Merrill Publishing Company
A Bell and Howell Company
Columbus, Ohio 43216

This book was set in Optima.
The production editor was Jan Hall.
The cover was prepared by Will Chenoweth.

Photo on p. i by E.F. Bernstein.

Library of Congress Catalog Card Number: 78–61205

International Standard Book Number: 0–675–08407–5

Printed in the United States of America

1 2 3 4 5 6 7 8 9 10/ 85 84 83 82 81 80 79

Foreword

Little children who fail at school, who lack social graces, or who have inferior cognitive abilities tug at most people's heartstrings. We are apt to assume immediately that young handicapped children's behavioral or cognitive faults are not much of their own making and that such faults are mostly due to cruel environmental circumstances. Working with tykes who are failures or misfits is often accompanied by a generosity of spirit, an attitude of pity, an emulation of the Divine imperative, "Suffer the little children to come unto me." But it is hard for most of us to be so sympathetic toward adolescents who need special help. We hold them more accountable (psychologically at least, if not legally) for their failures and misdeeds. Our pity is called forth by their victims. By the time behaviorally handicapped children reach adolescence, they have lost their status as innocents—they indulge in the iniquities of youth.

Differences in social attitudes toward handicapped young children and handicapped adolescents are reflected in programmatic differences for these groups at every level of the educational system. From the federal to local level, the emphasis is on programs for young children. The early years (so the argument goes) are the crucial ones, the malleable ones, the hopeful ones. We use a medical analogy to argue that academic and behavior problems, like cancer, must be caught early or the prognosis is bad. The most extreme argument is that we might as well write off the generation that has reached adolescence and concentrate our preventative and therapeutic efforts on the younger children with whom we have a reasonable chance of success.

There are understandable reasons for gloomy views of programs for adolescents. The behavior of adolescents is more complicated than that of younger children. Sex, drugs, cars, and jobs add their complexities to the scene. Academic work is often more difficult. Adolescents are typically able to use language and physical prowess as elaborate and effective weapons against their peers and adults in ways that younger children do not dream of or do not dare. Developmental changes come fast and furiously, making predictable behavior and steady progress unlikely. To work effectively with adolescents, one must, therefore, be able to control a very intricate set of interpersonal relationships and deal with a multifarious set of potential outcomes. It is no wonder that few people want to tackle the job.

This book says there is hope. It says the job is not impossible. It says the rewards to be obtained by working with mildly retarded, emotionally disturbed, and learning disabled adolescents can rival or surpass those that come from working with younger children. I hope it also represents a reassessment of our level of concern for handicapped adolescents and a determination to see that they must not be special education's slighted population.

James M. Kauffman
University of Virginia

Preface

People who are neither children nor adults exist in a state of dynamic limbo known as *adolescence*. This period is characterized by many exhiliarating, embarrassing, and bewildering new experiences often seemingly beyond the adolescent's control. Successful human adjustment calls for mastery of numerous social, cognitive, and other developmental skills. During adolescence, some individuals give the first indications that they cannot meet expectations. Other children already identified as having problems may continue in these deviant patterns of conduct and achievement or worsen during adolescence. There can be no doubt that these teen-agers challenge educators and other helping professionals to understand them and to help them deal effectively with their learning, adjustment, and career problems.

Despite their need for help, adolescents receive less attention to their problems than do children, especially in the area of special education. Compared to their younger counterparts, handicapped adolescents are less frequently addressed in teacher preparation programs, funding provisions, research efforts, and other manifestations of professional interest and concern.

How did this imbalance come about? First, "normal" adjustment for adolescents includes a greater range of possible behavior patterns than for younger children, so identifying adolescents in need of help is difficult. Second, because adolescents should and do have more to do with determining their own goals, educational and other objectives are less clear-cut for them than for younger children. Additionally, many professionals may prefer not to work with teen-agers because young people often fail to appreciate or even resist intervention efforts.

Understandable as the Lilliputian emphasis on adolescent handicaps might be, these individuals must now begin to receive long-overdue services. Recent legal and judicial mandates have underscored the calls for professional attention to handicapped youth. Teachers and other workers in the field who have been "doing the best we can" are now insisting upon advanced training opportunities featuring a strong orientation to intervention practices as well as current facts and theories. To comply, teacher preparation programs will need, more than ever, to draw upon the expertise of successful professionals across disciplines. Those who are best prepared to deliver effective services to handicapped adolescents need to be competent in the areas of adolescent development, diagnostic and curricular decision making, behavior management, alternative educational services, model educational programs, and professional issues. At this early stage of special education for adolescents, it is best to turn to some of the major individuals who have worked with this population. Their experiences and views can provide the logical foundation for the further development of a technology of special education for handicapped adolescents.

This book, designed to give students in special education for adolescents a firsthand account of the development of secondary school and related programs for handicapped youth, will help the reader gain a broad perspective. The contributors were chosen for their expertise in a particular topic, for their acknowledged accomplishments (most chapters were authored by individuals who have made and will continue to make a significant impact on the field) and for their suitability as professional role models in an area experiencing rapid growth. The authors were encouraged to recount in a personal manner some of their early professional experiences. Each chapter features a detailed exposition of a selected issue associated with the contributors or contributors' present and future involvement.

The first chapter provides an overview on the historical background, current developments, and future directions for special education for adolescents. Chapters 2, 3, and 4 discuss the characteristics of handicapped adolescents and the diagnostic, curricular, and academic programming considerations appropriate for these youth. The new areas of specialization in vocational education and training, orientation and education for a career, and drug education are described in chapters 5 through 7. Chapters 8 through 10 present current strategies of managing the behavior of adolescents in a variety of settings. In chapters 11 and 12, legal issues and obstacles to educating handicapped adolescents are discussed. In this book the pronoun *he* will be used for ease in reading. No sexual bias is intended.

We are grateful for the assistance of many people as we produced this book, including Susan Scarpitta, James Kauffman, and Jan Hall. Most of all, we appreciate the encouragement and patience of our families as we moved along to completion.

Contents

Contents

Education of Handicapped Adolescents: An Overview

1

Michael H. Epstein
Douglas Cullinan

The nature and role of secondary education in America have evolved a great deal during this century. In 1900, only about 10% of adolescents were educated in high schools, compared to over 90% of today's adolescents (National Panel of High School and Adolescent Education, 1976). At the turn of the century, the goals of high school education were predominantly scholarly and academic ones for children of the elite. Now the educational offerings of high schools are extremely diverse, and only a portion is concerned with the traditional academic subjects. The school is no longer merely *one* of society's institutions for acculturating adolescents, along with the home, the church, and job apprenticeship arrangements; today the high school is the major institution serving socialization and social engineering objectives and purposes for most adolescents.

Too frequently, however, secondary education has not been available to adolescents whose interaction with formal education is not satisfactory in some way. The intellectual, social, and educational performance of these youngsters is often in discord with expectations of educators and other pupils. To facilitate exceptional arrangements for these pupils, their problems are commonly designated *learning disability, behavior disorder, mental retardation, social maladjustment,* or some similar term indicating a "mild handicap."

1

The exceptional arrangements have not always provided much advantage to the designated individuals. For a variety of reasons, soon to be discussed, there is growing concern for the education of mildly handicapped adolescents. One certain consequence of this movement is that the American high school will have to become even more diverse than it is now. Regular secondary educators, special educators, vocational educators, administrators, educational support personnel, and other professionals involved with the education of adolescents will have to apply their talents to the task, learning from each other about service to mildly handicapped adolescent pupils.

The job can be botched, and no doubt will be in many cases; after all, there are ample difficulties to which unsuccessful efforts can be attributed. There will also be successful programs, each emphasizing somewhat different components designed to meet particular needs and harmonize with local preferences. It is not possible now to specify exactly the what and how of special education for mildly handicapped adolescents. We do know some important considerations for those who are or will be delivering such services, however; these include certain foundation concepts, principles related to the assessment, instruction, and management of the mildly handicapped, and issues closely tied to successful program delivery. These topics are addressed throughout this book.

Theories of Adolescent Development

Although writings on the psychological functioning of adolescents may not be quite as numerous as those dealing with infants and children, there is a wide variety of theories on adolescent development. Perhaps the first modern theory was that of G. Stanley Hall (1904), a pioneer American psychologist whose viewpoints shaped the study of adolescence for the first few decades of the twentieth century. Hall's position was strongly influenced by the work of Darwin and others who developed theories of evolution. He believed that the growth and development of an individual occur in a series of stages reiterating those through which Homo sapiens has evolved. Just as the stages of humans as a species were biologically determined, he thought that the stages in human development are environment or culture. Regarding the adolescent stage, Hall believed that it is characterized by "storm and stress," in that abilities emerge rapidly and abruptly, and emotions are more influential than the intellect in determining behavior.

Hall's theory of adolescence obviously leans heavily on biological factors, and in this respect it is like other influential viewpoints of the first half of this century. For example, Freudian theories of adolescence emphasize a resurgence of sexual urges that have been successfully repressed during the earlier latency stage of development. At the onset of latency, the child has had to repress sexual and aggressive impulses in order to resolve the Oedipus complex. By doing this, the youngster can retain the affection of and attachments to his parents and pursue the other matters of childhood. The resurgence of sexuality in adolescence revives the Oedipal feelings, but now the adolescent's task is not to repress but to totally relinquish incestuous and aggressive wishes, in order to move away from his parents toward an independent adult orientation. As a result, the adolescent alternatively loves and hates his parents, vacillates between dependence and revolt, is both idalistic and self-centered; and this pattern, to the Freudians, is perfectly normal adolescent behavior. Once the revival of the Oedipus conflict is resolved and separation from parents is achieved, the individual experiences grief and mourning at the loss of childhood.

Another biologically oriented theory of adolescent development, and probably the one which most heavily invokes innate maturational processes, is that of Gesell (e.g., Gesell, Ilg, Ames, 1956). Basing his research on a longitudinal study of boys and girls up to 16 years of age, Gesell came to believe that each individual passes through common developmental cycles repeated throughout development. Each cycle involves a characteristic pattern of development that occurs at progressively more advanced levels of maturation, like the repeating revolutions of a spiral. Within each cycle, he found that development proceeds unevenly, with dominance first shown by some systems, then others; the sequence and timing is largely determined by biological factors. The developmental progressions occurring between 11 and 16 years resemble those seen in the years between early infancy and 5, and again between 6 and 10 years.

Other theories of adolescence have given less emphasis to constitutional influences upon the development of the adolescent. For instance, neo-Freudian positions are frequently oriented to broad sociological, anthropological, and other environmental psychological viewpoints in which the adolescent personality is seen as largely culturally determined. For instance, Sullivan (1953) sees adolescence as divided into two periods, early and late. Early adolescence begins at puberty and is largely concerned with "social intimacy," a basic need; the adolescent must deal with the fact that the genital areas of the body are potentially available in the quest for social intimacy. The interaction of this basic motivation toward social intimacy and one's new bodily capabilities leads to a related but separate motivational system identified by Sullivan as lust. The early adolescent must attempt to bring these two needs into harmony with a third, the need for freedom from anxiety. Late adolescence begins, according to Sullivan, when the individual has resolved the sexual issues of early adolescence; it consists of participating in experiences which lead to a realistic picture of one's capabilities and other features of the self. The goals of late adolescence are the development of competence and respect for self and others.

Erikson (1963) describes social psychological development in terms of eight stages, one of which (stage 5) is primarily concerned with adolescence. Stage 5, which Erikson calls "identity versus role confusion," begins with puberty. At that time, although the individual is beginning to realize that the stability and continuity of childhood can no longer be depended upon, he still strives to achieve the old stability and continuity; this is not only futile, but it also revives a number of conflicts similar to those of childhood. The adolescent is increasingly concerned with how others view him; a great deal of effort is directed toward establishing an acceptable self-concept based on trying out a variety of social roles. There are relatively rapid shifts in role models and points of view. Along with these shifts comes a certain amount of unavoidable role confusion; the individual may feel that he does not actually belong in any role. The overall task of adolescence, then, is to experience the different roles and the period of role confusion, finally coming into a realistic appraisal of one's own identity.

Another viewpoint on adolescence is exemplified by Havighurst's formulation of developmental tasks of adolescents (1953). A developmental task is an event determined by cultural or biological factors (or the interaction of these two), occurring at a certain point in an individual's life, which must be successfully resolved if the individual is to develop normally and be able to face subsequent developmental tasks. The adolescent developmental tasks put forward by Havighurst include (a) achieving more mature relations with peers, (b) adopting the appropriate sex role, (c) recognizing one's bodily capabilities and limitations, (d) reaching emotional independence from parents, (e) recognizing that one is potentially economically independent, (f) initiating preparation for a vocational role, (g) beginning preparations for family life, (h) developing skills required for participation as a citizen of the community, (i) successfully pursuing and achieving social responsibility, and (j) acquiring moral judgment and moral behavior. In Havighurst's view, when there are several tasks appropriate to a particular age, the individual who successfully achieves one is likely to successfully achieve others, while the adolescent who fails at a particular developmental task is likely to fail at the others.

More recently, McCandless (1970) has put forward a theory of adolescence based on both biological and social learning principles. In this theory, puberty is ushered in by a new sexual drive which, together with the onset of additional social expectations and influences at this period of life, exposes the adolescent to an assortment of new problems and tasks to be mastered. The combination of biological and social influences assures that the adolescent period is one of great personal change for the individual, for better or for worse. McCandless posits four major areas in which the adolescent must strive for and achieve competence: (a) status, that is, skill and achievement competencies, and self-respect for possessing these competencies, (b) sociality, in terms of having friends, especially very good friends, (c) sexual adjustment, including the broader psychological implications of sexuality, and (d) moral development, the selection of appropriate models and behavior standards through identification and other psychological processes.

The foregoing brief descriptions hardly do justice to the ideas represented, and there are many other worthy positions which could have been reviewed. In order to have a broad foundation upon which to plan and implement specialized education for adolescents, the professional should understand these theories and their implications in depth through appropriate readings (e.g., Ausubel, Montemayor, & Srajian, 1977; Horrocks, 1969; Jersild, Brook, & Brook, 1978). For purposes of this discussion, however, it appears that there are two main features emphasized by the various theories: first, adolescence begins with the onset of puberty, consists of important individual challenges occurring on a very frequent basis, and ends as various aspects of personal independence are achieved; second, adolescence is a time of recognition of many aspects of one's own individuality—the "self"—especially those behavior patterns which indicate that new intellectual, physical, and social competencies are being acquired.

Because education plays such a central role in the lives of our society's adolescents, there should be and is a good deal of interdependence of developmental goals and educational goals of adolescents. That is, developmental goals can hardly be considered apart from the adolescent's participation in formal educational situations, and educational objectives and activities ought to be in harmony with developmental goals. Thus it should be possible to formulate a number of educational goals that have general applicability to adolescents as pupils, and that can facilitate the adolescent's development. Like most goals, these educational goals are idealistic in the sense that not all secondary school pupils will achieve them fully within desirable time limits, but most individuals will achieve them to some extent before leaving the secondary schools. In a real sense, mildly handicapped adolescents are defined by their failure to achieve one or more of these developmental educational goals to an acceptable extent within an acceptable period of time.

Developmental Educational Goals for Adolescents

Social Participation

Ideally, adolescents should use the school to test out, elaborate, and refine social skills. They must do so within the contexts of formal educational offerings, relationships to teachers and other school adults, and the adolescent school subculture. Such social skill building opportunities are reduced if the pupil does not attend school, misses classes, or is merely physically present at instruction. Thus, it is frequently an important first step in the education of mildly handicapped adolescents to increase school and classroom attendance and to build voluntary participation in classroom instruction.

Intellectual Competencies

It hardly needs to be said that a primary educational goal for adolescents is to assure that formal instruction strengthens developing intellectual competencies, provides relevant and extensive information in the tool and specialized subject areas, and leads the individual to self-directed independent exploration of areas for further knowledge. Of course, the vast majority of handicapped adolescents are characterized by—in fact, identified by—serious weaknesses in the ability to competently perform basic skills, including fundamental arithmetic, reading, and oral and written communication skills.

Community Contribution

Because human development takes place in community contexts, it is important that adolescents contribute to the efficient delivery of educational services within the school by working cooperatively with teachers, encouraging their peers to do so, helping maintain public materials, equipment, and other property, contributing positively to the policy making of the school by taking part in school governance, and so on. Pupils who cannot achieve this ideal fully are expected at least to avoid disrupting the educational process by refraining from verbal disorder, motoric disruption, physical aggression, and property destruction, so that the presentation of instruction is not interfered with.

Career Preparation

Another goal of secondary education involves the fact that secondary school pupils are approaching the time in their lives at which they must assume economic productivity and independence. In this society, healthy adult functioning is closely interwoven with career considerations; thus, it is clear that secondary education must help all pupils understand career possibilities, acquire employment or pre-employment skills, and face related considerations involving eventual employment.

In addition to these four major developmental educational goals for secondary pupils, there are other objectives schools should address. For example, it is generally desired that adolescents avoid using (or at least abusing) alcohol, controlled substances, and other intoxicants. The reader can easily think of other areas in which secondary education needs to be active.

For most of these goals and objectives, the greatest discrepancy between the ideal and the real exists with learning and behavioral disturbances. The daily experiences of special and regular educators in the secondary schools provide ample evidence of this, but it is worthwhile to review available data on the extent of critical problems among the nation's adolescents. Of course, not all mildly handicapped secondary pupils contribute to the figures on school nonattendance, academic achievement difficulties, behavioral disorders, and so on. There is little to indicate, however, that the mildly handicapped are less likely to be implicated than the non-handicapped; further, many adolescents are identified as learning disabled, behaviorally disordered, mentally retarded, or socially maladjusted precisely because they do fall significantly short of meeting the developmental educational goals previously described. Thus, although most of this prevalence of information is not specific to mildly handicapped adolescents, it clearly pertains to them.

Parameters of the Adolescent Dilemma

It is obvious that as adolescents pursue developmental educational goals, their behavior will frequently deviate from the desirable

7

and even the minimally acceptable. However, within the adolescent population, rates of school nonattendance, academic disability, mental illness, school violence and vandalism, unemployment, sex-related problems, and drug abuse have skyrocketed. Heavy coverage by the media has aroused citizen awareness of these problems, and the results of government, advocacy group, and other professional studies provide data to support many of the commonly held impressions about how serious the problems are.

School Nonattendance

The number of pupils out of school has become a national problem. According to U.S. Bureau of the Census (1972) data, in 1970 approximately 2 million children between 6 and 17 years of age were not enrolled in school, or 4.8% of school-aged children. The Children's Defense Fund, a nonprofit group organized to advocate on behalf of children and youth, recently analyzed school nonenrollment (1974). Nonenrolled children and youth were categorized as the "excluded" (incontinent, immature), "pushed out" (expelled, dropouts), "partially excluded" (institutionalized), "rejected" (minority youth, troublemakers), and "unknowns" (special needs, immigrants). Children and youth from some segments of society are least likely to be enrolled, of course; or as the Children's Defense Fund (1974) analysis puts it,

> If a child is not white, or is white but not middle-class, does not speak English, is poor, needs special help with seeing, hearing, walking, reading, learning, adjusting, growing up, is pregnant or married at age 15, is not smart enough or is too smart, then in too many places, school officials decide school is not the place for that child. In sum, out of school children share a common characteristic of differentiation by virtue of race, income, physical, mental, or emotional "handicap" and age. (pp. 3–4)

Even if a pupil is enrolled, he may miss much school due to suspensions. In the 1972–73 school year, over a million students were suspended from school, for a total of more than 4 million school days (Children's Defense Fund, 1974). The most frequent reasons for which suspensions occurred were fighting (36.6%), truancy (24.5%), behavior disorders (13.6%), and arguments with adults (8.5%). Secondary school students were suspended more than twice as often as younger students.

Deviant pupils—those with special needs, students with behavior, learning, and/or intellectual disabilities—comprised a significant proportion of the excluded and suspended populations. Unfortunately, these nonenrolled students are the very ones who could profit most from appropriate specialized education at school.

Academic Inability

Upon leaving the educational system, an adolescent needs to be proficient in basic reading, math, writing, and oral expression skills. Handicaps in these areas are obviously likely to restrict independence and opportunity in many areas of life in a technologically advanced society. There is ample evidence that many secondary pupils are handicapped in these areas, however.

For instance, the Department of Health, Education and Welfare examined the physical, psychological, and educational development of 6,227 youths aged 12–17 years, carefully selected to represent noninstitutionalized Americans in this age range (Oliver, 1974). Some of the key indicators of academic competence—grade placement, intellectual ability, and academic performance—are relevant to an overall picture of adolescent educational adjustment. The grade placements of approximately 8% of secondary school students were more than one year below aged-based expectations. About 16% had repeated a grade; academic failure was cited as the primary reason for most of the repeaters. About 20% of pupils showed below average intellectual ability and almost 30% were low achievers, as indicated by teacher judgments (and largely confirmed by standardized testing). Special education resources beyond the regular classroom were recommended for almost 20% of the students, of whom about one-third were recommended for remedial reading and an additional one-third were recommended for services for the slow learner. Compared to pupils who were not experiencing academic achievement problems, those whose achievement was poor were about four times as likely to show behavior problems of various kinds. Clearly, the findings of this massive nationwide survey indicate that many secondary schoolers are experiencing difficulties in their academic adjustment.

The National Advisory Committee on Dyslexia and Related Reading Disorders (1969) presented data suggesting that 8 million children and youth in elementary and secondary schools will not learn to read adequately. Approximately one student in seven is handicapped to such an extent that the ability to acquire reading skills is impaired. The committee further pointed out that reading and related academic disorders are found in all subdivisions of society.

9

Other reports (e.g., National Assessment of Educational Progress, 1975; Tolor, 1970) confirm that large percentages of adolescent pupils are unable to show even basic competencies in the areas of reading, mathematics, and communication. Many of these pupils need specialized intervention if they are to have a "fighting chance" to acquire fundamental academic competencies.

Psychopathology

Those who have closely studied adolescent mental health hold that this developmental period may demand the most complex and challenging set of adjustments in the life span (e.g., Joint Commission on the Mental Health of Children, 1973). Other authorities have noted that today's adolescent appears to be more alienated, depressed, and in need of assistance than his counterpart of a generation ago (Bronfenbrenner, 1974; Coleman, 1974).

Defining and assessing mental health is difficult, perhaps especially so for adolescents; however, there are a number of indicators hinting at the magnitude of the problems. For instance, mental hospitals are now admitting more and more young people diagnosed as having impulse disorders and acting-out behavior (Public Health Service, 1975). Approximately 20% of all psychiatric patients in 1971 were under 18 years of age (Social Research Group, 1975). In that same year, 140,000 in-patient psychiatric care episodes involved individuals 18 and under, a 32% increase over the previous 2-year period. The most dramatic indicator of mental health problems is the mounting rate of suicide among adolescents. For example, the annual suicide rate for white youths 15 to 19 years of age rose 171% between 1950 and 1975, from 2.8 to 7.6 deaths per 100,000 persons (Wynne, 1978), even though the general population suicide rate remained relatively stable. Presently, suicide is the third leading cause of death for older adolescents.

These mental illness data apply to adolescents in general, but clearly a significant number of the mildly handicapped are involved. Secondary school special educators are in the forefront of the effort to educate and treat adolescents who are alienated, depressed, aggressive, and show other disturbed and disturbing patterns of behavior.

School Violence and Vandalism

Throughout the country, school administrators, teachers, parents, and students are being confronted with a different educational problem, school violence and vandalism. Only a decade ago, school disruption and destruction of property were isolated problems, viewed as relatively minor; but today these same issues have risen to a position of pressing concern (Subcommittee to Investigate Juvenile Delinquency, 1975). The levels of violence and vandalism have escalated to the point where the task of education has been made visibly more difficult.

A special Senate subcommittee formed to study crime in our nation's schools released a report which documents the frequency and intensity of school violence and vandalism (Subcommittee to Investigate Juvenile Delinquency, 1975). Based on a survey of 757 school systems, the report found alarming increases in school violence between 1970 and 1973: homicides increased 18.5%; rapes and attempted rapes increased 40.1%; robberies increased 36.7%; assaults on students increased 85.3%; assaults on teachers increased 77.4%; burglaries on school buildings increased 37.5%; and weapons confiscated on school grounds increased by 54.4%. Other surveys support these alarming data, and more recent evidence indicates that the spiraling trend has continued (Neill, 1978). Concomitantly, school vandalism has mushroomed: the cost of vandalism, theft, and arson for 1973 has been set at $500 million, undoubtably a conservative figure because it does not account for the costs of security, extra staff, insurance, regular staff labor required to repair minor damage. Still, the half-billion figure is grim enough, especially when put in perspective:

> This $500 million vandalism cost represents over $10 per year for every school student, and in fact equals the total cost amount expended on textbooks throughout the country in 1972. (Subcommittee to Investigate Juvenile Delinquency, 1975, p. 6)

Dollar figures and prevalence data do not accurately portray the complete impact of school violence and vandalism on our educational system. Funds spent for security or repair purposes invariably reduce allocations reserved for institutional and supportive services for children. Worse, the atmosphere created by violence and vandalism negatively affects the feelings and productivity of students and staff. Students become fearful, distrustful, and alienated from the school environment; teachers must divert their energies away from instruction and may become more apprehensive of their students. Without question, the rise in school crime and destruction has brought schools precariously close to the point where their mission to children and youth is in jeopardy.

Vocational Problems

Although there are many yardsticks to measure successful transition from adolescence to adulthood, none is more meaningful than employment. The ability to train for and secure gainful and purposeful employment is, for better or for worse, used by society to ascertain an individual's success. If the adolescent has no general or specific vocational skills, if employment opportunities are scarce, or if job performance produces no satisfaction, the individual may be expected to have difficulty assimilating into society (O'Toole, 1973). For a variety of reasons, some beyond the control of the schools, secondary school pupils, especially the mildly handicapped, are frequently ill equipped to move from school to work.

The problem of teenage unemployment is not new, but the magnitude of the problem is increasing (Law Enforcement Assistance Administration, 1976). The proportion of unemployed workers who are youths has roughly doubled in the last two decades (e.g., 1955, 15.8%; 1973, 28.5%). The rate of youth unemployment is about triple that of all workers.

A number of critical factors have been identified as aggravating the youth employment situation (Congressional Budget Office, 1976; Law Enforcement Assistance Administration, 1976). Perhaps the most unfortunate of these is the isolation of the major institutions charged with the responsibility for career training: employers, schools, and manpower agencies. Specifically, employers have been divorced from educational institutions and are ill informed as to what youths can offer; schools have generally neglected the career and vocational needs of students; and public vocational agencies have provided minimal informational services to youths in school. Concern for the employment problems of youth has led to massive monetary commitments by public and private agencies to remedy the situation: between 1964 and 1974, 14,439 billion were invested in various types of manpower programs (Hoyt, 1977). However, this effort appears to have been fragmented; in any event, results have been equivocal.

The behavioral and learning problems of the mildly handicapped adolescent complicate the question of employment. Special education has infrequently afforded the optimum in employment guidance and training to its clients. The importance of specialized vocational and career education is readily apparent. According to the Deputy Commissioner of the Bureau of Education for the Handicapped, Edwin Martin,

> Most people would agree that an important index of fulfillment and competence in our society is to be appropriately employed. Yet our educational system for handicapped children is just beginning to point toward this end. From two-thirds to three-fourths of all special education programs are at the elementary school level, and in many, preparation for the world of work is only indirectly involved. Only 21 percent of handicapped children leaving school in the next 4 years will be fully employed or go on to college (1972, pp. 523–524).

Drug Abuse

Drug use can be defined as the introduction into the body of "any substance other than food which by its chemical nature affects the structure or function of the living organism" (National Commission on Marijuana and Drug Abuse, 1973, p. 9). By this definition, alcohol and cigarettes are no less drugs than psychoactive compounds such as heroin, cocaine, and marijuana. The definition of *drug abuse* is more difficult; cultural, temporal, situational, and other considerations complicate a clear specification of this point. What is certain is that drugs are used and abused widely by adolescents.

A wide variety of motivations have been put forward for drug use, including experimentation, social facilitation, countercultural rebellion, and mood alteration, to name a few. Some detrimental consequences of drug use include its risks to health, the danger of psychological and/or physiological dependence, and the potential for avoiding the need to confront realities. National surveys indicate that by 7th grade, 63% of boys and 54% of girls have experimented with alcohol, and that by 12th grade these percentages have increased to 93% and 87%, respectively (Social Research Group, 1975). Moreover, one of seven male high school students becomes intoxicated at least once weekly. Based on their own national survey and a review of other studies, the National Commission on Marijuana and Drug Abuse (1973) concluded that the incidence of drug use among secondary school students has increased, but the large majority of students do not intend to continue use in the near future. It was suggested that many adolescents who try drugs discontinue use after satisfying their curiosity. Data indicated that relatively few adolescents use hallucinogens (4.8%), glue (6.4%), cocaine (1.5%), heroin (.6%) and marijuana (14.8%). Even if the incidence of illegal drug use among secondary school students is low, the actual numbers are great; and for the particular youths involved and the school officials responsible for these students, there is a significant problem.

The increases in drug abuse have led to proposals and programs aimed at this problem, and large investments of time and money. Secondary educators are involved in this situation in several ways. At the most basic level, for example, many teachers report having to deal with pupils who come to class intoxicated on alcohol and/ or drugs. Also, many school drug-abuse prevention efforts involve general, school-wide campaigns rather than isolated instruction.

The nature and degree of drug abuse among mildly handicapped youth is not known; separate prevalence data have not been collected. Nonetheless, certain educational changes may bring the handicapped adolescent into greater contact with the problem. For example, as greater numbers of mildly handicapped adolescents are placed into the educational mainstream, the availability of illegal substances and drug-abusing models will probably increase.

Sex-related Problems

Whether sexual mores and activities of teenagers have changed significantly in the last two decades is an issue which has no doubt stimulated interesting conversations, debates, and publications. The unfortunate consequences of adolescent sexual activities are not in doubt, however; for example, teenage venereal disease and pregnancy are epidemic. According to Public Health Service (1975) data, reported cases of gonorrhea rose more than 200% between 1956 and 1974. During this period the general population rate of syphilis stabilized, but the incidence among adolescents increased over 100%. Paradoxically, these increases are occurring at a time when venereal disease information, prevention, and treatment services are widely available.

A second barometer of sex-related problems among adolescents is the rate of teenage pregnancies. Between 1950 and 1975, for example, illegitimate births for white females 15 to 19 years of age rose from 5.1 to 12.1 per thousand (National Center for Health Statistics, 1976). Current indications are that:

> One of every ten girls in the United States will give birth
> to a baby before reaching age 18. . . . One of every ten
> school-age girls is a mother, and 17 percent of these have

two children. This totals about 210,000 girls a year. One-sixth of this 210,000—or about 35,000—are less than 16 years old. . . . Only about 10 percent of the 210,000 are served by maternity homes, and only 15 percent place their babies for adoption. In other words, more than 85 percent attempt to mother the child. (Children's Defense Fund, 1974, p. 68.

Again, it is tragically ironic that these increases coincide with greater availability of information on sexual relations, contraceptive devices, and abortions (Wynne, 1978). The pregnancy statistics are alarming for several reasons. Children born to immature females may be "at risk" for central nervous system and other pathology (Ferreira, 1970; Public Health Service, 1975), due to higher rates of toxemia, labor and delivery complications, cesarean sections, and other pre- and perinatal problems than more mature women. Additionally, pregnancy is the major reason for excluding girls from school in the United States. Thus, the child of an adolescent is likely to be reared by a mother whose education has been prematurely interrupted or terminated. Thus, to the personal, individual difficulties in many cases of adolescents pregnancy may be added enduring societal responsibilities to the offspring of unwanted pregnancies.

It may be that increased integration of mildly handicapped adolescents into regular educational situations will heighten existing problems related to venereal disease and unplanned pregnancy. Certainly, youngsters with learning and behavioral disorders are no better equipped to face these problems than the nonhandicapped. The roles of special educators in sexuality education very much need to be addressed.

This listing of problems of adolescents could be extended, and other situations of particular local concern will most likely need to be considered as practitioners develop and adjust their particular programs of special educational intervention. The problems are undeniably massive, but little can be achieved through excessive hand-wringing or breast-beating. Perhaps these problems are central to the human condition; in some way they have probably confronted us throughout history, and it may be unrealistic to believe that they will ever be fully solved. At any rate, handicapping conditions of adolescence are much more than an educational challenge; they concern most facets of society. Still, one of the most important facets of society is education, so educators do have a major role in attacking handicapping conditions of adolescence.

The education profession has taken its lumps regarding how well it is suited to provide for adolescents' developmental educational goals; schools have been accused—justifiably, no doubt, to some extent—of bureaucratic ineptness, lack of creative teaching practices, role confusion, irrelevance to the real world, and assorted other transgressions (Coleman, 1966; Joint Commission on the Mental Health of Children, 1973). But education has traditionally been the springboard to upward mobility in our society and can similarly facilitate success for many handicapped youths. In fact, school may be the principal institution for servicing the handicapped adolescent. Hobbs (1975a, 1975b) cogently noted a number of reasons for assigning this responsibility to the schools.

1. Schools are the primary socialization agency designed to help the family induct the youth into our culture.
2. They are presently assigned to provide educational services; their responsibilities could be broadened to include the other necessary services.
3. Schools have more expertise in educating youth than other agencies, and the problems of mildly handicapped youth are largely educational in nature.
4. Schools are geographically central, an important practical consideration in providing a comprehensive program.
5. Schools have the physical facilities and space to house the comprehensive services.

Thus, formal education has the potential to promote the welfare of all youth; and of all of society's institutions, schools may be especially suited to take the lead in improving the lives of the mildly handicapped.

Legal Impetus

Although the viability of special educational services for mildly handicapped adolescents depends predominantly on the talents and efforts of individual practitioners and local working groups, some obstacles to service are of such general concern that they might best be resolved at a different level. For instance, many districts have historically hesitated to initiate or expand special education for pupils who have needed it, not out of malice but for various logical reasons. The action of parent organizations and other advocacy groups has often succeeded in convincing the proper officials that the needed services have to be provided.

During the present decade, legal developments have reduced the need to show that mildly handicapped adolescents, for instance, *ought* to receive special education. In the early 1970s, a "quiet revolution" began which eventually established the *right* of all handicapped children and youth to an appropriate education (Abeson & Zettel, 1977). Two court cases have been prominent in confirming the right to education: *Pennsylvania Association for Retarded Citizens (PARC)* v. *Commonwealth of Pennsylvania* (1972) and *Mills* v. *Board of Education of the District of Columbia* (1972). In 1972, PARC filed a class action suit charging that the Commonwealth of Pennsylvania failed to provide a public education to mentally retarded children and youth. The consent agreement signed by both parties established the concept of the "right to education" for all retarded children and youth in Pennsylvania. According to the agreement, the state was given 90 days to identify all retarded children and youth excluded from public education, and further, to begin teaching all retarded children and youth by September 1972. A similar case, *Mills,* was brought in 1971 by seven parents of the handicapped on behalf of *all* handicapped children and youth, that is, the behaviorally disordered, physically handicapped, and delinquent, as well as the mentally retarded. The court decreed that no child, regardless of handicapping condition, could be excluded from a public education in the District.

Based on these and other court decisions, recent federal legislation has set a national policy that for the first time guarantees the right of all handicapped children and youth to a public education. The Education for All Handicapped Children Act (P.L. 94–142), signed by President Ford in November 1975, was due to be implemented in September 1978. The purpose of P.L. 94–142, as specified by Congress, is to "assure that all handicapped children have available to them, within the time periods specified, a free appropriate public education which emphasizes special education and related services designed to meet their unique needs" (P.L. 94–142, 1975, Sec. 3, c). P.L. 94–142 establishes national policy regarding the education of handicapped children and youth. Beyond policy, the law insures a number of basic rights, as follows:

1. All handicapped individuals have a right to a free public education in the least restrictive environment.
2. Diagnostic and evaluation materials and procedures must be

appropriate to the child or youth; this provision is intended to eliminate discriminatory biases in testing minority and culturally different children and youth.

3. A written individualized education program has to be provided for each handicapped child or youth, specifying present levels of performance, educational goals, services to be provided, and evaluation procedures.

4. Due process is to be afforded each individual and his family, insuring that the rights of the handicapped child or youth will be protected.

Special Education for Adolescents: Past and Future

The number of potential candidates for specialized educational services at the secondary school level is very large. Estimates by the U.S. Bureau of the Census for 1973 indicated that there were 42 million individuals in the United States aged 10–19. If this group were to be considered "adolescents" and if a conservative figure of 5% were used as the incidence of handicapped adolescents, approximately 2.1 million adolescents would qualify for special services; the overwhelming majority would be considered mildly handicapped. That is, they would evidence mental retardation, learning disability, behavior disorder, emotional disturbance, and social maladjustment; further, they would have fallen short on one or more of the developmental educational goals described earlier. A large number would be receiving no specialized educational services and many would be underserved, despite the clear legal and educational obligations to provide services to this population.

There are a number of ways to determine the nature and scope of educational services available and professional commitment to a handicapped population. As will be apparent from available indices, a serious shortage of services and commitment to the adolescent has and does exist.

Historically, mildly handicapped adolescents have been ignored compared to their elementary-aged counterparts (Lerner, 1976; Nelson & Kauffman, 1977; Wiederholt, 1978). Although accurate information regarding youths served and those in need of services is difficult to obtain, a number of studies indicate that mildly handicapped adolescents are both unserved and underserved. A national survey by Metz (1973) revealed that many youths were unserved by their local educational institutions. Figure 1–1 depicts the percentages of all handicapped groups receiving educational services in 1970. Of 314,000 learning disabled adolescents, only 172,000 were receiving instruction; of 160,000 behaviorally disordered adolescents, only 20,000 were receiving instruction; and of 257,000 mentally retarded adolescents, 218,000 were receiving instruction. The data on learning disabled and behaviorally disordered indicate that approximately half of these adolescents were not receiving educational services. Although the figures for the mentally retarded portray a high degree of services, there is evidence that many of their "educational" programs are work-oriented with little supportive vocational and career education; not only do these inadequate programs remove retarded adolescents from the educational main-

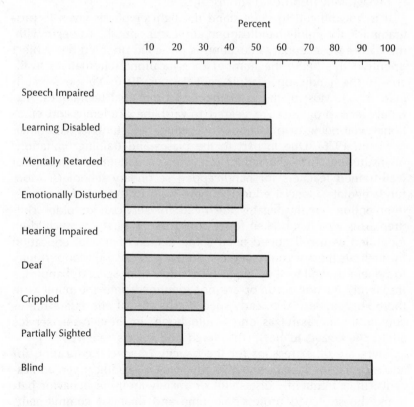

FIGURE 1–1
Percent of secondary school handicapped pupils receiving special instruction of assistance in school: spring, 1970.

stream, their efficacy has been seriously questioned (Dunn, 1968; Hutt & Gibby, 1976). Thus, the figures may appear impressive, but the retarded still are grossly underserved.

More recent information tends to confirm Metz's (1973) findings. Scranton and Downs (1975), for example, conducted a nationwide survey to determine the level of program development for elementary and secondary school learning disabled students. Data from over 10,000 districts in 37 states indicated that almost half of the districts offered elementary school programs, whereas only 9% provided secondary school programs. Regarding behaviorally disordered pupils, a study of Florida counties (Bullock & Brown, 1972) indicated that 69% of the counties examined served elementary-aged pupils, but only 15% of those counties were providing services to behaviorally disordered adolescents.

It is not difficult to understand the light emphasis given to programming for mildly handicapped adolescent pupils. To begin with, the nature of secondary education is not child oriented but subject oriented; this limits the number of educational alternatives available to the handicapped adolescent (Lerner, 1976; Nelson & Kauffman, 1977). Most of the assessment and remedial techniques, materials, and programs are geared toward the academic and emotional well-being of preschool and elementary students (Goodman & Mann, 1976). Due in part to the biases and training limitations of institutions of higher education, there is a definite shortage of well-trained teachers for handicapped secondary schoolers. More fundamentally, special educators have held to the belief that early intervention largely negates the need for services for older children. This idea is mistaken for several reasons. First, many children identified as handicapped need some degree of special education throughout their school careers if they are to have the opportunity to benefit as well as they might from education. Second, handicaps frequently do not occur or are not identified until the pupil is in the higher grades. Also, early special educational efforts are not as commonly successful as one would hope; in these cases, service alternatives have to be reconsidered and efforts renewed.

There are other reasons for the paucity of special education for adolescents: the lack of effective advocacy for handicapped adolescents, their frequently distasteful or anxiety-arousing behavior patterns, the stretched professional time and financial commitments of secondary schools, and so on. All of these have combined to limit the amount and quality of programs available to handicapped adolescents. Nonetheless, the basic fact remains: many handicapped adolescents are in dire need of appropriate educational provisions.

Fortunately, there are encouraging signs that this neglectful trend will be reversed. Activity on a number of fronts indicates that professionals are now recognizing the unique needs of this population. We are now entering an era in which handicapped adolescents are becoming a top priority among professional organizations, federal, state, and local education agencies, and to researchers. These efforts are exciting because they give indication of leading to the development of a range of programmatic alternatives, based on adequate research and evaluation, supported by renewed professional concern and appropriate governmental funding.

Several professional groups now acknowledge that drastic action must occur for handicapped pupils at the secondary school level. For example, the Division for Children with Learning Disabilities of the Council for Exceptional Children held a special conference in 1975 devoted exclusively to the plight of the learning disabled adolescent (Wiederholt, 1978). The following critical recommendations were stressed by the subcommittee:

1) that operational criteria for the identification of adolescents with learning disabilities be developed,

2) that the types of school programs needed at the secondary level be defined,

3) that a continuum of services from preschool to adulthood be established

4) that adolescents' academic, social, emotional, and career needs be the focal points of school programs,

5) that competencies of secondary learning disabilities teachers be defined and appropriate training programs instituted,

6) that a model for evaluating instructional strategies be developed,

7) that increased communication between parents and professionals be established, and

8) that funding and legislative agencies seek input from parents and professionals regarding the needs of learning disabled adolescents. (Wiederholt, 1978, p. 18)

Nelson and Kauffman (1977), writing in the official journal of the Council for Children with Behavioral Disorders of the Council for Exceptional Children, called for immediate, far-reaching educational reform for maladjusted and delinquent adolescents. They argued that educational programming for adolescents with behavior disorders should become a top priority at local, state, and federal levels, with particular effort put toward the preparation of teaching personnel and the search for meaningful alternatives within and outside public education. Further, they underscored the need for valid efficacy studies on educational programs available to adolescents with behavior disorders. In addition, other professional groups and commissions have articulated recommendations for the study and restructuring of educational programs for adolescents (Coleman, 1974; Joint Commission on Mental Health of Children, 1973; White House Conference on Youth, 1971).

The development of new professional organizations in this field is a further signal that changes are underway. Within the American Vocational Association, a new group has been founded: the National Association of Vocational Education Special Needs Personnel, which will advocate solely for the special needs of handicapped adolescents (Brolin, 1977). The Council for Exceptional Children has recently established a Division on Career Development, acknowledging that the career needs of handicapped individuals are a priority concern.

The number of educational programs available to handicapped adolescents will surely increase as state and local educational agencies begin to fully implement P.L. 94–142. There will be innovative programs, and well-trained personnel to staff these programs will be required. The federal government, acutely aware of the need to stimulate the establishment of model programs, has already funded a variety of model secondary school programs and teacher preparation efforts. One such funding service, Title VI–G, provides support for the development of Child Service Demonstration Centers, the express purpose of which is to implement model innovative programs for children and youth with learning disabilities. Presently, 50 such projects are funded throughout the United States, 23 of which include learning-disabled adolescents in their population. Because these programs were funded as exemplary models, their ultimate goal has been to disseminate information on the critical features of the projects, thus providing direction to the field about programming alternatives. Some of the more promising Child Service Demonstration Centers are discussed by Goodman (1978) and Goodman and Mann (1976).

University training programs to prepare teachers for assignments with the mildly handicapped in secondary schools appear to be moving in the right direction. Recently, the Department of Justice awarded 2.8 million dollars to the Office of Education to support continuation of a program to train teachers and community representatives how to cope with school violence and vandalism ("USOE Gets Money," 1978); five regional centers will teach personnel from 300 schools in problem-solving strategies to permit the local educators to search for and implement their own solutions. For the last several years, the Division of Personnel Preparation, Bureau of Education for the Handicapped (BEH) has encouraged institutions of higher education to prepare teachers in career and vocational education, and the development of a number of exemplary career education programs have been supported (Cegelka, 1977).

Over the next few years, the Division for Personnel Preparation is likely to increase support for efforts to train additional professionals to work with handicapped adolescents. Present estimates indicate that 130,000 teachers are currently serving exceptional children and youth, but that to fully implement P.L. 94–142, approximately 250,000 more will be needed (Harvey, 1976). Program development, professional training, and research pertaining to emotionally disturbed adolescents are also recommended BEH priorities (Brown, 1977).

A recent report of the Interagency Panel for Research and Development on Adolescence (Heyneman, Mintz, & Mann, 1977) shows that federal funding for basic and applied research on handicapped adolescents is increasing. In 1977, BEH funded five research institutes in learning disabilities, the major purposes of which are to conduct research on the educational treatment of individuals with learning disabilities, work directly with learning disabilities populations, and develop a set of viable educational interventions (Deshler, 1978). One of these, the Kansas Research Institute for Learning Disabilities, directed by Dr. Edward L. Meyen and Richard L. Schiefelbusch, will focus on adolescents with learning disabilities. The Kansas Research Institute will have three main emphases: conducting epidemiological research, developing and implementing educational intervention strategies, and replicating and evaluating these strategies across various populations and settings (Meyen & Deshler, 1978).

The BEH learning disabilities research institute program should be the model for similar institutes in the area of special education for mildly handicapped adolescents. The list of crucial research topics is long, due to a shortage of appropriate research attention in the past. The research institute model could generate much needed empirically based activity in the development, implementation, and evaluation of assessment, instruction, and other procedures for handicapped secondary schoolers.

Overview of Special Education for Adolescents

To recapitulate, handicapping conditions of adolescents, broadly defined are a continuing source of concern to society. In light of evidence that these problems may be deepening, particularly as they interface with secondary education, a much greater commitment is required of the educational profession and of the larger society. There is good evidence that beneficial changes will occur, and front-line educators will need to be ready to capitalize on favorable events and avoid foreseeable problems. The remainder of this book is intended to support professional efforts to provide appropriate educational services to mildly handicapped adolescents. This goal is approached through material designed to build a foundation of the required knowledge and to suggest and instigate some of the appropriate action.

First, those concerned with the education of mildly handicapped and alienated pupils must understand adolescent development. Professional educators need to know theoretical and philosophical viewpoints, major research findings, intervention techniques and structures, and other critical issues relative to special education in the secondary schools. Those who are going to identify, assess, and provide treatment to mildly handicapped secondary school pupils need to consider the criteria used to make a determination that an individual adolescent's behavior is deviant. Although it goes without saying that every adolescent presents a unique pattern of abilities and personality characteristics, it is sometimes helpful to discriminate major varieties of disability, deviance, and alienation. The prevalence and expected course of each of these types of handicap is of interest to practitioners, because this information may influence program decisions. In chapter 2, Clarizio addresses these points.

Few would take issue with the position that assessment is of central importance in provision of appropriate services to the handicapped. Assessment and the role of assessment in special education for adolescents has rarely been adequately addressed and is a stumbling block to concerned practitioners. In chapter 3, Wiederholt and McNutt have taken a major stride towards demystifying assessment by providing a useful perspective for assessment and outlining recommended guidelines for practice.

Assessment is shown to follow from decisions made about how service will be provided, including the theoretical model that guides service, the educational alternative chosen, and the curricular options selected. The authors propose a three-factor model for assessment, taking into account three major realities of special education for adolescents: that adolescents are rapidly approaching or even beginning to assume adult career and citizenship life roles; that the important variables to assess extend beyond the school setting; and that classroom learning situations are frequently inadequate to provide a medium in which handicapped adolescents can best acquire informational and performance competencies.

The widespread lack of basic academic skills of pupils in America's secondary schools is a source of major concern in our country. Alarm over this situation is expressed by parents, politicians, the media, governmental agencies, as well as by educators and the pupils themselves. Deficiencies in fundamental aspects of reading, arithmetic, and writing characterize the vast majority of disabled, deviant, and alienated adolescent pupils. Students' lack of proficiency in these basic skills is extremely debilitating in and of itself and complicate attempts to provide services of all types. In chapter 4, Goodman deals with this aspect of special education for adolescents by providing a conceptual model clarifying strategies for educational remediation of deficits in the basic skill areas. Those who are to provide such remediation must understand and take account of the several decision points identified and described in this chapter. Drawing on research and experience, Goodman presents recommendations for action to strengthen mildly handicapped adolescents' academic skills, recommendations which deal with the focus of educational efforts, the range of service delivery alternatives, and considerations for curriculum selection.

Schools are intended to structure the transmission of a society's culture, a principal aspect of which involves vocational phenomena. Those who would provide special education for adolescents must understand the historical and legal bases of vocational education for the handicapped, a meaningful definition of vocational education in terms of its similarities to and differences from regular education, and the essential oneness of these services. Brolin and Brolin, in chapter 5, provide this information and more: they capture the arguments for and against vocational education for the handicapped, clearly establish the need for vocational education, and articulate the interelationship of vocational education, career education, and special education. These authors provide a plan for meaningful specialized vocational education for mildly handicapped adolescents by addressing appropriate objectives of such programs, the individual and team roles which have to be carried out by professionals who will deliver these programs, recommended goals to be achieved in delivering specialized vocational educational service, and professional activities required to achieve these programmatic goals.

Few educational topics have received a greater level of interest, development, and debate in recent years than the concept of career education. Cegelka in chapter 6 briefly defines and explains career education, with particular reference to recent developments of importance to handicapped adolescents. Career education for the handicapped is described in terms of a series of recommended objectives, the stagewise components of career education as it should be delivered. The relationships of career education to vocational, occupational, and special education are discussed, with special reference to how career education fits into available special education delivery structures. The author offers concrete recommendations on implementing career education for the handicapped: performance assessment procedures, competency-based curricular options, and an enumeration of resources to help the practitioner flesh out the recommendations outlined. Finally, there are descriptions of operating programs illustrating the author's main points.

Those who would provide special education for adolescents must confront the issue of substance abuse, a problem which, although it has impact on our society at many ages and levels, is a particular impediment to effective education in the secondary schools. In chapter 7, Wong places drug abuse in its societal context. Recent drug abuse prevention education programs and evaluations of these are reviewed. Based on this background material, the author puts forward guidelines for drug abuse education.

One of the major models of intervention appropriate to helping mildly handicapped adolescents is the behavioral model. The behavioral model encompasses a wide range of theoretical principles and actual field applications; what these share is that each is guided to some extent by an operant behavior approach to learning and performance handicaps. One of the more hopeful developments in programming for mildly handicapped adolescents has been the application of the behavioral model to their problems. In chapter 8, Phillips and his colleagues describe the behavioral model and specific examples of how it has been used with adolescents. One prominent application, the Teaching-Family Model, is discussed extensively in terms of its basic premises, the youth re-education procedures employed, the roles and training of personnel, evaluations of the Teaching-Family Model, and its more general relevance to special education for adolescents.

The psychoeducational model is another prominent approach to helping the mildly handicapped. In chapter 9, Fagen explains a psychoeducational approach to understanding and teaching adolescents with learning and behavior problems, beginning with an analysis of the development and maintenance of failure in young people. A principal aspect of psychoeducational management—the concept of self-control—is defined and analyzed. The relation of self-control to overall psychoeducational management, and procedures for building and maintaining adolescent self-control are addressed. Application of self-control and other psychoeducational intervention procedures is described with reference to an ongoing school program. This program includes the student goals, and instructional, behavior management, and counseling techniques appropriate to each of three stages of psychoeducational intervention with adolescents.

Contemporary treatments of education for adolescents commonly make reference to *alternative education,* but there is little consensus as to the meaning of the term. Knoblock, who has had extensive experience with alternative education for handicapped pupils, describes in chapter 10 an encompassing viewpoint regarding educational alternatives for adolescents. The author discusses alternative education as it relates to the concept of an open learning environment, a concept that includes alternative views of the educational process and alternative roles for teachers, as well as alternative structure and content for secondary schools. Specific steps are recommended for secondary educators who desire to reduce the isolation and alienation separating students, teachers, and the education process as a whole. Examples of open learning environments are presented and sources for in-depth exploration of educational alternatives are given.

Within the past few years, legal issues related to education, especially education of the handicapped, have become more important and more complex. Those who provide services to handicapped secondary school pupils can ill afford to disregard relevant judicial, statutory, and related legal developments regarding education of the handicapped. In chapter 11, Martin describes the history of recent developments influencing the civil rights of handicapped pupils and their parents. This chapter specifies how these legal factors affect identification, assessment, individualized education programs, the least restrictive alternative concept, and other aspects of education for the handicapped, with special reference to mildly handicapped adolescents.

In chapter 12, Sabatino provides a sobering view of the current status of special education for adolescents. Evidence is presented which calls into question society's level of commitment to fully educating mildly handicapped adolescents. Organizational and ideological aspects of special education and secondary education are examined. The author also enumerates a range of factors that hinder the provision of adequate services, with suggestions for needed changes. Thus, each chapter addresses an important aspect of special education for adolescents. There surely are other areas that need to be dealt with, but the present chapters are concerned with the most critical ones that must be confronted by special, regular, and vocational educators, counselors, administrators, school psychologists, and other professionals who are, individually or in groups, concerned with learning and behavior disorders in the secondary schools.

Because the gestalt of secondary level special education cannot be neatly apportioned into compartments, certain points have been addressed in more than one chapter. Generally this is beneficial because alternative views and different shades of emphasis regarding important issues can be especially rewarding. No attempt was made to eliminate conflicting perceptions, positions, and recommendations across chapters, because these variances reflect the debates and uncertainties existing in the field. Given the enormity of the challenges and the early stage of development of special education for adolescents, too much harmony in the chapters would be unrealistic. New debates, issues, and challenges will continue to arise as efforts to provide adolescents specialized educational services to develop and mature expand; important societal problems are rarely solved "once and for all." Our task is to understand and come to grips with today's most pressing needs, in order to be ready to move on to additional missions. The chapters to follow have been designed to facilitate the required understandings and suggest some appropriate actions.

Adolescent Development and Deviance

2

Harvey F. Clarizio

In my junior and senior years in high school I can recall wondering about what motivated people. My interest in the field of psychology was not intense, but that curiosity, together with a fascination for foreign languages, constituted the only intellectual interests I had at the time. Not too surprisingly I graduated from college with a double major, one in romance languages and one in psychology. By the time I had completed my undergraduate training, I had decided to specialize in work with children and adolescents.

The next step in my professional development took place at the University of Minnesota where I studied for a master's degree at the Institute of Child Psychology. There I met the late John E. Anderson, first director of the Institute. At least two characteristics of his and others at the Institute are apparent in my own professional development, namely, a reliance on empirical data and a strong interest in how development changes with age. I also learned the importance of having a sound background in normal child development before attempting to fathom deviant development.

While studying for my master's degree, I worked for two years with many maladjusted youth as a recreation center director in an inner-city area, an experience that helped me to better understand the influence of community and familial forces. Shortly after receiving my degree, I worked as a clinical psychologist at Cambridge State School and Hospital with severely disturbed and retarded children and youth. The severity of their conditions convinced me of the need to help youngsters before they become seriously impaired. Programs in school psychology were developing about the time that I realized the need to work with less seriously disturbed youth in a more normal setting than that generally afforded by a residential center. So I entered the specialist program (S. Ed.) in school psychology at the University of Minnesota in 1958. After six months of active duty with the National Guard, I worked in the Loyola Child Guidance Center in Chicago. There, under the guidance of a former English teacher, I learned how essential (and difficult) it is for psychologists to write reports that were meaningful to parents and teachers. In the late summer of 1960, I was offered a job that was to alter significantly my professional career. The job offer came from Dr. Merle Karnes, then director of special education at the Champaign (Illinois) Public Schools and currently a leader in the Home Start Program. During my three year stint in the Champaign Public Schools, I did diagnostic and consultative work concerning a wide variety of handicapped youngsters. It was in this same setting that I received an introduction to doing research in the public schools with handicapped youngsters. Dr. George F. McCoy, who had had as much impact on my professional career as any single person, was chief psychologist at Champaign. I am also indebted to Professor Stew Jones at the University of Illinois for his support during my doctoral studies. I've always had the nagging suspicion that he has done me numerous favors, many of which I am unaware. To this day I value my exposure to Sam Kirk, James Gallagher, Herbert Quay, Ray Simpson, Tom Hastings, J. McVicker Hunt, David Ausubel, and the late Celia Stendler, all of whom were then at the University of Illinois. While earning my Ed.D. at the University of Illinois, George F. McCoy arranged for my interview at Illinois State University as a trainer of teachers of maladjusted youngsters. Upon completion of the doctorate in 1966, I began work for the Department of Counseling and Educational Psychology at Michigan State University, where I presently direct the School Psychology Program. For more than a decade I have cherished the gentle and steadying personal influence of Robert C. Craig, the stimulating daily debates with Robert L. Ebel, and the hard-headed logic of William Mehrens.

Perspectives on Normal Adolescent Development

Adolescence is a time of transition signaling the end of childhood and the beginning of a yet unknown adulthood. Virtually every aspect of development undergoes modification. Physical changes are often dramatic as youth experience a growth spurt and sexual awakening. Thinking becomes increasingly abstract, reflective, and evaluative. Old social roles are discarded and new ones evolve. Friendships become more intense, cliques appear, the crowd takes on added importance, and male-female relationships become of interest. In short, significant advances are customarily made on several fronts.

For many youngsters, adolescence is a period of enjoyment, preparation for the future, and of personal maturing, a time during which they become individuals. For others, it is a time of insecurity, defeat, and despair. This chapter will examine some of the problems that adolescents experience and the kinds of treatment schools can provide. Serious conditions, such as psychosis, will not be dealt with, because not many teachers have to cope with such severe pathologies. Instead, we will focus on some of the problems most often faced by special education teachers.

Probably every teacher, parent, and adolescent has a set of norms by which to judge the appropriateness of human behavior in different contexts. Like the norms for all human behavior, norms for adolescents arise from firsthand experiences, observations, reading, mass media, and direct instruction. Mental health specialists also rely on norms in making judgments about the normality of adolescents. Like teachers, clinicians must answer questions; for example, how significant must an academic deficit be in order to be diagnosed as a learning disability? What is the difference between the adolescent who has a problem and the one who is emotionally disturbed? Decisions of this nature are formidable, for the question of what constitutes normality is best understood not as a question of fact, but rather as a question of conventional definition.

The issue of normality among adolescents is more than an academic question to those who must render judgments about the behavior of adolescents. This question also has ethical and practical ramifications, for the adolescent often does not seek help on his own but typically is referred for treatment by an adult in the environment. Indeed, an adolescent might not even need treatment even though his parents or teachers believe he does. Many parents, for instance, see perfectly ordinary adolescent behavior such as reading pornography and experimenting with smoking as deviant (Ricks, 1974).

Clinicians have relied on two basic approaches in their attempts to distinguish between normality and abnormality. As you will see, both of these approaches—what is typical and what is ideal—have advantages as well as limitations.

What is Typical?

The *What is typical?* approach to normality uses a statistical yard-stick. According to this criterion, normal behavior is defined as what the majority does. The more that an individual is like the average or typical teenager, the more likely he is to be seen as normal. For example, anxiety symptoms and depressive phenomena are fairly common among adolescents (Masterson, 1967). Because these problems are common among teen-agers, they might well be viewed by many people as normal phenomena. In a similar vein, rebelliousness among adolescents might be regarded as normal because it is believed to be typical of adolescents. We almost expect the adolescent to thumb his nose at society. We could calculate among youths the average number of anxiety symptoms, depressive episodes, and number of refusals to follow a teacher's instructions. If a student deviated markedly from this average, to the point that he exceeded 95 or 98% of most adolescents, he would be considered abnormal from a statistical point of view in these aspects of behavior. Similar norms could be established for other aspects of behavior that we regard as important, such as the number of lies told, the extent of aggressive attacks, the frequency of porno-graphic reading, the amount of drugs consumed, the incidence of various forms of sexual activity, the number of friends, the fre-quency of truancy, the commonness of running away from home, the amount of stealing, the extent of various prejudices, and so on.

There are at least five noticeable shortcomings in this approach, however. First, the statistical concept of normality implies that what is common is normal and desirable. Racial prejudice is very com-mon, but is not regarded as desirable. Similarly, 95% of all boys have masturbated by age 15 or 16, yet some people believe mas-turbation is not healthy. Although a sizeable segment of youths take drugs, this behavior is not desirable.

Second, abnormality in a statistical sense is not always unhealthy. For example, the performance of a very creative youngster may be statistically infrequent and therefore deviate markedly from the average. Are we to say that this youngster is abnormal when his very talent may lead him to self-actualization and benefit society?

A third problem centers around the complexity of analyzing personality. It may be possible to gather norms on certain characteristics of a person, for example, the amount of nail biting, but it is difficult to isolate and quantify many of the subtle or more elusive characteristics of personality.

A fourth problem is that norms are frequently based on maladjusted populations; but studies of the incidence of problem behavior in the general population suggest that norms based on deviant groups can be misleading. This can produce inconsistent identification and placement practices within a district or across districts. For example, a moderately maladjusted student in School A, which has a high incidence of problem behavior, may not be considered eligible for special education assistance because he does not exceed 95% of his classmates in his deviancy. Yet, a mildly troubled student in School B, which has a much lower incidence of disturbed students, may be placed in a special class for the emotionally impaired because he does exceed 95% of his peers in deviancy.

Finally, there is the problem of cutoff points. What percentage of the adolescent population does a student have to exceed with regard to number of fears? How many times does a fifteen year old have to be caught stealing or vandalizing to be considered a wayward youth? It is difficult to give definitive answers to such questions.

What is Ideal?

Whereas the statistical approach describes the frequency of given behaviors, the use of the ideal criterion implies evaluation of desirability. Whereas comparison with social norms involves relativity, an ideal criterion is based on absolute standards assumed to be worthy of emulation. The statistical approach is concerned with "what is"; the idealistic approach is concerned with "what should be." An ideal of behavior is posited for each individual, and a determination is made as to whether the individual is functioning at this level. Maslow's (1954) hierarchy of basic human needs illustrates this approach. In ascending order, his hierarchy lists physiological needs, safety needs, needs for affection and belonging, esteem needs, cognitive needs (a search for knowledge), aesthetic needs, and self-actualization needs. When the need at a lower level has been met, the individual seeks to satisfy the need on the next step in the hierarchic structure. Self-actualizing people operate at optimal level. According to Maslow, anything that detracts from the course of self-actualization is pathological.

What characteristics might the ideal adolescent student possess? He would be functioning at or above grade level in all subjects and would be easy to teach. Abstract, deductive thought and the use of verbal propositions to solve problems with multiple dimensions reflect qualitative advances that ideally occur with the coming of adolescence and make for more efficient learning. Being able to create hypotheses and deduce logical conclusions affords the ideal adolescent with the opportunity to plan scientific investigations in a systematic way. A natural curiosity about academic learning and/or things outside of school would also be evident. In addition to self-motivation and a thirst for learning, the fully functioning person would exhibit creative problem solving, independence of judgment, self-control, and a unifying philosophy of life. Not only would this individual be competent and engage in environmental mastery, but he would also be free from disruptive worry about such things as examinations, grades, acne, and dating. Other people would find this ideal person kind and physically attractive.

The equating of normality with perfection has an undeniably positive air about it, but this approach, like the statistical yardstick, also has difficulties. Ideal criteria have little practical meaning and, therefore, are of limited value in the decision-making process. Guidelines derived from such criteria as self-actualization do not aid us in deciding whether the adolescent is normal or in need of professional help. Second, few people can ever attain the ideal; even those individuals who do seem to qualify have other human frailities and weaknesses. Finally, since ideal criteria are in terms of what ought to be, we run the risk of assuming that we know what the ideal attributes are and that these are supra-cultural in character, equally valid for child and adult, man or woman, socialite and slum dweller.

Implications of the Concept of Normality

The concept of normality in adolescents, whether as statistically typical or ideal, presents numerous perplexing issues to society. In essence, society expects adolescents to conform to norms or ideals based in large measure upon cultural values. It is certainly reasonable to judge deviancy by comparing behavior against social norms, but difficulty can occur when an institution or society is dominated by a particular set of social-political values. Is compliance a sign of normality or of personal maladjustment? In the 1960s, who were the maladjusted youth—those who opposed the Viet Nam war or those who went along with it? What about the adolescent who, in his search for autonomy, refuses to comply with the dictates of restrictive parents or a restrictive community? Consider the lower class youth who rebels against school. Is this student to be considered deviant because he feels school is not relevant?

Youth can suffer from overconformity. The problem of normality does not seem to be resolved by a strict adherence to conformity; for eventually, conformity reaches a point beyond which normality is apt to be threatened. Compliance to the point where one's personal integrity is sacrificed is conducive neither to personal nor societal harmony. Furthermore, as Havighurst (1966) argues, it is important that a society educate certain forms of deviancy, for example, creative behavior. On occasion, adjustment demands that we rebel and express dissatisfaction with social mores and institutions. The value for the individual and for society of certain expressions of nonconformity are, unfortunately, often overlooked. Finally, we must ask how to determine whose norms or ideals we are going to use in judging normality. One group in society often evaluates behavior by a different set of expectations than other groups. For example, how would ministers, teachers, social workers, doctors, cultural anthropologists, and laborers as separate groups view a child who habitually curses? In all probability, there would be widely differing views regarding the acceptability and desirability of such behavior.

A special problem arises in attempting to judge what is normal for youth because adolescence is viewed even by many psychologists as a developmental period characterized by instability and turbulence. Because of the alleged "storm and stress" of this period, adolescents are often thought to display pathological behaviors. Conflict between generations is regarded by many as inevitable because of the differences in values between adolescent culture and adult society. Adolescents are often described as nonconforming, promiscuous, frivolous, irresponsible, and alienated. Although these attributes may characterize extreme segments of the adolescent population, available evidence suggests that they are not typical of adolescents at large. Indeed, the gloomy picture portrayed of adolescents is rooted more in myth than in fact.

Studies of normative adolescent behavior indicate that adolescence is not typically the period of instability and maladjustment that many have made it out to be. In one landmark study of more than 3,000 adolescents representative of virtually the entire adolescent population in the United States, Douvan and Adelson (1966) found little support for the "storm and stress" notion of adolescence. On the basis of their interviews and questionnaires, they found that the average adolescent is stereotyped in thinking, conforming in behavior, and resistant to conflict and change. While parents and their teen-aged offspring may disagree about the appropriate length for hair and skirts, the value of certain kinds of music and dances, and the use of the family car, they are in agreement on basic standards of conduct and decency. Despite the "new morality," the vast majority of female and male adolescents disapprove of promiscuous behavior. The adult stereotype of the adolescent as a fun-loving, irresponsible individual, unconcerned about schoolwork, committed more to enhancing personal popularity than intellect, and uncaring about problems and values of the adult world has also been found to be a fallacious overgeneralization. In brief, there is little evidence to indicate that adolescents as a group are defiant, immoral, frivolous, or alienated.

A Developmental Perspective of Normality

While there is no universally acceptable definition of normality, there are certain ingredients that a suitable definition must include. Such a definition should take into account the youth's developmental level, since what is regarded as normal at one age may be viewed as abnormal at a later age. Another factor would be the individual's sex, because gender influences society's judgments about the appropriateness of behavior. Consideration must also be extended to cultural background. Since judgments concerning the desirability of a specific behavior vary from one group to another, the relativity of any particular behavioral pattern becomes an important consideration (Havighurst, 1966). Allowances for individuality must be made. Finally, the definition of normality must be multidimensional; that is, it must take into account how the child functions in various representative areas of development.

What would the mentally healthy person look like in the school setting? Bower (1970) expects the following characteristics.

1. *Managing symbols.* A mentally healthy youth is one who is able to deal with and manage the symbols of our society. Such sym-

bols include those used in language, math, music, and art. Without this skill, the child is unable to function in school and later on in adult society.

2. *Coping with authority*. Teen-agers must be able to manage rapid and sometimes arbitrary fluctuations in rules and be able to accept sanctions for violating rules. It is highly significant that no society of adults or youth can go on without goals, rules by which one reaches goals, and sanctions for those who do not play by the rules. Those who continually break the rules may be suspended from school. The more defiant adolescents may be sent to institutions that prevent them from functioning in our society. An individual has few alternatives; he must learn how to deal with authority.

3. *Living with peer groups*. As part of the skill of coping with rules, one must learn how to be an individual and yet function in a peer group. The mentally healthy person has learned how to deal with the "give and take" nature of daily associations with classmates and friends.

4. *Regulating emotions*. Youths must be able to control and manage their impulses. This does not mean that a youth must give up impulses or inner life in order to become mentally healthy. The ability to manage one's impulses must also include the capacity to loosen controls when such freedom is appropriate and desirable. It suggests freedom to be creative, to be natural, or to be emotional when such behavior is enhancing and productive for the individual. Inhibited behavior can be just as irrational in some contexts as impulsive behavior. A youth needs to have access to his impulses and must be able to use each success appropriately. Stable people achieve an integrative balance between emotional and rational capabilities.

Typical problems of adolescents center around these four skill areas. For example, learning disabled adolescents have trouble managing symbols; delinquents have difficulty adjusting to the dictates of those in authority; phobic and depressed teen-agers are unable to control their emotions and therefore behave in irrational ways.

Bower's criteria are helpful in assessing normal development, but they do not zero in on the adolescent period. While no developmental theory explains the varieties of deviant behavior in adolescence, it is essential to have a developmental framework that identifies the major developmental tasks of adolescence. The writings of Havighurst and Erikson provide a better understanding of the accomplishments that are prerequisite to healthy functioning in adolescence.

Havighurst (1972) has identified eight rather specific tasks the adolescent must accomplish. If the youth is successful in accomplishing these tasks, present and future adjustments will be facilitated. Conversely, failure stifles development and leads to disapproval by society and difficulty in later life. For example, if successful in achieving mature relations with the opposite sex, adolescents may learn many social skills, such as how to converse, dance, play social games, and develop a sense of intimacy. Successful accomplishment may lead to a happier and more effective adolescence, whereas failure may lead to unhappiness and rejection during adolescence and potential difficulty in later relationships (work and marriage) requiring skill in interacting with others as equals. Achieving emotional independence, another developmental task, is also a necessary but difficult accomplishment. Havighurst's developmental tasks are briefly listed in Table 2-1.

TABLE 2-1
Havighurst's Developmental Tasks of Adolescence

---

1. To achieve more mature relations with male and female age-mates.
2. To achieve a masculine or feminine social role.
3. To accept one's own physique and to be able to use the body effectively.
4. To achieve emotional independence from parents and other adults.
5. To prepare for marriage and family life.
6. To prepare for an economic career.
7. To acquire systems of values, ethics, and other principles needed to guide behavior.
8. To develop socially responsible behavior.

Source. From Developmental Tasks and Education, 3rd ed., by R.J. Havighurst. Copyright © 1972 by Longman. Previously published by David McKay. Reprinted by permission of Longman.

Adolescents want to become free from adult dominance, yet they also like the security of parental protection as they encounter the strange and complicated adult world. Parents want their teen-agers to grow up, yet they are apprehensive of what might happen to their inexperienced and innocent children. In this ambivalent and confused situation, adolescents are prone to rebel at home and/or at school, particularly if subjected to very strict and authoritarian rule. Adolescents who do not rebel run the risk of becoming indecisive, reliant on parents or other dominant substitutes, and incapable of having satisfying adult relationships in marriage and in work. Let us consider preparing for economic self-sufficiency as one example of how essential developmental tasks are during adolescence. Of all the ways to prove that one is grown up, none perhaps is more convincing than the ability to earn a wage. While achievement of this task was once important primarily to males, this is no longer the case, as large numbers of women have entered the world of work. Employers want workers who can read and write. A high school diploma is almost mandatory, even for menial jobs. Thus, the learning disabled or retarded adolescent is at a disadvantage, particularly when the labor supply is plentiful with many educated people.

Much of what Havighurst discusses in his eight developmental tasks of adolescence can probably be subsumed under Erickson's (1965) idea of *identity*. According to Erikson, adolescence is a stage in which the youngster begins to develop an awareness of what he has become and begins to realize what he could be. An adolescent is in the process of becoming a person in his own right, an individual who is in command of his own life and who knows what he has in common with others and yet how he is unique. The main task is to integrate the many factors of one's uniqueness while remaining loyal to group ideals.

The achievement of identity provides some sense of stability. The teen-ager who has successfully warded off threats of identity diffusion can, for instance, plan for the future by accurately assessing past accomplishments and current abilities. Failure to achieve a sense of identity can lead to a variety of problems. For example, the inability to assess one's personal assets and limitations can seriously interfere with one's ability to plan accordingly. The teen-ager characterized by identity confusion may not know when to stop pursuing a given goal or when to continue trying. The youth caught up in an identity struggle may take extreme positions, or engage in delinquent behavior in an attempt to define himself more clearly. People would rather be somebody bad than to be not quite somebody (Erikson, 1959); being a competent vandal may be less anxiety arousing than struggling with the problem of identity confusion. The adolescent who has no clear sense of who he is sinks to a low level of self-esteem. In brief, identity confusion places the adolescent in a very vulnerable position that may lead to norm violation and feelings of inferiority, shame, guilt, mistrust, and exaggerated dependency. Before turning to some of the more common problems of adolescents, we will examine the stability of various problems during this developmental period.

Stability of Deviant Behavior

Do adolescents tend to grow out of the problem behavior or show increasing pathology as they develop? The practical significance of this question is immediately evident. Knowing whether an adolescent is likely to grow out of his problems with advancing age or likely to become a mentally ill adult enables us not only to predict the course and outcome of various problems but also to focus help on the cases most in need of special education and psychological intervention. We now turn to an examination of this issue with respect to four categories of deviancy: emotional disturbance, learning disabilities, juvenile delinquency, and mental retardation.

Learning Disabilities

Longitudinal studies on severe reading disability indicate that this condition is best regarded as chronic, requiring long-term treatment (Balow & Blomquist, 1965; Silberberg & Silberberg, 1969). In one intensive investigation, Koppitz (1971) reported that only 30 of 177 special-class students with severe learning disabilities were able to return to a regular class. These youngsters did not catch up in their work and their problems did not disappear. Almost all of the learning disabled pupils who returned successfully from special class placement "lost" a year or two in the process; they were placed below their normal grade level. Koppitz notes that there is an initial misleading spurt in achievement that arouses unwarranted optimism. Though the results of short-term studies are often dramatic, the gains made are often "washed out" in subsequent years. Finally, Koppitz's data suggest that if a student is reading at only a preprimer level between ages 10 to 12, the chances are that this student will never get beyond a second or third grade reading level.

Whether mild or moderate learning problems are less chronic is not yet clear but we do know that the relationship between school achievement in the early grades and the high school years tends to be substantial. In fact, several years of schooling often fails to help those with low readiness for school catch up with those who start school with adequate readiness (Coleman, 1966).

Hyperactivity.   Hyperactivity, a condition often associated with, but not synonomous with, learning disabilities, is now attracting special attention. Contrary to popular belief, hyperactivity does not disappear in adolescence. Although it does diminish, the adolescent is still noticeably more restless, distractible, impulsive, and emotionally unstable than peers (Ross & Ross, 1976). Underachievement, attention problems, low self-esteem, and depression carry over into the adolescent years. While the hyperactive adolescent may not differ very much from classmates in actual academic skills as measured by standardized tests, his ability to use those skills in everyday classroom performance is impaired. In addition to the problems that persist from the elementary school years, some authorities believe that in adolescence, antisocial behavior appears for the first time in approximately one-fifth of hyperactive youth (Stewart, 1976). Since hyperactivity is often defined to include youngsters who are distractible, impulsive, and excitable, a number of these youths might also qualify for the diagnosis of unsocialized aggressive delinquents because they are disobedient, aggressive, and destructive (Stewart, 1976). Whether the antisocial component is new or merely more noticeable at adolescence is not totally clear.

Despite the association between learning disabilities and hyperactivity, some learning disabled pupils are actually listless. It may be that many hyperactive youngsters appear to be learning disabled because of a lack of goal-directed activity (Wender, 1971). So, although only about 20% of children classified as *learning disabled* or *brain injured* show noticeable hyperactivity (Keogh, 1971; Werry & Sprague, 1969), over half of these youngsters are given drugs to make them behave better. Furthermore, exhibition of hyperactivity behavior depends partly on the setting; higher levels of activity are seen in structured situations (Tarver & Hallahan, 1974). Thus all learning disabled children are not hyperactive, just as all hyperactive children are not learning disabled. In fact, some researchers have gone as far as to state that the learning disabled and the hyperactive constitute relatively distinct clinical groups (Campbell, 1975). Using a purely behavioral definition of *hyperactivity*, various investigators report that only a small percentage (less than 15%) of children studied had a definite history of brain injury, and that hyperactive children did not have histories of difficult delivery and similar events more often than control subjects (Stewart, Palkes, Miller, Young, & Welner, 1974).

The long-term prognosis for hyperactive youth appears to be generally favorable. Follow-up studies suggest that the lives of hyperactive youngsters improve considerably in their late teens. One major follow-up study (Borland & Heckman, 1976) found that none of the 20 individuals in the sample had problems of a psychiatric nature. The majority finished high school, a few went to college, and most attained a middle-class status. They changed jobs more often than their peers and worked more hours per week. They were still more nervous, restless, and aggressive than their peers. Thus, while many of their symptoms persisted to some degree, they nonetheless achieved a reasonable adjustment as adults.

Neurotic-like Behaviors

Fears and phobias in children under the age of 10 appear to arise and dissipate quickly (Miller, Barrett, & Hampe, 1974). A recovery rate of 80% within a 2-year time period is not unusual for this age group. There is little information on phobias during adolescence except for school phobia, which has a poorer prognosis during the teen-age years than during middle childhood. In general, about 60% of adolescent school phobias are recovered within a 1-year time span (Miller et al., 1974). Thus, the prognosis for adolescent school phobia is favorable (unless psychotic symptoms are evident). Phobias in adults are much more persistent, the adults showing a recovery rate of only 20–30%.

In general, "neurotic symptoms" of childhood (anxiety, panic sleep disturbances, frequent stomachache and headaches) are largely outgrown and have little prognostic significance (Robins, 1966). Up to middle adolescence, neurotic types of behavioral disturbance probably reflect a phase-specific reaction to developmental crises. However, neurotic-like problems of middle adolescence, when less age appropriate, show greater stability and their prognostic value might increase (Gersten, Langher, Eisenberg, Simcha-Fagen, & McCarthy, 1976). Data emerging from a follow-up of the Symptomatic Adolescent Research Project (Masterson, 1967) confirm the idea that neurotic symptoms (depression, anxiety, phobias) do not spontaneously disappear among middle adolescent outpatients. In fact, five out of every eight patients at age 21 had not outgrown their difficulties. Thus, it appears that age-appropriate behavioral disturbances may have little predictive value, while the same symptoms at other ages when less normative do have greater prognostic significance. It also appears that disturbed behavior becomes more resistant to change with age, although the ages at which problems become more entrenched varies from condition to condition.

Mild Retardation

How persistent is mild mental retardation? [1] According to several studies, although the mildly retarded remain deficient throughout their school careers, they are not perceived as deviant in nonschool contexts (MacMillan, 1977). Once they leave school either through graduation or dropping out, they are no longer seen as retarded. In a sense, their deviancy disappears. The majority become self-supporting; the higher ability retardates achieve more success. While their postschool adjustment (vocational and marital success) is not as good as their average IQ age-mates, or even that of their immediate neighbors, in the majority of cases they avoid designation as mentally retarded, they do marry and raise children, and they do provide food and shelter for their families. However, qualitatively, they do not live as well as the general public (MacMillan, 1977).

Juvenile Delinquency

Although delinquent conduct often has an early onset, it is most common during the adolescent period. Delinquency appears to be an age-bound phenomenon, reaching a peak around age 17 and then leveling off (Kvaraceus, 1966).

When trying to assess the permanence of delinquent behavior, it is necessary to distinguish three different dimensions of antisocial activity: neurotic or individual delinquency, subcultural or gang delinquency, and unsocialized or psychopathic delinquency. Of these three dimensions, the psychopathic delinquent has the poorest prognosis, with two out of three persisting in their antisocial ways well into adulthood (Robins, 1966). The subcultural delinquent who comes from a lower class home in a deteriorated area of the community has the best prognosis of the three types of delinquents (Clarizio & McCoy, 1976). That is, his criminal be-

---

[1] Mild mental retardation includes those of IQ 50–70.

havior is least likely to persist into the adult years. The neurotic delinquent, who is anxious, unhappy, and insecure, is also apt to relinquish his criminal ways as he advances in age.

Varieties of Adolescent Deviance

Neurotic Reactions

While there are various schools of thought regarding the causes of neurotic-like conditions, there is general agreement that a psychoneurotic reaction entails extreme anxiety, associated with ineffectiveness in meeting life's demands. The impairments tend to be more readily observable in one large life area. These areas include adjustment to work, friendships, school, or physical health. Inadequate functioning persists in the face of evidence of adequate intellectual ability, good physical health, and normal family and home background. A disproportionate amount of personal resources must be directed to coping with high anxiety levels. Complaints of personal unhappiness, inability to function, and nagging discomfort are common to this cyclical pattern of intense anxiety and compensatory effects to reduce the anxiety to a more tolerable level. This section will focus briefly on two examples of neurotic reactions among adolescents, school phobia and depression.

School phobia. Although the term *school phobia* is usually regarded as a problem of childhood rather than adolescence, it merits major attention in any consideration of adolescent deviance (Weiner, 1970). Of the many adolescents referred for professional help, refusal to attend school constitutes the neurotic behavior that most arouses concern among parents and educators.

Work with school-phobic children has led to the identification of two subgroups of this disorder. According to Miller et al. (1974), each has distinctly recognizable characteristics, and there are differential implications for treatment associated with each type. The major characteristics are summarized in Table 2–2, "Characteristics of Types I and II School Phobics." Stressing that not all the relationships between behaviors are understood, the presence of six of the nine characteristics is sufficient for classification as Type I or Type II. Children with the Type I disorder tend to be younger, have more cooperative parents, and make a comparatively rapid response to intervention, even though the onset of their disorder may be of an acute nature. In contrast, children with Type II school phobia are likely to be older, have less cooperative parents, and respond slowly to even intensive treatment, such as hospitalization. Type II school phobia is more common among adolescents than is the Type I variety.

Adolescence can be a particularly stressful time for a school-phobic youth. Cultural expectations dictate an increased assertion of independence. Yet, the phobic teen-ager is poorly prepared for independence because of maternal (and sometimes paternal) over-protectiveness. The coping skills needed for self-reliance are lacking. With entrance into junior and particularly senior high school, the adolescent is faced with new situations and challenges, many of which can be anxiety provoking. In elementary school, he attended a self-contained classroom run by a single teacher; now he must go to several classrooms and report to many teachers. The student must assume greater responsibility for directing his own affairs. There is no particular school person who looks after him. Teachers are less nurturant. He must budget study time and decide what subjects to take. The fact that high schools are less structured than elementary schools renders adjustment more difficult for the anxious adolescent who prefers to rely on others

TABLE 2–2
Characteristics of Types I and II School Phobics

Type I	Type II
1. The present illness is the first episode.	1. Second, third, or fourth episode.
2. Monday onset, following an illness the previous Thursday or Friday.	2. Monday onset following minor illness not a prevalent antecedent.
3. An acute onset.	3. Incipient onset.
4. Expressed concern about death.	4. Death theme not present.
5. Mother's physical health in question; actually ill or child thinks so.	5. Health of mother not an issue.
6. Good communication between parents.	6. Poor communication between parents.
7. Mother and father well-adjusted in most areas.	7. Mother shows neurotic behavior; father shows a character disorder.
8. Father competitive with mother in household management.	8. Father shows little interest in household or children.
9. Parents achieve understanding of dynamics easily.	9. Parents very difficult to work with.

Source. From "Phobias of Childhood in a Prescientific Era" by L. Miller, C. Barrett, & E. Hampe. In A. Davids (Ed.), Child Personality and Psychopathology. New York: Wiley, 1974.

in the face of stress. Excessive dependence and avoidance of challenging situations limit the phobic adolescent's opportunities to develop the skills needed for self-direction and increase his uncertainties about himself. Concern about physical and sexual maturation can also intensify school-phobic tendencies. The girl who is concerned about her breast size or the boy who is ashamed about the absence of pubic hair might feel extremely uncomfortable in gym class. The challenge associated with developing new relationships with the opposite sex (dating, dancing, kissing) can also contribute to school-phobic reactions among adolescents (Weiner, 1970).

Educational Intervention. The treatment of school phobia has become a matter of increasing concern, one of the major issues being whether the treatment plan calls for early return to school or the adolescent's development of insight into his difficulties prior to his return to school (Kelly, 1973). There is still considerable controversy concerning the timing of return to school, but all agree that the school-phobic youth should be returned as soon as possible so that his condition does not become increasingly incapacitating. Whether quick return to school or treatment of the underlying personality difficulty is the outcome sought seems to depend upon the theoretical orientation of the therapist. Because cases that occur at adolescence are likely to be more chronic in nature, treatment approaches will often involve psychotherapy or behavior therapy as well as such ancillary measures as tutoring, resource room assistance, or alternative education programs. There is a tendency to involve parents to a lesser degree in the treatment of older school-phobic adolescents. That is, the adolescent himself becomes the primary patient. In any event, the prognosis is generally poorer for the older school-phobic adolescent. At this time there is insufficient data to demonstrate the superiority of any particular method of treatment.

Depression. Depressive reactions are frequently diagnosed in troubled adolescents. Although depressive disorders appear to be more common in adults, the topic deserves attention in a discussion of adolescent behavior disorders. First, even though the primary diagnosis of depression is infrequent among disturbed adolescents, depressive reactions are fairly common among this population (Weiner, 1970). Moreover, the incidence of neurotic depressive reactions increases with age throughout the adolescent years, particularly among females. Second, depressive reactions may be suggestive of later psychiatric difficulties. Lastly, the relationship between depressive and suicidal behaviors warrants attention, for the literature on suicide suggests that of all mental disturbances, depression is the one that increases suicidal risk (Weiner, 1970).

Behaviors indicative of depression appear to change with age. The symptomatology during early adolescence includes boredom and restlessness, fatigue and bodily preoccupation, difficulty in concentration, acting out, and either a desire for constant companionship or a withdrawal from people. The gloom, hopelessness, and self-devaluation characteristic of adult depression is not evident in early adolescence. Traditional depressive reactions such as apathy, insomnia, fatigue, inability to work efficiently, lowered self-esteem, and suicidal inclinations do not make their appearance until later adolescence, age 16 or 17.

Certainly not all depressed adolescents attempt or complete suicide, although there is a much higher ratio of attempted to completed suicides in adolescents than in adults. The possibility of suicide—the second leading cause of death in the 15–24 age group—should never be dismissed when a youngster becomes depressed. Weiner (1970) offers three yardsticks for assessing the seriousness of suicidal attempts: the *onset,* the *method,* and the *intent.* The more acute the onset, the greater the probability that treatment will be beneficial. A previous history of suicidal attempts increases the likelihood of future attempts and calls for extended treatment and surveillance, however. As for method, hanging and shooting attempts should be considered more serious than ingestion of aspirin or superficial scratches on the wrists. That is, lethality of the means is an important criterion. In assessing suicidal intent, several factors should be considered. If the attack was consciously planned and attempted in isolation, the possibility of subsequent self-destructive acts looms large. On the other hand, an attempt meant to impress or communicate with others implies a less self-destructive tendency—although these efforts should not be taken lightly either, for people sometimes kill themselves even if they are not totally serious in their efforts. Teicher (Saltus, 1976) states that one-third of suicide attempts are cries for help. Another third are ambivalent; they are not sure that they want to die. The other third want to die.

Teachers, counselors, school nurses, and school psychologists can provide front-line help (a) by spotting signs of depression, for example, isolation from friends, teachers, and parents; declining school performance; sleeping and eating disturbances; vague bodily complaints; threats to do away with oneself, (b) by providing a supportive, communicative relationship, (c) by helping the adolescent to take greater interest in life, for example, by joining a group or organization. Fortunately, society appears more willing to lift the taboo that has surrounded death and dying. Hopefully, suicide prevention efforts will benefit from increased open discussion of this problem.

Learning Disabilities

In recent years there has been considerable interest in children with learning disabilities. The term *learning disability* refers to a handicapping condition associated with the inability of a child to perform school tasks at an expected level (Hobbs, 1975). Some 40 different terms have been used to describe this condition, which affects some 7,000,000 children under the age of 19 (Hobbs, 1975). Although interest in learning disabilities is still relatively new, terminology associated with this condition has already passed through three stages. These children were originally classified as *brain injured.* Later they were said to have a *minimal brain dysfunction,* and most recently, a *specific learning disability* (McIntosh & Dunn, 1973). In general, definitions fall into two broad categories, those placing emphasis on the behavior itself without specific reference to the cause, and those citing the central nervous system as the basis of learning disability (Kirk, 1972). Among those people stressing behavioral characteristics without referring to cause is Kirk (1972), who states that "a learning disability refers to a specific retardation or disorder in one or more of the processes of speech, language, perception, behavior, reading, spelling, writing or arithmetic" (p. 43). On the other hand, Clements (1966) says:

> The term minimal brain dysfunction syndrome refers to children of near average or above average general intelligence with certain learning or behavioral disabilities ranging from mild to severe which are associated with deviations of function of the central nervous system. These deviations may manifest themselves by various combinations of impairments in perception, conceptualization, language, memory, and control of attention, impulse, or motor function. (pp. 9–10)

Here the term *minimal brain dysfunction* is designed to differentiate between children who have mild versus severe brain disorders.

It is not surprising to find disagreement over the definition in light of the heterogeneous group of children included under this catch-all term and the heterogeneous group of specialists (pediatricians, neurologists, psychiatrists, psychologists, speech therapists, optometrists, special education personnel) who diagnose this condition. Despite varying emphases, there is a certain core of agreement among different professionals. This core includes the following elements:

1. There should be a significant discrepancy between expected and actual development. Some authorities state that learning-disabled students at the secondary level must lag two or more years behind grade placement in basic math and language arts skills and in all cases fall below the seventh grade level in basic skills (Goodman & Mann, 1976).
2. The learning disability should be specific and not a correlate of other primary handicapping conditions such as general mental retardation, emotional disturbance, sensory impairment, or cultural disadvantage.
3. The child should evidence definite patterns of weaknesses and strengths with respect to individual growth (the child should show marked intra-individual variations).
4. The deficits formed must be of a behavioral nature: impairments in thinking, conceptualization, memory speech, language, perception, reading, writing, spelling, arithmetic, and related abilities.
5. The primary focus of identification should be psychoeducational for it is almost impossible to directly examine the brain (Kirk, 1972). Learning disability programs at the secondary level should be reserved for students who have failed to master the academic skills usually acquired during elementary school (Goodman & Mann, 1976).

Characteristic dysfunction. Due to disagreements as to the proper definition, the heterogeneous nature of the youngsters considered to be learning disabled, and other unsettled issues in this field, it is difficult to list definitively the characteristics of the population. Furthermore, much of what is known about learning disabilities has come from clinical and empirical reports on preschool and elementary aged children (Goodman & Mann, 1976). Nonetheless, certain existing sources do identify the characteristic dysfunctions of learning disability. A U.S. Office of Education Task Force headed by Clements (1966) identified 15 major clinical categories including over 50 characteristics. Of those characteristics listed, the ones most frequently associated with a learning disability are

1. *Visual.* Frequent mention is made of visual (spatial) difficulties in the ability to differentiate figure from background, to recognize reversal or inversion of letters and forms, and/or to perceive forms with visual consistency in the face of measured "normal" visual acuity.

2. *Motor.* Another commonly encountered area of deficit entails motor disabilities: the inability to write or reproduce figures accurately, awkward and gross motor coordination, and/or clumsiness and ineptness in performing fine motor skills.

3. *Language.* Certain language disorders cited include conditions ranging from mutism, omission or substitution of sounds and words, to confusion of tenses and acceptable syntax arrangements.

4. *Auditory.* Included in the group of auditory disabilities are the inability to discriminate sounds when these are presented as isolated elements; the inability to repeat more than five or six words in a sentence, a group of "nonsense" words, or a series of digits; and auditory-visual integration impairments (inability to associate sounds with written symbols).

5. *Hyperactivity.* No symptom has received more attention than that of *hyperactivity,* a term that is used loosely to refer to the child's restlessness, inattentiveness, distractibility, excitability, disciplinary difficulty, and lack of frustration tolerance. Parents and teachers will say these children act nervous, constantly fidget, are "into everything," and often walk around the classroom to bother other students.

6. *Emotions.* A large number of specific learning disabilities may be recognized on the basis of an emotional condition that impairs effective functioning. In this category are disruptions associated with such characteristics as impulsivity, destructiveness, daydreaming, aggressiveness, emotional lability, negativism, and uncooperativeness (Clarizio & McCoy, 1976).

7. *Social.* A little understood and probably frequently unrecognized group of learning impairments may be classed together as social because they seem to represent deficits in organizing or relating to social surroundings. It is possible that misperceptions of social relationships figure prominently in this group of dis-

abilities which is also comprised of more easily identified dis-abilities as erratic judgment, irresponsibility, nonparticipation, and irritability.

8. *Intelligence*. Many authorities regard normal intelligence as a characteristic of learning disabled children. Any findings to the contrary are regarded as reflecting misdiagnosis. Yet several studies indicate that learning disabled children have lower I.Q.'s (Stewart et al., 1974).

9. *Combinations of disabilities*. Not infrequently, deficits are observed that involve several of these areas of functioning; such learning disabilities are referred to as visual-motor, social-emotional, or language-communicative problems.

In summary, many learning disabled youth will show some of the previously mentioned characteristics, but it is not clear to what extent students must exhibit them in order to so be labeled. In addition, the study of learning disabilities has focused exclusively on the elementary aged child to the exclusion of the secondary school adolescent. The characteristics of secondary school learning disabled youth have not been investigated, thus statements regarding their learning and behavioral characteristics are limited. Some of the aforementioned attributes may not be manifested at the secondary school level, may be compensated for, or may even appear as other problems. It is clear that further research is warranted to investigate the learning, social, and emotional characteristics of learning disabled adolescents.

Educational intervention. While counseling and drug treatment can be beneficial, they do not correct educational deficiencies. To recoup educational losses usually requires remedial instruction or special education. Appropriate instruction is becoming increasingly available as parents, psychologists, and educators now recognize the needs of the learning disabled child.

It is beyond the scope of this chapter to detail remediation procedures. However, the reader should be aware that remedial instruction can be provided for oral language disorders, visual discrimination problems, disorders in auditory discrimination, reading problems, handwriting problems, and problems with mathematics.

By and large, evaluation of *perceptual-motor* training indicates that such training is ineffective (Hallahan & Cruickshank, 1973; Myers & Hammill, 1976). At present there is little evidence to support the belief that perceptual-motor abilities are critical to the development of traditional academic skills. This is not to say, however, that under some presently unidentified circumstances perceptual-motor training cannot be of value to an individual child.

It is difficult to assess the value of *psycholinguistic* training, because teachers often use a pick-and-choose approach rather than using treatment approaches systematically. A number of authorities have leveled serious criticisms concerning the potential benefits of process training in general and psycholinguistic training in particular (Hammill & Larsen, 1974a, 1974b; Newcomer & Hammill, 1976).

Psychoneurologically based language programs are highly regarded in certain quarters but have not been subjected to empirical evaluation (Bryan & Bryan, 1975).

While studies of educationally oriented treatment programs have not been highly encouraging (Hammill & Larsen, 1974a; Koppitz, 1971; Serwer, Shapiro, & Shapiro, 1973; Silberberg, Iverson, & Goins, 1973), most clinicians recognize the need for instruction tailored to the child's specific educational strengths and weaknesses. It remains for future research to clarify whether the disquieting findings regarding educational treatment are due to (a) the severity of the problems in the populations studied, (b) the invalidity of the diagnostic measure used, (c) the inadequacy inherent in the remediation effort, or (d) the intractability of the disabilities treated.

The previously described remedial approaches attempt to correct deficits within the learner, for example, visual perception. Because of dissatisfaction with process-oriented approaches (such as training visual perceptual deficits), Goodman and Mann (1976) have outlined an alternative instructional program to correct academic deficits. Their recommended secondary learning-disabilities program:

1. Teaches the basics in math and language arts to students who have not yet achieved beginning seventh grade competencies in these areas.
2. Does *not* include process-based training that is geared for perceptual deficits and younger students.
3. Embraces the concept of mastery learning.
4. Stresses a comprehensive, cohesive approach rather than the teaching of splinter skills.
5. Strikes a balance between academic and career education. The program would be incomplete if it did not provide for both

the remediation of specific academic deficits and preparation for post-high school career pursuits.

6. Operates on an integrated basis, somewhere between the poles of total containment and total integration.

Juvenile Delinquency

Delinquency continues to be one of the critical social problems in the United States. Despite expanded efforts to reduce and control juvenile delinquency in recent years, youth arrests for all crimes rose 138% from 1960 through 1974 (Subcommittee to Investigate Juvenile Delinquency, 1975). In proportion to the general population, those under the age of 18 are the largest contributors to the nation's crime problem. The number of juvenile arrests in 1974 was approximately 1.7 million, more than one-fourth of total arrests for all age groups. The antisocial behavior of adolescents involves more than prankish pursuits, for in that same year, juveniles accounted for about 45% of all arrests for serious crimes, including 19% of all arrests for forcible rapes, 10% of all arrests for murder, 53% of all arrests for burglary, 33% of all arrests for robbery, 49% of all arrests for larceny, and 55% of all arrests for motor vehicle theft. Moreover, recidivism rates (repeat offenses) among juvenile delinquents are higher than those among adult offenders, with estimated figures ranging from 60 to 85%. The high recidivism rates are particularly discouraging in light of the cost of incarceration, estimated about $12,000 per child per year. The greatest costs—wasted human resources, loss of life, loss of personal freedom and security—cannot be estimated in dollars and cents (Subcommittee to Investigate Juvenile Delinquency, 1975).

Drug and alcohol use among young people has increased substantially in recent years (Johnston & Bachman, 1976). For example, whereas in 1969 only 19% of seniors said they used illicit drugs, in 1975, 54% of male seniors admitted to doing so. Using a wide array of illicit drugs has not become an "in" practice, however. More than three-fourths do not go beyond experimenting once or twice with any illicit drugs (other than marijuana). Almost half of the seniors did not disapprove of smoking marijuana occasionally. Whereas the use of marijuana in the 1960s appeared to be rebellion toward adult authority, its use in the 1970s seems to be an accepted part of adolescent life-style. Despite the increased acceptance of illegal drugs, alcohol is clearly the favorite of high school seniors; half of the males and more than a third of the females reported having five or more drinks in a row on at least one occasion during the preceding 2-week period. It is evident that alcohol use constitutes a serious drug abuse problem among young people of high school age. These data pertain to regular education students, but there is little reason to believe that the figures would be lower for deviant youth. The need for specialized instruction regarding drug use would seem particularly critical for those youth who already have more than their share of problems.

How much disruption, serious aggression and violence is there in schools? Since 1969, Gallup polls on American attitudes toward education have consistently shown "lack of discipline" to be the primary problem perceived to exist in the public school (Stalford, 1977). While official statistics do not permit an analysis of how much of the increased youth crime occurred in and around schools, educators are concerned about such norm-violating acts as vandalism, violence, physical attacks on teachers, weapons violations and gang fights, narcotic or protection rings, and theft. The perpetrators of these acts fit into the same general student profile: poor grades, frequent truancy, and dissatisfaction with school.

It is no easy matter for high schools to deal with acting-out adolescents. Alternative schools, vocational education, behavior modification programs, positive peer culture and crisis teachers are among the measures that schools must use to combat the problems posed by the aggressive adolescent. Through practical changes in school structure we should be able to help these students feel more comfortable with themselves and to become more constructive members of the community.

Theories of delinquency. Various theories have been advanced to account for juvenile delinquency, many of which have implications for the schools; McPartland and McDill (1976) cite five. One of the most commonly advanced theories of youthful crime is *restricted opportunities*. According to this view, the majority of young people adopt the American dream of a middle class way of life. Children from lower class homes often find that legitimate avenues for achieving this life are closed to them for a variety of reasons: job discrimination, lack of salable skills, manners. Thus, the lower class person cannot compete effectively; delinquency results from the ensuing frustrations. This theory fits well with the observation that much of the theft, attacks, and vandalism committed by delinquents is not for material gain. This theory is at odds, however, with the fact that only a small percentage of persons who have restricted opportunities because of discrimi-

nation or poverty actually express their frustrations in an illegitimate way.

Another well-known theory centers around the idea of *subcultural differences* in values and attitudes. According to this view,
gang delinquency among lower class youth is an expression of
values pervading lower class culture rather than a reaction against
middle class thwarting and devaluation. Activities like ridiculing
authority, engaging in daring group activities and acting tough or
masculine, are believed to take on unusual importance in the
subculture and lead to out-of-bounds behavior. Critics of this viewpoint note that there is little if any evidence to suggest that delinquents have failed to incorporate middle class values (such as a
desire for material possessions).

A third theme emphasizes *adult-youth alienation*. Proponents of
this theory state that adolescents become alienated from adults and
immerse themselves in a peer culture that provides them with
status-giving pursuits, norms of behavior, and distinctive training.
Participation in the peer culture reinforces their feelings of alienation from adult society and promotes compensatory antisocial
modes of conduct. Defying adult directives, engaging in illegal
activities to relieve boredom, and obtaining money illegally to free
themselves from parental dependence are examples of wayward
conduct that may result from a prolonged, disaffected adolescent period. This theory is consistent with the findings that criminal behavior is concentrated among the young and that it decreases
as youth become independent adults. Nevertheless, most authorities question the existence of an adolescent subculture and point
out that adolescents generally accept parental standards and values
except for taste in music, dress, and language.

A fourth theory contends that criminal and violent behaviors
stem from *emotional disturbance*. That is, delinquency is a symptom of an underlying maladjustment. Common emotional problems
experienced by delinquents include acute feelings of rejection, inadequacy, insecurity, jealousy, and unhappiness. There is no
question that a small percentage (5 to 20%) of delinquents are
disturbed, but the vast majority are free from pathological emotional upsets.

A fifth theme that has been receiving attention recently concerns the process of *labeling*. Advocates of this view believe that
a self-fulfilling prophecy is set into motion by the labeling process,
as follows. The person comes to see himself as "bad" or "delinquent" because others communicate to him that they think he is

bad and expect the worst. The individual internalizes this image and behaves in a way that reinforces this image. The self-fulfilling prophecy concept seems to have widespread appeal, particularly to educators, but critics note that the labeling process is probably more of an intensifier of the problem rather than a precipitating condition. Since labeling is based on a person's record of delinquent behavior, it would appear to be a contributing element rather than an originating factor in criminality.

Educationally oriented treatments.   The present discussion will be restricted to changes in the schools even though more fundamental changes in society would in all probability have greater impact. There is little doubt that most juvenile delinquents have behavior problems in school and that many of them have learning problems. Whether or not these disabilities caused delinquency is uncertain. Although most authorities view crime as a reflection of problems in the larger society, it is possible that school experiences do play a role in promoting delinquency. Figure 2–1 provides a schematic representation of possible cause-effect relations.

According to Schafer and Polk (1967) there are four ways in which school experiences can contribute to delinquency:

1. By stressing the need for educational success and yet simultaneously insuring educational failure, the schools block legitimate means of entering the mainstream of American life.
2. Educational activities often seem meaningless in relation to the students' needs. Hence, because school tasks and rewards are perceived as unrelated to the students' future role in life, education becomes an empty activity. Consequently, illegitimate alternatives assume greater attractiveness.
3. The school is often unable to elicit a strong degree of commitment to conformity and legitimate achievement from students. A sense of alienation results, rendering students more susceptible to delinquent pursuits.
4. The manner in which the school handles student misconduct is also relevant. For example, overly punitive sanctions of a degrading nature can serve to push the student toward illegitimate forms of commitment.

Since the conditions that give rise to these unfortunate debilitating effects are deeply rooted in existing notions and organizations of our education system, Schafer and Polk (1967) argue that edu-

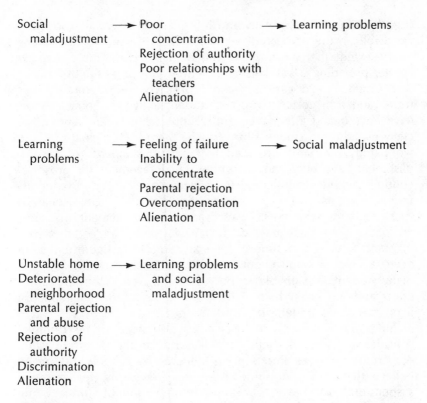

FIGURE 2-1
Possible cause-effect relations promoting delinquency.

cation must do more than adopt stop-gap measures that deal solely with surface problems. Adding more counselors and social workers, for example, constitutes a myopic viewpoint that ignores broader dimensions of the school's role in delinquency. These authors stress the need for fostering a belief in the educability of all pupils, expanding preschool educational facilities; developing meaningful and relevant instruction; innovating more appropriate teaching strategies; using flexible grouping; continuing re-education of teachers; providing alternative career-oriented programs; increasing the accessibility to higher education; and reintegrating dropouts. Unless fundamental and radical educational changes are made in the schools, these authors declare, schools will continue to contribute significantly to delinquency.

If schools are to have a impact on delinquency, they must become more responsive to socially maladjusted students. First, schools must become more rewarding institutions. Rewarding desired behavior both formally and informally is essential. Too often we dwell on the undesired behaviors that we want to discourage to the extent that we forget to encourage the desirable. For example, providing a vandalism depletion allowance might be one way to encourage care of school property by offering savings from vandalism costs to support student activities. Some schools have encouraged attendance and school achievement among socially maladjusted students by allowing them to participate in paid work-study programs provided that certain standards of accomplishment have been met at school. Encouragement for prosocial conduct should ideally come from many sources: school administrators, teachers, custodians, parents, and classmates. Unfortunately, those students who need rewards and encouragement the most are perhaps the ones least apt to receive them. Grades are a case in point. Report card time is for many socially maladjusted teenagers a time of punishment. Under our present grading system, many students are unable to be successful even if they put forth effort and are given help. Frustration, anger, and alienation are likely outcomes under such circumstances.

Punishments meted out by schools also need to be carefully considered. There has been little research on the deterrent value of various penalties imposed on students by schools, but many believe that some punishments are really rewards (for example, suspensions). Moreover, punishments often do not fit the crime (suspending a person for being truant). We must search for more meaningful and beneficial penalties. Saturday schools for truancy, control over student employment, parental fines, loss of extracurricular activities, and reduction in student activity funds hold promise. Bear in mind, however, that punishment of any variety must be used sparingly. If we are to overcome alienation there should be four or five rewarding experiences for every punishing one.

Allowing students a greater voice in the decision-making process is another way in which schools can enhance student commitment and involvement. Students should help establish rules and alternatives available to students regarding academic as well as nonacademic matters. In addition, they should participate in the day-to-day administration of the rules.

There are many other ways in which schools can become more responsive to the problem of social maladjustment. Several of the later chapters will cover topics relevant to the needs of troubled youth (vocational education, alternative education, behavior management).

Important in a discussion of delinquency is the Preparation through Responsive Educational Programs (PREP). Since PREP's introduction into public schools in 1971 (Friedman, Archer, & Lordeman, 1976), it has been field tested in suburban, rural, and urban settings. Most of the instructional program in each site has been individualized, and quick, specific feedback has been a central component. PREP relies heavily on peer and high school aides to provide the feedback, particularly in large classes. Students are graded noncompetitively, primarily on the basis of number of work units they complete at mastery level. They attend a skills center for language and math instruction. Development of interpersonal skills constitutes a special class taught by the school's counseling and teaching staff. Content areas include such topics as "Observing and Reporting Accurately," "Problem Solving—You and Behavior," "How to Follow Instructions," "Careers," and "Teen-agers' Rights and Responsibilities." Behavioral rehearsal, role playing, and group discussion are the primary methods of instruction. Teachers receive preservice training in the use of behavior modification methods such as the use of contracting. Inservice training and consultation services are also made available to teachers. While most of PREP's activities are for groups in the regular classroom, individualized programs are developed for those who failed to make adequate programs. Training and liaison activities are also an important part of the program. While it is not easy to clearly summarize the outcomes of PREP, and while the results have not always shown consistency, the overall picture has been favorable.

Mental Retardation

About 3% of newborns in the United States will be diagnosed as mentally retarded at some time in their lives (MacMillan, 1977). For more than a century, the mentally retarded have been divided into various levels according to the degree of retardation. A child with an I.Q. between 55 and 70 is often considered *mildly mentally retarded;* consideration is also extended to social competence as well. Children classified as mildly retarded often lose their retardation once they "graduate" from school and enter the world of work; but they do experience difficulty during school years. Their intellectual level as adults may be comparable to that of the average 8 to 12 year old. This mildly retarded group, or *educables* as they are often called, comprise the majority of retardates. The *moderately retarded* or *trainable* usually remain illiterate throughout life and can ordinarily function in a sheltered setting. Their intellectual level as adults may be similar to that of the average child in the 4 to 7 age range. Those below IQ 30, the *profoundly retarded*, are typically very dependent upon others for their care.

In the cases of severe mental impairment—an infrequent happening—physical causes can usually be identified; but usually, the causes of mild mental retardation are largely unknown (MacMillan, 1977). In the vast majority of cases, there is no obvious physical cause. Some hypothesize that mild retardation is due largely to lack of suitable early stimulation, cultural disadvantages, maternal deprivation, or emotional stress (MacMillan, 1977). Still others subscribe to an interactional hypothesis contending that low intellectual functioning arises from a combination of biological weakness and environmental deprivation. This type of retardation produced by both environmental and genetic factors is called *cultural-familial*. These retardates come from families of low intelligence and live under impoverished conditions. They tend to marry others of similar intelligence, receive poor prenatal care, and have low-paying jobs, thereby creating a vicious cycle.

A great deal can be done for retarded children. While attempts to raise IQ scores have not been encouraging, gains can be made in the social and vocational realms. Even the moderately retarded can learn more than was previously thought possible, largely due to advances in the application of behavior modification techniques. By the end of this century, a rich array of small, special-purpose community and residential services will be available for retarded individuals of all ages and levels of functioning.

Public school programs for educable mentally handicapped adolescents emphasize prevocational and vocational development and de-emphasize academic subjects. Development of sound work habits and attitudes is of central importance to programs for educable adolescents. Academic instruction tends to deal with the practical aspects of daily living. Development of high school programs for the mildly retarded has been slow but should increase under federal impetus. Much of the discussion in later chapters on vocational development, career education, and behavior management will elaborate on the provisions that can be made for the mildly retarded adolescent.

Problems and Prospects

This final section will point out the need for additional information, speculate about future directions in intervention programs, and touch upon some of the difficulties encountered in the delivery of services at the high school level.

First, there is a definite need for research in the area of normal adolescent development if we are to have a clearer idea of what constitutes normality for adolescents of different ages, backgrounds, and sex. Much of what we consider deviant may be fairly typical of adolescent development. Some of the phenomena that we concern ourselves with (for example, that adolescence is a period of storm and stress) may be, in varying degrees, figments of our imaginations.

Considerable work needs to be done concerning educational provisions for deviant adolescents. The appropriateness of available curricula needs to be studied, for example. Since there is no single curriculum guide for emotionally impaired or mildly retarded youth, teachers have typically devised their own patchwork curriculum. Seldom does one see carefully sequenced curricula for deviant adolescents. The problem of providing carefully sequenced and integrated curricula will be no easier matter under mainstreaming. Placing a handicapped adolescent in a regular classroom may well mean that the student will be presented with a curriculum that is not geared to his needs.

A few words are in order about mainstreaming since its use is increasing. While mainstreaming may be good when feasible, it is not a panacea. Simply legislating that handicapped youth be integrated into regular classrooms will not remove their behavioral and academic problems. High school teachers, who tend to be more subject-matter oriented than person-oriented, are not going to be eager to accept these hard-to-teach adolescents who often have little motivation to overcome their problems. The very nature of the high school poses problems for mainstreaming (e.g., the resistance of the secondary school to change). Whereas mainstreaming in the elementary school may involve basically one teacher, mainstreaming at the high school level requires the cooperative efforts of several teachers. And since teachers may change every 9 or 18 weeks, communication can easily bog down. Special education staff may consult with regular education teachers, but this consultative service will most likely prove ineffective because high school teachers are less person-oriented, have less time to develop individualized programs given the large numbers of students they have each day, do not have the training to deal with the more pronounced academic and behavioral problems of adolescents (a task that taxes even trained professionals), and do not perceive consultation as help.

Peer relations is another problem area. We know that mildly retarded youngsters are more likely to be rejected in regular classes than in special classes. Emotionally disturbed and learning disabled teen-agers are not well accepted either.

Mainstreaming also means that troublesome adolescents can move about a large high school building under minimal supervision. This situation can cause problems, in that many handicapped adolescents do not yet have the skills for acceptable self-direction. Handicapped teenagers will need more guidance and structure in organizing their study time, adjusting to several different teachers and classroom climates, and choosing subjects that may be feasible under mainstreaming.

In short, we still need a variety of programs (e.g. alternative programs, special classes, resource rooms) to meet the needs of the heterogeneous group that we call *deviant*. Mainstreaming will probably not prove to be the least restrictive environment for many troubled adolescents. After all, handicapped adolescents have often been excluded from regular education in the first place. Although educational programming for handicapped youth is still in its infancy, we will need a complete range of educational placement alternatives if we are to meet the needs of this heterogeneous group of adolescents whose numbers in our public schools will swell in the near future.

Assessment and Instructional Planning: A Conceptual Framework

3

J. Lee Wiederholt
Gaye McNutt

Currently there are numerous ways to assess handicapped adolescents and to plan instructional programs for them. Often the decisions regarding these matters are guided by the existing state-of-the-science, the philosophy of the educators involved, and the constraints of the situation. An examination of the factors that influence the making of decisions relative to the education of handicapped adolescents is provided in this chapter. First, a personal analysis of the authors' own professional development with regard to assessment and instructional planning is presented. Second, three factors that affect the selection and evaluation of assessment and instructional procedures are delineated. Third, a conceptual framework for educating handicapped adolescents is overviewed.

A Personal Analysis

In the development of our present position regarding assessment and instructional planning, we have made three major shifts. In the 1960s, we were advocates of the process-perceptual-motor orientation. In the early 1970s, we shifted to a behavioral orientation. Today we are becoming increasingly supportive of what we term a meaningful/natural learning approach to assessment and instruction. A brief discussion of these orientations and reasons for our changing is provided in this section.

When we began studying special education in the 1960s, one of the most stressed approaches to assessment and instructional planning was the process-perceptual-motor orientation. This approach has been recommended by such professionals as Marianne Frostig, Newell Kephart, and Samuel Kirk. We were trained to assess motor skills, visual and auditory perceptual abilities, memory tasks, and sensory modality strengths and weaknesses. The basic assumption for employing this approach was that once students performed adequately on these tasks, they would become more proficient in learning academic tasks. At the very least, it was inferred that these constructs were in some way useful in educating adolescents and children.

Limited experimental data to substantiate this approach was available at that time; but it was generally accepted by most professionals that the clinical insight of those who recommended these procedures was sufficient reason for the rest of us to accept them. However, as time went on, research data became available which cast serious doubt upon the usefulness of these approaches (Bibace & Hancock, 1969; Cohen, 1969; Goodman & Wiederholt, 1973; Hammill, Colarusso, & Wiederholt, 1970; Hammill, Goodman, & Wiederholt, 1971, 1974; Hammill & Larsen, 1974; Hammill & Wiederholt, 1973; Larsen & Hammill, 1975; Mann, 1970; Mann & Phillips, 1967; Robbins & Glass, 1968; Wiederholt & Hammill, 1971).

As a result of this research, in the early 1970s we shifted to a behavioral approach and focused on remediating basic academic skills. We adopted the methods of operant conditioning and specific skills assessment and instruction as recommended by such individuals as Vance Hall, Norris Haring, and Frank Hewett. The rationale for this approach was that in order to improve learning or behavior, the specific problem should be attacked directly. For example, if the problem was reading, the student's knowledge of particular consonants, vowels, blends, and digraphs might be assessed. The specific skills in which the student was deficient would then be taught using drill, repetition, and reinforcement.

We again shifted our emphasis in the mid-1970s. A change was necessary because we felt that the approaches used by many persons within the behavioral school of thought were too confining and doctrinaire for use with the youngsters we were seeing. For example, a strict behavioristic approach does not account for (in fact, ignores) causation, an often illusive but undeniably important aspect of many problems. Also, we now believe it is imperative that techniques used in assessing and planning instructional programs deal directly with the students' comprehension, synthesis, and application of information; personal attitudes, values, and beliefs; self-concepts; inner motivations; and interactions with other persons in their environments. Unfortunately, scant discussion of techniques for assessment and instruction related to these important variables is found in the present behavioral literature.

One should not assume, however, that we have totally disavowed behavioral techniques. On the contrary, we often employ and recommend the use of such methods as applied behavioral analysis as overviewed by Lovitt (1975a, b) and behavior modification in the natural environment as described by Tharp and Wetzel (1969), among others. That is, many behavioral strategies are still used and recommended by us; but we are no longer limited to this approach exclusively.

Currently, we have become increasingly supportive of a meaningful/natural learning approach, especially as articulated by Frank Smith (1975). His influence is reflected in the fact that we now focus upon assessment and instructional techniques that are geared to comprehension or understanding and the manner in which students apply their knowledge to aspects of their experiences. Many of the procedures we currently find interesting are reviewed in *The Resource Teacher: A Guide to Effective Practices* (Wiederholt, Hammill, & Brown, 1978) as well as materials emanating from the Adult Performance Level Research Project (e.g., *Adult Functional Competency: A Summary*, 1975). Of a more specific nature and related primarily to the academic area of reading, we recommend Fernald's (1943) techniques; the various works by Goodman and Goodman (1976) and their co-workers; and the *Test of Applied Reading Comprehension* (Brown, Hammill, & Wiederholt, 1978). Specifically related to the ecological approach to learning and behavior, we rely on the *Behavior Rating Profile: An Ecological Approach* (Brown & Hammill, 1978) as well as the publications by such individuals as Cantrell and Cantrell (1974), Hobbs (1966), and Rhodes (1967).

A rather simplistic example might help to clarify our shifting positions since circa 1965. Let us assume that a student is referred for a reading problem because he consistently substitutes words when reading orally (reads *mom* when *mother* is in the text, or *dat* for *that*). Prior to 1970, we would have stated that in the first case (*mom* for *mother*) the student might have a process deficit in auditory visual association and/or auditory visual memory. In the second case (*dat* for *that*), we might have hypothesized that the problem was one of auditory discrimination. Naturally, the instructional plan developed for this student would have been one geared to developing auditory visual association and/or memory (repeating sequences of digits) as well as discrimination ability (identifying whether pairs of spoken words were the same or different).

During the early 1970s, if the same problems were evidenced by a student, we would not have hypothesized any particular "process" problem. Instead, as strict behaviorists, we would simply have identified specific words or sounds that the student misread orally and taught them through drill, repetition, and reinforcement. Today, we probably would not count words that were read aloud incorrectly as errors or deficits as long as they did not interfere with the student's understanding of the written material. Instead, we would view these substitutions (*dat* for *that*) as the student's use of his natural language and consider them a possible reading strategy rather than a weakness.

The reader should bear in mind that the preceding examples were used only for descriptive purposes. Naturally, we would never have proceeded with instructional programming based on such limited assessment data. However, the example should help to clarify our shifts in theory and practice over the years regarding assessment and instructional planning. Additionally, from this example, the reader should now be aware that the choice of teaching procedures changes as the individual's approach to the learning process is altered or as other factors are changed. Because there are numerous factors and subfactors that affect assessment and instructional planning, we believe that teaching procedures are a highly idiosyncratic matter, varying from person to person. In the next section, a more detailed discussion of the idiosyncratic nature of assessment and instructional procedures is presented.

Factors in Selecting Assessment and Instructional Procedures

In deciding which procedures to use with handicapped adolescents, professionals are usually guided by three factors: the type of educational alternative through which services will be provided, the theoretical approach to learning that is advocated by the professional(s) working with the students, and the curricula to be taught. A brief discussion of each of these factors follows.

Educational Alternatives for Handicapped Adolescents

There are basically three types of educational alternatives for handicapped adolescents: remedial, vocational, and compensatory. A fourth alternative is the regular secondary program, but we have not included this type in our discussion because whenever handicapped students are placed in a regular program, some additional support to the teacher and/or the students is usually provided by a special educator. More often than not, this support is provided through the use of remedial and/or compensatory educational strategies.

Remedial education.   Remedial education for handicapped adolescents is usually provided administratively by special education and may be offered in conjunction with other alternatives (vocational education, compensatory education, or regular education). These services can be delivered in numerous settings (resource rooms, integrated classes, self-contained classes) within remedial education. The basic purpose of the service is to ameliorate the students' problems as much as possible with complete correction being the consummate, though often unattained, goal. This purpose of remediation is often based on the assumption that the evidenced problems (inability to read, overly aggressive) are intrinsic to the students and the students must be changed if they are to appear "normal." While the manner of assessing and planning instruction within remedial education varies a great deal, in this alternative attempts are made to identify specific weaknesses of the students. Once the weaknesses are identified, instructional techniques are implemented to ameliorate them.

Basically, remedial education has three strengths and three weaknesses. The strengths are (a) it encourages the identification of the skills that students lack, (b) it focuses on decreasing students' weaknesses rather than ignoring them, and (c) it offers an option to those students who are not able to cope with the regular education programs. Some of the weaknesses are (a) remedial education frequently fails to focus on the entire situation; it is more often than not assumed that the problems are within the students rather than considering that outside variables may be causing or contributing to the problems, (b) there is a tendency to fractionalize students in that the instruction is composed of bits and pieces that do not always fit into a cohesive whole (e.g., the skills learned in remedial education may have no applicability to the students' actual needs in other settings and environments), and (c) there is an unfortunate

67

lack of research validating many of the tests and materials used with adolescents in remedial education.

Vocational education.   The definitions of vocational education found in the literature includes both broad and narrow conceptualizations. Today it is probably best to hold to a rather narrow definition in order to be in agreement with such federal mandates as the Vocational Education Act of 1962 (P.L. 88–210) and the Vocational Education Amendments of 1968 (P.L. 90–576). Accordingly, vocational education is the process of providing individuals with training so that they may find gainful employment as semi-skilled technicians or technicians. The basic purpose is to provide students with job skills that are needed for specific occupations that generally are not considered "professional" and do not require college degrees.

The methods used by vocational educators often call for delivering services in (a) the traditional classroom setting and (b) on-the-job training, either on- or off-campus. In addition, vocational education programs may cooperate with the state vocational rehabilitation agency as well as rehabilitation facilities to further increase the alternative services. For greater detail on vocational education for the handicapped, the reader is referred to chapter 5.

Vocational education has several apparent strengths. First, students are prepared to enter the world of work by learning particular marketable skills. Second, viable alternatives to the traditional college preparation track found in most schools are provided. Third, it provides opportunities similar to apprenticeships and the learning of family trades that are seldom found today.

Vocational education has its weaknesses, too. First, individual differences in students are often not accommodated. For example, if students do not have certain prerequisite skills, such as minimum reading skills, generally no attempt is made to remediate or compensate for the deficiencies. Second, the focus of vocational education is often too restrictive. For example, vocational educators tend to train for rather specific occupations rather than exploring a wide continuum of occupational options. Writing to this point, Bailey and Stadt (1973) state that since the skills taught are often outdated and not in keeping with current technology, students may be prepared for skills and jobs that are not needed in the current job market. Third, these programs often ignore the affective development of adolescents and the teaching of functional living skills that are not specifically job related. That is, some students may complete a program with the necessary marketable job skills but lack the skills needed to be self-sufficient citizens. Finally, as noted in a federal report:

> . . . graduates of vocational programs tend *not* to be employed in the field of their training, . . . their earnings do not exceed those of nonvocational students, . . . materials and equipment used and skills taught in vocational courses tend to be out-of-date, and . . . little effort is made to relate training to job needs or to provide help in placement. *(The Education of Adolescents,* 1976, p. 6)

Compensatory education.   Compensatory education for the handicapped is geared to help students learn by circumventing, to some extent, their handicaps. For example, if the students cannot read but can understand when information is presented orally, then instruction emphasizing listening and talking is undertaken. In some cases, the compensatory alternative is used in conjunction with remedial or vocational education. In other cases, the compensatory alternative is implemented by special teachers to help maintain the students in the regular education programs. The aim is generally to support and aid the students in obtaining high school diplomas.

Since compensatory education often assists students in obtaining their high school diplomas, a brief discussion related to requirements for receiving a diploma seems needed. Currently, it is assumed that (a) a high school diploma indicates the recipient has a general background in language, sciences, social studies, the arts, and mathematics, and (b) this general knowledge is necessary for successful living. In addition, the assumption is made that a high school diploma is prerequisite to higher education and/or "good" employment. However, these assumptions may lack validity since, in part, most high school diplomas are based on the concept of the Carnegie Unit. The number of Carnegie Units (usually around 20 units) and types of units (e.g., units in English or mathematics) required by a state or local district for a diploma may vary; but, due to its historical background and connection with college requirements, the diploma based on Carnegie Units is generally oriented towards college preparation (Clark, Klein, & Burks, 1972; Davis, 1966; Walton, 1966). In fact, Siegel (1974) observed that 85% of high school course work is oriented toward college preparation, yet only 20% of the high school seniors earn a college degree. He also noted that 88% of jobs require no college degree.

In order for handicapped adolescents to receive high school

diplomas, compensatory education must change the format of the requirements or the actual requirements. These changes may be in the form of modifying the courses by simplifying the material (using an easier-to-read text), offering only parts of the curricula (eliminating concepts identified as less important than other concepts), or simply allowing the students to "pass" if they attend class and have tried (unsuccessfully) to meet the course requirements. Or, the students may be taught the identical subject matter but the method of presentation and testing may be different. For example, group discussions instead of lectures, tape recordings instead of reading the text, and oral rather than written exams may be employed.

There are three advantages to compensatory education. First, many employers require a high school diploma; therefore, if students want particular jobs, they must obtain a diploma. Second, if students are interested in post-secondary work, such as advanced vocational training or college work, a high school diploma is generally required. And, third, many students who participate in this program supposedly are in the "least restrictive environment," a requirement of Public Law 94–142.

Two of the three weaknesses are directly related to that aspect of compensatory education that assists students in obtaining a high school diploma. First, the high school diploma is aimed at preparing students to enter college and does not focus on preparing students for entering the "real" world. Second, the high school diploma as it currently exists is almost meaningless because it does not indicate that students possess certain skills but only indicates they have attended school. In fact, there are many instances where diplomas have been awarded to nonhandicapped individuals who could neither read nor do basic arithmetic. Third, most regular secondary teachers are trained only in a particular subject matter area and lack training in teaching prerequisite skills, individualizing instruction, and curriculum adaptation. Therefore, the regular education programs may not meet the needs of the handicapped student to any great extent.

The matter of what to assess and what to teach is usually predicted upon the type of alternative by which the student is to be served. Most certainly, if the alternative is remedial, as opposed to vocational or compensatory education, some differences in the selection of assessment tools and the development of instructional plans will exist. Other factors that influence the selection and development of strategies in the education of the handicapped adolescent are the stressed curriculum areas and the chosen approach to learning.

Approaches to Learning

The second factor that influences the selection of assessment and instructional procedures is the theoretical approach to learning of the professional(s) involved in this process. Several professionals have organized the various approaches to learning, usually in relation to the behaviorally disordered. For example, Rhodes and Tracy (1974) have grouped theories in the following manner: (a) behavorial theories, (b) psychodynamic theories, (c) biophysical theories, (d) sociological theories, and (e) ecological theories. Coleman (1976) has grouped the various theories somewhat differently. He identified (a) psychoanalytic, (b) behavioristic, (c) humanistic, (d) existential, and (e) interpersonal theories as the major approaches. In this chapter we have chosen to use Millon and Millon's (1974) five approaches as a description of the various learning approaches. Their organization of approach types follows:

Behavioral.   Behaviorism stresses overt and observable data (i.e., actions and behaviors exhibited by the individual). Modern theories grouped under behaviorism are classical conditioning, instrumental conditioning, and social learning.

Psychoanalytic.   Psychoanalysis is oriented to the understanding of intra-psychic processes and their development. Modern theories grouped under psychoanalytic approaches are neo-Freudian social and neo-Freudian ego.

Phenomenological.   Approaches within the phenomenological orientation stress that individuals react to the world in terms of their own unique perceptions of it. Modern theories included are existential, self, and humanistic theories.

Biophysical.   Included within biophysical approaches are theories stressing the biological basis of psychological functioning. Modern theories include heredity, constitutional, and neurophysiological.

Sociocultural.   Theories within the sociocultural school of thought stress that the individual person is not the prime focus; instead, the social setting and the forces which impinge upon the person and which he in turn influences are the center of focus. Modern theories are social systems, consultation, and crisis theories.

For a detailed analysis of these approaches, the reader is referred to Millon and Millon (1974). In addition to describing the development of these approaches and each of the modern theories subsumed within each approach, they have also alienated the ways in which behaviorally disordered individuals may be provided with special help according to each particular orientation.

The organizations provided by Coleman (1976), Millon and Millon (1974) as well as Rhodes and Tracy (1974) demonstrate an important dimension in assessment and instructional planning: The theoretical approach to learning used by a particular professional will influence the procedures he uses in teaching students. For example, an educator who employs a behavioral approach in vocational education will use different procedures than one who employs a phenomenological approach. The organization of learning theories points out quite clearly that assessment and instructional planning can be very diverse and idiosyncratic based on the professional's own personal view of the learning process.

Curriculum Areas

The final factor in the selection of educational procedures can be termed *curriculum areas*, or the content to be taught. The content is an integral part of assessment and instructional planning and is drawn from three learning areas: cognitive, affective, and motor. Each is briefly overviewed.

Cognitive curriculum area. This is usually the most emphasized curriculum area in an educational program and includes the following subareas: intellectual abilities, academics, functional living skills, and occupational skills. Intellectual abilities are often assessed by administering standardized intelligence or aptitude tests. Usually, the purpose of administering such tests is to qualify students for specific programs or services. For example, low intellectual ability plus meeting certain other criteria may qualify students to be labeled as *mentally retarded*, enabling them to enter a remedial education program. While intellectual abilities are often assessed for labeling purposes, they are seldom assessed to derive instructional information.

The second area of cognition is academics, which may be partitioned into three subcategories. First, there are *basic academics*: reading, spelling, arithmetic, and possibly spoken language. Such academics are usually taught at the elementary level, but handicapped adolescents are frequently deficient in one or more of these areas. The second type of academics we have termed *general academics*. At the secondary level, general academic courses build upon students' basic skills and increase their knowledge of the world around them. Courses such as consumer mathematics, introductory science, and civics may be classified as general academics. The final subcategory is *college-preparatory academics*, including courses that are considered prerequisite to entering a college or university, such as advanced sciences, advanced mathematics, and foreign languages.

The third category of the cognitive curriculum area is functional living skills, those skills that are needed in order to be productive members of society but are not specifically job related. General areas related to functional living skills include consumer-economics, effective use of community resources, health, and participation in and understanding of government. Naturally, within each of these general areas, certain basic academics (reading, writing, problem solving) are often assumed to be needed. Additionally, some of the functional living skills may be included in general academics courses.

The last component of the cognitive curriculum area is occupational skills, which are directly related to the world of work. These skills include specific marketable abilities (typing or bookkeeping) as well as more general skills (job-seeking skills, personal neatness). Occupational skills taught at the secondary level are usually in one of the following categories: (a) consumer and homemaking education, (b) business and office education, (c) agriculture, (d) distributive education (i.e., the distribution and marketing of goods or services), (e) health occupations education, and (f) trade and industrial education.

Affective curriculum area. Within this area, we have identified three overlapping subareas. The first focuses on the emotions or attitudes within the individual. Terms such as *self-concept* and *self-image* are often associated with this subarea, as well as the values or morals of an individual. The second subarea focuses on behaviors that students exhibit. While these may be termed *positive* or *negative*, negative behaviors often listed include aggressiveness, acting-out, and withdrawal. The final subarea of the affective curriculum area is interpersonal relations between the student and others. Naturally, emotions and attitudes of individuals affect their behaviors, their behaviors affect their interpersonal relations, and so on. However, assessment and instruction quite frequently focus on only one subarea of the affective area.

Motor curriculum area. We have identified two subareas within motor learning: fine motor and gross motor coordination and/or skills. Examples of fine motor skills include writing, artistic endeavors, and sewing. Gross motor skills are used in walking, active sports, and manual labor. Assessment and instruction in these areas is often undertaken in order to increase vocational skills or social competence.

Application of the Three Factors

In deciding which assessment and instructional procedures to use, professionals are usually guided by three factors: educational alternatives, approaches to learning, and curriculum areas. There are, of course, any number of combinations possible when the various areas and subareas are considered. To briefly illustrate the application of the three factors, two possibilities are overviewed: (a) a behavioral-remedial alternative emphasizing the cognitive curriculum area, and (b) a socio-cultural-compensatory alternative focusing on the cognitive curriculum area.

Behavioral-remedial-cognitive.   If an educator worked within this example, he would need to consider the following. First, with a behavioral approach to learning, should classical conditioning, instrumental conditioning, or social learning be emphasized? Second, which of the subcategories of the cognitive curriculum will be assessed and taught? For simplicity's sake, we will assume that instrumental conditioning, which teaches basic academics (reading, spelling), is chosen. Naturally, a more eclectic and comprehensive application is possible.

In diagnosing and ameliorating basic academic weaknesses, skills retrieval or skills management systems would probably be used. Basically, these systems consist of a set of specific skills usually stated in behavioral objectives and presented in a stated sequence (Wiederholt et al., 1978). In addition to the list of skills that is often presented in the form of a scope and sequence chart, skills retrieval systems include other components, such as (a) tests to measure each skill or objective, (b) rules for determining mastery, (c) references to various materials (either as a part of the system or available elsewhere) that may aid in teaching specific skills, and (d) a means of reporting which skills have and have not been mastered (Johnson & Pearson, 1975). Other methods of diagnosis that may be used alone or in combination with the skills retrieval systems include diagnostic tests, criterion-referenced tests, checklists, and teacher-made tests. The materials used for instructional purposes may be commercially produced or teacher made, and they usually focus on one academic area (reading or math) although they may attempt to incorporate some functional living skills within the content.

The implementation of this example would find a highly structured and organized classroom. Students would be expected to exhibit very specific, measurable behaviors (e.g., reading orally a 200-word passage with no more than five errors). When the specified behaviors are evidenced, rewards or reinforcement would be available.

Sociocultural-compensatory-cognitive.   As with the previous example, the educator would need to further delineate particular factors. First, should the social systems, consultation, or crisis theory be used? Second, should the manner in which the requirements are met be changed, or should the requirements be altered? And, third, which of the subcategories of the cognitive curriculum area should be emphasized? This final question is usually determined by the particular course(s) in which compensatory education is needed. As with the previous example, for simplicity we will assume that the consultation theory will be used to change the manner in which requirements are met in an United States government class.

In this example, the emotional-social adjustment and functioning of the student would be of primary concern even though the cognitive learning area is the designated area. This is because the consultation theory assumes that the student must be psychologically well adjusted before he can be successful in learning. Therefore, a special educator might assume the role of consultant. The special education consultant might offer individual- or group-therapy sessions for the student. In working with the regular teacher, the consultant could also work towards changing the way in which the requirements of the course are met to alleviate the anxieties and tensions the student might be experiencing.

It should be quite obvious that the emphasis that each professional places on the areas and subareas within each factor greatly influences the selection of assessment and instruction programs. It is important for educators to identify the particular category of each of the three major factors they use as well as to identify categories others use for educating handicapped adolescents. Where differences exist, commonalities among these different orientations may be identified, alternatives delineated, and meaningful communication increased. These may well be the first steps in providing more effective education for handicapped adolescents.

A Conceptual Framework

In this section, a conceptual framework for describing assessment and instructional planning is presented. We believe this framework encompasses the strengths of many of the current practices but adds some important dimensions often overlooked by educators. Basically, the concepts added are career education, ecological considerations, and meaningful/natural learning approaches. Each of these is discussed separately prior to the introduction of the conceptual framework. The implications of this framework are then delineated.

Career Education, Ecological Considerations, and
Meaningful/Natural Learning

Our proposed framework is based to a great extent on three key terms: career education, ecological considerations, and meaningful/natural learning. In this section, the meaning of each term is discussed separately.

Career education.   Increased attention has recently been given to the concept of career education. Yet, there exists some confusion as to what the term actually means. Some individuals view career education as being synonymous with vocational education. Others adopt a more comprehensive definition (Hoyt, Evans, Mackin, Mangum, 1974):

> Career education is the total effort of public education and the community to help all individuals become familiar with the values of a work-oriented society, to integrate these values into their personal value systems, and to implement these values into their lives in such a way that work becomes possible, meaningful, and satisfying to each individual. (p. 15)

This is the definition that is used in this chapter. Hoyt et al. (1974) stress that career education is the responsibility of the schools as well as the community and that it is a lifelong process. This means that career education should permeate all aspects of an individual's educational experiences, including the curricula, instruction, and counseling, both in the school and the community. Therefore, they reject the idea that career education should be relegated to only a small portion of the day or one unit in a school year. Furthermore,

Hoyt et al. (1974) note that career education is more than just preparing an individual for work. It does involve preparation for economic independence, but career education also focuses on an appreciation for the value of work and personal fulfillment for each person involved.

The U.S. Office of Education (1972) developed a model (Figure 3–1) that depicts how the career education concept may be applied. As indicated by this model, career education should begin at the kindergarten level and continue throughout life. Obviously, in order to have a program for adolescents, the students should have had appropriate experiences with career awareness in the elementary school. Unfortunately, career awareness is rarely taught systematically and comprehensively to handicapped children during their elementary school years. Therefore, it is often necessary to assess career awareness and include it in instructional planning at the secondary level. In addition, the career education model in

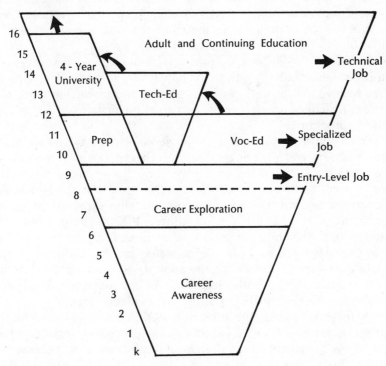

FIGURE 3–1
U.S. Office of Education's career education model.

Figure 3–1 does not take into account the fact that handicapped students may have different developmental patterns and may not be able to benefit from particular programs (e.g., career exploration) at the stated age/grade level. This problem indicates that educators should be prepared to offer the various programs at different age/grade levels based on the individual's need and readiness for learning as well as his background. Any assessment and program planning activities should take these factors into consideration.

Ecological considerations.   Ecology has many interpretations. As it relates to humans, "human ecology is the study of the dynamic relationship between the individual and his unique set of environmental circumstances, at a particular period of time" (Hobbs, 1975, p. 113).

In discussing the ecological approach, Wiederholt et al. (1978) state that many (if not most) of the problems that students encounter in learning are the direct effect of the environments rather than the result of "defects" in the students' physical makeup. Consequently, Wiederholt et al. (1978) recommend that assessment and instruction be undertaken in the students' natural environment so that outside variables may be considered.

Listed in Table 3–1 are the environmental elements that may contribute significantly (positively or negatively) to adolescent growth. We believe that procedures for analyzing and modifying these elements (teachers, peers, parents, curricula) be included in any educational program.

Laten and Katz (1975) describe an ecological/behavioral approach for assessing and planning for adolescents, which is composed of five phases. The first phase involves assimilating all of the intake or referral data from the various settings in which the adolescent functions. Second, the educator identifies the expectations or requirements that individuals in different settings have for the adolescent. The third phase is one of organizing the various behavioral descriptions. Data are collected on the interactions and skills of the people (including the adolescent) involved in situations where the student is both successful and not successful. The fourth phase involves summarizing all of the available data.

In the final phase, the educator establishes goals and plans a program for the student based on the preceding phases. When problems exist between a student and some part of his environment, three types of intervention may be planned during the final phase. First, the environment may be changed (the task may be restructured or the teacher's expectations may be changed). Second,

TABLE 3–1
Possible Settings/People Within an Adolescent's
Three Major Environments

Major Environments		
Home	School	Community
Immediate family members	Classes, such as English Math History P.E. (includes objects & people in each class)	Sports not sponsored by the school
		Volunteer work
Frequent visitors to the home (relatives, neighbors)	School clubs, organizations	Organizations/ clubs outside the school
	School sports	
	Counselors	After-school jobs
The adolescent's own room	Detention Hall	Religious groups
	Principal & principal's office	Gathering places for adolescents (e.g., the local "teen hangouts")

the student may be changed perhaps by modifying his behaviors or increasing his skills. Third, both the environment and student may be changed.

Meaningful/natural learning. We have already stated that we have become increasingly supportive of meaningful/natural learning. In part, our approach is based upon the writings of Frank Smith (1971, 1975) of the Ontario Institute for Studies in Education. Smith (1975) states ". . . the only effective and meaningful way in which anyone can learn is by attempting to relate new experiences to what he knows (or believes) already" (p. 1). In other words, students learn when the new material being presented is meaningful to them and meaning exists only when the new information is related in some way to what is already understood by the individuals.

Inevitably the information that particular individuals bring to a learning situation is unique and diverse, a situation that can make relating new information to what is known a difficult task (for example, creating a meaningful learning situation.) To decrease this difficulty, Smith (1975) suggests four strategies that increase meaningfulness:

1. If the material is not familiar, but the components or aspects of it are, meaningfulness is increased.
2. If the sequence of the components is familiar, meaningfulness is increased (e.g., 12345 rather than 42318).
3. Meaningfulness can be increased when the new material can be related to something already known (for example, when meeting someone new, associating the person's name with something familiar).
4. When the unfamiliar information "fits" with known information or fills in "gaps" (much like putting the last few pieces of a puzzle together), meaningfulness is increased.

We are strong advocates of making learning meaningful by employing the preceding strategies. In addition, we believe that learning should be viewed more as a natural phenomenon rather than an artificial condition that must proceed in a rigid, lock-step fashion. An illustration of this is provided by Smith (1973):

> The skill of riding a bicycle comes with riding a bicycle. We do not offer a child lectures, diagrams, and drills on the component skills of bicycle riding—we sit him on the saddle and use a guiding hand or training wheels to make sure he does not fall off while he teaches himself the precarious art of keeping balance. Forcing him to worry about laws of motion and centers of gravity would obviously confuse him. (p. 195)

The Conceptual Framework

By combining the terms career education, ecological, and meaningful/natural learning, a specific concept of education emerges. First, within this concept, education is viewed as a life-long process with the primary goals for each individual being economic independence, personal fulfillment, and productive participation in society. Second, education is viewed as taking place in the entire ecology of a student, not just within a classroom setting. Of particular importance is the dynamic relationship between the handicapped adolescent and his unique set of environmental factors. These factors include other people as well as materials, equipment, and events. Third, the process of education is viewed as making what the students need to learn as meaningful to them as possible and doing it in as natural a way as feasible. We believe that this concept of education should serve as a guide by which professionals judge and select assessment and instructional tools.

But how does this concept relate to the three factors mentioned in the second section of this chapter (see p. 66)? Specifically, how does the concept affect the curriculum areas, the types of alterna-

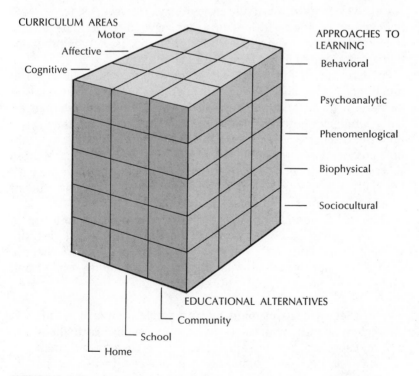

FIGURE 3–2
A conceptual framework for assessment and instructional planning.

tives, and the approaches to learning? Figure 3–2 graphically depicts this relationship in a three-dimensional conceptual framework.

The curriculum areas in our framework are the same as those identified in the second section of this chapter: cognitive, affective, and motor. However, we strongly believe that the focus of assessment and instructional planning for the handicapped should be upon those abilities and skills in each area relating to career education. Specifically, we believe that the particular learning emphasis should be a prerequisite to, or relate directly to, (a) career awareness, in which students become familiar with the general aspects and categories of work, (b) career exploration, in which students further explore and identify a wide variety of work roles, (c) career choice, and (d) career preparation. Intrinsic to each area is the belief that *career* does not infer a specific vocation but is broader and more comprehensive.

The second dimension of this framework depicts educational alternatives. In a previous section of this chapter (see p. 67) we discussed remedial, compensatory, and vocational alternatives as the alternatives that are primarily used today. However, since we adhere to an ecological orientation, we have extended the educational alternatives to include school programs as well as programs that are developed in the home and community.

For example, if the focus of the curriculum area is to establish functional living skills (within the cognitive area), assessment and instruction might take place in all three of the major alternatives. If the objective is to enable the student to use public transportation, the teacher would observe the student actually using the public transportation system in the community and then teach those skills that the student lacks. If the objective is to improve budgeting skills, the teacher might ask the parents to allow the student to assist in planning the family budget.

The third dimension of the framework is approaches to learning. For descriptive purposes we have retained the categories described by Millon and Millon (1974) (see p. 71). We believe each of the approaches to learning have some utility. Millon and Millon (1974) point this out quite clearly:

> . . . let us keep in mind that no single approach is sufficient to deal with all types of abnormality. Each theoretical school and therapeutic approach carves out a small slice of this vast complex for its special focus. Let us remember that theories are "inventions" created by man

to aid him in understanding nature, and are not realities themselves. (p. 27)

However, we have previously noted that we are advocates of meaningful/natural learning. Consequently, when professionals employ a behavioral approach or a sociocultural approach, for example, we suggest that they make the instruction meaningful to the students as well as present it in as natural a way as possible.

In summary, this three-dimensional framework can be viewed as the "what," "where," and "how" of assessment and instruction. The "what" is the curriculum areas, with the focus on career education. The "where" is the educational alternatives. And the "how" is the approach to learning, with meaningful/natural learning being an integral consideration.

Application of the model.   Three examples will be given to illustrate the application of our conceptual framework. The first example described is related to the upgrading of the general reading level/ability of a student (a subcomponent of the cognitive curriculum area). The second example is related to improvement of interpersonal relations, while the third focuses upon career exploration.

1. *Upgrading general reading level/ability.* To find out the student's reading ability, collect a variety of reading materials that the student comes in contact with every day. They should differ in difficulty and topic and relate directly to the student's present or extra needs. Find out how well he understands the material, not how many words he can read aloud. A student's reading ability may vary depending on his motivation for reading, his experience with the material, and the complexity of the presentation. If it is determined that a student is having some trouble with practically all material or with a specific type of material, a more comprehensive and specific assessment could be undertaken. For this, the *Reading Miscue Inventory* (Goodman & Burke, 1972) or an adaptation might be used. The results would likely indicate particular strategies that the student would be lacking (e.g., failure to use syntax clues). The educator would then attempt to aid the student in acquiring needed skills.

However, if it is determined that the student is close to being a nonreader and will soon be leaving school, the teacher may wish to concentrate on compensation skills rather than teaching reading. Going out in the community, as well as in the home, the teacher and student could identify cues which can be used (for example, particular insignia, such as the "Golden Arches," which could substitute for reading ability). The parents could assist in developing these compensation skills related to reading in the home (identifying key words on medicine bottles, using pictures on canned goods). The Fernald (1943) approach might also be employed to teach certain essential words.

This very brief illustration related to reading emphasizes several factors. First, the materials used relate in some way to the students' current or future needs/interests. If students do not identify the relevance of particular materials (either automatically or with assistance from the teacher), there is little chance of upgrading reading ability. Second, instruction does not have to be limited to a reading class organized by the teacher. Third, an acceptable alternative is to teach compensation skills. And, finally, comprehension, understanding, and application are emphasized rather than word recognition.

Related to this illustration, it should be noted that the general approach to learning would be phenomenological. However, depending on the particular students involved, as well as other variables, the educator might need to implement other approaches to learning. For example, a behavioral orientation could be used in teaching essential sight words (*exit, emergency*) where reinforcement might be employed each time the student identified a word or a contract might be written. The contract would likely state what the student was to do ("learn 20 new words") in order to receive a stipulated reward. Time limits might also be included in the contract which both the student and teacher would sign.

2. *Improvement of interpersonal relations in a social context.* This aspect of affective learning is often overlooked in current education practices because it is generally assumed that students will learn the skill "on their own." However, handicapped students frequently need assistance in learning how to interact with their peers socially.

If students are deficient in skills needed to enhance interpersonal relations, sociocultural approaches involving individual or group therapy could be used and combined with the phenomenological approaches based on the work of Rogers (1951, 1961), focusing on client-centered therapy. When such a technique is used it is assumed that the student improves or grows due to the quality and character of the student-educator relationship rather than because he receives special treatment procedures or specialized expertise in psychology. The educator assumes the role of a nondirective therapist and encourages the student to take responsibility for the subjects of the discussions. In addition, the educator reflects rather than interprets the student's thoughts and feelings and encourages (but does not recommend) efforts toward growth and individual expression.

The actual work with the students on improving their interpersonal-relation skills would likely take place in the school. However, the students would be encouraged to apply the skills in both the home and community. In fact, the objective (improving students' interpersonal relations in a social context) could not be judged successful unless the students were evaluated in the community and home as well as the school.

3. *Career exploration.* Career exploration usually indicates that students will be examining a variety of occupations they may wish to pursue. However, it may also indicate a time when students probe or learn the usefulness of particular functional living skills or subject matter areas. That is, the skills being taught become relevant to the students because their practical value in daily life is emphasized.

Evans, Hoyt, and Mangum (1973) illustrate the manner in which both aspects of career exploration can be incorporated into a mathematics class. One objective of the class might be to focus on the importance of keeping an accurate check register (checks written, deposits, service charges, and current balance). The students could interview various bank employees as well as local businessmen (how are checks cashed, what happens when one "bounces"). During this time the students would be exploring various occupations as well as identifying for themselves the need to keep an accurate check register. Concurrently, or later, lessons would be directed toward the specific skills needed. These skills would likely incorporate math as well as reading and writing skills.

In this example, the curriculum area focused upon is functional living skills within the cognitive component. The community is utilized as the educational alternative along with the classroom. Finally, sociocultural approaches to meaningful/natural learning are emphasized.

Implications of the Framework

Three major implications of the framework to assessment and instruction seem most evident. First, all handicapped persons' education should be geared toward career development. All assessment and instructional procedures used with the handicapped from kindergarten through adulthood should be critically analyzed regarding their relationship to career development. Where little or no relationship is found, other strategies should be located or developed that foster career education. Our analysis of career programming indicates that much work remains to be accomplished before it can be stated with confidence that the educational practices used with the handicapped in the schools relate to the development of successful adults in society.

The second implication of our framework is that special educators at the secondary school level need to expand their efforts into the home and community. It is important that individuals in other settings be included in the educational practices of the school for several reasons. First, it is necessary to begin longitudinal planning for the handicapped at the secondary school level. That is, most of the handicapped will need special support throughout their lifetime and, as the special educators end their responsibility for the handicapped at age 21 (according to P.L. 94–142), individuals from other settings must be ready and able to take up this responsibility. If educational practices are extended beyond the school, and into the community, longitudinal planning should assist in the shift of responsibility.

Another reason that the home and community must be involved in the educational program is simply one of efficiency. If individuals in these three settings work together on the educational process for the handicapped, we are more likely to have success with our students. Education in the natural environment where students can actually apply the knowledge and skills they learn in school is always a desirable practice. As with the other implications of this framework, much work remains for us in this area.

The final implication of our framework is that it provides us with a foundation from which to begin new and innovative approaches in the assessment of and instructional planning for handicapped adolescents. This is not meant to infer that we should throw out all the old practices and begin totally anew, but rather that we should expand upon what we do have and develop more appropriate, efficient, and relevant secondary programs.

Some readers may wish that we had provided in this chapter specific assessment devices and instructional techniques for use with handicapped adolescents. These same readers may believe that we have provided them with a somewhat complex and difficult system to operationalize. We readily admit that this is what we have done. However, a knowledge of special education history will attest that improvements are rarely easy and simple. It was not easy in the 1940s and 50s to get the public school system to accept the responsibility for the education of many of the handicapped. It was not easy in the 1960s and 70s to assist regular education teachers in accepting and integrating the handicapped into their classrooms. It will not be easy in the 1970s and 80s to improve the educational opportunities for the handicapped adolescent. But, is there ever an easy way to make significant improvements?

Programming for Academic Disabilities 4

Libby Goodman

An understanding of an author's perspective is perhaps more important for a chapter on secondary level minimally handicapped pupils than for most discussions in the realm of childhood exceptionality and special education. For one thing, the very topic of the "minimally handicapped" is as yet ill defined, one in which it is easier to recognize ambiguities and identify problems than to establish hard parameters and to clearly define programs and services. Secondly, the very nature of the educational services provided within special education until quite recently has been "elementary school" oriented, both in terms of the major focus of services and the technologies of instruction that have evolved. As a consequence, the special educator is not really prepared to deal with the complexities that he finds at the secondary school level.

These problems confronting a writer discussing secondary school minimally handicapped can be easily reduced to manageable proportions if one is willing and able to approach the topic from the standpoint of various over-simplifications. Thus the problems can be neatly packaged and written about (from afar) if one wishes to narrow discussion to problems of differential diagnosis, or individualized programs, the application of specialized techniques of management or skill development. It is quite another thing, however, to approach the topic with respect to the actual school experiences that the minimally handicapped must undergo within the traditional secondary school programs of a public school—the particular departure point that I, as a public school educator, must take. The neat, often simplistic, solutions that are so readily available from the pens of those who do not have to accept responsibilities for day-to-day operations—and year-end outcomes—do not then seem as facile or sure as they are professed to be. The realities of making do with what is available within a school to help the minimally handicapped, or, at best, of seeking new solutions that are realizable within the public school must instead be recognized and addressed. So will it be in this chapter, which recognizes, I believe, the state of the art of education for minimally handicapped youth, and the need to make this art practicable amidst some of the most complex social institutions ever developed to manage and educate man and womankind—the junior and senior high schools of this country.

Within such schools, the educator cannot expect the ultimate in diagnostic or individual prescriptive educational services to be readily available for all those whose cognitive problems have resulted in school failure. He must seek methods that can readily serve large groups of pupils, and must accomplish what is best for the majority of these. The educator has to recognize that if easy solutions were already available, there would be few minimally handicapped at the secondary level—the problems of most having already been solved during the elementary grades—instead of the many that confront us everywhere. In truth, there are now few ready and effective answers to remediating academic problems in these youths.

This chapter, then, is intended to orient the reader to the field of secondary level minimally handicapped, rather than to proffer any particular direction in which to proceed. Also, I will attempt to provide a framework within which the practicing educator may begin to work to seek his own solutions and to make a personal contribution in a fledgling field that needs practical approaches far more than theories and rhetoric. The problems of the minimally handicapped at all school levels, particularly at the secondary level, need to be approached from the standpoint of the schools wherein these pupils must cope and learn. Schools are where academic skills are taught and subject matter mastered; this is the perspective adopted for this chapter, and the one that I hope the reader will also come to understand.

Introduction

Recent federal legislation (The Education for All Handicapped Children Act, P.L. 94–142, and The Vocational Rehabilitation Act of 1973, Section 504) has affirmed the right of every handicapped child to a free, public, and appropriate program of education. However, even a cursory examination of special services at the secondary school level reveals a serious neglect of the older handicapped student (Kline, 1972; Wennberg & Hare, 1977). Undeniably, education for these academically handicapped students has been limited because the public school sector has been focused on the problems and needs of young handicapped children (Goodman & Mann, 1976; Scranton & Downs, 1975). Yet, in the face of inadequacies in both programs and services, the number of such students in need of special services appears to be increasing.

While educators today are becoming more sensitive to the needs of mildly handicapped youth in our secondary schools, public confidence in the quality of education at large is diminishing. There had been a great deal of public concern expressed about a trend of declining effectiveness of America's public school systems. Alarm has been created by highly publicized evidence that Scholastic Aptitude Test scores (which reflect the verbal and math aptitudes of high school graduates aspiring toward a college education) have been steadily dropping for the past 10 years (Angoff, 1971, 1975; Hechinger, 1974). According to a recent nationwide assessment of science achievement conducted by National Assessment of Educational Progress (1975), achievement in science is also on the decline. More disturbing still—because of its fundamental and critical relationship to overall school achievement and literacy—is the reported status of reading and nonreading among American children. For instance, the National Advisory Committee on Dyslexia and Related Reading Disorders (1969) reported that reading disability is a major problem in America's elementary and secondary schools, having found that one child in seven (15%) has serious reading disability. This report projected that eight million children in America's elementary and secondary schools would not learn to read adequately. Many would suggest that these figures are conservative. Dr. James E. Allen, commissioner of education at the time of the report's publication, drew an even more ominous conclusion: that one child in four had significant reading deficiencies, and that in large urban systems as many as half of the school population read below expectation (as reported in Lyman, 1973).

Perhaps some individuals can accept such statistics with equanimity, feeling that they reflect someone else's problem. But the social and far-reaching economic implications of massive school failure cannot be easily dismissed:

> The student's failure in learning to read can have enormous consequences in terms of emotional maladjustment, tendency toward delinquency, likelihood of becoming a dropout, and difficulty in obtaining employment. The economic loss to the nation as a result of these failures is incalculable. (National Advisory Committee of Dyslexia and Related Reading Disorders, 1969, p. 11)

Information pertaining to adult literacy does, in fact, reveal that the results of poor school performance persist beyond the conclusion of formal academic training. Government census figures on the rate of illiteracy among adults indicates that 2.4% of the population aged 14 or older are illiterate and that 8.3% of adults aged 25 or older are functionally illiterate (Lyman, 1973). Because these statistics are based on the number of years of school attendance (as reported by the respondent), rather than the result of direct testing of literacy skills, they most likely provide a gross underestimate of the problem. Time spent in school can hardly be equated with mastery of subject matter, and authorities generally agree that such governmental figures seriously underestimate the prevalence of illiteracy (Harman, 1970; Lyman, 1973).

The true enormity of the problem of illiteracy—as well as the real-life consequences—was recently revealed by the Adult Performance Level (APL) project, a federally funded project based at the University of Texas at Austin. The APL project defined *adult literacy* in terms of actual competencies performed in everyday life tasks. Life competencies were identified and categorized into one of five general knowledge areas: consumer economics, occupational knowledge, community resources, health, and government and law. Assessing the presence or absence of these competencies in a nationwide sample of adults aged 18 to 65, the project found that 20% of adults "lack minimal survival and coping skills" (Northcutt, 1976, p. 1).

The accumulation of facts and figures such as these has produced a call for action. The public has become increasingly critical of schools that give grade promotions for "social" reasons rather than academic performance. The Competency Based Education (CBE) movement seeking minimal performance requirements for promotion and graduation has been spawned by public opinion and concern (Walker, 1978).[1] Special education for the mildly handicapped will have to be responsive to the CBE movement; its implications for special education are discussed on p. 117. The CBE movement holds many potential benefits for handicapped youth in our secondary schools.

Nonachieving, sometimes disruptive, secondary school pupils clearly present critical educational problems. The number of students who can accurately be labeled *underachiever* is enormous, certainly a significant minority of our school population. There are many reasons for underachievement (Goodman & Mann, 1976); this chapter is concerned only with those students whose lack of achievement is the result of cognitive disabilities. These junior and senior high students, heretofore unserved or underserved, are candidates for educational assistance through special education. Though often considered as merely variants of the underachiever, they do, in fact, require specialized education. Let us more clearly define this special subpopulation of underachievers.

The Mildly Handicapped

The phenomenon of the mildly handicapped is becoming ever more salient as increasing numbers of children are identified and labeled under various categories of exceptionality. This is partially due to society's insistence that everyone, except for the most disabled, become academically competent; as society's demands have increased, more students have become "handicapped," unable to perform adequately and/or appropriately within traditional educational frameworks without the provision of "special" education services. The growth of the learning disabilities movement has also contributed to the trend toward using the term *mildly handicapped* and has focused educational attention upon greater numbers of educationally handicapped pupils. Compulsory school attendance laws are yet another factor in the identification of increasing numbers of mildly handicapped students in our secondary schools. These laws have prolonged the school programs for many students whose

---

[1] As of this writing, 27 states have enacted some type of educational competency requirement (Walker, 1978). The CBE movement is also attracting federal attention. Representative Ron Mottl (D–Ohio) has introduced a bill in the U. S. House of Representatives which would create a National Commission on Basic Education with the responsibility for setting national standards of educational proficiency for both elementary and secondary schools and for the development of the testing methodology by which to assess students' achievement of those standards. The proposed legislation would offer monetary incentives to states that undertake an active commitment to CBE.

cognitive deficiencies are most apparent within the academic environment. Because such pupils become, with increasing age, less and less capable of benefiting from traditional academic instruction, special educators are obligated to provide services and programs for many of them.

Any attempt to define *mildly handicapped* necessarily reflects the ambiguity of terminology and concepts in the field. It is a loosely descriptive, catch-all term arising from the attempts to noncategorically approach a range of exceptionalities. In comparison to the severely handicapped (children whose disabilities involve very serious and obvious physical deformities and/or seriously limited intellectual capacity), children who show no physical disabilities and who, outside the school, may be indistinguishable from the non-handicapped population, are indeed mildly handicapped. However, *mildly handicapped* has little information value beyond this superficial categorization and understates the severity of functional and academic disabilities displayed by many mildly handicapped children. Thus, a senior high school student with functional reading skills at the first grade level obviously has a serious disability. Many mild handicaps (poor penmanship, spelling difficulties, grammatical errors) are very resistant to remediation.

Mildly handicapped is an appellation that includes children with behavioral disorders, learning disabilities, educable mental retardation, and emotional disturbances; therefore, the heterogeneity of such children works against efforts to establish effective programs for the mildly handicapped as a group. A most important distinction among mildly handicapped adolescents can be drawn between pupils with cognitive disability and those with personality disorders, because priorities in educational programming are not the same for both types.

For the pupil with minimal cognitive handicap, the special approach to be taken is essentially an educationally remedial one; emotionally based learning problems warrant behavioral and/or psychotherapeutic intervention as their primary consideration. The remainder of this chapter will be devoted to discussion of academic problems of cognitively disabled youth: social and academic characteristics of these pupils will be discussed; a synopsis of Lerner's (1978) taxonomy of remediation will be presented; remedial instructional alternatives appropriate to the needs of the mildly cognitively disabled students will be explored. Finally, I will present a model of intervention for the mildly handicapped and address their specific programming concerns.

Alternative Remedial Approaches for Mildly Handicapped Students

The goal of remedial education for cognitively impaired adolescents is *to improve their academic achievement*. These pupils have deficits in their performance that are detrimental to their current well being and future life success. At least some of these deficits are amenable to treatment.

To accomplish the goal of remedial education, the special education teacher has at his disposal many methods, techniques, materials, and technologies from which to select; the problem is determining which are the most effective tools for any given student. It may assist the teacher in the selection process if he understands theoretically and methodologically the major "schools" of remedial approaches and techniques. Taxonomies can provide a useful perspective and starting point for effective individualization of instructional programs. Lerner (1978) provides a useful framework within which classes of remediation and subcategories of remedial methodologies are presented and contrasted. In this model, remedial approaches are classified under three broad headings: *analysis of the student*, *analysis of the curriculum*, and *analysis of environmental conditions*. The three approaches are further subdivided into more specific categories of remediation so that, in all, nine remedial subcategories are included in the model. Let us examine this model further via its three major categories.

Class I Remediation: Analysis of the Student

Analysis of the student subsumes (a) cognitive-process approaches, (b) test-related approaches, and (c) sequential stages of development approaches. These three approaches are similar in their focus on the status of the learner relative to predetermined standards for psychological and/or intellectual development. These approaches require that the educator be concerned about the child who does not measure up to age expectations for various areas of growth and development, that is, who does not achieve as well as the average youngster, with respect to rate, quality, or quantity.

Cognitive process.   The cognitive approach has been very popular with educators of the mildly handicapped, particularly regarding processes that are presumed to underlie an individual's ability to successfully process information. Extensively studied cognitive processes include memory functions, language abilities, and perceptual motor capabilities. Within each of these areas, hierarchies of skill development have been delineated, and despite gaps in our knowledge, general age expectancies for performance have been established against which we may evaluate student growth and progress. Adherents of the cognitive process approach to remediation attempt to identify specific deficit areas or deficiencies in process areas through clinical-educational diagnosis. Their remedial efforts are designed to ameliorate these deficits or to attenuate their effects.

Within the cognitive-process approach, interest and a good deal of literature have focused particularly on specific perceptual-motor abilities and disabilities and the related issue of modality functions and dysfunctions. Research and development activities in the area of perceptual-motor abilities in children has progressed from identification of specific cognitive abilities and disabilities, through the use of diagnostic instruments, to the development of training programs and materials designed to facilitate the growth and development of the processes assessed. However, available evidence on statistical qualities of the diagnostic instruments, the trainability of perceptual-motor skills they identify, and the generalizability of perceptual-motor training to academic performance has not favored a continuation of this remedial strategy (Cohen, 1967; Goodman, 1973; Hammill, Goodman, & Wiederholt, 1974; Hammill & Larsen, 1974; Newcomer & Hammill, 1976).

A related training approach is based on the concept of modality preferences. Many educators believe that an important component of a child's learning style involves modality functions; some individuals may more efficiently process information if they hear it, others if they see it, and so on. Thus, it is thought that knowledge of modality preferences and/or deficits should be used in the design of individualized instructional programs. Such instructional programs would either capitalize on a child's modality strengths and minimize his modality weaknesses, or strengthen deficit modalities. However, Arter and Jenkins (1977) recently reviewed 14 studies dealing with application of the modality concept to reading instruction; only one was found to demonstrate an interaction effect between modality preferences and type of reading instruction (Bursuk, 1971). Investigations of modality-based instruction with handicapped children have yielded a similar pattern of negative results (Goodman, Mann, & Proger, 1978). Thus, despite the widespread acceptance and application of the modality concept, appropriate research into this area has provided little validation of the idea on interventions based on it. Lerner's second remediation approach within Class I Remediation, test-related approaches, are closely aligned with and must be viewed as extensions of the cognitive remedial approach.

Test-related. In test-related remediation, specific cognitive functions are delineated through assessment with special diagnostic instruments such as the Illinois Test of Psycholinguistic Abilities (ITPA) and the Developmental Test of Visual Perception (DTVP). Results are used to develop profiles reflecting areas of pupil strength and weakness in specific psychological ability areas. Programs of ability development or remediation are then developed or prescribed on the basis of these results. Not infrequently, "canned" remedial programs accompany the test instruments.

The test-related approach is subject to many of the same criticisms leveled at the cognitive process approach. If a particular remedial format is based directly upon a test instrument, the shortcomings of the test must affect the quality of its associated training program. For example, factor analytic studies do not corroborate the existence of five discrete areas of visual development diagnosed by the DTVP; thus we must question the validity of the associated Frostig programs that provide materials and training for each of those five "discrete" skills. Very few of the testing devices that are widely used for assessment of perceptual-motor abilities have adequate reliability, construct validity, or predictive validity. Their use in individual diagnosis, where the most demanding statistical standards must apply, is clearly unwarranted.

In addition to weaknesses inherited from the testing devices on which they are based, training programs of test-related approaches suffer from a lack of documentation of training effects upon the specific psychological abilities claimed to be remediated by each training program, and sparse evidence that the training effects transfer to academic skills (Goodman, 1973; Hammill & Larsen, 1974; Newcomer & Hammill, 1976). The use of perceptual-motor training programs, in particular, is hard to justify in the face of so much contradictory evidence.

Obviously, test-related programs featuring process function and dysfunction, and remediation of the dysfunctions, are plagued by unresolved difficulties, including those reviewed previously. The issues continue to be hotly debated with respect to younger pupils, but there is general agreement that process training is rarely relevant at the secondary level. This agreement stems from the belief that the critical time for the development of cognitive skills is past by the time a youngster reaches his secondary school years. At approximately age 12 and beyond, the student is "operating within higher cognitive realms," even if defectively; so that the diagnostic-remedial tools of the process-oriented learning disabilities specialist, designed for "lower" processes of younger children, are no longer relevant (Goodman & Mann, 1976). For the secondary school population, even when process dysfunctions appear to be present, the direct teaching of academic skills is the preferred remedial approach (Goodman & Mann, 1976; Lerner, 1978; Ysseldyke, 1973).

Sequential stages of development.   Also focusing upon analysis of the student, the sequential stages approach views child development as a hierarchy of stages through which the normal child passes in the course of growing up. Piagetian psychology exemplifies this viewpoint, while Johnson and Myklebust (1967), and Getman (1965) are special educators who also hold to a sequential development perspective. Various models emphasize different specifics, but all varieties of the sequential stages of development approach propose a series of interrelated, and to varying degrees interdependent, stages that constitute the course of normal growth and development. While most children adhere to the normal sequence (allowing for a generous amount of normal variation), some will experience difficulties along the way. For these special children, it is recommended that remediation consist of (a) identification of the stage or level at which the child's development is arrested, and (b) provision of special instruction to help the child progress "as normally as possible" through to completion of the sequence. While this approach is widely accepted, Lerner (1978) notes that most hierarchical models of development apply to young children and have little relevance to adolescent education. The sequential stages approach, then, is of little direct concern in programming for cognitively disabled adolescents.

Class II Remediation: Analysis of the Curriculum

Lerner's second category encompasses three remedial approaches: (a) the skills-development approach, (b) the materials approach, and (c) the specialized techniques approach. In contrast to the first category of approaches, which hinges upon analysis of the student, approaches in this second category disregarded individual or personalized student characteristics in favor of in-depth analyses of subject matter, form, and content. While curriculum is the focus of all, each of these three variants of remediation uses a different vehicle to improve the pupil's academic achievement.

Skills development. The specific skills and the sequence of those skills within a particular subject area are focuses of this approach. Diagnosis and remediation involve the assessment of a learning-handicapped student's status relative to the skills mastered and those yet to be achieved. Various instructional methods compatible with this approach are available to assist the student toward mastery of academic skills; many criterion-referenced materials (Fountain Valley Teacher Support System, Wisconsin Design for Reading Skill Development) exemplify the skills-development approach in practice.

Skill hierarchies are at the heart of the skills-development approach, and this suggests potential problems. Lerner notes that there is little evidence that the specific skills sequences established in skills-development hierarchies are accurate. There is also the danger that a particular skill hierarchy will be applied rigidly, as when all students are expected to repeat identical developmental stages and achieve the same skills in the same sequence, even though their makeups, needs, and problems are quite disparate. While a specific skill hierarchy may outline the trend of academic training to be followed in a given curricular area, individual variation must be acknowledged and adjustments made accordingly. Despite these problems, this approach can readily be used with learning disabled adolescents. Its strong points include the focus on skills to be learned rather than weaknesses within the student to be remediated, and the direct involvement of the student in analysis of his own skill development needs and monitoring of his own progress. These aspects of the approach can greatly enhance motivation and learning, particularly in secondary school mildly handicapped pupils, who are likely to be academically turned off by school.

Materials. The materials approach involves the use of commercial, prepackaged curricula. Comprehensive curricular programs that embody entire instructional programs, including instructional objectives, materials, activities, evaluation, and supplementary materials, are widely available now. These programs minimize the time a teacher needs for instructional planning and preparation and provide for efficient academic instruction. There is, of course, danger in overreliance on such curricular materials: innovation and creative teaching may be discouraged, and as Durkin (1974) warns, overreliance on one particular material or a materials approach may lead to irrelevant instruction for an individual student. Irrelevant instruction may also result if the materials used are of poor quality or are inappropriate. Further, prepackaged approaches may even result in teacher insensitivity by giving the teacher a feeling that he is relieved of the commitment to make a personal contribution to the child's instruction.

A variation of the materials approach is one in which the teacher draws from a variety of commercial and/or teacher-made materials to design individualized instructional programs for the handicapped pupils. Such "clinical" teaching requires a teacher to have a wide range of skills: (a) knowledge of the scope and sequence of content in at least the basic skill subjects; (b) ability to translate subject content into instructional objectives; (c) ability to design informal diagnostic instruments; (d) ability to administer, score, and interpret a variety of formal, standardized, diagnostic-assessment devices; (e) ability to evaluate the relative merits of instructional materials. Also, the teacher must be willing to devote considerable time to the selection or even construction of materials, and to lesson planning.

On balance, despite limitations and possible dangers, prepackaged curricular programs can be recommended, especially to the novice teacher who lacks specific instructional skills. Reliance on good, comprehensive programs, properly implemented, should guarantee at least a minimum of adequate coverage and exposure to curricular content of concern. Personal experience with the large-scale use of a particular program of this type (Price, Goodman, & Mann, n.d.) implemented in all of our programs for learning disabled children at both the elementary and secondary levels has reaffirmed my belief that the materials approach can have considerable merit for the secondary school student who is mildly cognitively impaired.

Specialized techniques. The third variation conveys information to the disabled learner through specialized teaching techniques such as the Fernald method or the Orton-Gillingham method. Such methods prescribe specific teaching procedures, the contents to be taught, the sequence of instructional activities, and the nature of all instructional activities. They tend to be rigid but are useful for certain types of learning problems, particularly those which have been intractable to other instructional approaches, or in which children require a high degree of structuring. It must be said that the claims for the usefulness of such specialized techniques more often rest upon hope and experience than on empirical data.

Class III Remediation: Analysis of Environmental Conditions

Lerner's third category is expansive, involving analysis of the child's environment and the components thereof that shape his school performance. Three remedial approaches are subsumed in this classification: (a) behavioral approaches, (b) psychotherapeutic approaches, and (c) pedagogical approaches.

Behavioral.   The management of the student's in-class behavior is the focus of this approach. Through the application of reinforcement theory, the teacher attempts to increase desirable behaviors and/or decrease undesirable behaviors in order to improve the child's overall behavior and academic performance. Etiological factors underlying the student's difficulties are not of concern. Analysis of curricular content is secondary to the technology of behavior management.

The use of behavior modification technology is still growing rapidly within special and remedial education. Its effectiveness for both handicapped and nonhandicapped has been clearly demonstrated (O'Leary & O'Leary, 1977). Undoubtedly, it is a most powerful tool and one which every teacher should understand and be able to apply as needed in the classroom setting. However, behavior modification clearly has limitations and is not without its critics (Cronbach, 1975; Friedenburg, 1974; Goodman, 1974). Opponents of behavior modification cite its rigidity, dehumanizing qualities, and lack of generalization to other situations, among other objectives.

From the instructional perspective for secondary pupils with mild cognitive impairments, it is important to realize that behavior modification is not a replacement for curriculum. Rather, it is an adjunctive device which, when properly applied, should enhance classroom control and maximize learning outcomes.

Psychotherapeutic.   The remedial strategies dealing with feelings, emotions, and/or personality constitute psychotherapeutic remediation; the objectives of psychotherapeutic remediation are "rebuilding students' egos, giving students the confidence and assurance they lack, and letting them know that, as the teacher, you understand their problems and are confident that they can learn and succeed" (Lerner, 1978, p. 110).

Critics of this remedial approach point to a lack of evidence of its effectiveness. Even if it is successful in improving personality functioning, psychotherapeutic intervention will, by itself, do little directly to improve a student's academic performance. It may even create within the student an acceptance of his not learning: a danger exists that the pupil's academic deficiencies may become ego syntonic if his teacher loses sight of the ultimate desired outcome, improving academic functioning. However, for students whose major disabilities stem from emotional or personality disorders rather than from cognitive disabilities, an emphasis on psychotherapeutic intervention is obviously appropriate.

Pedagogical.   In dealing with the pedagogical approach, Lerner acknowledges a widespread problem that recently has been openly discussed within special education circles. The teacher is obviously a critical component of the child's learning environment. If through his actions he is hindering a student's achievement, then alteration of his teaching style is indeed a legitimate remedial strategy. The central role of the teacher has always been given lip service but is now receiving renewed attention through several avenues of research [e.g., classroom climates, ecological assessment of children with learning problems, behavioral management, effects of teacher expectancy on student performance (Rosenthan & Jacobson, 1968)[2]]. Bateman's (1974) observation that labels such as *learning disabilities* or *minimal brain dysfunction* may mask instances of poor teaching or nonteaching is very much to the point for special educators. We must recognize that at least part of a learning disability may reside in the technique of the teacher, rather than in the psychological or physiological makeup of the child. Forthright recognition of a teacher's problems can be the first step toward their solution. It follows that remediation for the mildly handicapped may require the improvement and upgrading of teaching skills.

Lerner's classification schema for remedial approaches has been discussed at some length in order to provide the reader with a useful perspective from which to judge the relative merits of different remedial approaches. There is a relationship in remedial instruction between the means and the ends. Varying remedial approaches will result in different definitions of the problem, goals of intervention, and materials and techniques employed with the problem learner. In the initial selection of a particular remedial strategy, the teacher may thus predetermine the remedial outcomes.

Remedial approaches emanating from an in-depth *Analysis of the Student* should probably be restricted to the younger populations to whom their theoretical constructs and practical methodology apply. *Analysis of Curriculum* and *Analysis of the Environmental Conditions* approaches have produced demonstrable positive results in behavioral and academic realms and are applicable to secondary as well as elementary school pupils. The teacher is ad-

---

[2] This study has not stood up well to critical examination, but it has focused attention on a critical issue.

vised, then, to draw from these two categories of remediation in dealing with the academic problems of adolescent students.

These three categories of remediation and the nine approaches they include are not perfectly discrete or mutually exclusive of each other; certain redundancies and commonalities have no doubt been apparent to the reader. Specific curricular methods or materials are not restricted to one remedial school nor are they successful with just one type of pupil. A student whose learning problems are affected by his emotional stress may require psychotherapeutic and/or behavior modification as well as academic intervention. A skills-development approach (e.g., the VAKT) may be relied upon for initiating academic remediation in order to give the student a taste of success and create an inroad to learning where none existed before, even when a materials approach is to be eventually employed. The use of curricular-based strategies does not preclude the concomitant application of behavior-management techniques; in fact, the methodologies of these two remedial approaches can mold to form a particularly powerful approach to remediation of learning problems.

Relevant Characteristics of Adolescent Learners

Selection of specific remedial methods for a given student should be based upon familiarity with the learner's characteristics and an understanding of the alternative methodologies available for teaching him in ways appropriate to his particular cognitive makeup and personality. Unfortunately, data regarding the psychoeducational characteristics of secondary school-aged, cognitively/academically deficient students are very limited with respect to instructional programming. Nevertheless, some broad characterizations and descriptive statements concerning these issues are possible.

Socio-emotional Characteristics

The concomitant emotional and social difficulties of adolescent students with learning problems have been widely discussed (Cox, 1977; Giffin, 1971; Gordon, 1970; Rosenthal, 1973; Siegel, 1974; Silver, 1974). The student in academic difficulty quite frequently exhibits a degree of socio-emotional difficulty. The probability of social problems in addition to academic ones increases with time, and disorders that may have been secondary to the learning problem in the elementary grades may intensify to major proportions at the high school level (Lerner & Evans, 1977) and even persist into adulthood (Cox, 1977). This situation appears to be particularly true when there is an absence of appropriate education and treatment for the student.

Disorders associated with learning problems include problems of social adjustment, social perception, self-concept, and motivation (Deshler, 1978). These disorders may evolve from the basic condition of learning disabilities and resultant school failure. Repeated failure and frustration inevitably cause stress, and each individual adopts an affective style to deal with it (Deshler & Alley, 1975). One student may withdraw from unrealizable demands and pressures, another may adopt an aggressive, acting-out posture, and another may exhibit both the inwardly and outwardly directed pathological behavior. When behavior problems are extreme, it may be that the pupil must be managed and educated in a way quite different than would be indicated by his learning problems alone.

Delinquent behavior has frequently been tied to academic deficiencies and specific learning disabilities (Berman & Siegel, 1974; Hogenson, 1974; Mulligan, 1969; Silberberg & Silberberg, 1971). The frequent co-occurrence of learning problems and social deviance in children who come in contact with the law has been interpreted by some professionals as evidence of a causal link between juvenile delinquency and learning disabilities. This conclusion is as yet unsubstantiated by the available data; other unidentified variables may be the causative factors underlying the correlation of delinquency and learning disability. Further investigation along these lines is certainly needed.

The need for a differentiation between emotional disability and cognitive disability has been pointed out, and its importance has to be emphasized. For the majority of students with learning problems, those whose behavior is manageable within reasonable bounds, an appropriate, comprehensive, academic program should be the preferred and primary approach. However, when a pupil's emotional and/or behavioral maladjustments are severe, management of his learning problems can no longer be the primary focus of remediation; amelioration of his emotional problems must precede academic remediation.

Emotional overlay is a term that has often been used to describe young students with learning problems, but it also applies to the older student with a long-standing history of poor school performance, whose added years of failure and frustration impair his personal adjustment to school. The important point is that such emotional problems are secondary to the student's learning problems; they are the result, not the cause, of the learning problem (DeWitt, 1977). An appropriate program of academic remediation, through which the student comes to achieve success, can lead to marked improvement in emotional status and behavioral control.

The difference between deep-seated emotional problems and cognitive disabilities was highlighted by deHirsch (1963), who found that educationally handicapped adolescents having similar behavioral and academic characteristics did not represent a homogenous group with regard to educational needs. For some of these boys (Group A), learning difficulties stemmed from "ego impairment and a manifestation of severe character disorder"; for the others (Group B), poor school performance resulted from persistent cognitive disability, usually language based. The primary treatment approach for Group A is psychotherapeutic, and the prognosis for academic success is not good. Group B boys require emotional support in addition to intensive academic remediation, but their prognosis is more hopeful: some go on to college and do quite well. The writer's own experience underscores the findings of deHirsh's study. Despite the behavioral and academic similarities of many mildly handicapped secondary school pupils, some show emotional difficulties that overshadow academic needs, require special assistance of a type and intensity the classroom teacher is unable to provide and have a poorer prognosis for progress than would be expected on the basis of cognitive factors alone.

For adolescents, social skills take on added importance; unfortunately, it is in this area that the handicapped adolescent is so often awkward and inept (Bryan, 1977; Deshler, 1978; Giffin, 1971; Johnson & Myklebust, 1967; Lerner, 1976; Wiig & Harris, 1974). Social skills require various social perception skills, encompassing an understanding of verbal and nonverbal communication, a sensitivity to the effect of one's own actions on others, and the flexibility to act appropriately in different social situations. Additionally, the personality of the older handicapped student is often one that repels rather than attracts those around him (Siegel, 1974).

While the normal experiences of growing up lead to sufficient socialization for most adolescents, the specific social deficiencies of mildly handicapped adolescents suggest that training in socialization skills must become part of the curriculum. One should not assume that minimally handicapped students will learn adequate social skills; deficient social skills areas must be systematically taught. This strategy will help insure the student's success not only in school, but also in the wider social and employment circles of adult life.

Academic and Cognitive Characteristics

The severity of academic deficiencies of secondary school students ranges all the way from mild to severe. Failure to perform up to the standards of the secondary school curriculum might only reflect a student's difficulties with a particular area of study, or it could also mean impairment of one or more basic abilities. Our concern in this chapter is for students who evidence moderate to severe learning problems, that is, students whose lack of elementary school basics stands in the way of success at the secondary school level. Careful study of their achievement reveals that these students have major gaps in knowledge and skills normally mastered during the elementary school years. The rudiments of reading, spelling, writing, and mathematics are seriously deficient, even almost totally lacking, often because of some type and degree of cognitive impairment that interferes with learning.

Academic underachievement.   Students with comparatively mild disabilities are those who experience difficulty in a particular subject area. There are many reasons for poor school performance, from lack of aptitude for the subject to lack of interest. Students with mild disabilities require tutorial assistance—best provided by content subject specialists (regular education teachers)—in addition to the regular program of instruction. The number of underachieving students in our junior and senior high schools far exceeds the number of students whose learning poblems are caused by cognitive disabilities. Underachievement in and of itself does not constitute exceptionality, but it provides one of the criteria by which the handicapped are identified. It is often the starting point for identification of a cognitively impaired pupil.

Chronicity.   Another characteristic that helps to identify the handicapped student at the secondary school level is the chronicity of his problem: he usually presents a long-standing history of academic difficulty. Cognitive disabilities generally appear early in the child's school career, typically when the child encounters the first requirements for reading and related language arts early in the primary grades. If there is no successful remedial intervention, academic difficulties result, tend to persist and become more severe. Unfortunately, early identification and remediation does not guarantee that disabilities will be totally ameliorated. The "catch 'em early and cure 'em" expectation may hold for some children, but there are others who do not respond even to the best early intervention; these pupils will require academic and other supportive services throughout their academic lives. In reality, most handicaps are not "cured"; some children compensate or circumvent and succeed despite their disabilities, and many do not. Early identification and intervention with cognitively disabled pupils will not eliminate the need for special programs in our secondary schools.

A decrease in assessed intellectual ability has often been observed among older disabled students. Myklebust (1973) attributes such decline to interferences and lags in student rate of learning, rather than to a drop-off in potential for learning. Maturational lag is also sometimes cited as an explanation for this phenomenon (Brutten, Richardson, & Mangel, 1973); this explanation is strengthened by reports of occasional spurts in cognitive ability and achievement during the early adolescent years for some learning disabled pupils (Brown, 1972; Stanford Research Institute, 1975). In the same vein as the Stanford studies, improvements in hyperactivity and distractibility are sometimes noted among older students (Bryant & McLoughlin, 1972), with or without remedial intervention.

Language problems.　While cognitive disabilities may be manifested in any and all academic tasks, the pivotal role of language ability in adolescents' learning and academic problems is unmistakable. The language and speech difficulties of adolescent students have been reviewed by Sitko and Gillespie (1978) and Wiig and Semel (1976). Both of these important sources highlight the fact that little is known about language processes in the older student; the younger child has been the focus of attention. The available evidence testifies to the vulnerability of the entire language system. Investigations have shown language deficiencies in the areas of reception, integration, and expression in learning disabled pupils. Impairments of written language are widespread, and in spelling, handwriting, and sentence production, spelling problems are often independent of reading problems (Bryant & McLoughlin, 1972). The oral language problems of older learning-handicapped pupils are often subtle and therefore overlooked in educational management (Wiig & Semel, 1976).

Because there is scant research on which to build, technologies of identification and remediation for language disability in the older pupils are limited: "Reliable, valid, and educationally relevant measures of adolescents' language competencies do not exist"

107

(Sitko & Gillespie, 1978, p. 156). The teacher must draw largely on his own resources in diagnosis and instruction and should consult Wiig and Semel (1976) and Johnson and Myklebust (1967) for remedial activities for language deficiencies, and Johnson and Myklebust (1967) and Otto, McMenemy, and Smith (1973) for remedial suggestions for written language problems.

Reading.   Reading difficulties continue to be of greatest concern to the teacher of minimally handicapped students. Gillespie and Sitko (1978) have concluded that clinical and empirical data indicate that "learning disabled adolescents possess reading characteristics that are similar to younger students with learning disabilities" (p. 190). These problems include the areas of basic sight vocabulary, comprehension, rate of reading, auditory and visual discrimination difficulties, sequencing of letters, and sound blending. Additionally, there are undoubtedly problems specific to the older age group, even if they have not been thoroughly researched. Because of basic reading problems, most older cognitively impaired pupils can be expected to have problems in many or all subject areas. An apparent lack of aptitude for a subject may be no more than a basic reading problem. Thus, one student may fail mathematics because of mathematical disability, while another student may be failing because he cannot read the problems (Cawley, 1978). It is critically important to distinguish between these two types of problems; the remedial help indicated in each case is drastically different.

The preceding litany of academic, cognitive, and social disabilities of handicapped adolescent youth should not discourage us. The first step toward remediation must be identification of the pupil's problem. The prognosis for remedial education is good. We have yet to see what can be accomplished with adequate resources and programs. The Stanford Research Institute report (1975) suggests that the adolescent years may hold added potential for learning:

> Fortunately, a growing body of psychological and educational research offers alternatives and details cognitive and psychological characteristics of adolescents that point to special potentials for learning. During adolescence the student gains the ability to take an objective viewpoint, which is crucial to the understanding and mastery of effective written communication. He also makes important decisions about his relationship to school and to society that affect his motivation. Perhaps most important

is the development of what is called "formal operational thinking," which enables adolescents to adopt whole conceptual systems rather than having to acquire bits of knowledge piecemeal. These and other abilities specific to adolescence make the intermediate and secondary grades periods of enormous learning potential, and a logical choice for compensatory intervention. (p. xii)

Although directed at compensatory programs, the comments of the Stanford researchers are germane to all students with learning problems, including the minimally handicapped.

To conclude, it is appropriate to ask if the atypical characteristics of cognitively impaired secondary school-aged students warrant the use of labels to distinguish them from other students. The controversy over this issue (Hobbs, 1975; MacMillan, 1977) has done much to sensitize educators and parents to the potential harm of indiscriminate and stereotypic use of labels to categorize children. We must consider the pros and cons of labeling cognitively impaired secondary school students.

Labels can only be justified if their use benefits the child. Kronick (1977) proposes that labeling, particularly the labeling of secondary school students with learning disabilities, has advantages that far outweigh the disadvantages. The adolescent with cognitive impairments surely is aware of his limitations and difficulties; having a name for the problem may help him, and the appropriate label may be far less threatening than the labels he imagined. Not only may the label make the student more comfortable by giving him an explanation for his difficulties, but it will often help adults who have frequent contact with the student to understand the student's disability and the effects of his disability on behavior and academic achievement. Adults are likely to be more tolerant of academic deficiencies and related social problems if they know that the student does indeed have a disability. Labels may help parents the most, giving "concrete assurance of what the child isn't" (Kronick, 1977, p. 102) as much as what he is. Labels are also a bridge to other parents of similarly handicapped children and to sources of help. Finally, labels give students access to programs and services. Even if categorical labels were done away with, at least two categories (*exceptional* and *nonexceptional*) would remain for the purposes of identification and placement of handicapped children, as required by P.L. 94–142. Perhaps the real problem has been the indiscriminate use of labels with scores of nonhandicapped children and the use of the wrong labels with many truly handicapped children.

Remedial Programming—A Model of Service

Secondary-aged students with cognitive disabilities who evidence moderate to severe academic deficiencies require remedial programming that addresses basic skill development. Goodman and Mann (1976) describe in detail a remedial model of basic education for secondary students with learning disabilities, one that emphasizes remediation of deficiencies in basic skill subjects: reading, mathematics, and language arts. The principles of this model can guide the education of all minimally handicapped pupils in need of remediation of academic problems. Major components are described following.

Educational Focus

Secondary remedial programs cannot undertake the tasks of both regular and special education and do them well. The scope of a special academic program intended for secondary pupils with minimal cognitive impairments should be restricted to instruction in basic skills at lower grade levels one through six. Students who function beyond the sixth grade level, even if their academic achievement is still below grade, age, or I.Q. expectancies held for them, should be considered candidates for other types of educational intervention, such as tutorial help. Special education academic instruction is thus restricted to students with severe academic deficiencies who are functioning below the seventh grade level.

Why have Mann and I held to this point for secondary level learning disabled pupils? Why am I suggesting it now for all secondary level minimally handicapped pupils? From the literature on adult illiteracy, we know that sixth grade competency in reading represents *functional literacy*, that is, the level at which individuals are "just able to read essential information for daily living and working at low levels" (Robinson, 1963, p. 417). Individuals who leave school functioning below this level tend to lose what skills they have and to regress to near or total illiteracy. Other basic skill areas also achieve functional level if full and effective sixth grade education has been accomplished. Viewed in this light, a sixth grade proficiency standard becomes revelant for the minimally handicapped. The goal of remedial academic programs, then, is to help all students achieve full sixth grade proficiency in reading, language, and mathematical skills. If this is accomplished, the pupils have usable skills sufficient for independent adult living.

Additionally, for students functioning beyond sixth grade academic achievement, reintegration into the regular classroom program is possible. The student who can function at a seventh grade level has a good chance of holding his own in regular secondary school programs. It is not unrealistic to expect that regular secondary education programs have sufficient flexibility and breadth in their course offerings and sufficient support services to accommodate students who have achieved at least seventh grade competency. Students who attain basic skill competency at this level are prepared to apply them to content subjects. Again, I am assuming a school system sensitive to individual pupil needs and the ability to provide some support services.

If the instructional scope of secondary special programs for the minimally handicapped is not restricted along the lines just suggested, the demands placed upon the teacher and school system become too great. It is unrealistic to expect a special education teacher to be proficient in teaching the content of various secondary level subject areas as well as basic skills to students with varied learning problems and academic achievement. Just as one would not expect any secondary teacher to be proficient in all areas, special education teachers cannot be expected to teach the basic subjects in addition to many of the content subjects as well. Conversely, we should not expect teachers specializing in a content area to also be skilled in the remedial instruction of students with learning problems who are achieving below sixth grade level. Teachers with dual expertise in both special education and secondary curricular areas would be ideal, but it is naïve to expect to find them. Thus, it seems best for secondary level regular and special teachers to carry out as best they can the particular responsibilities that they have been prepared to assume.

Alternatives in Service Delivery

Time is a critical factor in the delivery of services to secondary students with learning handicaps. Such serious learning problems require intensive remediation if we hope to alter established patterns of nonlearning and poor achievement. In schools, this remediation will typically proceed within a classroom framework. The different classroom models available for the secondary level program are the self-contained classroom, the resource room, and mainstreaming. Both the resource room model and mainstream programs are gaining in popularity (MacMillan & Semmel, 1977), while the self-contained classroom has become for most professionals the alternative of last choice. The advantages of the resource room program over other classroom models have been discussed in the literature (Wiederholt, Hammill, & Brown, 1978). But despite the trend toward less restrictive classroom models, the self-contained classroom model should not be dismissed too quickly.

The essential difference at the secondary level between the resource room and self-contained programs comes down to the amount of time the student spends in one classroom for the purposes of academic instruction. Totally self-contained programs in which students are completely shut off from contact with their nonhandicapped peers need rarely to be the case at the secondary school level. The varied curricular offerings of the junior and senior high school, including electives and special subjects, provide many opportunities for the integration of handicapped and nonhandicapped. The label attached to a classroom program, such as *self-contained* or *resource*, often has very little to do with the type of service that is actually being provided (MacMillan & Semmel, 1977). Thus, the debate over resource rooms versus self-contained classrooms is an unproductive exercise that detracts attention from the real problem: how to provide sufficient remediation, relative to the severity of the handicap, to reach the appropriate goals for each student. An indication of the importance of the time factor to remediation was recently revealed in a report on the impact of educational innovation on student performance. Project LONG-STEP examined the effects of "level of innovation" and "degree of individualization" across all grade levels (American Institute for Research, 1976). Various educational strategies were included in the investigation, many of which are frequently used in special education classrooms (e.g., multimedia emphasis, small-group activities, Individually Prescribed Instruction in reading/math). It was found that neither innovation nor increased individualization of instruction consistently enhanced student achievement; the positive note, however, was that additional instruction in language arts was related to substantial gains in reading achievement among second grade children, and further, that these children maintained these gains during the third grade even when the amount of instruction was reduced.

The point is that the needs of secondary level minimally handicapped students must not be subordinated to any one model of service. The question to be asked is whether the chosen program will enable the student to achieve educational goals, because academic failure may have lasting and devastating effects. Or as Miller and Switzky (1978) put the question: If the intent is to permit the individual to remain in a setting that is as normal as possible, is curtailment of individual freedom more likely to result from failure to achieve educational goals or from temporary placement in an atypical situation?

Setting is really of minimal importance. If a catchphrase like *resource room* translates into diminished instructional time for pupils who desperately require an intensification of remedial efforts, then surely a self-contained class is to be preferred. It may be that the "least restrictive environment" during his school years can condemn an individual to far greater restrictions in adult life if he has not developed social, vocational, and/or literary skills.

Curriculum Selection and Use

Curriculum is a major component of the basic education program. By *curriculum* is meant a cohesive and comprehensive approach to instruction in a given content area, as opposed to the teaching of isolated skills. A curriculum includes a specific program's materials, the modes of presentation used to impart a given subject matter, and a philosophy of instruction. Curricula help establish comprehensive frameworks to control, direct, and provide purpose to remedial programming. The burden for instructional decision making —that is, what the student will actually do while he is in the special education class—is greatly simplified by reliance on curricula. Based on years of experience in public school programming, I believe that carefully selected commercial curricular materials, modified as needed, offer the best approach currently available for a developmental-remedial instructional program that will meet the needs of the mildly handicapped adolescent.

For maximum instructional efficiency, such curricula must be "managed"; any curricular programs used with the mildly handicapped should be employed in concert with a curriculum management system. Such a system generally includes instructional objectives and a series of criterion-referenced evaluative tests for diagnosis and/or assessment at frequent intervals through the curriculum. Many commercial programs in reading and math now include a management component specifically designed for them. Others are not tied to a specific management system and can be used with available systems, but it is preferable to use curriculum programs with built-in management systems.

There are several reasons that curriculum management is essential. First, it is necessary to be able to place the student appropriately in an instructional sequence in any given subject area. Additionally, the teacher must evaluate student progress in an ongoing, continuous fashion for instructional purposes. Although pre–post assessment at the beginning and end of the year may be sufficient to evaluate the total program or gauge student growth over a long period of time, evaluation at frequent and regular intervals is necessary for effective daily educational programming. Further, management systems permit us to identify specific areas of educational difficulty or handicap to which we can bring additional help. Management makes it easier to recognize a pupil's strengths and capitalize on these. Finally, the teacher needs to be accountable for the educational planning for and progress of each student. It has become increasingly important that teachers be able to document what the course of study for a particular student entails. A management system simplifies this task by helping the teacher specify to administrators, evaluators, and parents the instructional goals, the materials and techniques to be used, and the outcomes of instruction.

A Look to the Future

Certain key points emerge from the preceding discussion of special education for adolescents. First, the designation *minimally handicapped* should be reserved for students who suffer from some degree of cognitive impairment and whose academic or behavioral problems are the result of such cognitive disability. Second, it is necessary to distinguish minimally cognitively impaired students from both the larger group of school underachievers and the smaller group of students whose school-related problems stem from severe personality or character disorder. The separation of the minimally handicapped students from general achievement is essential if we are to adequately address their unique learning problems. The prevalence of underachievement in some locations is so great that the financial resources for special education would be inadequate to provide the needed programs for such students—nor should special education resources be used in this way. The demarcation between students with cognitively based disability and those with emotionally based disability is necessary because, despite some possible surface similarities in academic performance, these two types of students may require significantly different treatment programs. Third, the adjective *mildly* has little value for instruction. Its use tends to mask the range and severity of functional and academic disabilities exhibited by minimally impaired learners.

Some principles for programming were also presented. The first emphasizes that the nature of the program follows from the need to maximize the intensity and quality of instruction provided the mildly impaired learner. Thus, there should be no subordination of the student to any particular service or instructional model. The pitting of one programmatic model against another (e.g., the resource room versus the self-contained class, mainstreaming versus special education placement) are examples of failure; we need to keep the needs of the student uppermost in our minds. It is important now, when our knowledge is so limited, that we have many options in hand and avoid uncritical acceptance of fads and trends, some of which may have considerable merit, others which may prove to be meretricious. We must ultimately evaluate the value of remedial programs not by their good intentions, fine rhetoric, or glowing testimonials, but by their power to remediate, to move the student toward attainment of appropriate goals. These recommendations proceed from the premise that our goals with the minimally handicapped are academic ones and that remedial efforts with these pupils will be judged by academic criteria.

A second principle of programming is that a managed curriculum is the single most effective way of programming for academic deficiencies within a public school setting. Further, for cognitively impaired adolescents a curriculum-centered program, not a process-based approach, is likely to produce the greatest benefits. The use of behavioral technology and/or mechanical aids in conjunction with academic programming can also be recommended as a possible means of enhancing learning.

The secondary school minimally handicapped student poses a "new" and serious challenge to educators. Heretofore the very existence of handicapped students in our secondary schools was barely acknowledged. Neglect of older students with special academic needs was in part due to a reliance upon early identification and intervention programs to eliminate the need for special programs in the higher grades. Time and experience have exposed the limitations of early intervention programs and the naïveté of such expectations.

The "newness" of the problem of cognitively impaired students in secondary schools is nowhere more apparent than in the lack of knowledge about this type of student and how to meet his educational needs. There is a critical need for research, both basic and applied, to provide data bases for sound program development. Research on the characteristics of the learner is important, but urgent, practical considerations require that immediate attention be given to those factors that predispose the student toward success or failure in the classroom. Thus, our research efforts must not be limited to analysis of the student *in vacuo*. Such efforts are not suited to the adolescent pupil who is participating within an expanded social and academic milieu. There must be an ecological perspective on the adolescent with academic problems that will encompass learner characteristics, environmental factors, and the interaction of these as they relate to academic learning. The increasing awareness of the methodology of ecologic assessment among special educators (Wallace & Larsen, 1978) may increase the momentum in this direction.

The supply of instructional technology for working with handicapped adolescents is meager indeed. Characteristics unique to the adolescent years (Brown, 1978) require that an instructional technology suited to the remedial needs of older students be developed, rather than borrowed from elementary school technology as has so often been done in the past. Research along these lines is imperative.

To meet the needs of handicapped youth in the secondary schools, special teachers and regular teachers will have to work together. There needs to be a "renegotiation of the relations between regular and special education" (Reynolds, 1978, p. 60). Special education programs at the secondary level will not be immune to the forces that are reshaping regular education; similarly, regular educators must anticipate more and more interplay with special education. The CBE movement of regular education and the Individualized Education Program (IEP) process in special education illustrate this point well. Let us explore this confluence a bit further.

The essence of the Competency Based Education (CBE) movement, as has been stated, involves the establishment of minimal performance competencies as prerequisites to promotion and graduation. Will secondary level handicapped students as well as normal ones be required to meet these competencies in order to progress through the grades and finally to earn a graduation diploma? The legal implications of the CBE for the handicapped are currently being explored and debated. At this juncture, it appears that CBE poses a potential "catch-22" (McClung & Pullin, as reported in "Law Center Outlines," 1978), in which either inclusion or exclusion of the handicapped can be subject to interpretation as discrimination. No doubt the issues will be resolved in time.

We must also recognize that the least restrictive environment provisions of P.L. 94–142 will result in greater participation and increased placement of handicapped students in programs of regular education. Students with relatively mild disabilities are the most obvious candidates for integration into regular programs of instruction, particularly at the secondary level. Mainstreaming, then, will bring more and more minimally handicapped pupils face to face with the demands of regular education, including the assessment of performance and the achievement of basic competencies, which brings us back to CBE.

As regards curriculum, the CBE movement's emphasis on mastery of basic skills is certainly compatible with priorities in special education, which have long included mastery of basic skills. I suggest that regular education's minimal competencies may well become special education's terminal competencies for mildly handicapped pupils.

If special education will have to adjust its goals to keep in touch with regular education, so will regular education have to accept the fact that it now is a full-fledged partner in the education of the handicapped child. This partnership will be expressed to the greatest degree in the help that regular education extends to the minimally handicapped child or youth. Under the provisions of P.L. 94–142, both regular and special education teachers have roles to play in the identification, assessment, and educational programming for the handicapped. There is one handicap category wherein participation of regular education teachers is mandatory: the learning disabled. Beyond the particular specificity for the learning disabled, the IEP document should establish the participation of a handicapped pupil, whatever his disability, in both the regular and special class. Thus, more regular class teachers will be asked to participate in the entire IEP process. The greater the degree of integration of the handicapped into regular education, the greater the involvement and responsibility of teachers from the realm of regular education. The impact of these developments will be greatest with the minimally handicapped pupil at the secondary level.

Vocational Education for Special Students 5

James C. Brolin
Donn E. Brolin

We became interested in vocational education for individuals with special needs in rather strange and circuitous routes. Interestingly, though our careers began in divergent areas we eventually arrived at the same goal.

James Brolin: I began my professional career as a teacher in the public schools of Zanzibar and Uganda. While teaching 3 years in East Africa, I not only experienced a completely different educational environment, but also reexamined and compared my philosophy of education with regards to objectives, methods, and processes. Teacher and student goals conflict in the educational system of those two countries. "Education for education's sake" seems to be the philosophy of most teachers, while the students know that their education, relevant or not, is the only ticket to jobs. If they do not do well in school, they will have to return to a primitive life-style that excludes them from most of the material benefits that the twentieth century society promises. The African student knows why he is in school.

119

Later, as a teacher and school counselor in American schools, my interests and concerns centered around vocational aspects of education, especially for young persons in special education programs. I felt that because of parent, student, and teacher attitudes and beliefs, many "special" students were being excluded from programs that could aid them in succeeding in the adult world of work.

After 9 years in formal education systems, I began work in a comprehensive rehabilitation center, Goodwill Industries of Milwaukee. Probably nothing influenced my career more than the staff and students (clients) at this facility. No client, no matter how severe his handicap, was vocationally "terminal." Everyone, given appropriate time and learning experiences, had abilities that could lead to employment. Furthermore, the clients and staff of this facility proved this belief to be true.

I maintained this philosophy as executive director of a rehabilitation facility in Grafton, Wisconsin, as an instructor in rehabilitation services at Emporia Kansas State College, and as a trainer of rehabilitation facility personnel at Auburn University.

Donn Brolin: I decided on a career in the business world, but soon found that business did not meet with my needs or interests. In 1961, I studied at the University of Wisconsin to become a school counselor so that I could "help poor misdirected people like myself." Instead, I received a degree in rehabilitation counseling and was hired in 1963 to develop a prevocational evaluation program for the mentally retarded at Central Wisconsin Colony and Training School in Madison, Wisconsin. Realizing that I better learn something about the mentally retarded, I re-enrolled at the University of Wisconsin and took several special education courses. My 6 years spent at Central Colony provided me with the opportunity to travel throughout the state, working with schools and agencies that were encountering major problems in serving retarded and other handicapped children and adults. My travels motivated me to undertake doctoral level training at the University of Wisconsin with the goal of becoming a university trainer who would be able to develop new approaches, personnel, and service delivery systems for handicapped persons. Those persons who were particularly significant in this decision were Harvey Stevens, superintendent of Central Colony, and George Wright, Mel Kaufman, and Paul Lustig from the University of Wisconsin. Since receiving my doctorate in special education and rehabilitation psychology, my professional life has been devoted to these goals.

Introduction to Vocational Education

With the passage of recent federal legislation, education for handicapped and disadvantaged students can no longer be considered an optional service provided by school boards who are sensitive to the needs of these populations. It now becomes the right of every child to receive a free public education in the least restrictive environment possible. Although this right does not mean that all disabled children will be "mainstreamed" into regular classrooms, it does mean that students can no longer be segregated into "special" classes unless this method can and will meet their special needs. Educators will now have to deal with disabled and disadvantaged youth who shall require more attention and/or alternative teaching strategies.

The Education for All Handicapped Children Act of 1975 (Public Law 94–142) has been hailed as the "Bill of Rights for the Handicapped." Special education teachers, vocational instructors, classroom teachers, and other school personnel are presently redefining their respective roles and responsibilities as they relate to services to the handicapped. Federal regulations for P.L. 94–142 promulgate that:

> Each public agency shall take steps to insure that its handicapped children have available to them the variety of educational programs and services available to non-handicapped children in the area served by the agency including . . . industrial arts, consumer and homemaking education, and vocational education (Section 102a, 305).

Already, we are hearing the protests of teachers who now have handicapped students as part of their regular classroom responsibility. During the 1977 National Education Association (NEA) Convention, the NEA executive director charged that the financing of the new federal law (P.L. 94–142) is "arbitrary and inadequate" ("New Law Requires," 1977).

The Vocational Education Amendment of 1976 (P.L. 94–482) mandates that each state spend at least 20% of their federal vocational dollars for disadvantaged individuals and 10% for handicapped individuals. Unlike the past, in order to get federal funds, state and local agencies must match the amounts to which they are entitled.

And finally, the regulations for Section 504 of the Rehabilitation Act of 1973 (P.L. 93–516) set forth requirements for nondiscrimination on the basis of handicap in preschool, elementary, secondary, and adult education programs and activities, including secondary and adult education programs.

School districts, state departments of education, legislators, and others are now attempting to define and direct these mandated services for the disabled. And it is at this point that we suggest that the schools take a hard look at vocational education for special students.

What Is Vocational Education?

Vocational education is a local, state, and federal endeavor focusing on the occupational preparation of individuals at less than a baccalaureate level. The Vocational Act of 1963 (P.L. 88–201) defines it as follows:

> Vocational education means vocational or technical training or retraining which is given in schools or classes (including field or laboratory work and remedial or related academic and technical instruction incident thereto) under public supervision and control or under contract with a state board or local educational agency and is conducted as part of a program designed to prepare individuals for gainful employment as semiskilled or skilled workers or technicians or subprofessionals in recognized occupations and in new and emerging occupations or to prepare individuals for enrollment in advanced technical programs, but excluding any program to prepare individuals for employment in occupations which the Commissioner determines, and specifies by regulation, to be generally considered professional or which requires a baccalaureate or higher degree. . . . (Sec. 108)

The Vocational Education Amendments of 1968 mandated vocational education for students with special needs. The term *special needs* refers to both handicapped and disadvantaged students, implying the need for special instructional services. The act defines vocational education for disadvantaged or handicapped persons as including special educational programs and services designed to enable disadvantaged or handicapped persons to achieve vocational educational objectives that would otherwise be beyond their reach as a result of their handicapping condition.

Vocational education relates directly and indirectly to employment. It differs from general education only in emphasis. Vocational education does not consist of a separate, distinct curriculum designed only to teach specific job skills to individuals who have already made definite career choices. It is concerned with the process of career exploration, vocational assessment, training, job try-outs, and job placement.

Vocational education for special students does not differ from regular vocational education in its goals, objectives, and emphasis. It does differ slightly in its process and design. In addition, vocational education can no longer be a program separate from the school's general academic curriculum. Everyone involved in the educational process plays an important role in vocational education. Almost all jobs require a basic level of competency in the areas of written and spoken communication and in basic computational skills. Indeed, even in the jobs that require the least academic proficiency, an employee who does not have these basic skills will find it difficult to cope with such elementary needs as keeping track of income, paying bills, understanding personal insurance policy coverage, and understanding the countless memoranda and printed notices that bombard us daily.

In addition, vocational education for special students does not exclude another primary function of general education, that of learning appropriate social or basic living skills. No individual in our society can survive independently from other people. Twentieth century American society has no place for the hermit. The better equipped an individual can become to cope with societal demands, the more likely that person will succeed vocationally. Most workers who lose their jobs do so not because they cannot do the work, but because they come into conflict with their fellow workers, supervisors, customers, or the organization structure as represented by management.

It should be apparent that vocational education is an important component to the career education concept discussed in Chapter 6. In addition to occupational preparation, it promotes self-awareness, self-confidence, career awareness, career decision making, and many other competencies needed by handicapped students for successful community adjustment.

We do not discount the need for a sound foundation in the traditional areas of general education. But it should be remembered that vocational education has been a major focus since early times. Historically, education meant the process of training an individual to do those tasks we now call occupations: hunter, warrior, priest, crafts and trades, and leader. Education took a nonvocational function in Western society only after the Greeks generated the notion of the "Seven Liberal Arts."

In this chapter, we plan to focus primarily on the vocational aspects of education for the handicapped. In doing this, we shall look at how vocational education differs from general education, arguments for and against vocational programming for the handicapped, the people involved in the process, and the role of special educator in vocational education.

Vocational Aspects of Education

Vocational education does differ from general education in the areas of preparation and focus. Its primary concern relates directly to preparation for meaningful participation in society through employment. The skills and knowledge gained through the vocational program must be relative and applicable to productive work in specific occupations. It maintains a close relationship to actual jobs existing in our society, and it concerns itself with the process of developing skills related to obtaining and maintaining employment. It concerns itself with work, the work process, and work skills.

Because the goals of vocational education are clear and specific, we can measure success easily. If, as a result of the vocational program, our students can enter the labor force and maintain their employment, we have succeeded. And because these objectives are so clear and measurable (unlike many educational objectives) they also can be extremely threatening. If these goals are not met, who and what can we blame?

Employment is the sole criterion for success. If, as has been historically the case in American public education, the teacher looks upon the special student as a poor candidate for future employment, and if he perceives the vocational education program as a dumping ground for pupils who cannot "make it" in the regular educational program, vocational education cannot be justified.

Arguments Against Vocational Education

The special educator who plans to implement a vocational program for handicapped and disadvantaged students should be aware of some of the beliefs that tend to create opposition to vocational education programs for this group. In many cases, this opposition remains silent and unspoken. But it exists, nevertheless. Many educators, parents, legislators, and the tax-paying public do raise questions when asked to support special programs with a vocational emphasis. Let us, then, look at three of these arguments.

Patty Pragmatic: I'm all for helping the handicapped and disadvantaged . . . but let's be realistic. In the *real* work world, special considerations are not made for "special" workers. They must compete with nonhandicapped workers for jobs; why not let them learn about the real world in school? Why can't they take the same courses in school that other students do? Why do they deserve special treatment? You sure don't get special treatment in the real world. My son doesn't get any special consideration. And really, aren't we overprotecting them anyway?

Fred Facts: Let's get our heads out of the sky for a moment and look at the hard facts. Seven to twelve percent of the labor force is already unemployed. We have a lot of good men looking for jobs they need to support their families. Government planners say we will be lucky to get unemployment down to five percent. And you bleeding-heart special educators are telling me that we need to spend my hard-earned tax dollars to train more workers. And crippled ones at that. For what? So more people can become unemployed? Come on . . . be realistic!

Bertha Budget: All of our schools work on an already tight budget. Why, we can't do all the things we need to do now. We need to set some objective priorities. It seems to me that since these special students of yours need more time and resources, it is not really fair to take needed money away from the vast majority of students to help just a few. Normal students have a much greater chance of succeeding vocationally and of making a real contribution to society. By helping a retard, we may miss another Einstein. Why don't we spend our limited resources where they will do the most good for society? Anyway, social welfare programs will take care of your people once they graduate. Our other students have no one to take care of them after graduation.

These three arguments represent real questions that must be answered by any educator involved in the development and implementation of special programs in vocational education. The questions raised were only representative of some of the very real barriers to special programs.

Arguments for Vocational Education

Let us look at some of the justifications for vocational education for special students. These concepts represent only a few of the many reasons for using time and personnel to provide vocational education for the handicapped.

A recent study by the Carnegie Corporation's Council on Children (1977) reports that equal opportunity in the United States is a myth and that whole groups in our society—including the poor, minority groups, and the handicapped—are confronted by a stacked deck against economic survival. The Council recommends a national program that would guarantee a job for all breadwinners. Would such a plan contribute to inflation? The report states that no inflation short of the "runaway" stage could inflict the damage on families and children now being caused by unemployment.

Every citizen has the right to become an active, productive, participating member of society. This right has been spelled out in documents ranging from the Declaration of Independence, to recent legislation dealing with employment discrimination, to laws regarding the education of the handicapped. The question no longer is, Do these people have a right to education? The question is, How best can we educate our handicapped/disadvantaged citizens so that they can become active, productive members of society?

No society can afford to maintain a large number of unproductive citizens. If education for special students does not assist them in entering the mainstream of American life by participating actively as producers, it would be difficult to justify educational and, later in life, welfare expenditures. American society places a great emphasis on the work ethic. Our experience indicates that the handicapped and disadvantaged share in this belief. In many cases, people identify us by our job titles. What right do we have to deny any portion of our population an opportunity to participate?

There is no evidence to indicate that by employing the handicapped and disadvantaged, we deny other persons employment. The economic and social factors leading to unemployment cannot be solved by denying a portion of our adult population opportunities to work. The costs of denying handicapped individuals the oppunity to enter the labor force have been clearly spelled out by deputy commissioner of education Edwin Martin (1971):

From two-thirds to three-fourths of all special education programs are at the elementary school level, and in many, preparation for the world of work is only indirectly involved. Only 21 percent of handicapped children leaving school in the next 4 years will be fully employed or go on to college. Another 40 percent will be underemployed, and 26 percent will be unemployed. An additional 10 percent will require at least a partially "sheltered" setting and family, and 3 percent will probably be almost totally dependent. (pp. 523–524)

Finally, the alternatives to unemployment remain unacceptable to society. The daily newspaper contains constant critcisms of the government's alternative programs: welfare, social security, pointless "make-work" jobs, and other "services." If, indeed, no acceptable substitute exists, then educators have no real alternative to effective vocational education programs in the public schools.

The Need for Vocational Education

The most important concept to consider when designing vocational education programs for our special students should be that *people are more alike than different*. Those of us who work with the handicapped and disadvantaged usually stress the differences in our students. In reality, our students only differ from other students in one aspect, their disability. Every human has limitations; but in order for our students to be eligible for special programs, their "differences" must be identified, labeled, and given legal sanction. If we, in turn, think of our students in terms only of their limitations, emphasizing only what they cannot accomplish, we shall place them at an additional disadvantage. We need to look at what our students can do, what potentials they possess, and how to assist them in using their *strengths* to advantage.

After all, what does *mental retardation* mean? It simply means that a person probably scored below 70 on a standardized intelligence test. Before making any additional assumptions about what this score means, we have to look much more closely at the individual. And what does *disadvantaged* really mean? It only means that the individual probably comes from a financially poor family. We must be careful not to draw too many assumptions from a label. Labels only serve to qualify a person for special programs. After that, we must stop looking at the label and begin working with the individual.

127

Components of Vocational Education

There are many ways of looking at vocational education. We propose that instead of considering academic subjects, we identify the major tools involved in the process. These components may be used in many settings, both formal and informal. The users of these educational tools may be both professional educators and nonprofessionals, but all are involved in the educational process.

The first vocational education tool is career exploration, which consists of the process of learning about the world of work, the role of the worker, career opportunities, and specific job requirements. Career exploration aids the student in the decision-making process. As he learns more about the work world and career opportunities, he becomes better able to make wise vocational choices. He may choose to investigate more thoroughly a specific occupation that appeals to him, and he may be able to eliminate those vocational areas that have no interest for him or will not meet his needs. Ideally, the career exploration process begins early in life. The individual learns about the type of jobs his parents have and perhaps what the neighbor does for a living. As the child is exposed to more and more adults, he begins to discover that work takes many forms. In elementary school, he learns something of the work of a teacher, bus driver, nurse, janitor, cafeteria worker, and administrator. If the school has an effective prevocational program, the student will enter secondary school with limited knowledge of many types of work. The career exploration program then enables the student to expand his knowledge of the world of work, the role of the worker, the requirements of these jobs and to expand the choices available to him.

The second tool, vocational assessment, consists of a process that identifies the student's vocational strengths, limitations, and interests and aids him in setting specific vocational goals. Psychometric testing has been one traditional device used in vocational assessment. For the special student, many psychometric vocational tests have severe limitations (Neff, 1968). In fact, standardized tests have recently come under attack by the NEA leadership. NEA President John Ryor ("NEA Again Says," 1977) issued a statement saying,

> NEA continues to urge a moratorium on standardized tests as valid learning measures because the tests are misleading at best and provide misinformation to students, parents, teachers, and the general public. In fact, they may actually interfere with the attention that should be given

by educators and the public to problems facing today's students as they attempt to cope with contemporary society. (p. 3)

We suggest that when using standardized psychometric tests in the vocational assessment process, extreme care be taken so that abuses will not occur.

Another instrument that can be effective in vocational assessment is the work sample, a real or simulated task on which a student can do an actual job and compare his performance against a norm group or industrial standard. Job tryouts also give the individual a chance to compare his performance with real-life expectations and demands of a work setting. And finally, observing student behavior in the classroom, on a job, and during testing can be a valuable tool in vocational assessment. The process of assessing vocational potential cannot be accomplished in a brief time period, nor can it be the responsibility of one individual. The student will continually evaluate and reevaluate his vocational progress prior to and during employment.

The third vocational education component that the school can use is on-the-job training. It is difficult to identify any other single experience so useful in motivating and teaching about the world of work than on-the-job work experience. In the past, many handicapped and disadvantaged students have not been given the opportunity to work on a job for money. This experience gives the student an opportunity to learn about the role of the worker, explore vocational interests, learn to follow directions and work under supervision, and to earn wages for work accomplished. In addition to finding our students part-time jobs in the community (which is sometimes difficult to do), meaningful part-time employment can often be arranged in the classroom (i.e., teacher's aide), the school (janitorial, cafeteria, office), or in a sheltered workshop environment at a local rehabilitation workshop.

Our fourth component, vocational training, can be used as the tool by which our students learn specific job skills that will make them competent to handle jobs in the work world. When the student begins vocational training, he has, through the process of assessment and career exploration, begun to narrow his vocational goals. The student has not yet necessarily determined a final vocational objective, but the training chosen in secondary school should reflect his interests and capabilities. Vocational training can take place in the regular school vocational training program, in cooperation with the local vocational school, or in cooperation with a government-sponsored job training program in a rehabilitation center or agency such as Concentrated Employment Training Act (CETA). Again, it is important to remember that education for the handicapped and disadvantaged need not necessarily be confined to the school building. The least restrictive environment may be found elsewhere in the community.

Finally, the last important component in the vocational education program consists of counseling. Actually, everyone with whom the student comes into contact can be useful as a vocational counselor. The key word here is *feedback*. In all activities, be it classroom instruction, career exploration, assessment, or on-the-job training, the student needs to know four things: How does this relate to the world of work? How well am I doing? What additional information or skills do I need? And what decisions must I make now? A common failing of many educational programs lies in what *students* perceive as lack of relevance. If the student can be involved in the decision-making process (after all, it is his future) and can receive adequate feedback in order to make sound decisions, we can eliminate many of the motivational problems inherent in the mandatory public educational system. We should also clarify that making decisions includes making "bad" decisions. We cannot be the judge of what is best for the student. If the individual makes what we consider a serious mistake in judgment related to the vocational program, why not let this also be a learning experience?

The five major components of a successful vocational education program for special students have been described as career exploration, vocational assessment, on-the-job training, vocational training, and vocational counseling. Our next question can be, What vocational competencies should be included in the vocational program?

Vocational Competencies

Six vocational competencies have been identified for special students (Brolin, 1976) and, indeed, for all students. These competencies will determine the content and direction of each student's vocational program and should aid in the development of the curriculum.

Knowing about and exploring occupational possibilities. This area includes an expanded knowledge of the world of work. Information must be both relevant and experiential. Field trips, community speakers, summer work experience, state employment service, films, and vocational literature must be made available in a coordinated fashion.

Selecting and planning appropriate occupational choice(s).   The students should be aware of their specific abilities, interests, and needs, and how this relates to their future life work. Periodically, students should be evaluated and guided so that they are presented with sufficient information about themselves and occupational possibilities to insure that they can make logical decisions about their future.

Exhibiting the necessary work habits required in the competitive labor market.   The students should possess a realistic conception of the characteristics required of a good worker so that by graduation they will have developed the type of skill necessary for an entry-level job.

Developing the necessary manual skills and physical tolerances required in the competitive labor market.   Special students should be able to demonstrate those physical abilities, such as fine or gross finger dexterity, standing, pulling, lifting, and others that are both relevant and necessary to the individual's vocational capabilities and potential.

Obtaining a specific and saleable entry level occupational skill. The special student should have a saleable skill in order to compete in the labor market. This specific job skill should not pigeonhole a student for life nor should it disqualify him later for other work or training in another trade.

Seeking, securing, and maintaining jobs appropriate to level of abilities, interests, and needs.   The student should know the strategies for securing employment and know the resources available to help him when he needs this kind of assistance.

Figure 5–1 presents the relationship between the general and vocational education components and the six vocational competencies. In all cases, the tools or components of vocational education assist the student to achieve more than one of the competencies expected of students completing a vocational education program in a secondary school.

Now that we have discussed the components of a vocational education program and the competencies we would expect our students to acquire, our next task consists of identifying the individuals who will carry out the program and their respective roles in the process.

The Education for All Handicapped Children Act (P.L. 94–142) contains many implications for vocational education for the handicapped. The law directs that an instructional team, which includes

131

Competency	Career exploration	Vocational assessment	On-the-job training	Vocational training	Counseling	General program
1. Knowledge of occupational possibilities	+	+	+	+	+	+
2. Occupational choice	+	+	+		+	
3. Work habits			+	+	+	+
4. Manual skills			+	+		+
5. Occupational skills			+	+		+
6. Job-seeking skills Employment	+				+	+

FIGURE 5–1
The relationship between the educational components and student vocational competencies.

vocational teachers, academic subject matter teachers, special educators, and counselors, along with the pupil's parents, shall be responsible for insuring that an appropriate program and services shall be provided. The evaluation and testing materials used to place the child cannot be racially or culturally biased. In addition, handicapped learners must be placed in the least restrictive environment. This term—*least restrictive environment*—will be the subject of much discussion for years to come. For the handicapped or disadvantaged pupil, it means that doors will be opened.

This legislation has many implications for vocational education. First, all students, regardless of the severity of their handicap, can receive a vocational education. Second, the tools we use in evaluating vocational potential must be designed for the individual, not the average or nonhandicapped student. And third, the school and the community can all be involved in this educational process. Vocational education becomes the responsibility of the team.

In the Comptroller General's Report to Congress (1976), two major concerns surface:

> The majority of handicapped students spend most of their school-day in regular classrooms, yet regular classroom teachers generally have not received training in the skills needed to effectively teach them. (p. 5)

> Handicapped students vitally need vocational instruction, yet they are intentionally excluded from the schools' vocational training programs by teachers untrained in methods for teaching the handicapped. (p. 28)

If, indeed, this situation exists, how is the school to play a role in the provision of vocational education? P.L. 94–142 mandates a team approach. But clearly the team generally does not have the training or expertise to move ahead. Or does it?

The Role of the Special Educator

The role and function of the special education teacher are and have been undergoing dramatic changes in recent years. Schwartz (1971) identifies the competencies of a clinical teacher of exceptional children with learning and behavioral problems as (a) the ability to diagnose children with varying exceptionalities, and (b) the ability to design and employ individualized instructional strategies including skills in educational analysis, planning, curricula development, and media utilization. Younie and Clark (1969) identified vocational related responsibilities for certain specialists as (a) evaluating occupational readiness, (b) correlating classroom experience with work experience, (c) planning, securing, and supervising on-the-job training situations, (d) counseling pupils and parents on social, personal, and vocational problems, (e) securing or assisting in securing job placements, (f) serving as liaison person between the school and the state vocational rehabilitation agency, (g) maintaining school and work evaluation records, and (h) interpreting the work-study program to school personnel and the community.

Other lists of special education teacher competencies have been offered by Bullock and Whelan (1971), and Brolin and Thomas (1972). It is apparent that the role of special educational personnel is both varied and extensive. And so, at this point, we shall suggest another list of responsibilities and competencies that will define the role of the special educator in vocational education of the handicapped and disadvantaged. This role consists of four major functions: program coordinator, case manager, consultant, and teacher.

As *program director*, the special educator assumes responsibility for getting needed services for the student from the best available sources at the most appropriate time. These services will be based upon the written Individualized Education Program (IEP) designed by the instructional team and the parents. The professional then will have to be fully aware of the student's strengths and limitations, each individual's stage of vocational development, services available in the school and community, and how best to integrate the student into these programs. Special educational personnel will need more than a list of programs for special students. They must know the programs well enough to decide whether a certain program meets the specific needs of their student, how best to use the program, and how to evaluate the impact and effectiveness of the service. In addition, the special educator will be aware of the real world of work and be able to relate each segment of the student's program to the vocational objectives. In school systems where vocational education provides a special needs coordinator, the special educator will work closely with this professional to coordinate the vocational training aspects of the program.

Closely allied to the function of program coordinator is that of *case manager*. The focus here lies in the educator's relationship with the student. Working closely with the pupil, the professional functions as a catalyst for the student and the vocational program. The case manager provides feedback to the student, continually assisting in interpreting and evaluating educational experiences and their relationship to vocational objectives. This feedback includes aiding students in decision making and providing vocational counseling as needed. The case manager is the individual who remains constant in the student's program. While the handicapped individual will have a great variety of teachers and other individuals working with him, the special educator remains the one person who knows him and his program and is available for consultation and assistance throughout the program.

As *consultant*, the special educator will be called upon to use his expertise in aiding other educators, parents, and persons in the community. Teachers who have handicapped children placed in their classrooms may ask for assistance in curriculum planning. They may need more information relating to the student's handicap, strengths and weaknesses, or overall educational plan. Or they may require consultation in methodology and techniques. Administrators may need consultation about student programming, mainstreaming, developing IEPs, or coping with the special needs of students. Parents may wish consultation on specific problems with their child. And finally, individuals in the community who have been called upon to assist in the vocational program can also use the special education teacher as a resource person. As the educator who is most involved with the student (case manager) and who is responsible for coordinating services (program coordinator), the special educator will be called upon for help by many individuals involved with the student.

The special educator as *teacher* will be expected to provide instruction in areas that are not available in the regular curriculum or through other resources in the community. Although the special education classroom can no longer be the dumping ground for unwanted students, the special classroom remains a center for providing instruction on a group and one-to-one basis. Vocationally, this instruction may take the form of tutoring, career exploration, vocational assessment, or skill learning in specific areas.

Generally speaking, the special educator's role in the vocational education process begins as early as possible—coordinating services with the elementary program to provide continuity with secondary education. The special educator provides a focal point for a coordinated vocational planning effort while in junior and senior high school. This strategy is accomplished through coordination and case management. And finally, the special educator provides for much of the special instruction designed to meet the needs that regular curriculum cannot meet.

Obviously, the special educator cannot function independently of the home, school, or community. Many persons are involved in the special vocational program. At this point, we shall discuss briefly the roles of other members of the vocational-educational team.

The Team

The classroom teacher can be expected to provide the student with an environment that will permit him to learn specific skills. These skills may be academic, such as English, mathematics, citizenship, or history. Or, the instruction in skills may be vocationally oriented in specific areas, such as typing, mechanics, wood and metal shop, or distributive education. In addition to instruction, the classroom teacher plays a vital role in the vocational assessment process. Feedback from the teacher concerning the pupil's skills, capabilities, interests, and performance in his area of specialty is a vital component in the vocational planning process. The interaction between teacher, student, and special educator provides a sound basis for decisions related to further programming.

The problem of placing severely handicapped and disadvantaged students in regular classroom settings will remain an issue for years to come. As clearly stated in the Comptroller General's Report to Congress (1976), most classroom teachers (vocational and academic) are simply not prepared to work with this group. Given the years and funding necessary to train teachers for this responsibility and the attitude changes necessary for integration into the regular classroom, we must ensure that in selecting regular classroom experiences, our special students are adequately served.

The school administration functions in the role of facilitator. The very nature of special vocational education requires that a program, staff, and schedule implement rather than impede the process of maximizing vocational opportunities. The school system must be sensitive to the needs of the handicapped and disadvantaged, and it must be willing to provide flexibility, staff, and the necessary incentives for individualized programming. If the administration sees education of the handicapped as just another federal requirement, the student will be viewed as a burden on the teaching staff, and it is the student who will be shortchanged. If, on the other hand, the administration makes a commitment to the spirit of the law, positive and meaningful programs can be developed for the handicapped.

Pupil services programs in the school (i.e., counseling and psychological) have traditionally played a minimal role in providing vocational services to the handicapped. The school psychologist has traditionally been given the task of identifying and labeling children with social, emotional, and cognitive handicaps. Often the psychologist has assisted the teacher by providing prescriptive measures in dealing with specific student problems. The school counselor has, in most cases, left vocational counseling up to the special education teacher. From now on, however, special educators can expect to be working more closely with psychologists and counselors, who can contribute greatly in the vocational education program both in the areas of assessment and vocational exploration.

An important reference and service center outside the school is the state employment office. This office maintains local files on job opportunities, job requirements, and projected personnel needs. The staff should be well acquainted with the community's job market, both at present and in the future. In some states, special employment counselors are assigned to work with the handicapped, and special vocational testing programs are available. Finally, the main goal of the state employment agency is to assist individuals in gaining employment. Many schools have working arrangements with their local employment agency to provide information on government work programs, job opportunities, and special job-training programs.

The Employment and Training Administration of the Labor Department also funds special programs (e.g., CETA) to provide job training and employment for economically disadvantaged, unemployed, and underemployed persons. These programs, designed to assure that the training and other services lead to maximum employment opportunities, are decentralized and include a variety of federal, state, and local programs.

Another resource available to handicapped students is the State Vocational Rehabilitation Service, a state-federal partnership providing services directly to handicapped persons. The 1973 Amendments to the Vocational Rehabilitation Act mandate that priorities for service be given to the severely handicapped. The State Vocational Rehabilitation Agency maintains local offices throughout the state. In many areas, there is a working relationship between the school and the agency; often rehabilitation counselors are assigned to visit public schools on a regular basis. An individual is eligible for services if it can be determined that he has a physical or mental disability, he has a substantial handicap to employment, and there is a reasonable expectation that providing vocational rehabilitation services will make him employable. Services to the individual may include counseling and guidance, vocational evaluation, physical restoration, training, maintenance, placement, follow-up, transportation, and *other goods and services necessary* to make the individual employable.

Working closely with state rehabilitation agencies, vocational rehabilitation centers provide vocational services specifically designed for the handicapped. The majority of these facilities are private nonprofit organizations founded by organizations and individuals interested in assisting the handicapped to become active, productive workers. Many of their programs are designed around the sheltered work concept, in which individuals who are not yet ready for competitive employment can work and earn a wage commensurate with their productivity. Other services available in vocational rehabilitation centers include work evaluation, work adjustment, job training, job readiness, and placement. Often, these facilities have cooperative programs with schools and provide evaluation and part-time employment for severely handicapped students. Rehabilitation workshops have been meeting an important vocational need of handicapped individuals. This can be seen by the fact that, without any federal mandate, the number of rehabilitation workshops in the United States has grown from 885 in 1966 to almost 3,000 in 1977 (U.S. Department of Labor, 1977).

Each community has additional services available to the handicapped and disadvantaged that can directly and indirectly benefit the school's vocational education program. If selected carefully, mental health centers, juvenile corrections, work activities centers, and special counseling services can provide valuable assistance to the individual. Schools cannot be expected to provide all the services that every handicapped student needs, but before we throw up our hands in desperation, crying that the job is impossible, let us look closely at all the programs available to our students and the expertise already existing in communities, as indicated in Figure 5–2.

The Employer

No discussion concerning vocational preparation of the handicapped would be complete without reviewing the role that the employer plays. After all, the whole purpose of the program is to have our students hired by someone willing to pay for their efforts. Many myths concerning employers, especially in the private sector, seem to prevent educators and other professionals from making an honest appraisal of the placement potential for their students. Often, employers are seen as hard, insensitive capitalists who want nothing to do with hiring the handicapped. From our experience, this is far from the truth. In fact, we know of many rehabilitation centers where employers actually make first contact with the facility, wanting to know if any "trained workers" are available.

Let us look at the problems of employment of the handicapped and disadvantages from the viewpoint of the employer. In the private sector, the company president is in business to produce a quality product or service and then sell that product or service at a price that will pay his costs and enable him to earn a reasonable rate of return on the investment (profit). In order to do this, the product or service must be something that the public will buy and can be priced competitively. If he cannot do this, then the enterprise will lose money and (in most cases) he will go out of

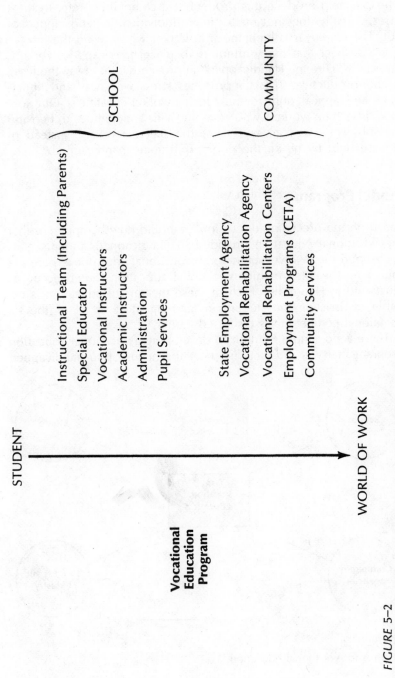

STUDENT

Instructional Team (Including Parents)
Special Educator
Vocational Instructors
Academic Instructors
Administration
Pupil Services

} SCHOOL

State Employment Agency
Vocational Rehabilitation Agency
Vocational Rehabilitation Centers
Employment Programs (CETA)
Community Services

} COMMUNITY

Vocational
Education
Program

WORLD OF WORK

FIGURE 5–2
Providers of service to the handicapped and disadvantaged.

business. In simple terms, then, the employer looks for employees who can help produce this product at a competitive rate. In most cases, it really does not matter if the individual is handicapped or not. The employer is looking for a worker who can do the job.

We suspect that many attempts to place handicapped workers, especially "Hire the Handicapped" approaches, are, to say the least, counterproductive. These approaches stress weakness and limitations and appeal only to the "social worker" instincts. Our job, then, is to train workers who have the skills and abilities to perform the job. Then we can say, "Hire the skilled worker," instead of "Please help by hiring the poor unfortunate handicapped."

Model Program

Based on the preceding discussion, it should now be apparent that the vocational education provided to handicapped students goes far beyond the involvement of only vocational educators. There are four main theaters in which vocational education should occur, as illustrated in Figure 5–3. Each of these theaters of education is capable of assisting the student in learning most or all of the six vocational competencies discussed earlier.

There is no simple solution to developing a vocational education program that will satisfactorily meet the needs of *all* handicapped

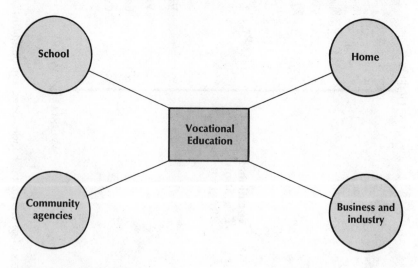

FIGURE 5–3
Theatres for vocational education.

students. Each student must be dealt with individually and alternatives will depend on the individual's unique characteristics as well as the school and community's resources for meeting these needs.

The development of a comprehensive vocational education plan should involve a variety of school personnel, as well as parents, agency workers, and employers. Parents in particular are known for their catalytic effectiveness in improving education for handicapped students. As we mentioned earlier, an integrated rather than segregated approach at least for the mildly handicapped is generally most appropriate. The special educator is a key to the coordination of appropriate educational programming for each handicapped student. We feel that a special educator, by working with other school personnel, parents, agencies, and employers (directly and indirectly) should be overall responsible for assuring that each student acquires the six vocational competencies to the extent they are within the student's capabilities. However, all school personnel must feel they too have a professional responsibility for educating the handicapped student. Administration must support this philosophy.

The following procedure is suggested for providing meaningful

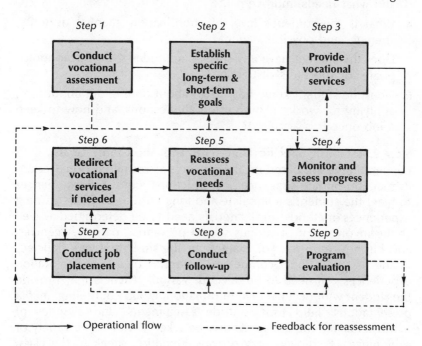

FIGURE 5–4
Systems model for secondary education services (10–12).

and comprehensive vocational education services to handicapped students. Each of the steps of the process presented in Figure 5–4 is discussed below.

Step 1. Conduct Vocational Assessment.   In the first semester of high school, the student should receive an initial assessment of the six vocational competencies. Using the standardized vocational interest and aptitude batteries, counseling, work/job samples, instructional packages, job-seeking skills packages, simulated work, campus work, parent interviews, and other techniques, an Individualized Vocational Plan (IVP) can be established either separately or conjointly with the overall Individualized Education Plan (IEP). The IVP should answer such questions as the following:

1. What does the student know about the world of work and specific job requirements?
2. What are the student's vocational interests and does he have any realistic choices at this time?
3. What type of work habits and behaviors does the student have and what needs improvement?
4. What is the student's level of coordination, manual dexterity, strength, and physical stamina?
5. Does the student have any specific aptitudes that appear appropriate for specific skill training?
6. Does the student know how to go about finding out about jobs, applying for work, filling out job applications, and how to keep a job once it is acquired?

Step 2. Establish Specific Long-term and Short-term Goals.   A cooperating team, based on the previous assessment, should establish an appropriate sequence of instructional units and experiences to meet the student's immediate and long-term needs. The learning experiences, methods, and materials need to be determined as well as the involvement of various school personnel, parents, agencies, and business/industry. For example, if the student is very deficient in the first vocational competency, a series of career exploration experiences will need to be devised. Various teachers may provide the student with occupational information, group counseling, media presentations, field trips, outside assignments, and a series of hands-on experiences. Parents may be asked to develop a variety of experiences. Employers may provide literature, speak to the class, conduct tours of their place of business, and then provide hands-on experiences.

Step 3. Provide Vocational Services.   Most likely, training and experiences in all six vocational competency areas will occur simultaneously throughout the high school program. The amount each is provided, by whom, how, and when depends on the student. The five components of vocational education are also continually part of the student's program. It is important that the various types of teachers work closely together in developing the student's skills. For example, if the goal is to prepare the student for community placement in a garment factory, the industrial arts teacher may help the student develop better manual skills and work habits; the special educator (work-study coordinator) may focus on teaching job-seeking skills; the school counselor may focus on making reasonable job choices within an occupational cluster; and the home economics teacher may help the student develop specific entry-level skills in the clothing construction area.

Step 4. Monitor and Assess Progress.   Someone will need to keep abreast of the student's vocational development. The special educator or whoever is designated as responsible must determine how successfully the short-term goals/objectives that were established are being met. The monitoring person should be available to suggest other methods and materials for students having difficulty. When it is determined that the student is not progressing satisfactorily, another vocational assessment should be conducted.

Step 5. Reassess Vocational Potentials and Needs.   The cooperating team may determine that the clothing construction area is not a viable occupational cluster, both in aptitude and interest, for the student. The student and parents may also agree and therefore, a reassessment of the student's vocational potentials, interests, and needs will be necessary. Vocational counseling and other classroom and home experiences should increase the student's vocational maturity. Thus, new interests and skills should surface from the counseling and testing experience. New goals and objectives can be established.

Step 6. Redirect Vocational Services.   Previous vocational services may have resulted in the acquiring of several vocational competencies. The only problem is the focus of occupational training. Thus, further career exploration may be needed before a specific occupational area can be determined.

Step 7. Conduct Job Placement.   Once the vocational training is sufficiently completed, the student is ready to be placed on a regular job in the community. The work environment (type of job requirements, physical characteristics, interpersonal relationships required) must be carefully analyzed prior to placing to assure placement will be consistent with the student's abilities, interests, and needs. The student should visit the job site, talk with the people there, and then decide on its appropriateness.

Step 8. Conduct Follow-Up. This activity is very important and should be done frequently. The real work place is much different than the school and home environments. If there are problems, every attempt should be made to resolve them there. If they cannot be, another placement should be sought.

Step 9. Program Evaluation. The ultimate test of the effectiveness of a vocational program is the extent to which the student secures and maintains satisfactory employment after graduation. Unfortunately, too little attention is given to this area. We recommend periodic follow-ups be made to determine former student, employer, and parent satisfaction. These three groups can also provide specific feedback on how the vocational program can be improved.

Vocational education is an important and integral part of the handicapped student's educational program at the secondary level; in fact, it should be the primary focus. It will, however, require the cooperative efforts of many types of school personnel, parents, community agencies, and employers. Systematic and cooperative planning are the keys to its success, combined with the meaningful involvement of both parents and community resources.

Where Do We Go from Here?

The first and easiest step has been taken: the legislation has been written and the mandate is clear. Now, it has become our responsibility to provide vocational education for the handicapped and disadvantaged. The task will not be easy.

We anticipate that during the next few years, the responsibility for carrying out vocational education programs will be given to professional teachers and other educators who have neither the training nor experience to work with the special-needs population. School administrators will be forced to make do with existing resources as they attempt to integrate special programs into the existing structure. Lack of adequate funding will necessitate many compromises in service delivery, so that as administrators determine new priorities and allocate resources, the place of vocational education for the handicapped and disadvantaged will be a controversial subject for all educators.

Institutions of higher learning have already begun to reevaluate their respective roles in the preparation of vocational and special teachers. A commitment to inservice training programs to meet the needs of teachers already in the schools will have to be made, and the role of the newest professional, the special needs coordinator/teacher, will have to be more clearly defined.

Two new professional organizations have been formed in order to bring together educators concerned with the vocational education of the handicapped and disadvantaged. The National Association of Vocational Education Special Needs Personnel (NAVESNP), affiliated with the American Vocational Association, has set as goals to:

1. Identify methods and procedures for improving and expanding the delivery of educational services to disadvantaged/handicapped persons through coordinating and consolidating resources of related agencies and groups.

2. Provide information for improving the effectiveness and encouraging the involvement of all vocational educators in meeting the special needs of the handicapped and/or disadvantaged learner.

3. Develop a systematic model of inservice training of teachers of vocational special needs students.

4. Encourage the involvement of NAVESNP in the development of legislative directions, strategies, and responses needed in support of Vocational Education with special attention to the disadvantaged and handicapped.

5. Develop a listing of resource persons with expertise in the various disciplines relative to programs and services for disadvantaged and handicapped persons.

6. Improve and expand preservice and inservice personnel development programs for persons working in the vocational education special needs areas. (National Association of Vocational Education Special Needs Personnel, 1976–77, pp. 1–4)

The Division on Career Development (DCD) became the twelfth division within the Council for Exceptional Children in October of

1976. The purpose of this organization is to "organize representatives from all disciplines who are involved in, or would like to be involved in, career development of exceptional children, youth, and adults." Some of the specific objectives of this organization include:

1. Provide a central or fixed point for the dissemination of career development information as they pertain to legislation, projects, research, techniques, training materials and other information that has applicability for exceptional children.

2. Stimulate and promote the implementation of pre-service/in-service training of LEA, SEA, and university personnel in career development concepts and methodologies to promote the professional growth of persons who are to deliver career development services to exceptional individuals.

3. Stimulate and promote research efforts on career development adjustment and need of exceptional individuals and to relate such information to programmatic changes on behalf of exceptional individuals.

4. Assist other organizations in identifying and promoting legislation needed to effect more appropriate career development services for exceptional individuals. (Division on Career Development, 1977)

The Council for Exceptional Children, with support from the U.S. Office of Education, has developed an administrative policy manual concerning vocational education for handicapped students. The manual is designed to be used as a guide by local educational agencies in creating or refining administrative policy that will serve as the basis for vocational education programming for these students. Policies included in the manual are those concerned with identification of students, vocational assessment, program placement, service delivery, facilities and transportation, personnel, fiscal management, and program administration. The manual contains actual policy language in the form of policy statements and administrative procedures that can be used as needed by a particular local educational agency. The policies and procedures included in the manual are based upon elements of good practice and are consistent with statute and regulations for Public Laws 94–142, 94–482, and Section 504 of 93–112.

The National Education Association, in its Resolution 77–33 ("NEA Resolution 77–33," 1977) recognizes that to implement Public Law 94–142 effectively,

a. A favorable learning experience must be created both for handicapped and nonhandicapped students.

b. Regular and special education teachers and administrators must share equally in planning and implementation for the disabled.

c. All staff should be adequately prepared for their roles through in-service training and retraining.

d. All students should be adequately prepared for the program.

e. The appropriateness of educational methods, materials, and supportive services must be determined in cooperation with classroom teachers.

f. The classroom teacher(s) should have an appeal procedure regarding the implementation of the program, especially in terms of student placement.

g. Modifications should be made in class size, using a weighted formula, scheduling, and curriculum design to accommodate the demands of the program.

h. There must be a systematic evaluation and reporting of program developments using a plan which recognizes individual differences.

i. Adequate funding must be provided and then used exclusively for this program.

j. The classroom teacher(s) must have a major role in determining individual educational programs and should become members of school assessment teams.

k. Adequate released time must be made available for teachers so that they can carry out the increased demands upon them.

l. Staff reduction will not result from implementation of the program.

m. Additional benefits negotiated for handicapped students through local collective bargaining agreements must be honored.

n. Communication among all involved parties is essential to the success of the program. (p. 52)

As we can see, the job of meeting the needs of our special students has just begun. Organizations are preparing to meet the challenge. But their success will depend entirely upon the individual professional educator. Organizations can set objectives, develop programs and offer services, but it is up to us to implement effective programs.

Special educators must become more knowledgeable of vocational education procedures so they can provide more of these experiences to handicapped students. Vocational educators must be trained to acquire the skills and abilities to work effectively with handicapped students. A truly team effort is required if these students are to receive a comprehensive vocational education.

Education for all handicapped individuals is a challenge educators must now face. Education for life implies the process of assisting our students in becoming participating members of society. And in American society, employment is a very important factor. Vocational education for the handicapped must be considered a right of each individual student, and it is our responsibility to provide this opportunity in a meaningful, flexible, obtainable manner.

In this chapter, we have discussed a rationale for vocational education, the major components of the program, and the services available to the handicapped and disadvantaged. Programming for the special student must be individualized, and so we have not spelled out a specific curriculum. But in Appendix A, p. 149, we offer the reader a list of materials that can be used by the special educator in preparing the vocational education program.

The task is difficult, but the objectives are clear. With your help, more individuals who have previously been excluded from fully participating in American society will have the opportunity to become contributing members of their communities.

Materials for the Student

The Job Box. Booklets in the Job Box are grouped together into seven different job clusters, describing in easy-to-read language a variety of jobs ranging from file clerk, to fry cook, to cattle ranch hand. Designed for the special-needs student at the junior high level. The Box also has information regarding working conditions, salary ranges, and possibilities for advancement. Includes 70 eight-page booklets. Fearon Publishers.

The Newspaper You Read by Turner, R.H. A 48-page student work-book, covering such topics as how to find information in a news-paper, jobs in the printing and newspaper industries, suburban life, reckless driving, and analyzing news stories. The teacher's guide covers this six-book series. It is suitable for reading levels 4-6. Follett Publishing Co.

Comprehensive Career Assessment Scales by Jackson, S.L., and Goulding, P.M. These scales measure student interest and familiarity with 75 occupations in 15 career clusters. In the elementary version, 75 written stimuli are orally reinforced by the examiner, and 3-point rating scales are used for responses in the familiarity and interest dimensions. A secondary version provides a 7-point scale for each dimension. The secondary version may be used in career counsel-ing. The package contains a test manual, reusable test booklets, 25 profile forms, and a scoring key. Learning Concepts.

Jerry Works in a Service Station by Wade, J.M. This book encour-ages students to experience a realistic job situation as they identify with a teen-age high school graduate. It includes exercises on the vocational content and language-arts skills. Fearon Publishers.

Occupational Notebook Program by Cook, I.D. This program deals with the basics of the world of work. The student becomes aware of the need for skills in various areas, including deciding on a line of work, filling out applications, interviewing, keeping a job, finances, travel and being a pleasant and productive worker. The book is 48 pages and comes with a 64-page teacher's guide. The kit costs $2.00; the teacher's guide is $3.00. Research Press.

PENNscript. One hundred job descriptions are available free upon request. *PENNscript* Production Center.

Finding Your Job Career Briefs. Detailed job descriptions are available for several occupations. Finney Publishing Co.

Jobs for Which a High School Education is Preferred, but not Essential. This booklet gives a brief description of a number of occupations, some of which appear appropriate for EMR students. It covers occupations, qualifications, training, and employment opportunities and trends. U.S. Department of Labor.

Help Yourself to a Job Workbooks. Part I covers the various steps leading to a job, including filling out an application form. Part II explains the difference between skilled, semiskilled, and unskilled jobs. It also includes lessons pertaining to base pay, withholding tax, fringe benefits, and social security. Part III explains employer-employee relationships, lists sources of employment and offers helpful suggestions for keeping a job. Finney Publishing Co.

Occupations by Blakely, C. (Ed.). This book contains information about job qualifications, pay, and advancement, taken largely from the *Occupational Outlook Handbook.* Information is organized into occupations in these areas: service, service occupations in government, paraprofessional, clerical, hotel and restaurant, driving, and skilled manual occupations. Reading grade level is 3–4. New Readers Press.

Occupations 2 by Schroeder, D. (Ed.). This second volume contains more information about job qualifications, pay, and advancement, again taken largely from the *Occupational Outlook Handbook.* Information is organized into these occupational areas: semiskilled, skilled, technical, clerical and sales, paraprofessional, self-employed, and supplemental. Reading grade level 3–4. New Readers Press.

The Job Ahead. This book provides reading instruction and information about the working world for nonacademic students. Its stories emphasize attitudes and skills for success on the job and in society. The book is printed in three reading levels, each containing essentially the same information: Level I (grade 2), Level II (grades 3 and 4), and Level III (grades 4 and 5). Science Research Associates, Inc.

Unemployed Uglies by Howard, R.D. A program of instruction emphasizing what not to do on the job, it includes teacher instruction book with 20 cartoons and jingles. Frank and Richards Publishing Co.

Job Attitudes: Trouble at Work. This kit explores typical on-the-job conflicts as crackling dialogue and on-location photography portrays tension between workers. Includes four color filmstrips, two cassettes, and one teacher's guide. Guidance Associates.

Your Attitude is Changing by Science Research Associates, Inc. Designed to close the gap between the untrained individual and the employment requirements of all organizations engaged in service and selling, this book helps to improve the attitude of the slow learner and prepares this person for a career. It is a guidance book written at the sixth grade reading level, oriented to adult work.

Clothing Services. Curriculum guide for teaching a clothing laboratory training course to students with special learning needs. Construction, assembly line production, alterations, repair, laundry, dry cleaning procedures, and packaging and storing clothes are included. Home Economics Instructional Materials Center.

Food Services. A curriculum guide for teaching a laboratory course in food to students with special learning needs. It includes job opportunities, equipment for commercial food production, sanitation, safety, food production, and customer service. Home Economics Instructional Materials Center.

General Power Mechanics by Worthington, R., Margules, M., and Crouse, W.H. This text enables students to acquire basic understanding and skills in the repair and maintenance of common prime power sources used in today's technology. Technical terms are highlighted in boldface type and are defined and explained when first introduced. Reading level is controlled at approximately grade 7. Webster/McGraw-Hill.

Basic Skills on the Job by Young, E.R. This kit has lessons printed on spirit masters for use with special education students. As one book in a series of six, this book covers want ads, measuring, pricing, alphabetical order, filing, and bar graphs. The kit contains 24 master lessons, each master guaranteed to make 250 copies. Warren's Educational Supplies.

The Jobs You Get by Turner, R.H. A student workbook covering such topics as job applications, how to read want ads, job interviews, letters of reference, private versus state employment agencies, and improving your speech and your handwriting. It is suitable for reading grade levels 4–6. Teacher's guide covers this six-book series. Follett Publishing Co.

Getting a Job by Randall, F. This book shows students the procedure for finding and applying for a job. It discusses on-the-job training and government programs, wages, taxes, social security, and work laws, and the reading level of the text is 3–6. Fearon Publishers.

How to Get a Job by Fraenkel, W.A. Written to be understood by an employable retarded person, this book describes the basic steps in looking for and holding a job. It is 30 pages. Single copies are free. National Association for Retarded Citizens.

Pete Saves the Day by Mafex Associates, Inc. This is a story approach to introduce varied employment concepts. Two specially prepared stories show students the basic elements in applying for employment. Mafex Associates, Inc.

Your Job Interview. Designed to guide young job-seeker through his first interview, it demonstrates why preparing is a vital step towards getting a job. The kit contains two color filmstrips, two cassettes, and one teaching guide. Guidance Associates.

Materials for the Teacher

Brolin, D. E. *Programming retarded in career education (Project PRICE). Working Paper No. 1.* Missouri: Department of Counseling and Personnel Services, Missouri University, 1974.

Brolin, D. E. *Vocational preparation of retarded citizens.* Columbus, Ohio: Charles E. Merrill, 1976.

Career planning program, grades 8–11. Boston: Houghton Mifflin, 1974.

Cegelka, W. J. *Review of work-study programs for the mentally retarded.* Arlington, Tex.: National Association for Retarded Citizens, 1974.

Curriculum materials for vocational-technical-career education. New Brunswick, N.J.: New Jersey Vocational-Technical Laboratory, Rutgers University, 1975.

DeBusk, C. W., & associates. *Vocational training and job placement of the mentally retarded: An annotated bibliography.* Lubbock, Tex.: Research and Training Center in Mental Retardation, Texas Tech University, 1974.

Distributive education for the disadvantaged. New Brunswick, N.J.: Vocational-Technical Curriculum Laboratory, Rutgers University, 1971.

Green, G. J. *Vocational education development project.* Oshkosh, Wisc.: Fox Valley, Special Education Instructional Materials Center, 1973.

A handbook for developing programs and services for disadvantaged students. Springfield, Ill.: Board of Education and Rehabilitation, 1975.

Lambert, R. H., Tindall, L. W., Davis, K. E., & Ross-Thompson, B. *Vocational education resource materials: A bibliography of materials for handicapped and special education* (2nd ed.). Madison, Wisc.: Center for Studies in Vocational and Technical Education, University of Wisconsin, 1974.

MacDonald, E., & Bridges, A. *Handbook for vocational programs for the handicapped.* Augusta, Me.: Bureau of Vocational Education, Maine State Department of Education, 1972.

National Association for Retarded Citizens. *This isn't kindness . . . It's good business.* Arlington, Tex.: National Association for Retarded Citizens, 1974.

Proceedings of the Conference on Research Needs Related to Career Education for the Handicapped. Washington, D.C.: U.S. Office of Education, Department of Health, Education, and Welfare, 1975.

Research in developing a program in basic vocational studies: Final report. Wellsburg, W.V.: Brooke County Board of Education, 1972.

Towne, D. C., & Wallace, S. *Vocational instructional materials for students with special needs.* Portland, Ore.: Northwest Regional Educational Laboratory, 1972.

Urban, S. J., & Tsuji, T. (Eds.). *The special needs student in vocational education: Selected readings.* New York: MSS Information Corporation, 1974.

Young, E. B., Stevens, G., & O'Neal, L. *Vocational education for handicapped persons: Handbook for program implementation.* (USOE No. 35096, Item No. 460–A–35). Washington, D.C.: U.S. Government Printing Office, 1971.

Career
Education 6

Patricia T. Cegelka

For the last few years I have been "in career education"—
meaning that I have identified it as my specialty area and that a
sufficient number of persons significant to my professional life
have been most supportive: my chairman has permitted me to
develop and teach career education courses, my dean has appointed me to career education study committees, and editors
have asked me to write chapters and articles on career education.
Notwithstanding this official sanctioning of career education as
an area of expertise, my interest in the career development of
handicapped children and youth is as long-standing as my initial
involvement in special education. My first teaching experience was
with junior high educable mentally retarded (EMR) youngsters in
Lawrence, Kansas. As a graduate student at the University of Kansas
I had the opportunity to work in the Kansas Work Study Project
under the direction of J. O. Smith and Jerry Chaffin. With Gene
Ensminger as my advisor, for my master's thesis I did a follow-up
study of former enrollees of that program. However, by the time I
finished my doctoral studies at the University of Kansas, concern
for occupational preparation and for secondary programs had
slipped as a national priority, so I spent my apprenticeship years
as a university professor in the general undergraduate teacher train-

155

ing programs, where most students were preparing to become special education teachers in the elementary school.

During this period of time I worked with and learned from such notable colleagues as Scott Wood of Drake University and James Tawney, C. M. Nelson, and Ed Blackhurst, all of the University of Kentucky. Our efforts, by and large, focused on competency-based instruction, mainstreaming, normalization, and litigation, all prominent features of special education during the first half of the 1970s. These developments have led us as a profession to reexamine the goals and objectives of special education. I believe that one by-product of this re-examination has been the identification of career education as a necessary component of meaningful educational programs for exceptional children. Further, we have come to recognize that this programming, as with other educational objectives, must be developmental and sequential, beginning early in the school experience with career awareness and continuing through the career preparation phase of the secondary programs, and beyond.

Each year I have required my graduate students to write a position paper on career education. In these papers they have had to review the development of the career education movement, the various definitions and approaches to career education, and its implications for special education. I have welcomed the opportunity to try my hand at my own course assignment.

Career Education

During the late 1960s and early 1970s, social and educational critics voiced discontent over the adequacy and relevance of public education. High dropout rates and high unemployment among youth were viewed as symptoms of the inappropriateness of educational programs. The frequently low academic achievement levels of both high school dropouts and graduates caused alarm. An erosion of work ethic was attributed, at least in part, to the failure of the schools to emphasize the value of work. Worker alienation was viewed by many as having its roots in school programs where no apparent relationship existed between what students were asked to learn and what they might do with the information after leaving school. Critics suggested that what the schools seemed to do best was to prepare children for the next level of education: first grade prepared them for second and twelfth grade prepared them for college, with little or no attention being given to the nonacademic aspects of life preparation.

Career education represents an attempt to respond to many of these concerns. The term was first used in this context by U. S. Commissioner of Education Sidney Marland in 1971 to describe an educational reform movement that was still on the drawing boards at U. S. Office of Education (USOE). As career education was only in the embryonic stage of conceptualization, no clear definition was offered at the time of its introduction. For several years following, the USOE avoided providing such a definition, stressing instead the evolutionary nature of the concept. Unencumbered by an official declaration, local and state educational agencies were left to develop both definitions and programs that corresponded to their varying needs.

The individualistic nature of these approaches has enhanced the appearance of career education as a "grass roots" movement, as opposed to a federally orchestrated one. While definitional flexibility has kept the concept elastic, capable of expanding and contracting in response to a variety of inputs, it has also contributed to the evaluation difficulties that career education has encountered. Due to the amorphous nature of these early conceptualizations, it was possible for proponents to casually dismiss criticisms of career education as based on misunderstandings of the concept or as responses to specific program efforts not truly representative of career education. More recently, the director of the Office of Career Education has called for improved evaluative efforts, emphasizing the need for program evaluations to become cleaner and more comprehensive and more able to stand up to tough scrutiny (Hoyt, 1977a). One step toward improved evaluation would be a clear conceptualization of the parameters, goals, and objectives of career education.

Conceptualizations of Career Education

The point of greatest disparity among the various definitional approaches to career education is in the emphasis placed on work. The narrowest conceptualizations define career education solely in terms of preparation for paid employment, whereas the broader definitions envision career education as comprehensive preparation for all aspects of life. In what perhaps had been the most conservative definition advanced, the former Executive Director of the National Council on Vocational Education stated:

> There is nothing mysterious or esoteric about Career Edu-
> cation. If it means anything at all, it means preparing for
> entry into the world of work. We can theorize it to death,
> or we can get down to the business of giving people job
> skills. (Dellefield, 1974, p. 11)

Conceptualizations of this nature have had a significant impact on the manner in which career education has been received. Many of the most scathing criticisms of this movement have focused on this narrowness of approach. Hansen (1977) notes that while the major roots of career education are to be found in both vocational education and vocational guidance, the role of vocational guidance has frequently been ignored. She suggests that this may be "one of the reasons that career education as a concept continues to be perceived, despite denials, as synonymous with vocational education" (p. 8). This interpretation has been further fostered by the facts that *(a)* early funding of career education efforts came from vocational education monies, and *(b)* the Office of Career Education was initially located in the Bureau of Adult and Technical Education.

Kenneth Hoyt, the first Director of the Office of Career Education, has been strongly criticized for the vocational education nature of his definitional emphasis to the neglect of vocational guidance (Hansen, 1977). In more recent years, his conceptualization of career education as preparation for paid employment has shifted to career education as preparation for work, including both paid and unpaid productive efforts. The first official USOE definition of career education was the totality of experiences through which one learns about and prepares to engage in work as a part of his or her way of living (Hoyt, 1975). Within this context, *career* includes all productive efforts that one engages in during one's lifetime, from self-directed early childhood learning experiences through the leisure-time pursuits of the retirement years. *Vocation* refers to the primary work role, paid or unpaid, in which one might be engaged at any given point in time, with *occupation* referring to that work role for which one does receive monetary remuneration (hence, employment). Therefore, while everyone who has an occupation also, by definition, has a vocation, not all people who have vocations can be viewed as having occupations (i.e., paid employment). Further, while one might have many occupations and vocations during his lifetime, he will have only one career (continuum of productive activities).

Despite this attention to a broadened concept of work, Hoyt's basic focus has remained on work as paid employment. He has heralded career education as leading to increased employability skills for students (Hoyt, 1977a), revitalization of the work ethic (Hoyt, 1977b), and increased economic productivity (Hoyt, 1976). Marland, who refrained from defining career education during his tenure as Commissioner of the U.S. Office of Education, has subsequently proposed a definition that stresses occupational/economic outcomes in a manner similar to that of Hoyt's (Marland, 1974).

Rejecting the narrowness of this approach, many groups have developed more encompassing conceptualizations of career education. Some have viewed career education as a means for attaining individual self-development through the clarification of values, needs, and goals, with work being only one of many ways in which the individual interacts with the environment. Others have extended this conceptualization to education for all life, thereby encompassing all of education. In this broader view, career education involves long-term involvement in activities that facilitate those competencies necessary for one to achieve satisfactory functioning in personal social, leisure, and career roles.

Super's (1976) broad definition of career is compatible with the more comprehensive conceptualization of career eucation favored by many. Super defines career as:

> The sequence of major positions occupied by a person throughout his preoccupational, occupational and post-occupational life; including work-related roles such as those of student, employee, and pensioner, together with complementary avocational familial and civic roles. (p. 18)

The Council for Exceptional Children Position

A position statement (Brolin, Cegelka, Jackson, & Wrobel, 1977) similar in many respects to these more encompassing conceptualizations is currently being considered by the Council for Exceptional Children (CEC) for official adoption. While the early paragraphs of the Brolin et al. statement focus on work, both paid and unpaid, the paper goes on to emphasize the encompassing nature of career education as preparation for all aspects of adult life. It addresses the career education needs of all exceptional individuals, from the most severely impaired to the gifted and talented. It stresses the appropriateness of the inclusion of career education objectives in the individual educational plans required for all handicapped children. Although a later section of this chapter will deal in more detail with career education for special populations, the position statement, in its entirety, is included here to facilitate comparison with other conceptualizations.

CEC Position Statement on Career Education

Career education is the totality of experiences through which one learns to live a meaningful, satisfying work life. Within the career education framework, work is conceptualized as conscious effort aimed at producing benefits for oneself and/or others. Career education provides the opportunity for children to learn, in the least restrictive environment possible, the academic, daily living, personal-social and occupational knowledges and specific vocal work skills necessary for attaining their highest levels of economic, personal and social fulfillment. The individual can obtain this fulfillment through work (both paid and unpaid) and in a variety of other societal roles and personal life styles including his/her pursuits as a student, citizen, volunteer, family member, and participant in meaningful leisure time activities.

Exceptional children, i.e., those whose characteristics range from profoundly and severely handicapped to those who are richly endowed with talents and/or intellectual giftedness, include individuals whose career potentials range from sheltered to competitive work and living arrangements. Exceptional children require career education experiences which will develop to the fullest extent possible their wide range of abilities, needs, and interests.

It is the position of CEC that individualized appropriate education for exceptional children must include the opportunity for every student to attain his/her highest level of career potential through career education experiences. Provision for these educational experiences must be reflected in an individual educational program for each exceptional child which must include the following:

* Non-discriminatory, on-going, assessment of career interests, needs and potentials which assures the recognition of the strengths of the individual which can lead

to a meaningful, satisfying career in a work-oriented society. Assessment materials and procedures must not be discriminatory on the basis of race, sex, national origin, or exceptionality.

* Career awareness, exploration, preparation and placement experiences in the least restrictive school, living and community environments which focus on the needs of the exceptional individual from early childhood through adulthood.
* Specification and utilization of community and other services related to the career development of exceptional individuals (e.g., rehabilitation, transportation, industrial and business, psychological, etc.).
* Involvement of parents or guardians and the exceptional student in career education planning.

Career education must not be viewed separately from the total curriculum. Rather, career education permeates the entire school program and even extends beyond it. It should be an infusion throughout the curriculum by knowledgeable teachers who modify the curriculum to integrate career development goals with current subject matter, goals and content. It should prepare individuals for the several life roles which make up an individual's career. These life roles may include an economic role, a community role, a home role, an avocational role, a religious or moral role, and an aesthetic role. Thus, career education is concerned with the total person and his/her adjustment for community working and living.

(Brolin et al., 1977)

The Study Committee went on to list ten objectives of Career Education for Exceptional Children. In tabular form, they are:

TABLE 6–1
Objectives of Career Education
for Exceptional Children

1. To help exceptional students develop realistic self concepts, with esteem for themselves and others, as a basic for career decisions.
2. To provide exceptional students with appropriate career guidance,

counseling and placement services utilizing counselors, teachers, parents and community resource personnel.

3. To help students know and appreciate the many changing avocational, domestic, and civic outlets for developed interests and abilities, outlets which in an automated society often supplement, complement, or even supplant paid work in making a satisfying career.

4. To provide the physical, psychological and financial accommodations necessary to serve the career education needs of exceptional children.

5. To infuse career education concepts throughout all subject matter in the curricula of exceptional children in all educational settings from early childhood through post-secondary.

6. To provide the student with the opportunity to leave the school program with an entry level saleable skill.

7. To provide career awareness experiences which aim to acquaint the individual with a broad view of the nature of the world of work, including both unpaid and paid work.

8. To provide career exploration experiences which help individuals to consider occupations which coincide with their interests and aptitudes.

9. To provide exceptional individuals programs with occupational preparation opportunities for a continuum of occupational choices covering the widest possible range of opportunities.

10. To help insure successful career adjustment of exceptional students through collaborative efforts of school and community.

(Brolin et al., 1977)

Sources of Career Education

Well before the 1971 articulation of career education, its bases were well established in educational thought and practices. Precedents for career education date back to the beginning of this century: Herr (1972, 1977) noted that elements of career education can be found as early as the American Revolution. Benjamin Franklin recognized the role education could play in facilitating success in business and in the mobility of the middle classes. He recommended that school curricula include furtherance of temperance, order, industry and frugality, good English, mathematics, the history of commerce, natural philosophy, and mechanics (Curti, 1959).

During the late 1800s, a time of rising industrialism and high immigration, a popular idea was that industrial education might provide a viable means of distributing manpower appropriately. The vocational guidance movement, attempting to explain occupational motivations and choices, grew out of observations of the apparently haphazard manner in which many people, particularly immigrants, were choosing occupations. Herr (1972) points out that during this time period the importance of education's stressing the "actualities" of life was voiced in many sectors, with the 1912 American Federation of Labor Committee on Industrial Education charging that:

> the present school systems are wholly inadequate . . . students are not directed toward the trades in our existing schools, but are actually often directed away from them by the books in education of those schools and their purely academic traditions. (p. 14)

By 1917, when the Smith-Hughes Act made the first federal monies available for vocational education, the place of vocational education in America was secured. The 1963 Vocational Education Act reaffirmed the role of vocational education while extending its services to populations not formerly included: those who had left school, either through graduation or otherwise; those who needed vocational training to gain entry into the job market or to maintain or advance in their present jobs; and, of particular interest to special educators, those who had academic, socioeconomic, or other handicaps that prevented them from succeeding in regular vocational education programs. This emphasis on the needs of individuals represents a fundamental philosophical shift in the approach of Congress to vocational education. While the Smith-Hughes Act in 1917 focused on the needs of employers for skilled workers, the Vocational Education Act of 1963 emphasized the importance of vocational skills to workers as a means of insuring their own welfares.

The specific inclusion of the handicapped as a target population for services was an important gesture. Unfortunately, it was not one, by and large, that was followed by meaningful action. The 1968 Amendments attempted to rectify this by specifying that each state must spend 10% of the Part B monies to provide programs for handicapped who were not already being served by vocational education. An additional 15% of the Part B monies were set aside for programs for the disadvantaged. For the first time, the term *handicapped* was defined for vocational education, with most categories of handicapped children being included, with the notable exception of learning disabilities. This oversight was corrected in the 1976 Amendments. Despite the expanded services provided for the handicapped following the 1968 Amendments, a government accounting office report in 1975 criticized the level of programming afforded. The majority of vocational education efforts for the handicapped involved special segregated programs, an approach deemed to be both educationally unsound and economically inefficient. The 1976 Amendments specified the inclusion of handicapped students in regular, ongoing vocational education programs, with special assistance in the way of equipment and instructional services being provided as needed.

Vocational guidance has also received attention in federal legislation. The 1964 amendments to the National Defense Education Act encouraged educational agencies to provide counseling and guidance activities that would assist students in achieving educational and career development commensurate with their abilities, aptitudes, interests, and opportunities. Amendments to the Elementary and Secondary Education Act reinforced this concept, with the 1968 Higher Education Act amendments providing for the training of school guidance counselors. As early as 1962, noneducational legislation in the form of the Economic Assistance Act promoted effective counseling as a part of its various programs (e.g., Job Corps, VISTA). Thus, it is clear that during the decade that preceded the christening of the career education movement, its antecedents were firmly established in legislation and in school practices.

Components of Career Education Programs

School-based programs in career education are usually conceptualized as including three developmental stages: career awareness, career orientation and exploration, and career preparation.

Career awareness. During the elementary school years (grades 1–6), initial examinations of the relationship of the world of work to the total life process begin. Occupations existing in the immediate environment are examined by the children, with their perspectives broadening as they mature. The work roles involved in various community resources are stressed by the teachers. For example, in a class visit to a zoo, the variety of occupations involved in maintaining a zoo could be emphasized. The relationship between various personal characteristics and attributes and the occupations are recognized. Development of pupils' awareness of their own skill potentials and preferences is an important part of career awareness. While career awareness is the focal point of career education at the elementary grades, it is conceptualized as

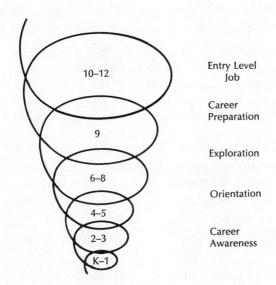

10–12

9

6–8

4–5

2–3

K–1

Entry Level
Job

Career
Preparation

Exploration

Orientation

Career
Awareness

FIGURE 6–1
Helical curriculum.

being a lifelong process, occurring concurrently with more advanced stages of career development. The helical curriculum approach (see Figure 6–1) described by Vinton, Pantzer, Farley, & Thompson (1976) best depicts fluid sequencing of career education experiences, with no distinct demarcation of stages. Movement along the continuum is a gradual extension and expansion of the knowledge and competencies obtained from the previous level. Numbers in this figure suggest the approximate grade levels at which a curriculum stage might begin.

Career orientation and exploration.   Due to the overlapping nature of these two stages, they are frequently combined for purposes of discussion. During the career orientation stage, generally recommended for grades 7 and 8, students become more involved in examining occupations through the study of several of the occupational clusters. Career exploration, slated for the 9th and 10th grades, is characterized by "hands-on" experiences, generally in simulated work environments. During these stages the students become more informed about the relationship of various vocations and occupations to specific human attributes, with career guidance being an important component of the program. In addition, the students examine a broad range of career potentialities in all areas of life, concentrate on a few of the possibilities, and relate them to predominant societal and personal value and belief systems.

Career preparation.   This final stage of a school-based program may involve the students in cooperative work experience, specific vocational training courses, and/or in preprofessional courses leading to advanced post-secondary preparation. Goldhammer and Taylor (1972) list six major features of programs at this level:

1. Continuous refinement and application of basic skills.
2. Development of specific knowledge and skills needed for family life, avocational citizenship, and cultural careers.
3. Exploration of the vocational opportunities within a specific cluster or area.
4. Provision of the opportunity for students to select a specific career.
5. Provision of opportunities for students to engage in initial preparatory knowledge and skill-building experiences while they explore post-secondary preparatory potentials; and
6. Acquisition by every student of some saleable skills before graduation.

From the preceding discussion, it is clear that career education is conceptualized as a continuous, sequential program, gradually shifting from a broad-based career awareness stage in the elementary years to more specific preparation and training at the senior high level. This is not to imply that career education ends with high school, or even college, preparation. Rather, it is conceptualized as a lifelong process, involving a continuum of career decisions and shifts. The rapidly changing nature of our society has created a need for what has been termed *lifelong learning programs.* Increasingly people have need of periodic retraining in order to maintain their current jobs, to secure promotions, or to change occupations. Such retraining opportunities are offered in a variety of sectors: industry-based inservice training, community-based adult education programs, and in colleges and universities. Testimony to the latter is the fact that the mean age of college students is increasing, as is the proportion of students enrolled in nondegree programs on a part-time basis. In addition to seeking occupationally related training, adults are looking for formal learning experiences that will enhance their avocational pursuits.

The need for a lifelong continuum of social and educational

services for the handicapped has long been recognized. Provisions for crisis counseling and semi-sheltered living environments, such as group homes and vocational rehabilitation services, are responses that have been made to this need. More frequently than not, these services have been offered on an intermittent basis and in a fairly disjointed manner. Under the auspices of lifelong learning, it is possible that·a more coordinated approach to the continuing career education needs of handicapped persons will be met, and long after graduation from high school these persons will be afforded opportunities that change their vocational, occupational, and leisure-time pursuits while engaging in a community-based life.

One unique continuing education program for handicapped students is offered at a Florida community college (Wood, Meyer, & Grady, 1977). The Educational Programs for Exceptional Adults (EPEA) is designed for educable and trainable mentally retarded students as well as those with orthopedic handicaps. A 2- to 3-year program offers noncredit course work in human growth and development, vocational adjustment, music appreciation, personality insights, home management, use of leisure time, health education, and consumerism. Additional coursework is also available in survival reading, writing, and math. Students have access to all college services and can participate in all student activities, such as dances, sports events, dramatic productions, and concerts.

Special Education and Career Education

Much of career education does not seem very new to special educators who recall the emphasis of early textbooks on the development of occupational adequacy, social competence, and personal adjustment for the mentally handicapped. The 1958 Illinois Curriculum Guide recommended a unit approach built around what were termed the *Ten Life Functions:* citizenship, communication, home and family, leisure time, management of materials and money, occupational adequacy, physical and mental health, safety, social adjustments, and travel. Ingram (1935) was one of special education's foremost advocates of this unit approach which makes educational enterprises vital and closely related to life's needs. Career education activities are found in many of the units traditionally recommended for special education, such as the classroom store and the simulated restaurant themes of primary level units.

Hungerford's (1948) conceptualization of occupational education is also reminiscent of much of career education. He stresses:

> The whole program for the mentally retarded must be built around the achieving of vocational and social competence, for here, if anywhere, the retarded will most nearly approach normalcy. This different developmental program is called Occupational Education. (cited in Kirk & Johnson, 1951)

The occupational education program was conceptualized as including five major areas: occupational information, vocational guidance, vocational training, vocational placement, and social placement. Teachers were to assume responsibility for the first three areas, with the last two being carried out by placement personnel, the U.S. Employment Service, and by other social agencies.

Kirk and Johnson (1951) proposed a core curriculum divided into "experience areas" of occupational education, societal relationships, homebuilding, and physical and mental health. They advocated that "as the learner matures in social skill and job ability, he must devote an increasing number of hours daily to exploration and learning in actual work situations" (p. 213).

The vocational rehabilitation/special education cooperative work-study programs of the 1950s and 1960s corresponded by and large to the career-preparation stage of career education. These programs featured a sequence of experiences that included prevocational activities in the junior high, job exploration in the form of work samples during the tenth grade, followed by job tryouts and, finally, permanent job placements. The emphasis of these experiences was not so much on specific skill training, or even on the development of work skills generalizable to several jobs within one or two occupational clusters, but, rather the basic emphasis was on the development of work attitudes and general work behaviors. Usually, program efficacy was measured in a binary fashion, which listed former program participants as either employed or unemployed as adults. Most efficacy studies of work-study programs did not attend to the quality or level of employment achieved. Chaffin, Davison, Regan, and Spellman (1971), noting that handicapped students who did not receive work-study training tended to become employed as adults, suggest that the function of secondary programs should not be conceptualized as making students employable (which, apparently, they were) but to maximizing that employability. They recommend that evaluation of programs be in terms of the kinds of jobs held, the reasons for changing jobs, the number of occupational promotions received, and so forth.

The mere fact of employment, regardless of job attributes or their match to the individual, is no longer acceptable for the handicapped any more than it is for the nonhandicapped. The following summarizes current thinking:

> We have, for far too long, seemed to act as though a handicapped person should be both pleased with and grateful for any kind of work society provides. Unlike other persons, we seem to assume that, if a person is handicapped, boredom on a job is impossible. Worse, much of society has seemed to assume that, while most persons should seek work compatible with their interests and aptitudes, such considerations are not necessary when seeking to find employment for handicapped persons. If any job in the world of paid employment can be found for the handicapped person, we seem far too often to be personally relieved and surprised when the handicapped person is anything less than effusively grateful. (Hoyt, 1975, pp. 6–7)

Career education can be an improvement upon the work-study model in that it entails a more coordinated and better conceptualized sequence of experiences, beginning no later than the primary grades and continuing through high school and post-high school preparation. The broadly conceptualized career education program offers several advantages over former curriculum efforts. First, the fact that it is not identified as an exclusively secondary program encourages special educators to identify sequences of experiences and competencies needed by handicapped children prior to reaching the career-preparation stage. Without this attention to the developmental sequence of skills, secondary programs can become what D'Alonzo (1977) has termed *latter-day headstart programs,* in which secondary teachers must develop the prerequisite skills before they can focus on career preparation itself. Second, career education is not identified as a mental retardation program, as was the work-study program. Rather, the career development needs of *all* exceptional children are recognized as relevant to their educational programs. Further, encouraged by the mandates of the Vocational Education Act of 1963, its amendments, and P.L. 94–142, more specific vocational training and/or postsecondary training is becoming a prominent feature of career preparation efforts with the handicapped. This fact enhances the probability that the career preparation afforded will, in fact, *maximize* the employability of the students. Clearly, secondary work-study programs can no longer be justified in terms of the placement of students in dead-end, minimal skill level jobs.

There are two additional ways in which career education is of significance to special education. The goals and programs of special education become "normalized" by the very fact that career education is promulgated as a program for *all* students. Hence, special education becomes less different both philosophically and psychologically. In addition, the timing of the career education movement has been particularly propitious for special education. It has provided a statement of goals and outcomes that often were neglected in the mainstreaming mania for placing children out of special education settings and into regular classrooms. The focus of special eduction in recent years has been on the remediation of academic deficits, frequently at the expense of substantive or content concerns. The implicit assumption has seemed to be that anything available in the regular classroom was inherently better than anything that the special education teacher could offer and that the best thing that could happen to a handicapped child was to be placed in a regular classroom. However, as Clark (1975) points out, the emphasis on mainstreaming can result in limiting the options available to the mildly handicapped. Since the curriculum focus of programs into which children are mainstreamed is not always compatible with the identified instructional needs of secondary students, mainstreaming could mean that the handicapped student would receive a watered-down curriculum that does not develop needed competencies. A sensible approach to mainstreaming is that suggested by Brolin (1975). His competency-based approach places primary responsibility on the special education teacher to coordinate and monitor the educational programs of exceptional children. He recommended that, where appropriate, the exceptional student be placed in those regular classrooms that offer the best methods of competency attainment and remain in these classrooms only as long as required to obtain the specified competencies. This approach is compatible with the following definition of mainstreaming:

> Mainstreaming refers to the temporal, instructional and social integration of eligible exceptional children with normal peers based on ongoing, individually determined, educational planning and programming process and requires classification of responsibility among regular and special education administrative instructional and support personnel. (Kaufman, Gottlieb, Agard, & Kukic, 1975, p. 4)

Career Education Activity in Special Education

In a 1973 report, the Bureau of Education for the Handicapped (BEH) projected a dismal future for the approximately 2.5 million handicapped youths who would be leaving the public schools during the following 4 years. The paper predicted that:

1. 525,000, or 21%, would be either fully employed or enrolled in college;
2. 1,000,000, or 40%, would be *underemployed* and at the poverty level;
3. 200,000, or 8%, would be idle much of the time in their home communities;
4. 650,000, or 26%, will be unemployed and on welfare;
5. 75,000, or 3%, would be totally dependent and institutionalized (p. 1).

Concerned over the implications of these figures for the adult adjustment of handicapped individuals, BEH established as a priority that by 1977, every handicapped child who leaves school shall have had career educational training relevant to the job market, meaningful to his career aspiration, and realistic to his fullest potential. Many states have recently added career education as a competency required for special education certification. Career education has become a funding priority for both the personnel preparation and research divisions of BEH, with numerous research and demonstration projects, university training programs, and special conferences being funded.

P.L. 94–142 and Career Education

The passage of The Education for All Handicapped Children Act (P.L. 94–142) has been heralded as an indication of the maturity of special education (Kokaska & Kolstoe, 1977). Essentially, the law requires that when a state undertakes to provide free education to some children, it must provide it for all children, including the handicapped. This education must be provided in the least restrictive environment feasible and it must be appropriate to the individual needs of the child. Although the law does not specify career education, its acceptance as appropriate for nonhandicapped children mandates its inclusion in the educational programs of handicapped children. The law does specifically speak to vocational education and, in fact, its provisions supercede those of the Vocational Education Act and its amendments. Consequently, it can be expected that the individualized education plans developed for most handicapped children will specify both career and vocational education training as appropriate; and that for many children at the secondary level, the regular vocational education program will be determined to be the least restrictive environment in which the requisite training can be provided.

Cegelka and Phillips (1978) list the basic components involved in the development of the Individual Educational Program (IEP) for secondary students. These five considerations (assessment, placement, curriculum, program management, and evaluation) comprise the structure for the delivery of services to secondary level handicapped students. The first three of these factors and their respective relevance to the IEP will be described in the following.

Assessment.   Assessment includes testing that occurs prior to the development of the IEP as well as the ongoing assessment of abilities and interests that occur as the student participates in a developmental sequence of academic and career preparation experiences. There is a wide variety of academic and vocational assessment instruments and techniques that have potential utility with the adolescent handicapped student. Brolin (1976) provides an excellent review of many of these.

The academic skills of the student can best be assessed through a combination of standardized tests, informal assessment procedures, and behavioral observation techniques. These assessments will provide a basis for decision making regarding the identification of the youngster as exceptional, the appropriateness of placing the youngster in selected mainstream classes, and the prescription of optimal instructional procedures. The academic assessment, in combination with data from appropriate vocational interest and aptitude assessments, can suggest a general direction for the career preparation components of an individual student's program.

One of the most popular means of prevocational evaluation of the handicapped involves the *work-sample* method. The work sample is a simulated task or occupational activity representative of those existing in various employment settings. Examples of work samples included in the various standardized evaluation systems include drafting, clerical, electronics, assembly, mail clerk, machine shop, woodworking, packing, sorting, industrial housekeeping, plumbing, cosmetology, data calculation and recording, and mechanics. Work samples provide the evaluator/counselor with an opportunity to observe a wide range of personality characteristics as well as skill aptitudes. The similarity of work samples to actual job skills provides a prevocational orientation to the world of work. In using the work samples, it may be best to forego standardized testing procedures; with many handicapped students, several attempts at each work sample will provide a better indication of vocational potential.

Commercial evaluation systems using a work-sample approach include the Philadelphia Jewish Employment and Vocational System (JEVS) Work Sample Battery, and the Vocational Information and Evaluation Work Sample (VIEWS), developed specifically for the mentally retarded; the Singer Vocational Evaluation System (sometimes called the Singer/Graflex System); and the Comprehensive Occupational Assessment and Training System (COATS).[1] While all the systems have some problems in terms of validity and reliability, they do afford the educator with an objective and systematic approach to prevocational evaluation.

Situational work assessment is a popular nonstandardized approach to systematically observing work behavior. By employing direct observation and recording of behavior, preferably by means of rating scales, the evaluator can determine the progress of the worker toward meeting the job standards. Situational work assessments can be used in simulated work settings, workshop settings, and on-the-job training, as well as in follow-up studies of former students. This type of assessment can assist the evaluator in pinpointing the particular areas of difficulty and in prescribing remediation.

Placement.   Although the decisions leading to initial special education placement usually occur at the elementary level, of no less importance are those decisions that are required as the student's program is reviewed and revised by the placement committee throughout the educational experience. The committee's ongoing review can have great impact upon the quality of adult adjustment that the handicapped individual will be able to attain.

If it is determined that placement in a special education program continues to be the appropriate placement for the student, a wide range of program alternatives are available, ranging from self-contained special education programs to almost all mainstreamed

---

[1] For more information on the JEVS and the VIEWS, write the Vocational Research Institute, 1913 Walnut Street, Philadelphia, PA 19103. For more information on the Singer System, write the Singer Evaluation Division, 80 Commerce Drive, Rochester, NY 14623. For more information on COATS, write Prep Inc., 1575 Parkway Avenue, Trenton, NJ 08628.

ones. Vocational education training affords an excellent opportunity for many exceptional children to receive specific skill training that will improve their opportunities for job entry and adjustment. The inclusion of students with handicaps into vocational education programs requires several adjustments on the part of vocational education teachers. They frequently must alter instructional methods (e.g., not relying heavily on reading), provide for adaptations of machines and tools, and, in some cases, differentiate instructional goals for the students. In other words, a student with a serious learning problem might not complete the entire vocational training program designed to produce skilled workers, but instead would complete vocational training sufficient for the less skilled entry-level jobs of a particular occupational cluster. It is important to keep in mind that while an initial IEP may call for only a limited level of skill training, the ongoing assessment of the student's progress and abilities may indicate that these objectives should be revised to include more sophisticated skill training.

As vocational education placement will not be appropriate for all handicapped students, some IEPs will specify other career-preparation experiences. For some students, college or other post-secondary training may be targeted. For others, work experience programs will be the critical feature of their secondary programs. Typically these programs involve job exploration in the sophomore and junior years and a supervised work experience placement in the senior year. This work experience may or may not develop into a permanent job placement, usually a final step in a work experience program. The National Association for Retarded Citizens (NARC) On-the-job Training Project, funded by the U.S. Department of Labor, can provide assistance in this final phase of the program. In those instances where job placement can lead to permanent employment, NARC will reimburse the employer half of the handicapped worker's starting wage for the first four weeks and one quarter of the starting wage for the second four weeks. This incentive is to reimburse any employer costs that might accrue due to the potentially longer training period required by the handicapped worker.

Curriculum.   Each program alternative available to meet the needs of any handicapped student must be considered in light of the curriculum design. An excellent framework for the development of the secondary curriculum is the competency-based approach developed by Brolin (1976). This curriculum, initially developed in conjunction with their work on the federally funded Project PRICE

174

(Programming the Retarded in Career Education) lists 22 competencies and 102 subcompetencies that are organized into three
curriculum areas: daily living skills, personal-social skills, and occupational guidance and preparation. A fourth area, academic skills,
is conceptualized as being supportive of these other competence
areas; such skills are to be taught as the means of attaining the
22 competencies. Table 6–2 depicts the basic 22 components.

For each competency and subcompetency, a PRICE competency
unit (Brolin, 1976) is outlined. The three components of these units
are (1) a statement of objectives for the subcompetency, (2) a
listing of activities and strategies for accomplishing each of these
objectives, and (3) suggested adult/peer roles or interactions (with
teachers, peers, parents or community) that can assist the student
in acquiring the objectives of the PCU. Brolin recommends that
each student be certified for each competency before being permitted to graduate from his secondary level training. To assist in
ascertaining student achievement of the competencies, a competency rating scale is included in the PRICE materials. This rating
scale provides for periodic assessment, beginning early in the
seventh grade, through program completion of each competency
and subcompetency. A final column on the rating scale requires a
yes/no designation of competency completion.

The PCUs are not grouped into course offerings, nor are they
conceptualized as being attainable only in segregated special education settings. Rather, they are to be integrated into a variety of
course offerings in both the regular and special education curriculum. The curriculum leaves it up to the individual school programs to determine the progression in which the PCUs are taught,
the relationships that exist among them, and the curriculum subjects into which they can best be infused.

Resources for Special Education/Career Education

Despite the recent federal mandates, cooperative efforts toward
providing improved career preparation opportunities to the handicapped are not yet a widely prevalent practice. Several factors
account for this problem. First, the historical orientation of neither
special educators nor vocational educators has been toward programming for the adolescent handicapped person. Vocational educators have developed programs for youth of average or above
average intelligence, whereas most special educators have concentrated their efforts on programming for young children. Furthermore, few professionals in either discipline have been trained to

TABLE 6–2
A Competency-Based Career Special-Education Curriculum Model
for EMR Students, Grades 10–12

Curriculum Area and Competency (Primary Responsibility: Special Education Teacher)	Suggested Other Relevant Personnel [a]
DAILY LIVING SKILLS	
1. Managing Family Finances	Home Ec./Math
2. Caring for Home Furnishings and Equipment	Home Ec./Industrial Ed.
3. Caring for Personal Needs	Home Ec./Phys. Ed./Health
4. Raising Children, Family Living	Home Ec.
5. Buying and Preparing Food	Home Ec.
6. Buying and Making Clothing	Home Ec.
7. Engaging in Civic Activities	Social Studies/Music
8. Utilizing Recreation and Leisure	Phys. Ed./Arts & Crafts/Music
9. Getting Around the Community	Driver's Ed.
PERSONAL-SOCIAL SKILLS	
10. Achieving Self-awareness	School Counselor/Teachers
11. Acquiring Self-confidence	School Counselor/Teachers
12. Achieving Socially Responsive Behavior	School Counselor/Teachers
13. Maintaining Good Interpersonal Skills	School Counselor/Teachers
14. Achieving Independence	School Counselor/Teachers
15. Making Good Decisions, Problem-Solving	School Counselor/Teachers
16. Communicating Adequately with Others	School Counselor/Teachers
OCCUPATIONAL GUIDANCE AND PREPARATION	
17. Knowing and Exploring Occupational Possibilities	School Counselor/Home Ec./Ind. Ed.

18. Making Appropriate Occupational Decisions	School Counselor/ Ind. Ed.
19. Exhibiting Appropriate Work Behaviors	Employer/Ind. Ed.
20. Exhibiting Sufficient Physical and Manual Skills	Phys. Ed./Arts & Crafts/Ind. Ed.
21. Acquiring a Specific Salable Job Skill	Vocational Ed./ Employer
22. Seeking, Securing, and Maintaining Satisfactory Employment	Employer/ Counselor

ᵃ Parents and other community personnel should also be included in competency attainment wherever possible.

Source. From *Vocational Preparation of Retarded Citizens,* p. 202, by D. E. Brolin. Columbus, Ohio: Charles E. Merrill, 1976.

meet the unique needs of the adolescent handicapped. Skills and attitudes needed to teach vocational education to special-needs students have rarely been emphasized to teachers.

In recent years a variety of attempts have been made to remedy this situation. Vocational education monies have funded preservice and inservice educational programs for special-needs teachers. In addition, several national conferences have been funded by monies from the Bureau of Occupational and Adult Education and the Bureau of Education of the Handicapped in an effort to encourage cooperative programming among university-level vocational education and special education teacher trainers. Invitational conferences of this nature have been held at the University of Illinois, the University of Kentucky, and at the University of Nebraska. Attention should now be turned to providing joint cooperative training for personnel from both disciplines, because all too frequently communication among special educators and vocational educators at the public school level is absent or unproductive. A cooperative training and programming effort such as this should include not only those special education and vocational education teachers at the secondary, career-preparation level, but the elementary and junior high special education teachers who are responsible for the career awareness and career-orientation phases of the program. This type of inservice training would assist the teachers of younger children in conceptualizing the entire sequence of career development experiences for their children. Conversely, the secondary teachers will be better informed as to what they can expect in the way of entry-level behaviors of students.

Career development of handicapped individuals has been an increasingly prominent concern of national organizations and agencies. The 1977 White House Conference on Handicapped Individuals stressed the need for prevocational and vocational training programs for all school-aged children and youths. Specifically, its key recommendation was the establishment of career education programs that would feature career awareness, increased vocational guidance, more job placement and exposure experiences, and an adequately trained staff. A forum sponsored by the President's Committee on Employment of the Handicapped developed several specific recommendations for improving the employment opportunities of the handicapped. The final report of this forum, *Pathways to Employment* (President's Committee on Employment of the Handicapped, 1976) reports these recommendations.

The Council for Exceptional Children (CEC) is expanding its support for career education for the handicapped through the scheduling of a National Conference on Career Education, a series of related training institutes, and other relevant professional meetings. The Division on Career Development, chartered by CEC in 1976, is the primary advocacy group for career education in special education. Comprised of university and public school personnel, as well as others interested in the career development of exceptional individuals, the Division has as its basic purpose "to organize representatives from all disciplines who are involved in, or would like to be involved in, career development of exceptional children, youth, and adults." Curriculum Development Center (CDC) [2] at the University of Kentucky is a notable example of a center that focuses on special-needs populations. Funded out of state vocational education monies, CDC has developed a set of comprehensive resource guides that annotate instructional materials for student use (e.g., texts, supplementary books, multimedia kits), curriculum guides, films and other multimedia packages. In addition, the CDC has developed over 20 excellent curriculum guides on a variety of career education topics for use by classroom teachers. Project PRICE materials also provide an excellent extensive annotation of curricular materials.

The U. S. Office of Education (USOE) has funded a number of curriculum development projects focusing on the 15 USOE career clusters (See Figure 6–2.) One such project developed a career

---

[2] For more information on these guides, write: Resource Center for S.V.E. Teachers, Curriculum Development Center, Taylor Education Building, University of Kentucky, Lexington, KY 40506.

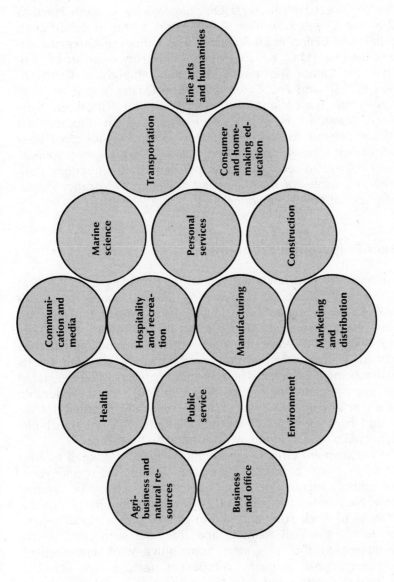

FIGURE 6–2
U.S. Office of Education 15 job clusters.

program in the leisure occupational cluster (Vinton, Pantzer, Farley, & Thompson, 1976).

Other sources of information on career education include the Office of Career Education (USOE), directed by Kenneth Hoyt, as well as the Career Education Coordinators found in departments of public instruction in all 50 states. *The Journal of Career Education,* edited by H. C. Kazanas of the University of Missouri, Columbia; the *Career Education News* (Bobit Publishing, Glenview, Illinois 60025); and *The Career Education Quarterly,* published by the National Association for Career Education (Glassboro State College, Glassboro, New Jersey) are also excellent resources. Of particular interest to special educators is the Division on Career Development's newly established *Career Development Journal.* Also of interest to secondary level personnel is the quarterly publication *Newsnotes* of the National Association of Vocational Education Special Needs Personnel.

Career Preparation Programs

The number of innovative approaches to providing career education for the handicapped is increasing. Several sources have dealt with exemplary programs (Blackburn, 1976; Bureau of Education for the Handicapped, 1973; Cegelka, 1977; Kokaska & Kolstoe, 1977; Lake, 1974). Various career education programs can be identified as illustrative of the broad range of program efforts currently being conducted. These include segregated and integrated programs, programs for the learning disabled (LD), the educable mentally retarded (EMR), the trainable mentally retarded (TMR), deaf and hard of hearing students, students with emotional disturbance (ED), and students with orthopedic handicaps.

The Employment Orientation Program (EOP) is designed to integrate mildly handicapped secondary students into the regular vocational school programs of vocational-technical schools in Camden County, New Jersey (Cegelka, 1977). The program affords a graduated series of work experiences from general prevocational experiences to specific skill training, and from the segregated school environment to the integrated, competitive work environment. The prevocational program component features an extensive vocational-evaluation and orientation phase followed by a basic-skills phase. During this latter phase, the student works in one of the 15 occupational areas for further exploration and evaluation and does initial skills training in the area where he has demonstrated interest and ability. On the basis of their performances during this program component, the students are placed in segregated, specialized skill-training programs, regular vocational school program and/or on-the-job (work-experience) programs. Teacher aides, special training recommendations, and other support services are provided on a needs basis to the regular shop instructors in whose classes the special-needs students are integrated. At the end of each grading period, the shop instructors submit progress reports on their special-needs students. In addition, frequent meetings are held by various members of the special-needs supportive staff and child-study teams to exchange information, monitor student progress, and coordinate activities. Along with the specific skill training, the EOP students participate in a 4-year sequence of related technology courses designed to provide information pertaining to a particular vocational area. Students also receive academic training in developmental, remedial, and/or regular courses.

Another integrated approach is found at the Calhoon Area Vocational Center in Battle Creek, Michigan (Cegelka, 1977). This program serves all students from the 13 public schools and 2 parochial schools of the area. It is fully integrated, with the students attending their home high schools for half of each day and the vocational training school for the other half-day. There are 30 occupational training programs.

Project SERVE is a vocationally-oriented interdistrict secondary program located in the St. Paul, Minnesota area (Lake, 1974). SERVE involves the cooperative efforts of the three state agencies for which its name is an acronym: special education, rehabilitation, vocational education. SERVE features formal assessment of vocational readiness and skills, a series of semi-sheltered work experiences, and during the final year or two of high school, specific vocational training and/or job placement.

The Pre-Vocational Work Study Program in Peoria, Illinois also involves a cooperative arrangement among special education, vocational education, and vocational rehabilitation (Cegelka, 1977). Located in all four regular high schools of the district, the program serves all of the district's mildly handicapped secondary students. Academic and vocationally oriented classes are featured during the freshman and sophomore years. A minishop provides sophomores and others with early "hands-on" work experiences. During the summer before the junior year, students participate in an intensive work evaluation and training program. During the junior and senior years, the students attend school in the mornings and work on school and community jobs during the afternoons. The students have regular homerooms and are enrolled in regular sections of physical education, study hall, and other courses as appropriate.

For half of each day, students work in their home high schools under the guidance of a teacher/job counselor, who designs the individual programs for each student. These programs combine academic and skill development, with more emphasis generally on the latter. Academics are viewed as supportive to the practical skills stressed for independent adult living. For the other half day, students are integrated into regular vocational training programs at the area vocational school, or they may participate in job training experiences in the school or community. Generally, each student receives a number of work experiences in different locales before graduation, with sophomore level students normally assigned to semi-sheltered jobs, such as custodial and cafeteria work, within the school community. In the eleventh and twelfth grades, placement outside the school community is a primary goal. Based on evaluations of student performance in both classroom and semi-sheltered work experiences, as well as on community-needs analysis, students are placed in a variety of work-experience situations, including gas stations, greenhouses, and nursing homes. Job coordinators monitor each student's work experience by visiting the job site, maintaining close contact with the supervisors, and counseling with students about any job problems.

Project Worker, located in 23 special education classrooms of Fullerton, California high schools, is designed to enhance the employability of EMR, LD, and orthopedically handicapped (OH) students by providing training to meet specific employer needs (Lake, 1974). Two prominent features of the program are the level of community involvement and the extensive use of videotapes. Videotaping is used as a primary teaching and evaluation technique, with local industry supplying much of the video material. All entering freshmen are given pre-employment training via videotapes, stressing such things as reasons for working, job attitudes, and job responsibilities. As a next step, each student selects a specific job area and is taught the job skills needed for actual job placement. These skills, in the areas of food services, medical services, general manufacturing, and machine trades, are taught through simulation and presented on videotapes. Frequently, various industries loan machines so that students can practice a skill in the classroom. Once a student has learned a skill, his performance is taped and comparisons are made by both the student and the teacher of his performance and that of the worker on the skill tapes. The student requests a final taping when he feels competent in the skill. This tape is shown to the perspective employer as a part of the student's portfolio. Students also participate in a series of on-campus and off-campus work placements designed to assist them in adjusting to normalized work situations. Following permanent job placement, follow-up records are maintained, again using videotaping.

The Multi-Regional Post-Secondary Program for Deaf Students, located at the St. Paul, Minnesota Technical Vocational Institute, is designed for hearing-impaired students who graduated from high school but who terminated post-secondary programs before completion (Lake, 1974). The program length varies from a few months to more than 2 years, depending on the needs and objectives of each individual. Various types of remedial assistance are provided to the students who, with the aid of trained interpreters, are integrated into the regular vocational programs. Prevocational preparation is another important feature of this program.

The Keefe Technical High School Special Needs Program in Farmingham, Massachusetts serves all special education students over 16 years of age. During the initial year of this 4-year program, students spend the first three quarters exploring each of the three vocational areas (housekeeping, basic shop, and food service). During the last quarter, they choose one of these areas for further exploration. The second year involves intensive study in the selected area, with the third and fourth years being spent in paid on-the-job training experiences. All participants other than the trainable mentally retarded receive remedial instruction in the academic areas. A final phase of the program involves follow-up counseling for the students.

Conclusions

An educational reform movement, career education, has developed as an attempt to make education more relevant. A plethora of definitions and conceptualizations concerning career education have been articulated, ranging from those that are very work oriented to those that encompass all aspects of life preparation. Career education requires the sequential development of attitudes, skills, and knowledge, beginning in the primary years or before, and continuing throughout life. Vocational education is one program option for the career-preparation stage, generally occurring during the final years of high school as well as during college and other post-secondary preparation programs.

The Bureau of Education for the Handicapped, declaring career education a priority for special education, has supported a variety of research, demonstration, and personnel preparation efforts. Competency-based approaches to career education have been advocated for special education. While mainstreaming is one approach to obtaining the specified competencies, it should not become an end in itself, particularly at the secondary level. A wide variety of instructional resources are available to practitioners wanting to implement career education programming for the handicapped. The exemplary programs discussed in this chapter are illustrative of the diversity of approaches to career education that have been developed for exceptional children.

The past half-decade has witnessed an impressive growth in the acceptance of career education, as evidenced by the development of career education programs in over 5,000 of the nation's school systems. It can be expected that this number will increase as state-wide career education plans currently being developed are implemented and as the monies authorized by the 1977 Career Education Incentives Act are allocated to state and local educational agencies for new career education projects. With the increased emphasis on mainstreaming, handicapped students' career education programs and projects developed in the general curriculum should also have impact on special populations as well. The requirement of P.L. 94–142 that appropriate, individualized educational programs be developed for handicapped students should further serve to guarantee the inclusion of career education experiences for this population.

Drug Abuse Prevention and the Special Education Student

7

Martin R. Wong

In the late sixties and early seventies, the "drug abuse problem," as it came to be called, achieved prominence in the local and national press. Since the costs of alcohol abuse in terms of human suffering and economic losses were already well known, "drug education"—the education of people about the dangers of drug use—appeared to hold the possibility for the meaningful application of knowledge and principles of psychology toward potentially useful social ends. When the opportunity arose in 1972 for me to be fully engaged in putting together materials, working with teachers, and doing research in the area of drug abuse education, I took it. At that time the field of drug education was chaotic. Supposedly enlightened people were trying every new fad, and the public outcry was so great that around every corner appeared a new savior with his or her own true road to salvation.

Much of this has settled down now and drug education is more appropriately termed "drug abuse education." Reason seems ready to prevail, and the area is one that holds great portent for its limited sphere and more importantly for the society in general. The problem of drug abuse—in some ways a particularly American problem—is increasingly being seen, in part, as a problem of American culture. It is a fact that America is committed to the use of drugs for recreational as well as therapeutic and other mood-altering purposes. This makes drug abuse prevention somewhat frustrating. Clearly there is no instant answer; drug abuse is a problem that will require the efforts of people engaging in a process leading to the greater fulfillment of people. The issues in drug abuse and drug abuse prevention are seen more as issues with which society needs to deal. I am glad to have had a chance to be a part of the development of the process leading to these conclusions.

I began in drug abuse prevention education in 1972 and have worked to some extent in this area since that time. I have witnessed the pulling together of those innumerable threads and "sure-fire" methods into coherent programs that respect the people to which they are directed and extract out of the myriad directions some meaningful goals. I have seen a gradual evolution of drug abuse education from the "frighten them to death" era through the "drug education is part of the problem" era to the present steady application of reason and the opening of options for people. It is reassuring to know that the winds often do blow in the direction of truth.

Presently I am continuing to work as an educational psychologist, with the bulk of my efforts going toward attempting to affect the quality of teaching in the public schools. Like drug education, it is a frustrating yet rewarding experience. The blossoming of a thousand flowers in nature, however, usually settles down to the alternatives that prove workable and provide meaning for those who seek them. The era of options in drug education seems to be budding. I would like to be part of seeing them bloom.

Introduction

America is a drug-using society. Billions of dollars are spent each year on "social drugs" such as alcohol, caffeine, and nicotine, and further billions are spent on prescribed and nonprescribed over-the-counter drugs. It hardly needs to be argued that moderate and conservative drug use is an accepted part of our society. As distinct from drug use, *drug abuse* is usually defined as the over-use of psychoactive substances to a degree that interferes with the individual's normal functioning (Wiggins, 1972). For most of the adult population, that is an adequate description, distinguishing between excessive, compulsive use, and medical or social use. It allows for moderate use of some kinds of psychoactive chemical for stimulation, pleasure, relaxation, recreation, or as a facilitator of social intercourse. This allowance is important because social drugs have always been available and used by many adult Americans, and societal experience with total prohibition of one of its favorite drugs, alcohol, resulted in widespread lawlessness and the expansion of organized crime.

As recently as 10 to 12 years ago, the alarm was sounded on a "new" drug problem, the abuse of drugs by American youth. Abuse in this case included use of any kind. It was not the use of the traditional American drug, alcohol, that triggered the public outcry, but rather the use of drugs with which the public had only minimal familiarity. Some of these drugs, such as marijuana, had always been around, but their use had been centered primarily in the lower classes. In the 1960s it became apparent that young people of the middle and upper classes were beginning to use marijuana and other drugs. Fed by publicity in the media (Brecher, 1972), the drug craze seemingly began to take on epidemic proportions. A small proportion of young users began to experiment with any kind of drug available and even discovered unlikely new substances to use: solvents, propellants in aerosol cans, cooking sprays, and lighter fluid, to name a few. Drug use among the young became widespread, climbed steadily each year and only recently has begun to show a slowdown in its overall rate of increase (Abelson & Fishburne, 1976).

If the lack of published data and other information is to be considered evidence, drug abuse has not been considered much of a threat to special populations such as the mildly or moderately mentally retarded, learning disabled, behaviorally disordered, or socially maladjusted. This sparse literature on this topic is primarily anecdotal, with only fragments of empirical data results. It has been said, for example, that the childhood use of medication by some handicapped pupils tends to inoculate them against later abuse of chemicals in general. Some correlational evidence seems to suggest this, but firm conclusions await further evidence (Beck, 1975; Eisenberg, 1972; Loufer, 1971). Although drug abuse may not be a problem with this group, clearly there must be more investigation.

In the past few years, practices regarding the education and care of part of this population have changed. In an attempt at more equitable educational treatment, laws were passed that were interpreted to mean that it is no longer enough to provide a reasonable level of amenities and education separate from the mainstream population. Every attempt has to be made to provide for each youth, to the degree possible, the same advantages and same level of education provided for the average population. Unless it could be shown to be absolutely needed, separate care is not equal.

Recent mandates and new practices designed to promote handicapped youth into the educational mainstream are widely applauded, but this integration may bring about some problems related to drug abuse that may not have been encountered before. For instance, separate facilities for these youths previously may have shielded them from the increase in drug experimentation that was occurring among regular secondary school. Now that they are being mainstreamed whenever possible, handicapped youth may constitute a special and perhaps naïve group with regard to drug abuse: naïve because recreational and experimental drug use may be new to them, special because the intellectual, emotional, or other handicaps that set them apart may make them more susceptible to drug abuse problems.

In the following pages, drug abuse prevention education will be treated by describing, in turn, a brief history of the movement, some recent programming efforts, issues related to implementing and evaluating educational efforts, and a suggested model based on three essential factors that seem to emerge from available information. Where appropriate, points and issues of particular relevance to special education populations will be noted.

Drug Abuse Prevention Education

Historical Review

In the 1960s the realization that there was increasing use of psychoactive chemicals among America's youth produced what can only be described as hysteria. This realization was followed by an infusion of funding by federal, state, and local governments into programs of drug education. Most of these preventive education programs were to be implemented in schools. In these early attempts to bring drug use under control, two tactics were popular. Both of them were based on the hypothesis that if some questionable source such as a street person or peer drug user could influence youths to use drugs, a credible source ought to be able to counteract the influence. Thus, policemen, judges, and other authoritative figures were brought into the schools to give "educational" lectures about the evils of drug use. In some cases, even reformed drug addicts gave talks. Often the main function of the message was to scare listeners with stories of the wretched fate that awaited anyone who fell under the influence of drugs. The second tack, sometimes combined with the first, was to provide extensive (if somewhat biased) information about the use of drugs, in the belief that rational minds would, when presented with the "facts," avoid drug use (Wong, 1976). Unfortunately, the information presented was often biased, intentionally inaccurate, and tended to stress drastic outcomes of drug use that were possible but not necessarily probable.

It did not take long for educators to realize that the many youths who used drugs constituted a virtual forum for drug education outside the classroom. Biased information dispensed by the schools, purported to be objective, detailed the adverse consequences of drug use but ignored the widely reported pleasures and benefits of drug use. Thus, the school's version became less and less credible in the face of evidence coming from peer and other pro-drug sources (Anthony, 1974).

When it was realized that scare tactics may in fact be counterproductive in an open society, the drug education community turned to other methods. Drug education became "drug awareness" education, with the emphasis on unbiased information about the effects of psychoactive chemicals along with believable information on the risks and dangers. This new approach, based on the revised theory that enlightened youths would be better able to resist the temptation of drug use, was usually employed as one part of a total drug abuse prevention program.

More recently, drug abuse prevention education programs have been founded on various psychological principles, with the details of a program reflecting the designer's favored principles. Many of these programs have been based on one or more hypothesized reasons why people might turn to the use of drugs. Perhaps the most simple hypothesis is that drug use is a reinforced act and that other ways of feeling good need to be developed to replace those induced by a drug. Other hypotheses assume that there are needs, drives, or similar intra-psychic phenomena that lead to drug use, such as death wishes, adventurousness, and risk-taking drives (Randall & Wong, 1976). Still other programs were built on the notion that the desire to alter one's state of consciousness is a normal motivation inherent in the human makeup. At any rate, these and other theoretical assumptions have stimulated the growth of countless school programs to reduce drug abuse.

Drug Education Programs

A variety of drug education programs have been developed within the past decade to combat the significant increase in drug abuse among our youth. The growth in educational programs has out-paced the limited resources of educational researchers to ade-quately design studies to evaluate the merits of these programs. Most reports of these drug education projects are limited in their experimental rigor (i.e., unreliable and invalid instruments, lack of experimental control, ill-defined treatment procedures) and often present conflicting evidence (Randall & Wong, 1976). It is there-fore difficult to make supportable generalizations about the effect of drug education to date. Nonetheless, some of the more em-pirically sound reports are discussed.

A multimedia drug abuse prevention program developed for the junior high school was reported by Kline (1972). On the first day of the study, all students were exposed to several hours of audio-visual presentations having primarily pharmacological and physio-logical information content. During the next 2 weeks, one class hour each day was devoted to role playing, lectures, and educa-tional games focusing on drugs and drug use. Approximately 3 weeks later, students anonymously filled out questionnaires devised for this program. Kline reports that 25% of the students who in-dicated that they had been drug users prior to the program claimed to have been influenced by the program not to use drugs again. In addition, 49% of students reported that the program had changed their minds against experimenting with drugs.

Blauat and Flocco (1971) report another short-term drug abuse program with some evaluation; this program was applied to 3,300 high school students in grades 10–12. During the one-week pro-gram, drug information literature was available in a display area during lunch and free-time periods. In the mornings, 15–25 ex-addicts visited the school and "rapped" with the students. In the afternoons some of the ex-addicts remained to rap further with interested students. A post-program survey of student drug use revealed that of the 31% of students who were drug users prior to the beginning of the program, 59% felt that the program had in-fluenced them to stop drug use. Furthermore, 65% of all partici-pants reported that the program had influenced them not to take drugs. These survey findings may indicate some immediate be-havior changes resulting from the program, but there were no follow-up measures to assess stability of results.

Swisher and Crawford (1971) compared a number of programs developed for different educational levels. A different program involving either small-group discussion, lecture group, or a com-bination lecture and discussion was applied. One program was applied to each of three groups of subjects, private school students in the ninth, tenth and eleventh and twelfth grades. School faculty members took no part in these programs; they were run by psychiatrists and rehabilitated drug users. Prior to participation in the groups, each pupil was administered four scales: a drug abuse issues attitude scale; a drug knowledge inventory about five drugs (narcotics, marijuana, LSD, amphetamines, and barbituates); a health habits inventory dealing with the use of cigarettes, alcohol, and marijuana; and a scale for students to assess the drug education program. These four scales were again administered one week after all groups had completed the discussion activities. Analysis of the attitudinal data revealed no significant differences among treatment groups. However, mean pre/post changes on the knowledge test for all treatment groups were positive and significant. There were no significant differences for the test results by grade level on pre- and posttests. All treatments seemed to impart knowledge equally. There were no significant decreases in marijuana use among the groups following the program. The authors concluded that (a) short-term programs, however sophisticated and intensive, may have little effect on students' attitudes on drug abuse, and (b) almost any discussion regarding drugs will have some impact on students' knowledge.

Virgilio (1971) investigated the differential effectiveness of a lecture-discussion drug education program and the School Health Education Study (SHES). Each program was integrated into established social studies classes for 3 weeks at a high school, with 18 sections (777 students) assigned to one or the other program. Regular faculty members were trained through inservice explanation programs and an inservice practicum in the SHES method. Following training each faculty member taught 2 sections of each treatment. Participating students were pretested 2 days prior to the program about drug knowledge and were given an attitude scale. Immediately following completion of the programs, posttests on the same instruments were administered; additionally, 4 months later students were retested to determine retention of drug knowledge. There were no significant differences between the two programs in achievement or retention of knowledge. A significantly greater change in attitudes resulted from the lecture-discussion program. There was also significantly greater achievement and retention of knowledge by students who were in the school's college preparatory division as compared to those in the noncollege preparatory division. However, overall gains in knowledge and attitudes for both programs were so small as to be nearly meaningless.

There have been numerous attempts to use values-clarification approaches (Raths, Harmin, & Simon, 1966) to change drug-abusing behavior. For example, one values-oriented program, "Operation Future," was conducted with 851 students in grades 5 through 10 (Warner, Swisher, & Horan, 1973). The program design included no formal control group, but the experimental group's results were compared to data from other area students. Students were administered pre- and postprogram surveys designed to assess actual drug use and attitudes that were assumed to be compatible with drug abuse. The program made extensive use of values-clarification methods and provided a variety of small- and large-group strategies for developing students' decision-making skills and understanding of their own values. Special procedures were employed to alter or strengthen value-related behavior among the students. Some success was reported in fostering appropriate value patterns in the students and in reducing the amount of drug abuse, but these findings were not consistent across all groups. Compared with young students, less program effectiveness was reported with students of high school age and with students on probation.

Another program that emphasized values clarification was conducted with over 3,000 students and extended over 3 years (Warner et al., 1973). There were four treatment groups: drug facts only, values only, drug facts and values, and no treatment. The drug facts treatment placed emphasis on presenting students with accurate information on drugs. The values-only treatment emphasized identification of individuals at high risk for drug abuse, development of students' value systems, and provision of drug information. Treatment was integrated into the daily classroom interactions of students and teachers. Results indicated that the values-only and drug-facts–and–values groups were more effective in developing antidrug attitudes and reducing drug use than the drug-facts–only and no-treatment groups.

Carney (1971) describes a values-oriented drug abuse education program that extended over a 3-year period and involved over 700 students in grades 4 through 12. The program goals were to convey drug information and develop values incompatible with drug abuse; the methods emphasized values and making decisions in risk-taking situations. Instructors of the experimental groups received training in "valuing" and in affective and cognitive aspects of drug abuse. Despite problems with the research design, there was evidence that the program had a positive impact. For example, drug-related behaviors and attitudes changed in the desired direction and drugs were perceived as more risky by some groups.

Warner et al. (1973) describes a small-group approach with 119 ninth grade students enrolled in required health classes, conducted by three counselors trained to conduct goal-directed counseling. Students were randomly assigned to 12 counseling groups, each of which was then assigned to one of four treatment conditions: (a) a behavioral counseling group emphasizing values, attitudes, and alternatives to drugs; (b) a cognitive-dissonance group in which counselors attempted to induce attitude change through cognitive dissonance; (c) a placebo counseling group in which the counselor's role was to stimulate discussion of drug problems and accept student comments nonjudgmentally; and (d) a control group consisting of a regular health-class unit on drug abuse. All participants were pre- and posttested on a 14-item Likert-type scale of attitudes about drug use. The analysis indicated that the behavioral counseling groups showed the greatest gain in healthy drug attitudes but was not significantly better than the no-treatment control group. Differences between placebo, dissonance, and no-treatment groups were also nonsignificant. Other studies by the same authors (Swisher & Horan, 1970, 1972; Swisher, Warner, & Herr, 1972; Swisher & Warner, 1971) showed conflicting evidence. Treatments were usually equally effective in increasing knowledge about drugs and equally *ineffective* in producing any impact on attitudes on drug abuse and degree of drug use.

Stuart (1973) describes the results of an information-oriented drug abuse education program for 509 seventh graders and 426 ninth graders in an upper-middle class suburban community. The program provided information on various aspects of drug use, pharmacology, drugs and the nervous system, and classes of drugs; it consisted of 10 weekly sessions. Sessions were offered in either teacher-directed or student-directed formats, and there were three varieties of program content: lesser drugs only, major drugs only, and both lesser and major. Instructors were a pharmacist with extensive drug counseling experience and an experienced teacher of junior and senior high inner-city students. Before and after participation in the program, students completed a self-report measure of attitudes and information about drugs. It was found that neither format nor content factors had any influence on the self-reports. Compared to a control group, the program participants increased in their knowledge of drugs, their use of alcohol, LSD, and marijuana, and their reported sales of LSD and marijuana; their worry about drugs decreased. Examination of the interaction among drug use, knowledge, and worry showed that use tended to rise as a function of a combination of more knowledge and less worry. However, the combination of factors was not sufficient to predict drug use, indicating the existence of untested factors.

The Rosemont Drug Education Program was developed to investigate a moral development and growth program for prevention of drug abuse (Briskin, 1974), and involved 656 sixth graders at four schools. This program was based on the theory that youths at higher stages of moral development will make decisions leading to avoidance of drug abuse. The objectives were to present information about drugs and stimulate students' growth into higher stages of moral development. The program's major technique involved the presentation and discussion of moral dilemma situations involving drugs. Two schools received the experimental program and two schools received a control program, a nationally published drug education curriculum. Over the 7 months of the project, instruction time was the same for experimental and control programs: sessions lasting 45–60 minutes, held one to three times per week. All participants were pre- and posttested on knowledge about drugs, communication skills, and stage of moral development. At the conclusion, both groups evidenced considerable gains in knowledge, with no significant differences between the groups on these gains. However, there was very little change in either group with respect to communication skills or level of moral development.

Geis, Morgan, Schor, Bullington, & Munns (1969) have published a comprehensive report on the development and evaluation of a narcotics education and prevention program that was planned and conducted with the help of former addicts. The program, lasting 5 weeks, was oriented toward increasing knowledge about drugs and preventing drug use. Junior high students from four schools in a predominantly Mexican-American area of Los Angeles took part. Ex-addicts trained teachers in special workshops and also led group discussions in the classrooms of the two experimental-program schools. The other two schools received traditional drug education programs. Compared to the control students, the experimental students showed significantly greater gains in drug knowledge and significantly greater antidrug attitude changes.

One final study illustrates the degree of variation in attempts to affect youthful drug-using behavior. Clark and Sieber (1977) extensively interviewed primary school students who had received a curriculum aimed at training recognition of situations that warranted uncertainty about attitudes toward drug use and drug-using behavior. A 3-year follow-up yielded correlational evidence that

students who could recognize when it was warranted to be uncertain about drugs reported less hard drug use and more soft
drug use.

Issues Related to Implementing and Evaluating Educational Efforts

As the preceding review indicates, a wide variety of approaches
have been used in attempting to change youthful drug attitudes
and behavior. There are few consistent results, and certainly it is
not possible at this time to select a single best approach. There
does seem to be some indication that unbiased information about
drugs, coupled with training in processing skills, may positively
affect attitudes and behavior with regard to drug abuse. On the
other hand, there is some evidence that the provision of information about drugs can increase the desire to use them. Very little
is known about long-term effects of drug abuse prevention education.

Methodological shortcomings of available drug education studies,
and suggestions for their improvement, have been addressed elsewhere (Randall & Wong, 1976). Certainly there is great need for
more and better evaluations of drug abuse education programs,
but drug abuse education will continue while further studies are
being conducted. Those who provide drug abuse education should
consult current reports of previous efforts to get ideas for their
own programs. Also, educators should consider the following realities when designing programs (c.f., Randall & Wong, 1976): (a)
drugs are and will continue to be easily available to youths; (b)
people enjoy feeling good, and using drugs frequently can produce
this effect; (c) mental and/or physical deterioration is not an inevitable consequence of the illegal use of drugs; and (d) some of
the highs achieved by drug ingestion can also be achieved without
drugs. These points can be helpful in planning and implementing
drug education programs for regular and mildly deviant pupils.

Model for Drug Abuse Prevention Education

The following three-pronged model has been devised in light of
available research and evaluation; it would appear to be as applicable to pupils in special education as to those in regular programs. This model suggests activities in three separate areas based
on the following assumptions:

1. Drug use may represent a wish to use drugs to cover up a personal deficiency.

2. To experience a mind-altered state may be in fact a positive and acceptable thing; most states achievable through the use of drugs are also achievable without. Therefore, one tenable mode of drug abuse prevention is to provide alternate ways of achieving desired states of mind.

3. The provision of accurate, believable information from credible sources will reduce confusion and aid young people in making decisions about drug usage.

Each of these three approaches and their accompanying assumptions are labeled and discussed next.

Psychosocial, Human-Skills Approach

The psychosocial, human-skills approach to drug abuse prevention education assumes that the excessive use of mind-altering chemicals indicates some personality or emotional disturbance on the part of the user. This model is based on the need or deficiency theory of motivation. Put simply, the theory implies that the motivation for much of human behavior can be directly attributable to some needs or deficiencies on the part of the individual. Varying levels of emotional disturbance can be explained in great part by the number and intensity of personal unmet needs.

Some psychologists have gone to great lengths to enumerate putative human needs. Bernard (1924), for example, lists some 6,000 needs. While few people accept all of the needs on this list, most seem to agree that some human activity is motivated by drives to fulfill learned or instinctual needs (Cofer & Appley, 1964; Maslow, 1970; Murray, Barrett, & Homburger, 1938). For example, Maslow (1970) sees psychological growth as movement toward a state wherein fewer and fewer needs remain to be fulfilled.

The hypothesis that links this theory to drug abuse is that the states produced by drugs may temporarily alleviate some of the discomforts associated with the need states. If persistence of a need state is uncomfortable or anxiety producing, the use of a chemical that at least reduces this discomfort must be negatively reinforcing in its ability to remove the discomfort. Correlational evidence lends support to the idea that certain aberrations of personality are related to drug abuse. For example, Braucht, Brakarsh, Follingstad, and Berry (1973) reviewed evidence for psychosocial factors related to deviant drug use in adolescence. They found that lack of family cohesiveness, use of drugs in the family, self-definition problems, high levels of anxiety, and sex-role conflicts are related to drug abuse. Other research has also pointed to family adjustment problems as important in distinguishing potential drug abusers (Blum, 1972; Goodman, 1972; Green, Blake, & Zenhausern, 1973). Emotional disturbance and low levels of self-esteem have also been shown to relate to drug abuse problems (Green et al., 1973; Kaplan & Mergerowitz, 1970; Norem-Hebeisen, 1976). It has been reported that soldiers who become addicted to opiates tend to have a history of deviant behavior before entering the armed forces (Warner & Swisher, 1971). In addition, a national drug survey (National Commission on Marijuana and Drug Abuse, 1973) shows that drug use among adults is related to psychic distress and life crises. Taken as a whole, these data indicate that certain psychosocial factors contribute to drug use.

Wiggins (1972, 1974) and Johnson (1974) have done much work in the area of psychological and social deficiencies that may lead to problems of drug abuse. Wiggins defines problem drug use as "a way of dealing with the environment . . . usually directed toward avoiding the user's personal problems" (1972, p. 11). Wiggins elaborates a comprehensive program to train teachers to facilitate interpersonal and intrapersonal skills in others. *Intrapersonal skills* include a person's ability to know himself, especially private feelings. *Interpersonal skills* refers to the ability to relate to other people. Wiggins explicitly assumes that teaching students to handle intrapersonal and interpersonal problems will ultimately decrease or eliminate drug abuse problems.

Johnson (1974), while not as specific as Wiggins on teaching methods and techniques, is more categorical in defining the areas of psychological functioning in which a person may be deficient: His "Theory of Social Effectiveness" has been the basis for other attempts to tie the drug abuse problem to psychological functioning. In Johnson's theory, psychologically sound behavior is subdivided into the basic social competencies necessary for development toward psychological health. Six of these particularly relevant to the etiology of drug abuse are (a) trust, (b) confidence in one's capabilities, (c) a sense of directing purpose in one's life, (d) self-identity, (e) taking perspectives other than one's own, and (f) interpersonal skills.

Trust refers to a basic underlying attitude that one can rely on others to provide affection and support when it is needed. Erikson (1963) suggests that this basic trust is developed very early in life, implying that the basic orientation may not be very amenable to change. Johnson holds that trust is built through the individual's interactions with his family, peers, and members of other reference groups. He suggests that programs specifically focusing on the development of trust skills will be effective in causing specific change in individuals having drug abuse problems. Johnson's concept of trust may be particularly related to the behavior and growth of special education students, who often find themselves dependent on others to a greater degree than normal students.

Confidence in one's capabilities refers to a belief in one's capacity to effect changes in the environment that are personally desired. Thus, this concept is similar to personal characteristics variously labeled *fate control* (U.S. Commission on Civil Rights, 1967), *locus of control* (Lefcourt, 1976), or *personal causation* (De-Charms, 1969, 1976). Johnson (1974) hypothesizes that a lack of this sense of personal confidence may be related to excessive use of drugs, and there is tentative evidence that this may be the case (Jessor, Young, Young, & Tesi, 1970). Mentally retarded, behaviorally disordered, and other mildly deviant secondary pupils may tend to have the histories of dependence on others and failure that preclude healthy development of this sense of personal power.

Johnson sees a *sense of purpose* as a basic need for healthy personality development. The lack of this sense may be characterized by chronic states of despair, depression, and alienation, which are affective states related to drug abuse. For example, Carman (1974) found that adolescents who have low expectations for achieving valued goals were more likely to be involved in drug use; other research has also linked drug use to personal feelings reflecting lack of a sense of purpose, such as depression, alienation, and loneliness (LeDain Commission, 1970, cited in Brecher, 1972; Pittel, Gryla, & Hoffer, 1971; Robbins, Robbins, & Stern, 1970). It is possible that socially maladjusted and other special education students are likely to experience these feelings. Perhaps their disabilities and social handicaps limit the options open to them; certainly it would seem that such limitations could predispose these populations to a sense of a lack of purpose and direction in life.

The development of an integrated and coherent *self-identity* continues throughout life, but has its greatest opportunity for growth and variability during the school years. Johnson defined this need for a coherent self-identity as a "distinct image of himself . . . an identity differentiated and discernable from others . . . autonomous and independent from others" (1974, p. 8). In line with this need, drug users often report that one of the motivations for using drugs is to "get your head together" or provide insights into the self (Brecher et al., 1972; LeDain Commission, 1970, cited in Brecher et al., 1972; Robbins et al., 1970). In supposing that there is a linkage of self-identity and drug abuse, Johnson probably meant that if the self-identity is not coherent and integrated, it is likely to be of a negative nature. Special education students may be particularly susceptible in the development of a poor self-identity due to the frustration and failure experiences that may often be part of their lives.

To take another's perspective refers to the ability to see the world through another person's eyes, to walk in another's shoes; it is the opposite of egocentrism. This is a skill that develops through learning in interaction with other people. Individual differences in this ability may relate to variations in experience with people of different cultures, different viewpoints, and different life experiences. Learning experiences that require the individual to actually assume another's point of view may also help build the necessary cognitive structures. Johnson suggests the following exercises: debating a position one does not believe in, psychodrama in which one needs to create a coherent character different from one's own, and simply role playing with required role reversals. Failure to develop this skill presumably encourages egocentrism, isolation, and a lack of opportunity to develop skills needed to function successfully in society. The individual would then be more likely to seek out other ways of coping, including the use of mind-altering chemicals.

Johnson lumps a group of other *interpersonal skills* together to round out the model of successful functioning. Skills in initiating contact with other people, promoting mutual understanding, building trust, communicating with others, cooperating successfully, expressing support, resolving conflicts, and the like are included. These skills in part follow from the previously mentioned deficiencies; their absence presages limited success in interpersonal interaction, leading to feelings of isolation, loneliness, alienation, and unstable relationships with others, all feelings related to drug abuse.

These six basic social competencies, and particularly the last two, require extensive human interaction to build and foster the special skills necessary for adequate human functioning that will preclude the need for abuse of drugs. The trend to include special education students in the educational mainstream can be helpful to this process. As mentioned before, it might also be dangerous in that it exposes them to a greater degree of contact with drug abuse temptations.

Johnson's basic social competencies seem relevant to drug use, but may not apply to every individual. Special education students are as individualistic as other youths, in some ways more diverse. Still, certain dysfunctions may make some of them more susceptible than others to deficiencies in one or more of these skill areas. Programs leading to the development and reinforcement of these skills would seem to hold promise for helping to pre-empt the need to use drugs.

Alternatives Model

The second model of this three-pronged attack on drug abuse problems is the elaboration and provision of alternate ways of attaining the desired feelings induced by drugs. This alternatives approach assumes that inherent in everyone is the need to feel good, to take part in experiences that will lead to pleasurable states. Some writers refer to "peak experiences" (Maslow, 1970), "fully functioning levels" (Rogers, 1961), and "altered states of consciousness" (Weil, 1973). For others the drive is merely to experience novel, curious, and satisfying experiences, and to attain competency over one's environment (White, 1959).

It is clear that many of the states and feelings brought about by ingestion of chemicals can potentially be brought about in more natural, self-controlled ways. These feelings are ultimately products of the individual's mind. Thus, the alternatives approach begins with those consciousness states induced by drugs and attempts to identify the feelings and cognitions that make these altered states attractive and desirable. A few writers have analyzed the chemically induced state of consciousness, arriving in general at the following characteristics: (a) a sense of euphoria, of high, of feeling good, a feeling that everything is all right; (b) a physical and mental relaxation coupled with a peace of mind; (c) a feeling that there is a meaning to life; (d) a feeling of oneness, of unity both within oneself and with the rest of the world, a harmony; (e) a sense of communication and communion with others, of involvement, of closeness and trust; (f) a feeling of insight about self, life, and associated problems; (g) altered perceptions of time, space, touch, vision; new ways of looking at things, problems, ideas; and (h) a certain ineffable, inexplicable quality that cannot be put into words (Brantner, 1974; Cohen, 1971).

The next step in this approach is to identify nondrug experiences that can bring on these same mental states. For example, Cohen (1971), Dohner (1972), Masters and Houston (1972), and Payne (1973) have described alternative experiences that are said to produce the same kinds of feelings and cognitions as certain drug-induced states. Cohen breaks the experiences down into a number of levels and addresses each level: physical, sensory, emotional, interpersonal, social, political, intellectual, creative aesthetic, philosophical, spiritual, mystical, and miscellaneous. For each of these levels, he suggests alternatives to drugs. For example, in place of the physical highs with drugs he suggests athletics, dance, exercise, and hiking. In the interpersonal area he describes sensitivity groups, therapy, confidence training, and emphasis on assisting others. As alternatives to spiritual/mystical experiences he mentions yoga, meditation, applied mysticism, and study of world religions. In each area he lists several alternatives, many of which are easily available.

It appears that most of the alternatives suggested have at least one common component: the requirement that the individual get intensely involved in an activity to the point where drug use loses its attraction because it will get in the way of the activity. This requirement may be an essential key. One can supply appropriate alternatives for youngsters to take part in, then induce the youngsters to get involved in the experiences. This involvement needs to be powerful; when people are truly invested and involved, alterations in their mind state that render them incapable of the full experience become less attractive.

If a primary goal of education is to provide experiences for young people that will maximize their growth, it is unfortunate that experiences such as those suggested by Cohen (1971) need to be called "alternatives." Viewing them as alternatives sets them aside as special and not normal. Actually, these experiences should be viewed as integrated parts of a youth's educational experiences, rather than as alternatives and substitutes for drug abuse. The alternatives model seems particularly relevant for the special education student. Its message of the provision of many options and the need for involvement and active investment should be consciousness-raising for these pupils and their teachers.

Information Provision

The third approach relies on the provision of accurate, complete, and unbiased information about drugs, the effective use of drugs, the short- and long-range consequences of drug use, and the pleasures as well as the hazards. There may be some wisdom in withholding information from pupils who obviously do not need it or who are not capable mentally to process the information at levels that will lead to independent decision making. But for the most part, the withholding of accurate information about drugs may have negative effects when erroneous and perhaps titilating drug information is readily available from peers and other sources.

Used as the only mode of drug education, mere information may place undue demands on gratification-delaying and decision-making abilities of youths. This approach, then, should be used in conjunction with the other two. The psychosocial, human-skills approach is intended to provide the skills necessary to make adequate, prosocial decisions. The provision of numerous alternatives and the reinforcement of meaningful involvement in those alternatives will provide options for decision making.

Conclusions

An attempt has been made to review the recent history of drug education as it has been applied to the normal student in the public school population. Three models relevant to drug abuse prevention education were elaborated on and an attempt was made to relate them to the education of the special education student. Particular reference was made to the possibility of the special education student being susceptible because of physical and emotional handicaps to drug abuse as it is seen from a psychological and social skills deficiency model. A case was also made for the needed provision of alternative experiences for special education students who might otherwise have more limited options.

Now the general trend of American society seems to be toward more openness. Recent legislation efforts attempting to ensure equal educational opportunities for all youths are part of this trend. In an open society it is difficult to depend on information censorship as a method of controlling drug use and drug abuse. The movement of drug abuse prevention education toward a more open stance based on individual choice of an enlightened populace seems to reflect this reality. It is difficult to make prescriptions about drug abuse prevention with special education students. The population is diverse with a wide range of individual needs. It is hoped that the three-pronged model may provide some basic principles for dealing with this diversity.

The Teaching-Family Model: A Comprehensive Approach To Residential Treatment of Youth

Elery L. Phillips, Dean L. Fixsen
Elaine E. Phillips, Montrose M. Wolf

The collaboration of Lonnie Phillips, Elaine Phillips, and Mont Wolf began in 1967 when Lonnie and Elaine responded to Mont's news ad and accepted the position of houseparents at a new group home, *Achievement Place*. After an unsuccessful search for model programs that might help in establishing Achievement Place, they sought funding from the National Institute of Mental Health (Center for Studies of Crime and Delinquency) to help them develop a model group home treatment program. In 1968, the grant was funded, Joan Fixsen was hired as the secretary for the grant, and the Achievement Place Research Project was created as a joint effort of the group home (Achievement Place), the Bureau of Child Research, and the Department of Human Development and Family Life. In 1969 Dean Fixsen became part of the Project. The team of "Phillips, Phillips, Fixsen, and Wolf" thus assumed responsibility for program development, research, training, and dissemi-

We greatly appreciate the contributions and advice of Dr. Curtis Braukmann of the University of Kansas, Department of Human Development and Family Living, and Dr. Joe Evans of Boys Town, Nebraska, in the development of this chapter. Also, we want to thank all the Teaching-Parents of the various Teaching-Family homes for their untiring efforts that have made the Teaching-Family Model the success it is today.

nation efforts that continue today after 10 years. The goal of the project from the beginning was and continues to be to develop a practical and effective residential treatment program that could serve as a model for others to use to benefit youths nationwide. It is called the *Teaching-Family Model*.

During their years of collaboration, Lonnie, Elaine, Mont, Dean, and their colleagues generated dozens of publications, a movie, and two books describing the results of their efforts. During this time, Lonnie and Dean became adjunct assistant professors and, later, adjunct associate professors in the Department of Human Development and Family Life; Elaine became director of evaluation for the project; and Mont became a full professor in the department. In addition, Mont was elected as the first editor-in-chief of the *Journal of Applied Behavior Analysis* from 1968 to 1971 and Lonnie and Dean were elected to the board of editors of the journal in 1973.

In 1975, Lonnie, Elaine, and Dean left the University of Kansas and went to Father Flanagan's Boys' Home in Boys Town, Nebraska, one of the most famous childcare institutions in the world. There, at the request of the Executive Director (Father Robert Hupp), they developed an institutional program based on the Teaching-Family Model. At Boys' Home, Lonnie is presently director of youth care and Dean is director of evaluation. Elaine has retired from full-time work but still remains an active member of the National Teaching-Family Association. Mont has remained as co-director of the Achievement Place Research Project (along with Kathryn Kirigin and Curtis Braukmann) at the University of Kansas.

We feel we have learned a great deal from our experiences. First, applied research is very difficult and requires the cooperative efforts of many people. The tasks of developing and maintaining cooperative research teams are of critical importance and deserve to be the subjects of analytic research itself. Second, applied research is expensive and complex. It requires the cooperation, good will, and support of a funding agency and an administrative umbrella. We were most fortunate to have the support of the Center for Studies of Crime and Delinquency at the National Institute of Mental Health (NIMH) and the Bureau of Child Research and Department of Human Development and Family Life at the University of Kansas. And, third, applied research is time consuming. To develop a program, evaluate it, learn to teach people to replicate it, and learn to administer it has taken 10 years so far and the program is still incomplete. However, the effort has been personally and professionally rewarding and our commitment to applied research methods as a solution to social problems has increased greatly over the years. We recommend it to all our friends.

Treatment Models for Residential Care

Each year many children are removed from their natural homes and placed in special residential settings. They may be placed in foster homes, group homes, halfway houses, or child care institutions. They may be placed in these facilities due to no fault of their own (the homeless child), or they may be placed due to misbehavior in which the youth has been involved (delinquency, emotional disturbance). In any case, the greatest problem facing these residential settings is the treatment model that they will employ to help these youths.

Mental Illness Model

The failure of residential-treatment programs to help deviant children, as well as the inhumane and debilitating conditions of many residential programs for children, have been documented by many authorities (Goffman, 1961; Stuart, 1970). These reports have indicated that the treatment programs for many children are not preparing them for the kinds of lives they will need to lead outside the program. Instead, these children live in an unrealistic environment where they are taught dependency on a hospital-like routine that provides few opportunities to learn productive skills. Essentially, the children are taught to live on the welfare system of the program rather than to be as responsible as possible for their own needs.

The mental illness approach to child care typically has resulted in a treatment model in which the youth spends the majority of his time in a custodial environment where he can learn very little of (nor is he responsible for) the day-to-day living skills and decisions that are so necessary. Indeed, many routine responsibilities such as doing dishes, cooking a meal, washing clothes, and cleaning the living area are done by various staff members. "Professional" treatment takes place when a psychotherapist sits down with a youth to determine what underlying inner-psychic problems have resulted in the youth coming to the treatment facility. Upon discovering the presumed underlying causes and having the youth "work through" the problems, he is returned to his original environment. He may or may not have learned any specific skills in how to deal with life during the time he was in residence. This, of course, leads to the phenomenon that most of us are familiar with; that is, a youth returning from a treatment facility seemingly unchanged, although the treatment facility claims that the youth is "cured."

Behavioral Strategies for Youth in Trouble

The lack of demonstrated effectiveness of the mental illness model with juvenile offenders is in part responsible for the increased interest in behaviorally oriented treatment programs (Schwitzgebel, 1972). Most behavioral strategies have been developed from classical conditioning efforts and by the more recent operant conditioning principles (Stumphauzer, 1973). Skinner's *Science and Human Behavior* (1953) has been cited as a major source for operant treatment and Wolpe's *Psychotherapy by Reciprocal Inhibition* (1958) as a major source for respondent therapy (Stuart, 1970; Tharp & Wetzel, 1969). While there has been some application of respondent therapy with juvenile offenders, especially with alcohol, drug, and sexual problems (Cautela, 1967; MacCulloch, Williams, & Birtles, 1971), most of the application of learning principles to juvenile problems has been based on operant principles. Underlying operant treatment procedures is the view that behavior (including deviant behavior) is learned through feedback between behavior and its environmental consequences (Bandura, 1969). This has been termed an *educational model* as opposed to the traditional mental illness model, which views deviant behavior as a symptom of some underlying pathology (Shah, 1966). The educational model suggests that the deviant youth has a behavioral deficiency (Wolf, Phillips, & Fixsen, 1972) in that he has not learned socially appropriate behaviors that will allow him to successfully interact with others in an appropriate way (Sarason, 1968; Shah, 1966, 1968, 1970).

Behavioral treatment typically involves the effective implementation of reinforcement principles in the differential reinforcement of desired prosocial behavior. That is, appropriate behavior is rewarded while inappropriate action is not rewarded. Bandura (1969) has identified three sets of variables involved in effective implementation of reinforcement principles. First, it is essential to devise an incentive system (reward or positive reinforcement) that is capable of maintaining a high level of appropriate behavior over long periods. Second, reinforcing events must be made contingent upon occurrences of desired behavior. Third, methods must be used that are powerful enough to teach or elicit the desired behaviors with sufficient frequency for them to be strongly established through positive reinforcement or systematic feedback.

The first of the set of three variables necessary for the effective implementation of reinforcement principles is a reward system. Two types of rewards are used in the consequation of behavior in most behavioral treatment programs for troubled youths: the token economy and the behavioral contract. Token economies use tokens, or "generalized conditioned reinforcers" (e.g., plastic chips, checks on a card, points) that can be exchanged for various "back-up" privileges (e.g., tangible reinforcers, such as food, free time, watching TV). A token economy in its practical application is usually administered by a youth engaging in a desirable behavior (such as sharing with others) and then receiving tokens from a supervisory adult. The youth in turn may later exchange these tokens for more tangible rewards, such as toys or privileges. Token systems have been used with a variety of populations including chronic hospitalized patients (Ayllon & Azrin, 1968; Krasner, 1968), retardates (Birnbrauer, Wolf, Kidder, & Tague, 1965; Girardeau & Spradlin, 1964), school-aged children (see O'Leary & Drabman, 1971), adult felons (McKee, 1973) and with predelinquent and delinquent youths in institutional settings (Cohen, Filipczak, & Bis, 1968), community-based residential settings (Phillips, 1968), community-based day treatment settings (Davidson, 1970) and classroom settings (Meichenbaum, Bowers, & Ross, 1968).

Kazdin and Bootzin (1972) delineate the following advantages of a token economy: (a) it allows the consequation of any response at any time, (b) it bridges the delay between target responses and back-up reinforcers, (c) it can maintain performance over extended periods of time when the back-up reinforcers cannot be given out, (d) it allows sequences of responses to be reinforced without interruption, (e) the reinforcing effects of tokens are relatively independent of deprivation states and less subject to satiation effects, and (f) it allows the use of the same reinforcer for subjects with different preferences for back-ups.

The reward system provided by a behavioral (contingency) contract is based on the specification of various consequences that will be provided contingently upon the occurrence of specified target behaviors. These contracts are usually negotiated agreements between the youth and someone in authority (e.g., his parents, treatment personnel). Stuart (1971) states that good behavior contracts contain five components: (a) a detailed list of privileges, (b) a detailed list of responsibilities essential to secure each privilege, (c) a system of sanctions for failure to meet the responsibilities, (d) a bonus clause specifying positive reinforcement for compliance with contract terms, and (e) a means to keep track of the rates and consequences of behaviors.

The second of the set of three variables necessary for the effective implementation of reinforcement principles is providing reinforcement contingent upon the occurrence of the desired behavior. This action requires the monitoring of the behavior of the youth by a contingency manager and the accurate and systematic consequation of that behavior. Monitoring can be of two types: direct observation and remote monitoring. In the latter case, behaviors that occur in settings that are not easily monitored by the contingency manager can be monitored by others in those settings and reported (e.g., by phone, checks on a card) back to the contingency manager who can then provide appropriate consequences. The procedure has been used in behavioral contracting and in token economies (Bailey, Wolf, & Phillips, 1970; Cohen, Keyworth, Kleiner, & Brown, 1974; Stuart, Tripodi, & Jayaratne, 1972; Tharp & Wetzel, 1969; Thorne, Tharp, & Wetzel, 1967).

In contingency contracts the consequences for the occurrence or nonoccurrence of each target behavior is prespecified. In token systems, on the other hand, such consequences are not always prespecified. A token economy can be standardized or individualized (Kazdin & Bootzin, 1972). In an individualized economy, the same behavior by two different subjects might result in different token consequences depending on the subjects' individual problems and histories. This flexibility has obvious advantages since each youth has different behavioral deficits that are the result of different learning experiences.

The last of the three sets of variables that Bandura (1969) identifies as being involved in the effective implementation of reinforcement principles is the use of methods powerful enough to teach the desired behaviors with sufficient frequency of positive rewards. When the youth does not know how to behave correctly, the teaching of more adaptive and socially acceptable behaviors is necessary to help him. Token economies and behavioral contracts are motivational tools but cannot teach new behaviors. One method to develop the desired behaviors is to shape those behaviors through selective reinforcement of behaviors that are closer approximations of the desired behaviors. For example, a teacher may want a youth to learn to read an entire book before he receives a reward. However, because of the youth's lack of skill in reading, the teacher may need to give the reward for approximating the desired behavior, such as reading a few pages or even a few lines. Then, as the youth becomes more skilled, the task can be made more difficult. However, Bandura (1969) suggests that "in most cases complex responses can be more rapidly created by the provision of performance guides in the form of appropriate verbal or behavioral modeling clues" (p. 283). Such teaching involves breaking down complex behaviors into their component behaviors, describing the component behaviors to the youth, and giving the youth feedback on his performance (Kaufman & Wagner, 1972; Phillips, Phillips, Fixsen, & Wolf, 1972; Rose, Flanagan, & Brierton, 1971; Sarason, 1968; Sarason & Ganzer, 1973). Bandura (1969) describes still another method of inducing desired models of responses when responses are already known by the youth, but rarely exhibited. In more common language, these are the "reminders" and cautions that we often give children. The method depends upon initially prompting the desired behavior, then fading out the prompts as the behavior becomes more frequent.

Of primary concern is that the generalization of behavioral changes from a treatment environment to the natural environment needs to be programmed (Baer, Wolf, & Risely, 1968; Kazdin & Bootzin, 1972). Generalization, or "internalization" of behavioral changes, is facilitated if the behaviors changed are likely to meet with reinforcement in the natural environment (Ayllon & Azrin, 1968). It also has been suggested that the probability of generalization is enhanced the more the treatment setting approximates the youth's posttreatment environment (Bandura, 1969). Therefore, community-based treatment settings would seem to be preferable to institutional settings, family-style group homes preferable to halfway houses, and so forth.

Another method for programming generalization is through the gradual fading of the youth's environment from one involving extrinsic incentives, such as tokens, to one involving natural consequences, such as verbal feedback. Programs that use a token economy sometimes have a system in which a youth can earn his way through various levels. At each level his responsibilities as well as his privileges increase. Also, as the responsibilities increase, the clarity of the contingent relationship becomes less obvious, and the youth needs to work on more ambiguous relationships. The final level usually involves the removal of the token system to approximate more natural conditions and reduce the dependency of behaviors on immediate consequences. The fading out of tokens can be done by increasing the delay between (a) the occurrence of a target behavior and token reinforcement or (b) the delivery of the token and the purchase of back-up reinforcers. In addition to being faded out of tokens, youths can be faded out of the treatment program by spending more and more of their time in the natural environment (Kazdin & Bootzin, 1972). In the discussions to follow of the Teaching-Family Model, these principles and procedures are employed in a comprehensive model of residential youth care.

The Teaching-Family Model

The mental illness model of deviant behavior, with its hospital-like treatment philosophy, generally is becoming less accepted because of its history of repeated failures and great expense. The credibility of the mental illness model is also lessened as the relationships between learning variables and deviant behavior become better understood. In the behavioral approach, the goal is to teach a youth as many different ways of handling a problem as possible so that when he is faced with a problem, he will be able to choose from many solutions. We firmly believe in the importance of choice in a person's life; however, unless a person has the skills necessary to behave in at least two different ways when a decision is needed, that person really does not have a choice. The skills we teach the youth in no way guarantee that he will pick the solution that we would prefer, but it does guarantee that at least he has the choice. We contend that if a youth is brought into a realistic environment and taught how to deal with that environment, he will learn the necessary skills to make choices once he returns to his original community and family. Naturally, a youth's underlying problems are not to be ignored; this skill-development approach is just another level of concern for his problems.

A child care program must teach a youth to live in a complex social world, to achieve the vocational and academic prerequisites for a happy and productive life, and to learn to work and to spend and save money for his needs. Our residential-treatment model is based on the belief that behavioral deficiencies in these areas are a result of inadequate histories of learning and instruction. Accordingly, our treatment programs, based on the behavioral-deficiency model, were designed to establish and teach the important behavioral competencies that the child has not learned.

The model that we have developed, which reflects a behavioral approach in a 24-hour residential program, is called the *Teaching-Family Model* (Phillips, Phillips, Fixsen, & Wolf, 1973). Through this model, the day-to-day events in a youth's life become the basis for meaningful lessons on how to deal with these events. Such events range from working out interpersonal conflicts and the development of willpower to learning skills that make mundane tasks like washing dishes at least tolerable duties.

Most of this teaching takes place in a family-style setting that attempts to create an environment similar to one that the youth will face throughout life. The adult personnel are a husband-and-wife team who live-in full-time. The facility is usually a self-contained home (a typical house with bedrooms, living room, kitchen, washer, dryer) in a community or campus situation. The home usually has six to nine youths living together; their backgrounds can range from homelessness to emotional problems. Homes can be specialized and handle only specific types of youths, such as boys between the ages of 11 and 16 who have committed an act of delinquency, while another home may have both boys and girls with problems ranging from waywardness to retardation.

Evolution of the Teaching-Family Model

Some treatment programs start with the premise that treatment need only take place at a specific location for a few hours each week. In the Teaching-Family program, treatment is provided throughout each day and almost everything that happens during a day can be used to teach or learn an important lesson. Another difference between the Teaching-Family Model and some other models is that the Teaching-Family techniques were not developed from any one theoretical framework. It was developed slowly and components were added as they were needed. The primary basis for developing or adopting a treatment procedure was whether it solved a particular problem and did not create any new problems. Thus it is a mixture of different theoretical frameworks but integrated into an approach that, if used as designed, can be a very humane and effective child care treatment model.

The original component of the Teaching-Family Model was the token economy or motivation system (Phillips, 1968). However, it was soon evident that more was taking place in changing behavior than the systematic consequences. A critical component, along with motivation, was the detailed description, observation, and teaching of specific social behavior. Both of these components were shaped by our early training and research in the field of applied behavior analysis, which revealed the importance of testing the effectiveness of our procedures.

However, we soon realized that the teaching and motivation components did not guarantee sensitivity to the feelings of the youths; thus, two more components were added to the model. The first was a self-government system, which was originally designed to insure that a time was set aside each day to hear the opinions of all youths. Although these early self-government sessions were primarily an opportunity for youths to air their concerns, sessions soon developed other aspects, such as peer judgments, problem solving, family decisions, rule establishment, and growth in youth responsibility. The second addition was an individualized counseling component, which was designed to occur at the end of each day or week in conjunction with the motivation system. This component was created from procedures derived from the field of guidance and counseling. There was also emphasis on insuring that if a youth was having mood problems, the Teaching-Parents would immediately engage in a teaching interaction that stressed the importance of positive reinforcement and praise statements.

The concern for youths' input into the program was also a major motivation for the Teaching-Family Model's development of a children's rights program. The Teaching-Family Model requires a very specific informed consent statement to be signed by the youth, parent, and legally responsible agencies before a youth is accepted. In addition, Teaching-Family staff takes great pains in the training program to insure that Teaching-Parents are alerted to various legal issues, such as avoiding the use of certain rights as privileges, the total prohibition of physical punishment, and the importance of providing legal counseling for all youths.

It would take too much space to describe how all the components were developed. It is important for the reader to understand that each component is there for a reason and if any aspect of the Teaching-Family Model is removed (without an effective replacement), then quality will be substantially reduced. In any case, when only parts have been employed, the results have been disappointing, if the model is attempted without proper training for the personnel involved.

Because the Teaching-Family Model was developed with the aid of the Department of Human Development and Family Life at the Kansas University (known for its development of innovative behavioral programs), many feel that the program is a total behavioral approach. A major part of the model is based on the behavioral approach, but many parts also are used in child care programs that are not considered behavioral. For example, the self-government component of the Teaching-Family Model is similar to Guided

Group Interaction or Positive Peer Culture that has become very popular in many residential programs. The important point is that while self-government is only *one* component of the Teaching-Family Model, it may be the *only* procedure for other treatment programs. Another example of concerns shared with other treatment modalities is the topic of children's rights. Many programs with an entirely different treatment philosophy have concerns that youths not be mistreated or rights ignored. In fact, a program not concerned with children's rights must be considered out of step with modern child care practices.

Major Components of the Teaching-Family Model

The Teaching-Family Model has many components, but we have selected 10 to describe in some detail. These components can be divided into two primary areas: the environment the youths live in and the treatment techniques used. Those dealing with the environment include (a) isolation of responsibility to specific staff, (b) training of treatment facilitators, (c) professional consultants, and (d) the encouragement of a realistic environment. Treatment techniques include (a) development of a child care curriculum, (b) a systematic approach toward motivation, (c) discovery of the power of teaching as an individualized change technique, (d) the use of self-government as a responsibility-building tool, (e) a program for the youth's school behavior, and (f) a program for the youth's natural parents.

Creating the Environment

Regardless of the quality of the treatment techniques employed, the quality of a program is dependent on the selection of the treatment personnel, the training and supervision of the staff, and the type of situation in which the staff and youth will live to achieve the goals of the program.

Isolation of responsibility. In many child care models, especially in shift-work arrangements, the division of responsibility makes it very difficult to pinpoint the individual responsible for the progress of the child. For example, the responsibilities of teaching the youth day-to-day living skills may be handled by a cottage counselor. If the cottage is on a shift-work schedule (three different shifts of staff, each working for 8 hours), even the cottage counselor will vary. Psychotherapy may be provided by a social worker, a psychiatrist, or a psychologist. The education of the youth may be handled by a teacher and an educational coordinator, while other services, such as health care and dental work, may be scheduled by the cottage administrator. This division results in a tremendous amount of confusion for the youth, who may not be sure to whom he should go to ask for help, nor to whom he is responsible for making improvement.

In the Teaching-Family Model, these responsibilities have been restricted to the husband and wife team, known as *Teaching-Parents*, who live in the home with the youths, 24 hours a day, 7 days a week, 52 weeks a year. They are responsible for running their home. As Teaching-Parents, they teach the youths how to care for a home, work together, solve conflicts, and other important skills that they will need in the future. The Teaching-Parents must manage their time so that they are available to talk with and counsel the youths, and they must help the youths schedule their time for such special events as school activities, medical care, home visits, and athletic activities. Usually the Teaching-Parents will hire an assistant to help with some of these duties and to give them time off. However, they retain complete responsibility for the operation of the home, even during their periods of respite.

The heart of the Teaching-Family Model centers around this husband and wife team and their development as child care specialists. They are hired as a couple, evaluated as a couple, and if need be, terminated as a couple. Although we have not as yet determined what selection variables are important in choosing effective Teaching-Parents, the following are the four most prominent characteristics of successful Family-Teachers: (a) they are between the ages of 21 and 30; (b) they have had 2 to 3 years of college (however, no educational degrees are required and no specific academic area appears to be important, as many of our best Family-Teachers have come from non–social science programs); (c) they have one to two children of their own; and (d) they have been married for at least 1 or 2 years.

Although we have not determined that placing certain types of youths with certain types of Teaching-Parents has any significant value, one selection variable is becoming more apparent than others; that is, the modeling aspect of the Teaching-Parents. We attempt to select Teaching-Parents as representative of the models we want our youths to emulate. They must have value systems that are very similar to the ones that we feel the youths need to learn. At this point, we have uncovered very few other selection components that are indicative of success, but continued research may prove useful in finding variables that will help us select Teaching-Parents.

Training.   The training for the Teaching-Parents is a 1-year program leading to certification. This training starts with a preservice workshop, which is approximately 70 hours of intensive, practical instruction and behavior rehearsal, during which the Teaching-Parents learn the basic teaching and organizational skills needed during the early days of their lives as Teaching-Parents. During the months following this preservice workshop, the Teaching-Parents are given hundreds of hours of in-home training by their consultant and out-of-home training by the training staff.

During the first year, Teaching-Parents go through a series of evaluations. The first, occurring approximately 1 month after they have been in the home, is called a *mini-evaluation*; a crew of independent evaluators go into the home and assess the Teaching-Parents' skills, the youths' skills, and the general condition of their program.

At the end of 3 months, the Teaching-Parents have their first major evaluation, a 4–5 hour visit to the home by a group of independent evaluators. These evaluators investigate more closely the Teaching-Parents' skills in running the program and the youths' progress; they also ask everyone with whom the Teaching-Parents have had contact about the development of the program. In addition, they talk privately to each youth concerning his view of the program. During this time, the evaluators study such data as the average number of youths in the home, the number of runaways, youth employment records, and school attendance. The report of this evaluation, called a *comprehensive progress report*, is used to determine whether or not the home appears to be progressing.

Additional evaluations take place over the first year, but the most important evaluation is the certification evaluation, which occurs 1 year after the Teaching-Parents have gone through the original preservice workshop. At that point, the Teaching-Parents either must meet stringent criteria and be certified, or else recycle through a retraining program and take more evaluations that could lead to certification. They could also be terminated from the profession.

Thus, training and evaluation are extremely important in maintaining the quality of the Teaching-Family Model. They have proven to be the most important and powerful aspects of the Teaching-Family Model in keeping the quality of the homes at a high level. Based on changes in the technology of the field, many components have changed; the training and evaluation, however, have remained amazingly stable in terms of how we teach and analyze the quality of the program.

Professional consultants.　　The consultant is a child care professional who serves as a informal administrator, an independent consultant, and an advisor for problem solving. The consultant-administrator has certain responsibilities with the Teaching-Family program; among these are cooperative decisions concerning admissions for the home, how and when youths can be terminated from the program, or whether or not youths receive additional treatment from sources outside the program. They also have the responsibility for problem-solving consultation with the Teaching-Parents and for giving advice on child-related problems.

The relationship between the Teaching-Parents and the consultant is an especially sensitive one. Teaching-Parents have the responsibility for working with the youths while they are in the home, as well as the major responsibility for input into any treatment decisions dealing with the youths. However, a consultant-administrator may have to make certain administrative decisions (with the input of the Teaching-Parents) concerning various aspects of the program; the degree of specific involvement depends on whether the program is community-based and run by a board of directors, or a campus setting with an administration that oversees the operation of several homes. The major role of the consultant, however, is to give advice to the Teaching-Parents about children who are having particular behavioral difficulties. Obviously, the consultant must be a technologist in problem behaviors of children and youth and act as an objective and innovative advisor to the Teaching-Parents.

Traditionally, we have tried to have as the consultant-administrator an ex-Teaching-Parent or someone who has had ample experience in direct work with children. Once a Teaching-Parent becomes certified, the need for a consultant is drastically reduced, as most Teaching-Parents will have considerable experience working with children at that point. However, the need for an outside independent voice remains a useful aspect of an objective child care program.

Realistic environment.　　We often describe the home environment of the Teaching-Family Model as a family-style program, leading many people to assume that it is a "normal" family program. That is anything but the case. We attempt to develop a realistic environment in the sense that the youths need to live with both male and female adults, as well as to learn the daily routine of living in a family. But, unlike most families, the goals of a Teaching-

Family home are to take several adolescents with problems and to solve those problems in a fairly short period of time (typically, 6–18 months). We expect the husband and wife team to become effective therapists by developing an environment that will assure that the youth will meet challenges and be taught how to overcome problems in an appropriate manner.

The development of this realistic environment is an extremely demanding and important task. If the Teaching-Parents become too tolerant of misbehavior, the treatment will be ineffective because it will not relate to the type of environment that the youth will have to face. If, on the other hand, the Teaching-Parents become unrealistic in their demands on the youth, he will reject both the Teaching-Parents' relationship and their lessons as impossible, and he may abandon the program. Thus, although we attempt to have the Teaching-Parents develop a challenging environment, we want them to set goals that the youths can achieve.

This balanced environment is created by first asking the youth to deal with problems that he should already have the ability to solve. For example, during the first few hours of the program, the youth may be asked to follow simple instructions, such as helping another youth with his chores, filling out some routine forms, or reading a house rule book. The important result of these early hours and days is the development of his ability to follow instructions.

The next step is improving the youth's ability to handle the more difficult task of being sensitive to feedback when he receives it. During this early stage of the program, effort is devoted to teaching the youths to accept routine criticism on ways to change their behavior. Once the youth has learned the basic premise of the home (i.e., the Teaching-Parents are there to teach), the youth will move on to more difficult problems; these include being able to handle the word no when he really desires something, being able to apologize when the need to apologize appears appropriate, being able to maintain study habits for an extended period of time, and being able to learn difficult skills so that he becomes confident that he can overcome problems.

Day after day, the youth's challenges become greater; however, it is the skill of the Teaching-Parents in determining when the youth is ready for the next challenge that makes the program effective. Not only must the youth develop the social skills needed to help him in his environment, but he must also become aware that many routine tasks are not always pleasant but must be accomplished anyway. Thus, the youth has a major responsibility in the Teaching-Family home for taking care of his own room, for helping prepare the meals, and for cleaning up after the meals. These responsibilities, too, are developed in such a way that they are realistic and similar to the ones that he will be facing when he returns to his natural environment.

Treatment Techniques

Some components of the child care curriculum have already been alluded to in the section on creating the environment. Below are some of the specific tools that the Teaching-Parents use to help change the behavior of the youths in their care.

Curriculum. The curriculum has been derived from our experience in working with youths and from the various skills that the youths have to be taught before we can have any realistic expectation that they will be able to handle their normal environments.

The curriculum outlines a course of study for youths with serious behavior problems to learn skills necessary for successful family and community living. It is assumed that improved social and self-help skills will increase the youths' opportunity for acceptance by their families, schools, and communities. Therefore, the development of this curriculum arose out of two primary needs: (a) the need for a program that identifies the special skills necessary for a successful existence in the community, and (b) the need for an evaluation system that insures the accomplishment of the program's goals and objectives.

The curriculum itself offers an extensive outline of specific behavioral skills necessary for successful existence in a community. It is not inflexible, however, and can be updated as necessary by additions and deletions.

The curriculum is an assessment tool to aid in identifying the youth's present skill level and in defining those skills that remain to be developed. A program can then be outlined to respond to each youth's individual needs. It also aids in the development of staff training procedures that are aligned with the needs of youths. Both staff and program evaluations can use the curriculum as the basis for determining whether or not the goals of each youth and the goals of the program are being met. The curriculum was not designed to take away the youth's present behavior repertoire, but rather to improve and expand his repertoire in order to help teach him how and when to use what he knows.

To develop the Family and Community Living Skills Curriculum, several classes of behaviors were initially identified as areas essential for successful survival within a social structure. Once the classes were specified, it was necessary to analyze the skills characteristic of each class. Skills were stated in terms of the youth's ability to perform a task and were described as the result rather than the process.

Teaching interaction.   In addition to using the curriculum as a tool, the Teaching-Family Model attempts to change behavior through a special teaching technique. This teaching technique includes an objective and detailed description of an appropriate behavior that should be learned or of an inappropriate behavior that needs to be corrected. The proper behavior must be demonstrated, and when the youth attempts to develop that behavior, his behavior, or a close approximation, must be reinforced. Long-term consequences must then be developed to insure that the behavior will become a part of the youth's typical behavior. Although this technique appears on the surface to be one that almost everyone would agree with, it is very seldom used with as much detail as it is in the Teaching-Family Model.

If a youth comes to a typical child care worker and asks if his task is complete, the child care worker often will concentrate on whether or not the youth successfully accomplished the originally assigned task (e.g., cleaning the floor, carrying out the trash). But, trained Teaching-Parents will concentrate not only on the quality of the task but on the manner in which the youth asks the question, the manner in which the youth receives feedback, and even more critically, how the youth asks the question the next time. The Teaching-Parents will be sensitive to several behavioral signs: eye contact, tone of request for checking the job, whether or not the youth attempted to do a good job or simply tried to get by, and whether the youth tried to con the Teaching-Parents into letting him slip by this time. Although the Teaching-Parent will certainly be interested in the successful completion of the task, the Teaching-Parent is also concerned with teaching the youth a new way of interacting with people. Every opportunity will be used to teach the youth how to go about reaching this point.

Systematic motivation.   Teaching techniques used in the Teaching-Family Model center around the unique application of the teaching technology to new and innovative behaviors. However, it is essential that in the process of teaching, positive consequences be delivered when the youth has achieved the desired level of behavior so that the newly acquired behavior can be strengthened until natural reinforcers are available. We call this systematic application of consequences the *motivation system.* Although many youths are motivated to learn without extrinsic rewards, the typical youth who comes into the Teaching-Family Model is not motivated to learn many of the skills necessary for survival and must be given some help by the development of external controls that will, hopefully, later lead to the development of an internal desire to learn.

The effectiveness of the motivation system is determined by a diagnostic approach toward the types and magnitudes of reinforcers that are needed to motivate a youth. For example, when a youth first comes into the program, he is immediately placed on what we call the *assessment system*. The assessment system is designed to determine the extent of external motivation that a youth will need during his stay in a Teaching-Family home in order to learn all the skills that he will be taught. If it appears that he can learn with natural consequences (i.e., those consequences that are naturally available in the environment), no further systematic reinforcement techniques are likely to be needed. Simply saying to him "No, you can't do this," or "Good, Johnny, I think you have done a fine job" will be sufficient to produce the desired effect necessary to teach the youth how to follow instructions and accept feedback. On the other hand, if the youth does not respond to these normal reinforcers and the negative consequences that are typically used in the environment, he will need to be given a much more structured environment. We call this the *negotiation system*. This system is designed to allow the Teaching-Parents to keep a record of the important behaviors, both positive and negative, that occur during the day and then to discuss those behaviors during a private conference with the youth each evening. How the youth performs during the day on these designated target behaviors determines the types and qualities of privileges that the youth may negotiate for the next day. During this private conference, which will last anywhere from 5 to 30 minutes, the youth has an opportunity to express his point of view about how he feels the day has gone, and the Teaching-Parents have the opportunity for individualized teaching and counseling during that period of time.

The negotiation system is simply a systematic way of delivering consequences on a day-to-day basis. It is important to note that natural consequences are still used for immediate events. That is, if a youth engages in an inappropriate behavior during the day, he may immediately lose a privilege, such as watching television, having a snack, or going into town to visit with one of his friends. On the other hand, if the youth completes a task exceptionally well, he may be rewarded instantly by a pat on the back, praise, or even an extra privilege. The end-of-day negotiation session is designed so that the youth and the Teaching-Parents may sit down to look over the behavioral record to determine if the day has been good or not so good and to decide what privileges the youth will have available the next day.

However, in many cases this negotiation system does not provide enough structure for the youth who needs more immediate rewards. In such a case, the youth will be placed on the point system, which is a token economy. The token economy is a way of immediately bridging the time between the behavior occurrence and the rewards. If a youth engages in appropriate behavior, he is immediately reinforced by receiving a certain number of "points" that he marks down on a card. If the youth engages in inappropriate behavior, he loses points, which he also indicates on a card. At the end of the day, the youth adds up all the points made, subtracts all the points lost, and determines how many points he has left to buy privileges for the next day. This is the most structured system in the Teaching-Family Model and is used only in the event that a less structured system (such as the negotiation system) fails to work.

On the other end of the continuum, if the youth engages in very appropriate behavior while on the negotiation system or learns very quickly from natural consequences, he will immediately advance to what we call the *progress system*. That is, a system where natural consequences such as those used in most homes (i.e., praise, looking for adult approval) are used almost exclusively. A youth normally has all his privileges and does *not* have to earn them on a day-to-day basis, but it is still possible, as in most natural homes, for him to lose privileges. While on the progress system, the Teaching-Parents still maintain a record of the types of behaviors that the youth is learning, to prompt them to teach new behaviors.

When the youth reaches the progress system, he is usually well advanced and is no longer engaging in massive inappropriate behaviors. This is the time when the Teaching-Parents find it most difficult to seek their own motivation to teach since the youth is no longer a potential problem in the home. However, this is the most important time for the Teaching-Parents to evaluate the types of skills that the youth should be learning. This is the time when the vocational skills, independent-living skills, and the most sophisticated social skills should be taught.

Once a youth has advanced on the progress system, he will probably be a candidate for returning to his natural environment. The youth's readiness for return will be documented by a progress report, which will reveal the behaviors that he has learned and what the likelihood is that he will be able to advance significantly by staying at the home for an additional period of time. At this point, the Teaching-Parents will intensify their work with the natural parents to teach the parents how to work with their off-spring, how to develop a systematic approach toward consequences, and how to develop a fair way of dealing with youth-parent problems.

Self-government. A major component of the Teaching-Family Model is the self-government system. This aspect of the model is divided into three areas: (a) family conference, (b) youth manager, and (c) responsibility development. In the family conference, all the youths and the Teaching-Parents gather each day as a group to discuss accomplishments, rules, and the problems of day-to-day life. It is a semi-democratic system; each issue brought before the youths is voted upon by the family. However, some problems are not voted upon by this group if the group has not yet learned the necessary self-government skills or the decision to be debated is not amenable to a vote. For example, the group cannot vote on whether or not marijuana usage is legitimate; such a consequence is determined solely by the Teaching-Parents. However, many rules can come before this group for solutions; among these are curfew hours, problems with other youths in the home, and the fairness of consequences.

The second area of self-government centers around the youth manager. A youth is elected or chosen at various times to perform the role of youth supervisor in the home. His task is to solve various squabbles between the youths in a fair and systematic manner and to make routine decisions, such as whether to save a particular leftover food and shower schedules. It is also his responsibility to report to the Teaching-Parents any event he feels should be handled by them. At the end of the day, everyone evaluates the youth on the basis of his firmness, fairness, and general quality as a manager.

Responsibility development is the third area of self-government in the Teaching-Family Model. Youths can readily learn to make a decision concerning whether a peer is or is not guilty of an offense and whether he should or should not have any major consequences. However, it is very difficult for the voting youths to accept responsibility for that decision. If they make the decision, and there are no future consequences, the youths will usually choose to take the easy way out and not deliver any consequences at all, thus, not risking the potential wrath of the accused youth. In the Teaching-Family Model, when the youths make a decision about another youth, they must accept considerable responsibility. If the youth engages in the inappropriate behavior again, the voting youths will be held to the same consequences that the misbehaving youth receives. This approach creates a relatively conservative self-government system in a Teaching-Family home. It is not just a matter of passing judgment; it is a matter of accepting responsibility for the effects of their decisions on the behavior of their peers.

Programming for school behavior. Once effective procedures have been discovered to help a youth in the Teaching-Family home, the next step is to generalize those effects to other environments. The school is considered a testing ground and a major indicator of how well the youth is improving. The classroom teacher is basically an objective observer who will give feedback concerning the youth's behavior.

When a youth enters a Teaching-Family program, the first step is to interview each teacher of the youth, his counselors, and the vice-principal or principal. The goal of these interviews is to help the teacher and others to clearly state the youth's most critical problems. The teacher may express his concern in nonbehavioral terms; thus, the major task of the Teaching-Parent is to determine the objective components of the youth's problems. Teachers may complain of poor attitude, nervousness, mild retardation, or aggressiveness. These comments are not sufficiently detailed to explain to the youth how he needs to change his own behavior. The Teaching-Parents must politely help the teacher describe the problem in enough detail so that an objective definition can be obtained. For example, a junior high school teacher once said that a new Teaching-Family youth was disruptive, dumb, and aggressive, and since he never followed her instructions, she thought he might be hard of hearing. After a 20-minute interview, the Teaching-Parent and the teacher were able to arrive at the following behaviors:

1. He talks to and bothers all the students around him.
2. He often disrupts the class by talking out loud and being out of his seat.
3. He complains that he can't understand how to work the problems but sometimes he does them well.
4. When kids walk by him, he often pokes or hits them.
5. He does not follow the teacher's instructions.

Once the problem behaviors have been defined, the next step is to have the teacher provide feedback as to whether these behaviors occurred in class. One of the most convenient feedback systems is the daily school note that the youth takes to each class in which he has problems. In Table 8–1 is the school note that was made up for the youth in this example.

When the youth returns from school with his daily report card, the Teaching-Parents and the youth discuss the school day. Each youth has various expectation levels determined by his ability, history, and length of time in the Teaching-Family home. When his note is compared with these expectations, he is given rewards or penalties. For example, if the youth was on the point system, he would receive a positive point reward for each appropriate behavior marked on the card. He might also receive a negative point penalty three times greater than the positive reward for each inappropriate behavior marked on the card. This differential reward/penalty ratio would vary depending upon the severity and persistence of the youth's problems.

Programming for the youth's natural home.   One goal of a Teaching-Family home is to educate the youths in the social and self-help skills they need for success in their home and community. These skills are taught throughout each day by the Teaching-Parents

TABLE 8–1
Daily Report Card

Name __Jack__

Class __math__

YES	NO	
—	—	Did Jack study and pay attention the whole period?
—	—	Did Jack get out of his seat without permission?
—	—	Did Jack talk out loud during class?
—	—	Did Jack trip, hit, poke, or in any way disturb other students?
—	—	Did Jack follow your instructions?
—	—	Did Jack complete _____ percent of the assignment?
—	—	Did Jack obey all classroom rules?

Signed _____ (please use ink)

and are tested often. The system ensures that the youths have continued contact with their parents and have free time in the community. The feedback the Teaching-Parents receive from the youths' parents and members of the community is critical in evaluating how well the newly learned skills generalize outside the group home.

Typically, the parents of the youths who come to the group home have had previous contact with community service workers who have attempted to teach the parents better child-management techniques. These efforts have generally failed as evidenced by the fact that the child continued to get into trouble. When the youth's problems became severe, he was adjudicated, and the Teaching-Family home assumed the responsibility for training the needed skills. The Teaching-Family program is designed to help the youths' parents learn how to maintain the youths' appropriate behavior even though they may have been unable to establish it originally.

Soon after a youth enters the program, he begins earning his way back to his natural home. One privilege available to a youth is to return to his home from Friday evening to Sunday evening. While the youth is at home, his parents are asked to fill out a home note. The home note asks the parents to rate the youth's behavior over the weekend and to indicate when the youth left the house and where he went. When the youth returns from the weekend visit, he gives his home note to the Teaching-Parents. If his natural parents answer each question positively, the youth will receive positive consequences, and if marked negatively, the youth will receive a penalty.

The home note, illustrated in Table 8–2, is a simple, practical feedback system. By looking at the home note, the Teaching-Parents can deliver consequences for weekend behavior. In addition, the verbal or written feedback the parents provide regarding specific behaviors give the Teaching-Parents additional problem behaviors to directly modify in the Teaching-Family home.

Parental reports of a youth's behavior on the weekend should be viewed with some caution. Reports of inappropriate behavior often can be believed since such reports reflect either the youth's actual behavior at home or at least the parents' dissatisfaction with the youth's behavior. Parental reports of appropriate behavior should be viewed with considerable caution, especially when the parents only rarely report any misbehavior. When this occurs, the Teaching-Parents talk with the parents as often as possible to make sure they understand the function of the home note, what the various categories refer to, and to allow the parents to verbalize

TABLE 8–2
Example of Home Note

Please rate your child's behavior for his or her home visit on the following scale. Please circle one.

EXCELLENT   VERY GOOD   AVERAGE   FAIR   POOR

Also, please answer the following questions, circling YES or NO in INK.

YES NO Did the youth give you this sheet as soon as he/she got home?
YES NO Did the youth accurately let you know where he/she was at all times?
YES NO Did the youth take a bath, brush his/her teeth, etc.?
YES NO Did the youth volunteer to help around the house?
YES NO Did the youth get in on time and stay around the house enough to suit you?
YES NO Was the youth polite and well mannered? (Did he/she avoid talking back or arguing?)
YES NO Was this note helpful in controlling your child's behavior during his/her stay at home?

FRIDAY	Home	Out	SATURDAY	Home	Out	SUNDAY	Home	Out	MONDAY	Home	Out
8AM			8AM			8AM			8AM		
9			9			9			9		
10			10			10			10		
11			11			11			11		

12PM	12PM	12PM	12PM
1	1	1	1
2	2	2	2
3	3	3	3
4	4	4	4
5	5	5	5
6	6	6	6
7	7	7	7
8	8	8	8
9	9	9	9
10	10	10	10
11	11	11	11
12AM	12AM	12AM	12AM

Time the youth left home to
return to Teaching-Parents _____

Parent signature _____

any complaints they might have about their son's behavior at home. Many times parents rate a behavior as inappropriate only if it is extreme. Usually, though, the Teaching-Parents can discuss the need for more sensitive reporting and produce more "discriminating" parental reporting.

For the first few weeks after a youth leaves the Teaching-Family program, the youth and his parents meet with the Teaching-Parents weekly. The parents are often very strict in the demands they wish to impose on the youth. They are sometimes unwilling to compromise on a privilege even though the youth is willing to compromise in order to obtain that privilege. In these discussions, the Teaching-Parents become arbitrators. They offer alternatives and make suggestions on how the dispute can be resolved. The goal of this arbitration process is to teach the parents and the youth to negotiate and compromise. After a few weeks, the parents and the youth are increasingly able to resolve their own disputes through compromise and negotiation and the Teaching-Parents play less active roles in the discussions. The parents and the youth then begin to meet with the Teaching-Parents only once every other week and eventually the meetings take place about once each month. After 6 months of the less frequent meetings, the scheduled meetings cease altogether. Thereafter, the youth, parents, and Teaching-Parents meet only when there is some problem. The Teaching-Parents, however, continue to call the parents or the youth every few months to see how things are progressing at home.

Usually, the parents and the youth become skilled in negotiating and compromising when disagreements arise and the youth continues to do well. Occasionally, however, problems become critical and the parents are unable to handle their child. Under these conditions, the Teaching-Parents take the youth back into the group home for a short time. While the youth is in the program, the Teaching-Parents modify the behavior that caused the problems and have meetings with the parents to resolve the problems at home. Depending upon the problem behavior at home, the youth may return to the group home for only a few hours each day, may spend a few days, or may return for a few weeks. In some cases, the youth simply cannot stay in his natural home and will look at the Teaching-Family program as his permanent home.

Youth Characteristics

A question that often arises in the description of any program is, What are the types of youths served by the program? To answer this question, a survey was conducted of the demographic characteristics of the youths admitted to one Teaching-Family program from January, 1975 through May, 1976. During this period, a total of 199 youths were admitted to this program and displayed the following characteristics:

FAMILY HISTORY

Parents' marital situation. Of those 199 youngsters admitted to a program using the Teaching-Family model, data were available on the majority of their parents' marital situations at the time of final placement. Only 17% of the youths had parents who were living together as a family unit. Reasons for placement in these situations varied from economic difficulties to severe youth behavioral problems. The remaining 83% of the youths came from backgrounds that would be considered broken homes. These included family situations in which the parents were divorced, separated, divorced and remarried, never married, or in which one of the parents was deceased. The majority (60%) of the youths were from families in which parents were either divorced or separated.

Legal planning responsibility. Legal responsibility for the 199 youths admitted to the program during the year and a half ranged from responsibility being with natural parents, to cases of court custody, to responsibility residing with public or private agencies. Of the 199 youths, only 16% were in the custody of parents living in a joint marital relationship. A full 17% of legal planning responsibility was in the hands of court systems, 13% with public and private agencies, and 47% with single parents, either natural mothers or fathers having been divorced, separated, or widowed. The remaining 7% were divided between grandparents, sisters, and other relatives.

Prior placement history. Youths admitted to the program arrived from a variety of sources. Only 13% of the youngsters came from a family situation of living with both natural parents. The number of youths coming from homes in which the youngster was living only with the natural mother was 41%, while 2% came from homes in which the youth was living only with the natural father. A full 14% of the youths were direct placements from other institutions or detention facilities, while 6% arrived directly from foster placement. The remaining 24% of the youths came from a variety of settings, including living with grandparents, brothers, and sisters.

Number of parental changes. Of the 199 youths admitted to the program, 52% had lived with one or both of their parents continuously prior to admission. The remaining 48% of the youths had a history of at least one and, in one case, as many as ten parental changes. A parental change, in this context, is defined as a change in the living situation of a youngster such that he moves his residence from living with one or both of his parents to living with a relative or foster parent, or to an institution. Of those youngsters experiencing parental changes, the average number of changes was two.

AGE. Of the youths admitted, 18% were 12 or under, representing youths of elementary school age. Youngsters between the junior high school ages of 13 and 15 comprised 59% of the population admitted, while 23% of the youths fell into the 16- to 18-year-old bracket, representative of high school aged youths. The average age of youths admitted to the program was 14.

RACE. Of the 199 youngsters admitted, 64% were Caucasian, 18% Black, 13% of Spanish-American origin, and 3% of American Indian ancestry.

GRADE. Analogous to the situation with age, 16% of the youths entering the program were placed in elementary school, 56% were placed in the junior high school grades, and the remaining 28% were placed in high school. The grade placement at admission averaged grade 8.5.

INTELLECTUAL ABILITY. Of the 199 youngsters, IQ scores were available for 136, or 68% of the youths. Of this number, 26% had recorded IQ's that would be considered in the below-normal ranges of intellectual ability; 49% of the youngsters had IQ's in the normal range; while 25% of youngsters had recorded IQ's above normal. Thus, the average reported IQ level was within the normal range.

ACADEMIC ACHIEVEMENT LEVEL. Data regarding academic achievement was available for only 73 youths, or 37% of those 199 youngsters admitted to the program. Of this total, 56% had recorded achievement scores at the sixth grade level or below and 30% of the youngsters had academic achievement levels between seventh and ninth grade levels. Only 14% had recorded achievement scores at the tenth grade level or above. In relation to age and grade levels, it can be seen that most youths have poor academic performance backgrounds and would be considered as several years behind their peers in academic achievement.

COURT CONTACTS. Of the 199 youths admitted, 50% had had some contact with juvenile court authorities; and of these, 20% (18) had more than one contact with court authorities.

INSTITUTIONAL HISTORY. A total of 27% (54) of the youths had some history of institutional placement prior to entering the Teaching-Family program. Of this number, 14 had a history of multiple placements involving two or more institutional stays prior to admittance.

Application and Evaluation of the Teaching-Family Model

The Teaching-Family Model currently is being used in many homes. The first Teaching-Family home was a boys' home developed in Lawrence, Kansas, in 1967 with the cooperation of the University of Kansas and a local nonprofit organization (known as "Achievement Place, Inc."). Very carefully, other homes were established in nearby communities, including a home for girls. Approximately 150 Teaching-Family homes are now in existence in the United States and in a few foreign countries. In recent years, Teaching-Family homes have been established in Arizona, Louisiana, Minnnesota, Montana, Nebraska, Nevada, New Jersey, North Carolina, and Texas. Many other states are currently in the process of establishing programs. In addition to these group-home efforts, the Teaching-Family Model has been applied to institutional campus-style homes at Father Flanagan's Boys' Home at Boys Town, Nebraska. The Teaching-Family components also have been applied to family therapy, youth counseling, and educational programs. Recently, the National Teaching-Family Association was established to monitor the quality of the various training sites being developed.

Research and Evaluation

This model is a heavily researched and evaluated group home residential model. The University of Kansas Department of Human Development and Family Life and the Bureau of Child Research have received funds from the National Institute of Mental Health (Center for the Studies of Crime and Delinquency) since 1968 to evaluate the effectiveness of it. Recent efforts at independent evaluations of the model have resulted in almost $1 million being granted to research groups not affiliated with the Teaching-Family Program. Research efforts also have taken place at various sites across the United States where this model is being employed.

The research has been divided into three different areas. The first is termed *procedure research* for comparing various techniques for changing behavior. Almost 100 different publications or presentations of specific studies have dealt with the experimental comparisons of the effectiveness of these techniques. Although the studies are too numerous to list in detail here, they have demonstrated the effectiveness of procedures used in the model. The second area of evaluation has dealt less with experimental efforts and more with progress evaluation. In this area, the major concern has been the tracking of progress; that is, the improvement of a youth's grades and school attendance, the characteristics of the programs that pass evaluations, and various individuals' perceptions of which social skills are important for the youths to have. The third level of research deals with outcome evaluation. The most notable of these efforts is concerned with the recidivism of youths who have been out of the Teaching-Family Model for some time. Typically, these results are compared with the outcomes of comparable programs. One of these studies, an independent evaluation now underway, will compare the outcome results of about 30 Teaching-Family homes with about 30 homes using other treatment approaches.

Conclusion

The Teaching-Family program has been demonstrated to be a practical and effective method of dealing with children who have a learning problem in the skill areas necessary to live and work in a free society. Without remediation of these deficits, the youths we serve would likely suffer social and career limitations that would result in unhappiness and unproductiveness. In our opinion, most of the skill deficiencies are the result of poor learning on the part of the youths and/or poor teaching by the adults and peers responsible.

Our society has attempted to remediate these social problems by various programs but many of these programs have fallen short due to the lack of accountability that these programs felt for the total youth. Educational programs may sometimes only feel responsible for the time the youth spends in their classroom. Recreational programs are satisfied if their facility has a high utilization rate. But staff in a fulltime residential model such as the Teaching-Family program is responsible for the youth all day, all year, and even if the youth has left the program for many years, the staff is held responsible for how the youth turns out. With this level of accountability being placed on a residential program, it is critical that a comprehensive 24-hour treatment program be developed in the residence if any hope of success is forthcoming. The Teaching-Family Model is one example of such an effort.

Psychoeducational Management and Self-Control

9

Stanley A. Fagen

Not long ago I was invited to return to Children's Hospital of Washington, D.C. to speak to a group of child psychiatry residents about training teachers to work with emotionally disturbed students. I had been employed for 6 years by Montgomery County Public Schools, Maryland, as supervisor of professional development. Having learned the hard way that teaching was much more than filling the air with clinical jargon, I brought with me a rather simple, dittoed handout. I must admit that a wave of warm nostalgia came over me as I slowly passed the doors of the child therapy offices on my way to the seminar room. As a practicing child clinical psychologist, I had spent a good part of my 7 years at Walter Reed Child Psychiatry Service, Children's Hospital, and Hillcrest Children's Center in those offices.

In introducing my topic, I commented with amusement, "I feel like my fifteen years of work as a psychologist have been reduced to this one-page handout." And in fact it had! It is no coincidence that the essence of this handout reappears as the "life space components" of Figure 9–1 in this chapter.

For me, the handout symbolizes much of what I have learned, believed, and shared with others at this point in my life. It says to me that all people need to be understood in terms of their thoughts, their feelings, their behaviors, and their influence by and upon their immediate environment. It says to me that people cannot be cut up into little pieces, their heads stuffed with knowledge, their thoughts revealed as cures, their actions prized because they are desired, or their emotions released merely because they are. It says to me that one-sided views and singular belief systems are false, and that human behavior cannot be easily labeled, typed, or discarded. One more thing—it reminds me of Joseph Addison's words: "The grand essentials to happiness in this life are something to do, something to love, and something to hope for."

I have had the good fortune to have been associated with professionals who cared about their work and about people. At the University of Pennsylvania, I studied with Jim Diggory, who helped me to appreciate that significant human issues were amenable to controlled investigation. As part of a close-knit group of graduate students doing research on self-evaluation, I became keenly aware of how one's valuing of self is affected by ability, social influence, and experiences of actual or perceived failure (Diggory, 1966). As I moved into clinical work in the U.S. Army from 1962–1966, I continued to be interested in people's reaction to stress situations. Through supervised practice in psychodiagnostic assessment and child and family therapy, I came to understand how behavioral symptoms could be dynamically related to subjective perceptions and feelings. Earl Janda encouraged me to apply my understandings to preventive programs with parents, and we collaborated with others in a series of studies on the effects of father absence on the family. Our research impressed upon me the importance of emotional support and acceptance in enhancing coping with stress.

In 1966, I joined the staff of Hillcrest Children's Center and Children's Hospital of Washington, D.C. as director of psychology training. My initial responsibilities included clinical child functions in the outpatient clinic and therapeutic school and residence programs, as well as design and execution of a full-time psychology internship program. Nick Long became a tremendous influence in my life, both as a friend and a supervisor. He guided me in my efforts to translate clinical principles to educational settings, and together we launched the Hillcrest-American University Teacher Training Program. I became increasingly motivated to work with teachers, feeling strongly that the hope for positive mental health was largely in their hands. Don Stevens, an older teacher at Hillcrest, welcomed me into his classroom, and for the first time I began to realize how discrepant classroom behavior could be from psychological test or individual interview—therapy behavior. My empathy and respect for the classroom teacher became genuine during that year, and I found it difficult to continue to participate in psychiatric staffings conjecturing negatively about teacher contributions to child psychology. Shortly thereafter I shifted to full-time work in Hillcrest's Psychoeducational Institute.

During 1968, Nick, Don and I came to a realization that student disruptiveness typically occurred in relation to specific classroom events or requirements. We hypothesized that weaknesses in self-control were due to limitations in skills for coping with classroom pressures, and through systematic observation and review of current literature we identified a core set of eight skills that seemed to determine capacity to maintain control over one's own behavior. A major portion of the next 4 years was devoted to developing, implementing, and evaluating a curriculum for teaching children self-control (Fagen, Long, & Stevens, 1975).

In 1970, as a result of budget problems at Hillcrest Children's Center, I was faced with a decision to return to outpatient clinic responsibilities or look elsewhere. With Nick's help I applied for the position of supervisor of professional development at the to-be-constructed Mark Twain School in Montgomery County, Maryland. I have never once regretted my decision to move directly into public education.

My years with Montgomery County Public Schools have been exhilarating. From the planning for Mark Twain School, to the establishment of the Mark Twain Teacher Internship in special education, to my latest involvement in preparing inservice trainers for mainstreaming, I have been challenged and enriched. Bill Porter and Gerry Meltz, each of whom served as director of Mark Twain Programs, patiently cultivated my skills for serving as a resource to staff and administrators. With support from the Bureau of Education for the Handicapped, Herman Saettler in particular, it has been possible to install a graduate-level teacher-preparation program in a public school system, funded 100% locally. Lyndall Bullock, Frank Wood, and Ed Schultz have provided outside encouragement for dissemination and as a consequence several publications on inservice training have been recently completed (Fagen, 1977a; Fagen & Guedalia, 1977; Fagen & Hill, 1977).

Now I am especially interested in discovering and teaching techniques for adaptive management of frustration and conflict. In my opinion, the key tests of self-control occur at moments of adversity, and we are still very much in need of humanistic curricula for development of student and staff coping skills. Finally, I am privileged to work with a team of competent, dedicated teacher specialists for inservice training, namely, Tom Beuglas, Len Guedalia, Jeff Hill, and Harry Klugel. These inservice trainers are making great strides toward helping school personnel meet the needs of all children, promoting "something to do, something to love, and something to hope for" in many more of the children for whom we work.

Overview to the Psychoeducational Approach

In many ways, adolescents and the problems of adolescent pupils may seem difficult to understand; thus it may be helpful to keep the following thought in mind:

> Adolescents are people—not people isolated from us in a painful period of struggle, or separated from adult cares in a peaceful age of bliss; but people who, as you and I, are learning how to live by facing as best they can the problems of everyday living. (Fedder, 1967, p. 43)

This chapter focuses on the needs and problems of adolescents who have been unsuccessful in schools and advocates both a purpose for re-education and a developmental sequence of strategies for psychoeducational management. We start with the viewpoint that experiences of failure in schoolwork, human relationships, and self-understanding are extremely painful. Such failures lead to intense and repeated efforts to avoid these situations previously associated with emotional upset. As a result, unsuccessful adolescents become adept at covering, evading, or depreciating valued school objectives, and have difficulty accepting responsibility for their own actions. It is crucial that they be reintroduced to basic developmental tasks so that a "failure identity" may be replaced by a sense of competence and worth. Educators must proceed planfully; gradually increasing difficulty, stress, and responsibility without destroying sparks of hope that they renew.

The purpose of all re-education must be to promote self-control and responsibility in the learner. *Self-control* is defined as the capacity to flexibly and realistically direct and regulate personal action or behavior so as to effectively cope with a given situation. Moreover, *effective coping* is defined as an adjustment or change that increases self-esteem, prospects for more successful striving towards constructive goals, or understanding and helpfulness between self and others (Fagen & Hill, 1977). To achieve this purpose, schools must demonstrate genuine respect for the whole person by providing for cognitive, emotional, and social-behavioral needs. A psychoeducational management approach is recommended as an effective means of caring for the whole person. *Psychoeducational management* may be defined as the planful influence of the teacher, the curriculum, the peer group, and the educational system to promote balance and adaptiveness in a learner's cognitive, affective, and behavioral development.

This chapter presents an interpretation of the roots of adolescent educational failure, a framework for implementation of a psychoeducational management approach intended to impact three major areas of programming, and specific strategies that can be used to assure sequential progress through three stages of psychoeducational management.

Dynamics of Adolescent Failure

Adolescence is often viewed as a period of major developmental change, during which time the individual moves from the dependencies of childhood to the rights and responsibilities of adult status (e.g., Erikson, 1950; Freud, 1969). This transition has been commonly regarded as a time of conflict and emotional turbulence, a kind of "revolution resolved by an evolution" (Josselyn, 1975). Other research studies have disputed this "storm-and-stress" assumption, finding instead that behavior progresses in a continuous, consistent manner from childhood to adolescence (e.g., Bandura, 1964; Offer, 1969). At any rate, there is strong agreement that secondary school-aged experiences have a crucial impact on both the outcomes of adolescence and the potential for adult adaptation (Bayh, 1975; Holt, 1969; Phillips, 1968; Silberman, 1970).

In a sense, secondary schools represent a last large-scale opportunity to develop positive respect for self and others in our nation's young men and women. The consequences of failure to fulfill this opportunity appear to be devastating for our schools and our country's well-being, as indicated in a recent report to the U. S. Senate Judiciary Committee:

> It is alarmingly apparent that student misbehavior and conflict within our school system is no longer limited to a fist fight between individual students or an occasional general disruption resulting from a specific incident. Instead our schools are experiencing serious crimes of a

felonious nature. . . . Moreover our preliminary study of the situation has produced compelling evidence that this level of violence and vandalism is reaching crisis proportions which seriously threaten the ability of our educational system to carry out its primary function. (Bayh, 1975, p. 3)

Protecting the Self Through Avoidance

In a powerful publication which reports the results of a questionnaire completed by 1,603 teen-agers regarding their feelings about parents, schools and teachers, Sabine (1971) quoted one student's response to the question, "If you were invited to make a speech to the principal and teachers of the high school you attend, what would you like to say?" The student replied in free verse:

I wish I wish
That I could
say what
I wish
so that you
would not laugh
at it
at me.

        And you say you would
        not laugh
        out loud
        but inside you would
        be laughing
        so loud
        that I could hear
        it from there, too.
        So I will remain
        quiet
        exposing my wishes only
        to this paper
        which cannot laugh. (p. 107)

Feelings of failure hurt badly. The emotional pain which follows unappreciated or rejected efforts to achieve is the most dangerous threat to mental health and self-actualization (Maslow, 1954;

Shostrom, 1973). Regardless of which theory of motivation one adopts, whether psychoanalytic, drive-reduction, competence, self-actualizing, or social-learning, it is accepted that all people set goals that are intended to fulfill wants. By caring enough to reach towards a goal, however, we become vulnerable to pain and disappointment. The unpleasant, often distressing effect, combined with the realization that the sought-after goals were not attained, forms the experience of failure.

Glasser (1969) considers the major problem of the schools to be a problem of failure:

> A person functions at any time feeling either that he is a success and enjoying the psychological comforts of success or that he is a failure and desperately trying to avoid the attendant psychological discomforts . . . If a person cannot develop an identity through the two pathways of love and self-worth, he attempts to do so through two other pathways, delinquency and withdrawal. Delinquency and withdrawal do lead to an identity, a failure identity.
> (p.15)

In other words, to protect oneself from a continuing emotional and psychological hurt, a person learns to avoid striving towards the goal associated with pain.

Unsuccessful adolescents have endured extreme doses of past hurt sometimes related to school work, sometimes to social relationships, sometimes to confusion about themselves. Very often the hurt is multiply determined. For example, a student who is unable to discriminate visual symbols is laughed at for falling far behind, blamed by teacher or parents for not trying, and totally bewildered about his own defects (Gordon, 1970; Kronick, 1975). Keogh and Sitko (1977) affirm this overlap between learning and social-behavioral problems:

> By the time a given child has experienced several years of school failure, it is often impossible to determine primary etiology in terms of neurological or social-psychological variables. Examination of patterns of referral for specialized services suggests that the same children are apt to turn up in both LD (learning disabled) and BD (behaviorally disordered) categories. Is the learning failure caused by the behavioral and social disturbance, or does pro-

longed and severe learning failure lead almost inevitably to behavioral disruption? (p. 130)

Holt (1964) has observed that students adjust to the fear of failure by employing strategies that preclude public disgrace and the discomfort of failure, even if these strategies prevent further learning.

The strategies of most of these kids have been consistently self-centered, self-protective, aimed above all else at avoiding trouble, embarrassment, punishment, disapproval, or loss of status. This is particularly true of the ones who have had a tough time in school. (p. 73)

Bloom (1973) offers a useful summary of this discussion in accounting for individual differences in classroom achievement:

Repeated evidence of success in a particular set of learning tasks is likely to increase a student's confidence in himself with this type of task and increase his interest in further learning tasks of this sort. Repeated evidence of failure or inadequacy in a set of learning tasks is likely to decrease the student's interest in further learning tasks of this type. (p. 141)

Helpless to prevent the sense of failure and defeat that accompanies repeated efforts to attain the impossible, such a student shifts to a failure identity, abandoning attempts to succeed. Hopefulness gives way to discouragement, resentment, and "I can't do" thinking, and creative energies are replaced by self-defeating techniques for avoiding the painful tasks or social situations. In turn, the avoidance perpetuates and hardens the inability to master the problem area, simultaneously strengthening further avoidance behavior because of its effectiveness in reducing or preventing unwanted pain. Furthermore, many students escalate their protective strategies beyond staying out of trouble; they may instead lash back through overtly disruptive actions. Like children who become immune to spankings, these students reach a stage where they seem almost impervious to school sanctions. The result is often a final admission of educational defeat: exclusion, "pushout," "force out" (Bayh, 1975; National School Public Relations Association, 1976).

This dynamic relationship between school-based failure and

avoidance behavior appears to have profound significance for understanding the unsuccessful adolescent. Thus, the lower class student who is unfairly regarded as incapable may protect himself by devaluing school and attacking it through vandalism, truancy, and verbal abuse (Coles & Piers, 1969; Greene & Ryan, 1965). The middle class youth who is subject to the perfectionistic expectations of adults may protect himself by withdrawing investment, seeking antiestablishment outlets, and resisting instruction (Divoky, 1969; Holt, 1964; Leshan, 1967). The anxious child who is pushed to perform may protect himself through withholding and inhibiting output (Gaudry & Spielberger, 1971; Swift & Spivack, 1975). The learning disabled student who is given the same text as everyone else may protect himself by bothering peers, fidgeting, daydreaming, and "fooling around" (Connolly, 1971; Gearheart, 1976; Hewett & Forness, 1974).

The Teacher and Unsuccessful Adolescents

In addition to understanding that students are motivated to avoid the intense stress or discomfort that has been associated with past learning (academic or social), educators need to keep several other points in mind. First, the concept of avoidance of failure experiences is essentially a derivative of the pleasure-pain principle and the laws of reinforcement (Ross, 1967). Moreover, avoidance behavior usually occurs after genuine efforts to achieve have been frustrated; in other words, the student who says he hates a teacher may well have started out wanting a positive relationship. The task or situation that is presently avoided was at one time positively valued and has the potential to be re-valued; for instance, students who have given up on learning to read and avoid it like the plague often feel joyful when they begin to experience step-by-step progress in a developmental or remedial sequence. Additionally, it is important to separate the dimension of striving or goal-seeking (*effort*) from the dimension of outcome (*consequence*). Learners will strive to achieve a goal up to a point; if the outcome of their efforts results in perceptible accomplishment and warm social feedback, continued effort can be expected; if, instead, they receive only critical or no feedback, avoidance can be expected. Desire and effort can be rekindled in all learners, but only if consequences reflect appreciation and support.

Teachers of unsuccessful adolescents are constantly taking risks to facilitate re-education. The act of setting clear limits and consequences risks student protest; establishing a definite contract with a student risks demonstrable letdowns; allowing freedom of verbal expression risks embarrassment or personal criticism; entrusting increasing responsibilities to students risks abuse to property and person. The hardest risk of all is accepting responsibility for another person, especially one with fragile self-esteem and marginal social adjustment. Reality insists that we accept our imperfection, prepare for failures, and give our best without self-pity or condemnation. It is also realistic to plan for positive outcomes to the fullest extent possible, as suggested in the section on stages of psychoeducational management.

Stotland (1969), in his fascinating book on the psychology of hope, defines *hope* as "an expectation about goal attainment." Based on a comprehensive review of research relating to goal-seeking, several propositions of relevance are offered to teachers of unsuccessful secondary pupils.

I. An organism's motivation to achieve a goal is, in part, a positive function of its perceived probability of attaining the goal and of the perceived importance of the goal.

II. The higher an organism's perceived probability of attaining a goal and the greater the importance of that goal, the greater will be the positive affect experienced by the organism.

III. The lower an organism's perceived probability of attaining a goal and the greater the importance of that goal, the more will the organism experience anxiety.

IV. Organisms are motivated to escape and avoid anxiety; the greater the anxiety experienced or expected, the greater the motivation. (pp. 7–10)

Students who have been unsuccessful in their schoolwork, interpersonal relationships, and self-understanding enter a new program with extremely strong motivations to escape and avoid anxiety (proposition IV). Furthermore, they have frequently mastered techniques for achieving their avoidance objectives. The critical task for the teacher is to renew hopefulness and motivation toward the avoidance goals, without creating massive anxiety (proposition III), and to heighten the perceived probability that these previously thwarted goals can realistically be achieved (proposition II).

James (1890) remarked that "with no attempt there can be no

failure; with no failure no humiliation" (p. 311). The risks of hope entail the dreaded prospects of another round of attack on self-esteem (Diggory, 1966; Felker, 1974; Wylie, 1974). It is no wonder that educators are reluctant to commit themselves to teaching unsuccessful students, and particularly, unsuccessful adolescents (Saettler, 1976). The mature teacher recognizes that re-education of adolescents with learning and emotional problems means exposing oneself to defiance and impulsive outbursts, feelings of personal inadequacy and discouragement, and lots of patient, hard work with limited immediate gratifications. Fortunately, there are many skilled educators who possess both the professionalism and the courage to care (Fagen, 1977a). Given this type of educator, it is indeed possible to gradually rebuild the unsuccessful student's sense of trust and competence (Hobbs, 1967, 1969).

Let us consider the risks of hope, as applied to a former Mark Twain student. Walter, age 14, entered Mark Twain School after having failed in most subjects at a regular junior high. He had been underachieving in schools for most of his years, and his negative attitude had reached unmanageable proportions during the past year. The junior high staff was concerned about predelinquent behavior (e.g., shoplifting, truancy) and was unable to cope with his constant refusal to comply with classroom expectations. Walter had been getting daily help from the student resource teacher in his regular math class, as well as tutoring and counseling on a regular basis in the student resource center. Despite these services, he continued to evade responsibilities and finally ceased to meet any learning requirements. The Mark Twain School staff decided to prioritize development of basic math and reading skills, and improvement in problem-solving behavior. Since Walter had demonstrated almost total avoidance of academic tasks and failure to accept any responsibility for his own behavior, these objectives seemed major. At the point that Walter entered Mark Twain, he was unconcerned about attaining goals set by the staff and essentially unwilling to commit himself to any definite tasks. His avoidant behavior had successfully precluded feelings of failure, since he attached no importance to vital learning activities. The challenge to the teaching staff was to arouse Walter's desire to accomplish something purposeful by gradually demonstrating that he could succeed in areas where he felt hopeless.

It was important for the staff to understand that as Walter became hopeful of the possibilities for success, his anxiety over failure would also increase. As he began to care about school-related goals he would become vulnerable once more to feelings of inept-

245

ness and rejection. And, as Walter began to trust that staff cared about him, he would become sensitive to disappointments, disrespectful communications and lack of responsiveness to his genuine efforts.

A Psychoeducational Solution: Self-Control

Regardless of theoretical or professional identities, educators and other mental health practitioners agree that a fundamental value is to prepare learners for the responsible exercise of freedom. Bower (1969) suggests that "forces which increase or enhance the degrees of freedom of man's individual and social behavior are mentally healthful, and those which reduce such freedom are unhealthful" (p. 298). Continuing his discussion of "behavioral freedom," he states,

> Behavioral freedom may be regarded as the inability of the organism to develop, maintain, and enhance resiliency and flexibility in coping with problems. Operationally, the degree of such freedom may be defined as the number of behavioral alternatives available to an individual personality under normal or stress conditions. (p. 299)

Goldiamond (1974) arrived at a similar place in espousing an ethical basis for behavior modification. He argues that behavior change should be "constructional" (i.e., advancing constructive behavioral options).

> This is defined as an orientation whose solution to problems is the construction of repertoires (or their reinstatement or transfer to new situations) rather than the elimination of repertoires. . . . The focus here is on the production of desirables through means which directly increase available options or extend social repertoires, rather than indirectly doing so as a by-product of an eliminative procedure. (p. 5)

Dunn (1973), in summarizing emerging dimensions for special education, states that the practice of segregating children into self-contained programs will be markedly reduced, adding: "The focus is on the individual and his optimal development as a skillful, free, and purposeful person, able to plan and manage his own life and reach his highest potential in society" (p. 53).

The conviction expressed here is that *critical aspects of intervention for unsuccessful students are not a matter of free choice or preferred ideology, but are implemented "because it is right."* Specifically, it is right that all conceptual models of child variance strive to promote increasing self-control and responsibility in the learner. This position was strongly advocated in *Teaching Children Self-Control* (Fagen et al., 1975):

> This book is about freedom and responsibility. . . . The notion of forced, external control is inherently repugnant to a liberal, freedom-seeking society. The spirit of democracy calls for an atmosphere conducive to nurturing the free expression of feelings and behavior. At the same time, however, we are concerned that this freedom not become a license to infringe upon or injure the rights of others. It is an implicit rule that the exercise of personal freedom requires modulation of behavior in conjunction with concern for the needs of others. (pp. v, 21)

As Polsgrove (1977) notes in a thorough review of the self-control literature, "the issue of freedom versus control has recently turned behavioral researchers to designing techniques that can be used to teach children self-control" (p. 30). This mobilization of effort promises great advances in effective helping during the next few years (Kanfer & Goldstein, 1975; Karoly, 1977; Mahoney & Thoresen, 1974; Stuart, 1977).

The concept of self-control has been developed at three different levels of meaning: as a capacity, as a process, and as an outcome. Thus, Fagen et al. (1975) define *self-control* as "one's capacity to flexibly and realistically direct and regulate personal action or behavior in a given situation" (p. 34). In contrast, O'Leary and O'Leary (1976) emphasize a process for self-management consisting of self-determination of goals and reinforcement standards, self-recording, self-evaluation, and self-reinforcement. Thoresen and Mahoney (1974) define *self-control* in terms of outcome: "A person displays self-control when in the relative absence of immediate external constraints, he engages in behavior whose previous probability has been less than that of alternatively available behavior" (p. 12). The position taken here is that while each of these meanings is important in understanding self-control, there is a need to integrate various approaches into an overall model. The author's preferred model, and the one relevant to the ensuing discussion of psychoeducational management, involves several key points.

Capacity.   Self-control is the *capacity to flexibly and realistically direct and regulate personal action or behavior so as to effectively cope with a given situation.* In this conceptualization, (a) the locus of control is in the person, (b) capacity implies degree or amount of control that is variable within and across individuals, (c) self-direction and regulation of action means having alternative choices of response to external pressures or inner impulses, (d) to effectively cope with a given situation means "an adjustment or change which increases self-esteem, prospects for more successful striving toward constructive goals, or understanding and helpfulness between self and others" (Fagen & Hill, 1977, p. 179). With regard to the point (d), this definition requires that behavior displayed not be destructive towards self or others. In other words, it is stipulated that a human and social ethic be applied to the criteria for effective coping and self-control. An expanded treatment of most components of this definition may be found in Fagen et al. (1975); the element of "effectively coping" is newly introduced.

Enabling skills and methods.   Self-control is a function of basic enabling skills and systematic enabling methods. The relationship between enabling skills and enabling methods is delineated in Table 9–1.

Corrective and preventative self-control.   Self-control may be strengthened by (a) *building enabling skills* so that a wider range of behavior is subject to personal direction and regulation, or by (b) *specifying a particular behavior* to be controlled and employing systematic enabling methods to increase desirable behavior that is incompatible with previous actions. An example of the skill-building (preventative) approach would be teaching students to generate and evaluate alternative possibilities for behavior in a variety of situations, and expecting them to transfer this skill to other instances when action-decisions must be made.

The specific behavior (corrective) approach might instead teach the student or students to smile or nod their heads instead of looking down or away when being addressed by an authority figure. Whereas the specific behavior approach requires *in situ* analysis of an existing problem (corrective), the skill-building approach may not (preventative). Another difference is that skill building may start at a more general or group-instructional level and more toward specific problems or weaknesses, while specific behavior approaches begin at a pinpointed, individualized problem

TABLE 9–1
Summary of Enabling Skills and Methods for Self-Control

Basic Enabling Skills	Systematic Enabling Methods
Cognitive	*For Antecedent Events*
selection (attention, discrimination)	(cognitive methods: covert self-control)
storage	self-instruction
sequencing and ordering	problem-solving
anticipating consequences	modeling and rehearsal
Affective	*For Behavioral Consequences*
inhibition and delay	self-determination of goals and reinforcement standards
appreciating feelings	self-recording (monitoring, observation)
managing frustration	self-evaluation
relaxation	self-reinforcement (reward, punishment)
References	*References*
Valett (1967); Hewett (1968); Mann & Suiter (1974); Fagen et al. (1975); Palomares & Logan (1975)	Thoresen & Mahoney (1974); Kanfer & Goldstein (1975); Meichenbaum (1975); O'Leary & O'Leary (1976); Polsgrove (1977)

and may be spread to more students and behaviors. Thus, the two approaches differ primarily in their precision of analysis, and breadth or narrowness of behavior taught.

It is important to recognize that these two approaches often converge at a midpoint of instruction, that is, when skill building moves to concrete, individual needs and when specific behavior shaping moves to a class of behaviors or students. In reality, these approaches are not independent of one another, but are at different points on a continuum for instruction. Finally, it should be noted that systematic methods are commonly applied to developing basic self-control skills. For example, in teaching students to cope with feelings of frustration, cognitive methods of self-instruction, modeling, and rehearsal are indispensable (Fagen & Long, 1976).

Psychoeducational Management

Psychoeducational management was defined earlier as the planful influence of the teacher, the curriculum, the peer group, and the educational system to promote balance and adaptiveness in a learner's cognitive, affective, and behavioral development. Various attributes of a psychoeducational approach have been described elsewhere (Fagen et al., 1975; Long, Morse, & Newman, 1976); the present discussion will highlight the framework and key techniques of psychoeducational management as practiced at Mark Twain School.

Central to psychoeducational management is a respect for the whole person in the learning environment. Educational programming is correlated with the "life space" of the learner to prevent depersonalized instruction. Figure 9–1 illustrates this overall relationship between programming components and life space components.

For an adolescent to develop self-respect and respect for others he must experience success in relation to three basic areas: schoolwork, relationships with peers and adults, and self-understanding. Rollins (1968) addresses these areas in terms of the problem of self-understanding, the problem of developing new ways of relating to others, the problem of teacher-student relationships, and the problem of the teaching-learning situation. Similarly, Felker (1974) discusses building positive self-concepts during adolescence through the sense of belonging, and the sense of competence, and the sense of worth. Glasser (1969) reduces the sources of failure to two main ideas: failure to love and failure to achieve self-worth. In sum, it is clear that an overall psychoeducational management system must develop explicit strategies in three programming areas: *(a)* instructional, *(b)* behavior expectations and interventions, and *(c)* counseling.

Using case material, Figure 9–1 can be illustrated as follows. Susan has difficulty decoding complex verbal messages and is acutely sensitive to adult and peer disapproval. As she is presented with environmental (school) influences that require advanced verbal comprehension, she perceives herself as dumb and feels sad and fearful of ridicule. In turn, she retreats from social interaction and does not share her talents or interests. Consequently, adults and peers overlook her and take no time to understand her strengths and limitations (cf. Fagen & Guedalia, 1977).

Applying a psychoeducational management approach to this sort of interaction between thoughts and feelings, behavior, and school

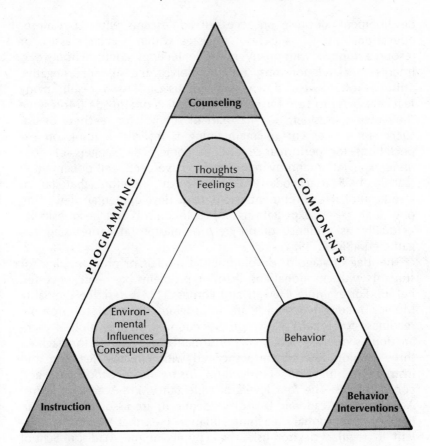

FIGURE 9–1
Relationship between programming components
and life space components.

influences or reactions requires that programming components be
created to support each life space component. As shown in Figure
9–1, instructional interventions provide the most direct input to
school influences; behavior interventions provide support for meeting behavior standards and limits; counseling interventions provide
assistance for dealing with thoughts and feelings.

Stages of Psychoeducational Management

In addition to the three-pronged program for intervention into
educational, social, and self-related problem areas, it is important
for teachers to consider sequential stages or phases of student

251

development. Because unsuccessful adolescents enter special re-educational programs (schools, classes within regular classes, or resource rooms) with many negative feelings about schoolwork, interpersonal relationships, and themselves, the student's negative attitudes often wear down staff enthusiasm. As a result, many teachers cease to care for certain youngsters or struggle to preserve their own self-esteem. A vital part of survival for teachers of unsuccessful adolescents is maintaining a realistic outlook on expectations for performance and outcome. The dangers of both underexpectation and overexpectation have been well documented (Larsen, 1975; MacLeod, 1973). It is critical, therefore, that staff of re-educational environments hold to a developmental viewpoint, one that raises expectations for self-control and responsibility gradually, as evidence of progress or mastery at earlier stages is gathered (Block, 1971).

The idea of stage or developmental models or programming for students with emotional and learning problems has been suggested before. For example, Hewett and Forness (1974) describe the Santa Monica Madison School Plan, a program designed to promote readiness for regular classroom functioning. In this model, there are four sequential levels of performance expectancy for each of three "major determiners associated with effective learning and instruction" (p. 398): *curriculum, instructional conditions,* and *consequences.* The four levels of expectancy, Pre-Academic I, Pre-Academic II, Academic I, and Academic II, are associated with an increasingly "normal" teaching situation (i.e., that situation prevalent in regular classrooms). Thus, pupils in the Madison School Plan are encouraged to sequentially progress from an initial emphasis on readiness skills, such as attention to task and orderly responding in individual work with the teacher, with checkmark tokens backed up by frequent tangible rewards (Pre-Academic I level of curriculum, conditions, and consequences); all the way to an emphasis on grade-level academic performance in large-group situations, with grades and occasional social praise as consequences (Academic II level of curriculum, conditions, and consequences). This developmental program is more fully described in Chapter 11 of Hewett and Forness (1974).

Wood (1975) has successfully applied a developmental therapy approach to special school programming for preschool and early elementary disturbed children. Her work has provided a rich resource for creating a continuum of psychoeducational experiences in relation to behavior, communication, socialization, and academics. Like Hewett, her five stages are arranged to progressively prepare children for a normal classroom environment. Wood's five stages are I—responding to the environment with pleasure; II—responding to the environment with success; III—learning skills for successful group participation; IV—investing in group process; V—applying individual and group skills in new situations.

Swap (1974) outlines a developmental and ecological approach, based upon Hewett's and Erikson's hierarchies of developmental stages. She cautions that student behaviors that are below developmental expectations frequently trigger ineffectual responses from teachers. For these triggering behaviors she presents suggestions for adaptive environmental responses.

The following recommended stages of psychoeducational management have much in common with Hewett's and Wood's levels or stages. Based on staff experience with secondary students in special programs, three stages are proposed: I—renew hope and motivation for learning; II—develop caring and ownership for own efforts; III—strengthen self-control and internalization of responsibility.

Education for Troubled Youth: Mark Twain School Program

The experience gained in conducting the Mark Twain School strongly corroborates the concept that unsuccessful adolescents have had frequent difficulties in achieving academic, interpersonal, and personal goals. Mark Twain is a specially designed public school that conducts a short-term psychoeducational program for pre-adolescents and adolescents of normal intelligence who are having serious difficulties with academic tasks, human relationships, and self-organization. Students are referred by local school personnel through area offices when it is determined that their needs cannot be met by the resources available in the local schools.

To establish a school environment with balanced groups of students in small units based on age, physical maturity, and social development, Mark Twain was designed as three schools within one. The Lower School is composed of 110 students, ages 10–12; the Middle School has 110 students, ages 12–14; the Upper School has 55 students, ages 14–18. The primary objective is to prepare the student for a successful return to a local school program.

Mark Twain School provides for major areas of psychoeducational programming in several ways. It offers an individualized and personalized task-oriented curriculum, which includes (a) assignment to an instructional team on the basis of age and grade level, (b) assessment of academic, personal, and social functioning prior to setting priority objectives, (c) scheduling into classes and groups appropriate to the student's cognitive and affective needs, and (d) continuous diagnostic-prescriptive teaching. Each student is assigned a teacher-advisor who becomes a sponsor and counselor. The teacher-advisor coordinates the student's instructional program, establishes goals and schedule with the student, conducts group and individual counseling, and serves as a resource to other teachers. A code of school-wide rights and responsibilities has been established, and all staff are expected to reinforce the announced standards and limits in accordance with the school's discipline policy and sequential steps.

In developing individual educational programs for students admitted to the school, the staff has found that student needs can consistently be prioritized within several of the following "change variables": (a) academic learning in subject areas of English-language arts, math, social studies-geography, science, physical education, and arts; (b) basic skills (reading, computation, language, reference, psychomotor); (c) classroom participation, including attendance, cooperation, and task orientation; (d) interpersonal relations, such as acceptance of authority, respect for others, and social skills; and (e) personal adjustment—a sense of self-worth, self-responsibility, emotional control, and problem solving. Individual educational programs are prepared for each student prior to placement in Mark Twain, identifying needs improvement areas, priority objectives, strategies, and resources for promoting progress. These priority objectives (e.g., arithmetic computation, respect for others, a sense of self-worth) then become the basis for parent and student conferences for a designated period of time (usually 9–10 weeks).

Psychoeducational Programming

Intervention efforts at Mark Twain are largely directed toward the three major realms of adolescent failure: academic, interpersonal, and personal goals. That is, psychoeducational programming must encompass *instructional* needs, must address *behavior expectations and interventions* and must provide various *counseling* opportunities. Additionally, the stage at which the student is operating, as discussed previously, must be taken into account as programming in each of these three areas proceeds.

TABLE 9–2
Parameters for Areas of Psychoeducational Programming

Instructional	Behavior Expectations and Interventions	Counseling
Work format	Limits and expectations	Relationship
Academic contracts	Physical holding	Small-group meetings
Monitoring	Planned sequential response to violations	Parent conferencing
Tasks	sponse to violations	
Stress	Rewards	
	Life space interviews	

In order to more clearly indicate the nature of psychoeducational programming that takes place at Mark Twain, each stage will be described in terms of student entry characteristics, student goals, and management strategies for each area of psychoeducational programming (i.e., instructional, behavior expectations and interventions, and counseling). The reader should keep several points in mind as this material is studied. First, the programming strategies presented are not meant to be all inclusive, nor is the absence of a given strategy a censure. Additionally, the strategies presented are meant to be emphasized in programming. Taken together, the strategies could comprise or facilitate construction of a checklist for psychoeducational program design. Finally, programming strategies are presented as general practices. Much individualization would be required in terms of learning content, specific student objectives, rewards, and contracts.

Stage I: Renewing Hope and Motivation for Learning

Student entry characteristics. Many teachers become quickly discouraged in their attempts to help unsuccessful adolescents. During the early days of the Mark Twain School, staff would often feel disillusioned about the possibilities for improving academic and social performance. As talented teachers in regular secondary schools, many hoped that their own skills and personality would spur dramatic gains for their students. When it became clear that finding student potentials and turning them on to learning were to be arduous, frustration-filled processes, many staff began to question the reality of their own competence and the wisdom of their decision to teach emotionally handicapped teen-agers. This occurred despite the fact that an intensive inservice program had been conducted prior to the opening of the school in order to prepare staff for the difficult times ahead. On an intellectual level, the teaching faculty had heard that years of student failure would be tough to crack, but on a gut level they yearned for immediate success.

It is important for staff who receive unsuccessful adolescents in re-educational settings to understand that the students who enter their classrooms may have already developed a strong set of negative learning characteristics. Such students often feel defeated, resentful, and reluctant to risk new failures; expect repetition of previously negative school experiences; mistrust staff and are insecure in schools; and lack self-esteem and peer friendships.

Student goals. For those students who enter a program without much hope or motivation for new learning, it is critical that program goals be matched to their fundamentally negative and defensive orientation. We have seen parents and teachers who generated near-fanatic optimism about such students, wishing to ignore the blemished past, only to retaliate with anger and accusations when early progress was lacking. For example, Mr. Lansing refused to be biased by cumulative folder reports of Michael's fearfulness in new situations. Instead, he chose to show trust by allowing his student to read in the instructional resources center, in another area of the school. A half-hour later, the school psychologist found Mike trying to hitch a ride along the busy highway that passed the school. When Mike was returned to the classroom, Mr. Lansing angrily expressed his disappointment that Mike could not be trusted.

At this beginning stage of re-education, the goals for psychoeducational management are to help the student become willing to try again; to develop faith and comfort in the new setting; to experience positive reactions within self and from others; to gain confidence in his own strengths; and to form friendships with one or two peers.

Psychoeducational management strategies.

Instructional. Work format should be individually paced by the teacher, using learning activity packages or a modularized approach (Charles, 1976; Kapfer & Kapfer, 1973). Precision teaching is useful for specific skill development (Kunzelman, 1970; Meacham & Wiesen, 1969). Students must be involved in enjoyable individual or paired-partner projects (Council for Exceptional Children, 1977). The student chooses or is assigned high-interest activities in school programs (Bauer, 1975; Goodlad, 1970; Rohwer, 1971). The teacher structures the learning environment for private work and break periods (Abeson & Blacklow, 1971; Hewett, 1968; Phillips, 1967; Stellern, Vasa, & Little, 1976; Volkmor, Langstaff, & Higgins, 1974).

• *Academic contracts.* The teacher initiates simple, written and signed contracts covering no more than a week's work (Gearheart & Weishahn, 1976; Homme, 1970; Kiesler, 1971).

• *Monitoring.* The teacher checks work immediately or at least within the work period and takes responsibility for charting and displaying progress (Kanfer & Goldstein, 1975; Lawrence, 1971).

• *Tasks.* Tasks are set by the teacher on the basis of prescriptive assessment and analysis of student needs. Instructional tasks need to be well within the student's skill range, concrete, and clearly sequenced for developmental mastery. Student understanding of the assignment should be checked before work is attempted (Bloomer & Ducharme, 1974; Engelmann, 1969; Gold, 1976; Lovitt & Smith, 1972; Mann & Suiter, 1974; Moran, 1975; Tawney, Kruse, Cegelka, & Kelly, 1977).

• *Stress.* Exposure to school stress has to be minimized. The teacher must offer emotional support during personal stress. Limits need to be clearly stated and enforced fairly and objectively in order to avoid guilt feelings (Lipe & Jung, 1971; Long & Newman, 1971; Morse, 1976; Swift & Spivack, 1974).

Behavior expectations and intervention.

• *Limits and expectations.* Desirable and unacceptable behaviors should be clearly stated in written form as rights and responsibilities. Students may often have to be reminded of these expectations through visual (e.g., posters) or verbal (e.g., teacher reminders) means (Madsen & Madsen, 1974; National School Public Relations Association, 1973).

• *Restraint.* It may be necessary to physically hold the student at times in order to prevent or curb harmful or dangerous behavior (Redl & Wineman, 1952; Samuels & Moriarty, 1975).

• *Planned sequential response to violations.* Planned response means that the teacher anticipates possible rule violations and prepares to employ successive levels of intervention. For example, one sequence might be *(a)* respectful but firm reminder or request to desist, *(b)* warning, time out, or regulated permission (i.e., channeling deviant behavior into acceptable outlet such as punching a boxing bag), (c) isolation/time out within the classroom area, (d) isolation/time out outside the classroom area, (e) immediate counseling session; (f) temporary suspension as an enforced conse-quence, requiring parent-school conference before readmission (Montgomery County Public Schools, Maryland, 1977; National School Public Relations Association, 1976).

• *Rewards*. For sincere improvement efforts on the student's part, the teacher can frequently and contingently apply rewards, such as tangible and basic rewards (e.g., food, material objects, money), praise, classroom recognition, and special individual ac-tivities and privileges (Martin & Lauridsen, 1974; Nolen, Kunzel-mann & Haring, 1967; O'Leary & O'Leary, 1976; O'Leary, Poulos & Devine, 1975; Reinert, 1976).

• *Life Space Interview*. The life space interview is an im-portant intervention that may be employed following an incident that disrupts classroom learning. It assumes that students who vio-late expectations or are emotionally upset can manage their be-havior more effectively if they are helped to understand the situation that triggered the disruption. The method calls for an emotionally accepting relationship and structured interview process, conducted by an adult close to the problem incident and as soon as practical. In most cases, the adult is the classroom teacher.

The goal of the life space interview will vary depending upon the student's emotional stability at the time. When students are extremely distressed, the goal is to provide immediate ego-support so as to prevent deterioration of impulse controls. More often, however, the goal is to establish an empathic understanding that facilitates new learning and possibilities for personal and environ-mental change. During Stage I, the emphasis is on emotional sup-port and adjustment of the environment to better accommodate student needs (Fagen & Hill, 1977; Morse, 1976; Redl, 1959).

Counseling.

• *Relationship*. There must be brief regular individual meet-ings with the teacher-advisor on approximately a weekly basis. The teacher-advisor emphasizes responding with respect, empathy, and support (Carkhuff, 1969; Fagen & Guedalia, 1977; Ivey, 1971; Rogers, 1969; Sklansky, Silverman, & Rabichow, 1969).

• *Small-group meetings*. At least once per week, a group of 6 to 10 students meets for structured, enjoyable, activity-oriented sessions led by a teacher-advisor. Topics for discussion are combined with audiovisual presentations (e.g., films, records, slide-tapes). Problems are discussed voluntarily, with the focus being the individual as a part of the group. The teacher-advisor encourages vicarious learning such as clarifying one's own problems through identification with or talking about another person or literary characters; praise and other rewards are provided for staying on-task in the group (Alschuler, Tabor, & McIntyre, 1970; Gorman, 1974; Hawley & Hawley, 1972; Lyon, 1971; Ohio State Department of Education, 1971; Pfeiffer & Jones, 1969, 1970; Schrank, 1970; Stanford & Stanford, 1969).

• *Parent conferencing.* The teacher meets with each student and his parents to discuss progress within 6–10 weeks of student enrollment in Mark Twain. Immediate conferencing with parents follows disciplinary actions or crisis situations (Barsch, 1969; Kroth, 1975).

Stage II: Developing Caring and Ownership for Own Efforts

Student entry characteristics. Once it is evident that the student anticipates or appreciates positive experiences and relationships in school, it is time to move to the second stage of psychoeducational management. Perhaps the angry defiance has changed to a watchful coolness, or the frightened withdrawal to a hesitant approach, or the flagrant apathy to a casual interest. Regardless of the manifest changes in behavior, the crucial fact is that the adolescent has begun to feel that good things can happen in this school setting. Energies previously devoted to avoiding failure and rejection are now available for new academic and interpersonal pursuits.

As the adolescent enters this stage, he is beginning to feel hopeful; willing to try some new tasks and relationships; able to perceive positives in self and others; tentatively interested in challenge; partially comfortable and trusting with some staff; and developing some meaningful relationships.

Student goals. At this point the teacher must recognize that while the student may be ready to invest sincere efforts in the learning environment, he has become openly vulnerable to failure once again. The re-educational tightrope calls for strengthening self-esteem through genuine accomplishment, while guarding against massive defeat. Staff should be keenly attuned to ways in which they can set up a student for major letdowns.

For example, Greg constantly demanded sympathy and support from adults. He was always "hurt" or "gypped" or "ripped off." In an effort to meet his unfulfilled dependency needs, Mrs. Freedman went out of her way to nurture and protect Greg, even if it meant bending rules in his favor. In time, Mrs. Freedman, like everyone else, including staff and peers, grew tired of Greg's incessant whining. On soapbox derby day all the students wheeled out the woodbox racing cars they had made in the industrial arts shop. Greg placed his car on the starting line with tremendous pride, between two other cars. The starter's gun went off and suddenly Greg found his wheel jammed. The boy next to him had placed a stick in the spokes. Pulling it loose, Greg sped down the raceway, barely losing the race at the finish line. Tearful and greatly distressed, Greg spotted Mrs. Freedman and rushed to her, only to hear her respond, "Greg, if it wasn't you, I'd believe it. Go move your car out of the way—there's another race."

The primary goals for psychoeducational management at this stage are to help the student to begin to deal with his own problems and self-defeating behavior; to acquire strength to face adversity and conflict; to identify and prize positives in self, gaining courage to risk and feel badly; and to cope with group stresses, giving and receiving feedback about behavior.

Psychoeducational management strategies.

Instructional.

    • *Work format.* At this stage the teacher still individually paces work in remedial or weak areas, but there is self-pacing and small-group pacing by the teacher in areas of relative strength or grade-level performance (Hewett & Forness, 1974; Noar, 1972; Stellern et al., 1976). The student works on both preferred and nonpreferred activities, strengths and deficits (Johnson & Myklebust, 1967). The student is taught to request help or learning supports such as a cubicle, study time, or a tutor (Randolph & Howe, 1966; Rosenberg, 1972). Effort is directed toward broadening student initiative and involvement in the school program (Jackson, 1968; Swift & Spivack, 1975).

    • *Academic contracts.* The student is ready for more complex, short-term (1–2 week units) written contracts. More student input in the determination of learning tasks arises from mutual student-teacher requests and negotiations, leading to the signing of a jointly constructed contract by the responsible persons (Fagen & Hill, 1977; Gearheart & Weishahn, 1976).

    • *Monitoring.* Regularly, on a weekly basis or more often, the teacher should check work. There is peer checking and feedback, teacher and self-recording and charting of work, leading to the display of work and progress charts (Broden, Hall, & Mitts, 1971; Dreikurs, Grunwald, & Pepper, 1971; Gottman & McFall, 1972).

• *Tasks.* Tasks are selected for reasonable challenge, with skills especially extended in high-motivation areas. The teacher consults with the student on the nature of task and supports or resources required; the teacher offers help if needed, but the student is encouraged to explore alternative methods of learning (Gallagher, 1972; Minskoff, 1975). Student completion of less preferred tasks leads to highly preferred events (Premack, 1959; Stevenson, 1972).

• *Stress.* Students are intentionally exposed to mild, realistic types of instructionally related stress (e.g., tests, deadlines, projects, new skill areas). The teacher creates opportunities for the student to vary levels of risk in learning (Bower, 1964; Hollister, 1965; Kohl, 1967; Phillips, 1968; Sharp, 1971; Swit & Spivack, 1975).

Behavior expectations and intervention.

• *Limits and expectations.* Standards and limits are consistently modeled and reinforced. Behavior contracts are developed based on mutual student and teacher needs. Conflicts are discussed and resolved through enforcement of consequences or commitment to constructive alternatives (Glasser, 1974; Kounin, 1970; Krumboltz & Krumboltz, 1972; O'Leary & O'Leary, 1972).

• *Restraint.* Physical restraint should be avoided and replaced by signal interference (e.g., prompts, gestures, looks), proximity control (e.g., standing near or gently touching) and awareness-heightening reminders (e.g., "If the test gets to you, just take some deep breaths or get a drink of water—no acting up") (Cheney & Morse, 1972; Gray, 1974; Long, 1969; Long & Newman, 1971). The teacher takes care to reinforce all desirable behaviors demonstrating improvement in delay and inhibition skills (Epstein, Hallahan, & Kauffman, 1975; Fagen et al., 1975; Kauffman, 1977).

• *Planned sequential response to violations.* At Stage II, the following sequence illustrates the possible successive levels of intervention after violations: *(a)* time outs and regulated permission on prearranged signal basis (e.g., student writes note or crosses arms in seat), *(b)* respectful reminder or request to desist, *(c)* warning of consequence, *(d)* isolation/time out within or outside the

261

classroom area, followed by life space interview, *(e)* temporary suspension as an enforced consequence, requiring parent-school conference before readmission, *(f)* expulsion, requiring parent-school conference and consideration of alternative placement before readmission (Fagen & Hill, 1977; Montgomery County Public Schools, 1977; National School Public Relations Association, 1973).

• *Rewards.* The contingent use of points or tokens mediates delayed access to tangible and school-related or group-related rewards (e.g., notebooks, pens, magazines, bowling, free time, field trip). There is also the use of intermittent teacher praise and public recognition, peer recognition and approval, letters to parents, a phasing-in of self-evaluation (e.g., self-charting, keeping diaries, rating one's own behavior), as well as opportunities to earn privileges and leadership opportunities (e.g., work on interest project, time with liked staff member, peer counseling or tutoring, news reporting on school TV, film making or preparation of teaching materials) (Frederiksen & Frederiksen, 1975; Gartner, Kohler & Riessman, 1971; Hosford & Brown, 1975; MacDonald, 1971; National Commission on Resources for Youth, 1974; Nelson, 1976; Rosenberg & Graubard, 1975; Stephens, 1975; Thoresen & Mahoney, 1974; Worrell & Nelson, 1974).

• *Life Space Interview.* The emphasis in Stage II is on awareness and consideration of alternatives. The primary strategies used to promote personal change include "reality rub," "new tools," "arousing doubt," and "clarifying numb values" (Fagen & Hill, 1977; Hammill & Bartel, 1975; Redl, 1959). When possible, videotape playback is used to enhance the life space interview.

Counseling.

• *Relationship.* On alternate weeks, there are brief individual meetings in which the teacher-advisor emphasizes initiating direct encounters and disclosures and maintains responding with respect and empathy (Fagen & Guedalia, 1977; Glasser, 1965; Gordon, 1971; Harris, 1967).

• *Small-group meetings.* Meetings of small groups led by the teacher-advisor, occurring weekly or more often, reflect a balance of structured activity and free discussion, with student involvement in agenda setting and problem sharing. There are emphases on constructive expression of feelings, clarification of one's own values, management of conflict and frustration, and responsible self-assertion. Also, the group plans to be engaged in enjoyable activities contingent upon purposeful group work (Covington, Crutchfield, Davies, & Olton, 1972; Ellis, 1972; Fagen et al., 1975; Glasser, 1969; Ivey & Alschuler, 1973; Lange & Jakubowski, 1976; Mosher & Sprinthall, 1971; Palomares & Logan, 1975; Shaftel & Shaftel, 1967; Simon, Howe, & Kirschenbaum, 1972; Wren, 1971).

• *Parent conferencing.* The teacher meets with the student and his parents to discuss progress about every 2 months, with immediate conferencing with parents following disciplinary actions or crisis situations. Parents are encouraged to become involved in a planned series of group meetings with other parents, with an emphasis on promoting compatible school-home relationships and expectations (Clements & Alexander, 1975; Dinkmeyer & McKay, 1976; Gorham, 1975).

Stage III: Strengthening Self-Control and Internalization of Responsibility

Student entry characteristics. The third stage of psychoeducational management begins when the adolescent demonstrates pride and emotional investment in both work and social relationships. At this point, the student evidences optimism for success and a desire to attempt new goals; willingness to accept difficult tasks and satisfaction from the accomplishment of them; comfort with most staff and trust in some; respect for himself and a willingness to share personal ups and downs; a few enduring friendships; and empathy for others' feelings. These characteristics need not be consistently or totally displayed, but they are clearly present to an identifiable degree.

For example, when Eddie entered Mark Twain School he was critical and antagonistic to staff and students. He saw most of the school activities as worthless; he picked at assignments like they were unappetizing vegetables. Over time, he began to take interest in setting learning objectives, such as preparing a detailed outline for a report on civil rights protests in rock music. Eddie's complaining decreased as he completed agreed-upon tasks, and he was able to talk about how hard it was to "find that stuff." The staff knew he was ready for the stage of preparation for regular school return when he and band members from the upper school wrote, rehearsed, and happily performed original music at a school-wide celebration.

Student goals. Perhaps the most painful part of teaching adolescents is exposing oneself to rejection for "letting them down." Teen-agers tend to perceive adults in accordance with their own ideals: adults who are open, flexible, trusting, modern, and approachable are "right on," while those who are strict, conservative, and detached are "out of it." The adult world is commonly divided into good guys and bad guys, and when things do not go right, a bad guy can easily be found. Often a good guy can also be found to give support to this dichotomy. Many staff are unwittingly drawn into these good-bad judgments and wind up criticizing or undercutting other teachers on their own faculty in order to maintain favor with the student.

As the student comes to care about and accept ownership for his own ideas and actions, he also reacts more strongly to persons or situations that differ or interfere. Real disappointment and disillusionment become possible as striving gains importance. It is natural to seek external fault when a problem surfaces, and usually adult bad guys are abundant. Sometimes, however, the problem or conflict is experienced directly with a good guy—often resulting in exaggerated self-blaming on the part of the adolescent. An important developmental milestone is attained, however, when a young person develops the inner strengths to share responsibility for a problem and accept emotional hurt within a caring relationship.

Special educators must become more sensitive to the importance of phasing in opportunities to experience and work through conflict and frustration in re-educational programs (Fagen, 1977b; Fagen & Hill, 1977; Fagen et al., 1975; Palomares & Logan, 1975). Too often students do well in protective, highly structured special environments but are ill-prepared for the stresses of less restrictive settings. We do not pay enough attention to the meaning of separations or transitions from more to less intensive programs, for staff as well as for students. It is typical in good programs to find staff and students increasing their commitment and caring for the program and each other. As the time approaches for return to a regular school program, staff and students are at the most intense point of relationship and involvement. Ironically, the staff often handles its anxiety about the students' readiness for separation by working even harder to build academic and social abilities as time runs out. Parents and students frequently move on to the next school program wondering why they had to go and feeling unprepared, even abandoned.

In the past few years, the Mark Twain School staff has sought to face these issues directly. As students enter the final stage of programming, they are planfully exposed to both simulated and real stresses of the regular school setting to which they will be returned. Thus, class periods are structured for larger group instruction, more authority-oriented teacher-student relationships, and more formal curriculum content and media. Students who are outward bound are placed in a regular secondary school program for a 6-week period before leaving Mark Twain. After this outside trial placement, they return to Mark Twain to process their regular school experience, complete unfinished business, and prepare for graduation.

In this culminating stage of psychoeducational management the teacher's goals are to help the student to deal directly with his own problems, deciding among choices for actions and accepting consequences for those decisions; to maintain respect for self and others in the face of adversity and conflict; to demonstrate the courage to risk and feel bad; and to model coping with group stresses and provide group leadership.

Psychoeducational management strategies.

Instructional.

- *Work format.* Work pacing remains similar to that of Stage II, but additional types of work are phased into the student's program. For instance, the student may contribute to the school program (e.g., preparing audiovisual material, building wall displays, arranging a greenhouse) (Armstrong, 1973; Swift & Spivack, 1975). There is guided independent study, with research in the media center (Taylor, Artuso, Stillwell, Soloway, Hewett, & Quay, 1972; Torrance & Myers, 1970; Wilson & Armstrong, 1976). Teachers must bring about a balance of high-interest choices and lower-interest requirements (Stellern et al., 1976).

- *Academic contracts.* Contracts become more challenging, covering both short-term and long-term objectives. They may be written and signed or strictly verbal agreements. The learning tasks should be initiated by the student, with teacher agreement (Polsgrove, 1977; Uhlman & Shook, 1976).

- *Monitoring.* At Stage III, the emphases are on self-recording and charting and peer feedback. Only periodically does the teacher check on priority student objectives (Gottman & McFall, 1972; Solomon & Wahler, 1973; Swift & Spivack, 1975).

- *Tasks.* Tasks are selected to require application of skills to practical, real-life situations (e.g., division in handling a budget, spelling in filling out an employment application). Based on student initiation and student-teacher consultation, the teacher promotes challenging projects that link several skills and steps (e.g., a slide-tape on bees, building a model of a Japanese sampan, conducting and writing an interview of the school principal). Difficult tasks in areas of relative weakness are assigned to be attempted with teacher help, and the teacher has to be ready to modify these if necessary following appropriate student involvement (Bowe, 1970; Colella, 1973; DiTullio, 1974; Gronlund, 1970; Kohl, 1976; Weiss & Weiss, 1974).

• *Stress.* The student is exposed to moderate, realistic types of instructionally related stress: the teacher creates opportunities for the student to risk failure and achieve success through repeated efforts; he provides for mastery of simulated stress situations and the development of skills for effective coping with conflict and frustration (Bower, 1964; Fagen, 1977b; Fagen & Hill, 1977; Fagen & Long, 1976; Fagen et al., 1975; Hobbs, 1974; Johnson & Bany, 1970; Ohio State Department of Education, 1971; Palomares & Logan, 1975; Rothman, 1970; Sherry & Franzen, 1977; Swift & Spivack, 1975).

Behavior expectations and intervention.

• *Limits and expectations.* Standards and limits are discussed, negotiated, agreed upon and mutually reinforced (e.g., each student reminds peers, holds the teacher accountable). Conflicts are discussed and resolved through commitment to constructive alternatives; behaviors that deviate from limits and expectations are viewed as decisions subject to either natural or established, logical consequences (Dreikurs, 1964; Felixbrod & O'Leary, 1973; Krumboltz & Krumboltz, 1972; Phillips, Phillips, Fixsen, & Wolf, 1972; Sarason & Sarason, 1974).

• *Restraint.* Holding or other physical restraint is avoided; restraint is provided by signal interference and awareness reminders (as in Stage II) as well as direct "I messages" requesting or promoting change in behavior (e.g., "I'm having trouble concentrating with the talking going on" or "I won't allow teasing in here"). The teacher shows appreciation for desirable behaviors that demonstrate self-regulation and consideration for others (Fagen & Guedalia, 1977; Gordon, 1971; James & Jongeward, 1973; Kauffman, 1977; Long & Newman, 1971).

• *Planned sequential response to violations.* At Stage III, successive levels of intervention are initiated as follows: *(a)* time-outs and regulated permission on self-managed or prearranged signal basis; *(b)* respectful reminder or request to desist; *(c)* request that the student go to a private area or office, followed by a life space interview (e.g., "John, I want to speak to you in my office" or "Please go to the conference table—I'll be there in a few minutes"); *(d)* temporary suspension as an enforced consequence, requiring a parent-school conference before readmission (Fagen & Hill, 1977; Kanfer & Goldstein, 1975; Montgomery County Public Schools, 1977; National School Public Relations Association, 1973, 1976).

• *Rewards.* Rewards are employed as in Stage II, except that there is a much greater emphasis on self-reinforcement through group sharing and individual conferencing sessions (e.g., "I wasn't as bossy this week and even enjoyed having someone else call the plays in the football game") (Allen, 1976; Gartner et al., 1971; Kanfer, 1977; National Commission on Resources for Youth, 1974; O'Leary & O'Leary, 1976). Also, peer recognition and status events are used to reward achievement of goals (e.g., leadership responsibilities, peer counselor, or tutor role).

• *Life Space Interview.* There is a major emphasis on resolutions in which responsibility for personal or environmental change is accepted by the student. Major strategies include role reversal and coping-with-frustration techniques (Chelser & Fox, 1964; Cheney & Morse, 1972; Fagen & Long, 1976; Fagen et al., 1975; Morse, 1971; Redl, 1959).

Counseling.

• *Relationship.* There may be individual meetings with the teacher-advisor at the request of either party. At this stage, the emphases are on initiating direct encounters and disclosures, value clarification, and working towards resolution of problems. Again, responding is maintained with respect and empathy (Carkhuff, 1971; Fagen & Guedalia, 1977; Lange & Jakubowski, 1976).

• *Small-group meetings.* Weekly meetings reflect a balance of structured activity and free discussion, with much student involvement in agenda setting and problem solving. Leadership of the group meetings is shared by the teacher-advisor and students. The main objectives are constructive expression of feelings, clarification of own values, management of conflict and frustration, responsible self-assertion, and dealing with separation and transition to a less restrictive environment (Fagen et al., 1975; Johnson &

Johnson, 1975; Lazarus & Fay, 1975; Mahler, 1969; Newman, 1974; Palomares & Logan, 1975).

   • *Parent conferencing.* The parent conferencing component is unchanged from Stage II except that the emphases in the parental group meetings turn to dealing with the students' upcoming transition to a less restrictive environment and maintaining parent-student and parent-school communications following program completion (Abidin, 1976; Brownstone & Dye, 1973; Ginott, 1969; Gordon, 1971).

Future Developments in Psychoeducational Management

Public education has arrived at a moment of truth, as a result of demands for accountability and Public Law 94–142. Never before have school systems been clearly required to provide a free, appropriate education for all students, including many who have suffered from repeated experiences of failure. Obviously the mandate for least restrictive appropriate placements and individualized education programs prohibits disownership of students who are difficult to teach. The question that must now be faced is whether we have the means of programming for students who have not responded favorably to previous educational interventions.

   Given these circumstances, the psychoeducational management approach described here could have the following impact on educational practices: *(a)* increased respect for the integrity and uniqueness of the individual student, *(b)* development of individualized education programs that are relevant to priority developmental needs, *(c)* enhancement of prospects for progressive inclusion in less restrictive environments, and *(d)* promotion of the student's ability to cope with adversity and manage his own behavior, even under conditions of stress and frustration.

   People who believe in psychoeducational management insist that those individuals in the educational environment deal with students as integrated beings, rather than fragmented objects. By focusing on the interaction of academic achievement, self-understanding, and social behavior it is possible to formulate goals and objectives that represent valid priorities for individual growth and mastery. Such priorities may reflect personal and interpersonal goals, as well as academic and basic skill needs. However, it will be necessary for psychoeducators to provide leadership in translating life space analysis into the precise language of objectives and strategies required for individualized education programs.

In the next few years, educational programming should achieve a balance between personal and interpersonal goals, and strictly academic goals. Individualized education programs should evidence a variety of objectives related to personal and interpersonal goals, for example:

The student will demonstrate confidence in his own ability to express an important idea by ————.

The student will ask to borrow someone else's property instead of taking it.

The student will take a time out in the reading area when the work gets too hard instead of ————.

The student will directly state his negative feelings or differences of opinion using "I messages" rather than "you-blaming" messages or disruptive-destructive behavior.

The psychoeducational approach regards the management of conflict and frustration as indispensable to successful attainment in schoolwork, human relationships, and self-understanding, and self-control. If adolescents with emotional and learning problems are to be reintegrated into regular school environments, teachers must develop the capacity to absorb the emotional pain that erupts from the student's struggle to master increasingly more difficult life tasks. As Kauffman (1977) writes: "Disturbed children cannot be depended upon to learn by some magical, mysterious, internally guided process; their learning will be assured only by a skillful and sensitive adult who makes the expectations for their behavior appropriately difficult" (p. 265).

Now most regular educators feel inadequately prepared to teach adolescents with special needs. For example, our own studies of regular teacher attitudes toward these students indicate that teachers overestimate the frequency and intensity of acting-out behavior and worry about their own reactions to such behavior. However, with exposure to sound principles and techniques for handling and preventing behavior problems, these same teachers can gain confidence in their ability to maintain classroom order and discipline.

It is clear that the combined initiatives of The Council for Exceptional Children and the Bureau of Education for the Handicapped have launched an era of inservice training in the education of students with special needs. The fate of this massive inservice training effort is largely in the hands of school-based special educators, for it is they who must become inschool consultants, trainers, and models for their regular education colleagues. In effect, just as regular educators will be asked to regulate levels of stress to help students master learning and emotional problems, so will special educators be expected to serve as managers of stress for their teammates in regular education. The old polarization between special and regular education must be replaced by a functional continuum of educational services, meaning that special educators can no longer be satisfied with a singular identification as "student-advocates." Instead they must evolve a more progressive identity as "facilitators of mainstreaming," adjusting dimensions of curriculum and materials, teacher-student interactions, peer-group relations, and classroom organization to match realistic individualized education programs.

Of course, school-based special educators cannot be expected to meet these emerging challenges without steadfast support and assistance from teacher-training institutions and school administrators. Staffing and scheduling patterns must allow for resource roles that provide direct support and inservice training to teaching staff. Federal, state, and local funding must be allocated to programs that develop school-based expertise in the content and delivery of competency-oriented inservice training. Suitable training materials and formats need to be developed and disseminated, particularly in the areas of assessment-programming for developmental needs, counseling, strategies for individualizing instruction, and behavior management. Secondary curricula that focus on self-control and the development of student alternatives for coping with problem situations must be incorporated into the general instructional program.

In selecting new teachers for the secondary level, priority will need to be given to those with experience in genuine encounters with adolescents. Preservice programs that prepare secondary teachers to deal with a wide range of student thoughts, feelings and performance should be considered as exemplary models for replication. Employment procedures that assess a candidate's interpersonal and communication skills with adolescents, as well as his instructional competencies, should be disseminated as methods for the primary prevention of adolescent failure.

Effective implementation of a psychoeducational management approach can be advanced through concentrated research in several major areas, namely: methods for identifying the individual adolescent's status in relation to stages of psychoeducational management; techniques for promoting mutual assessment and goal-setting in relation to individual growth needs; effects of psychoeducational programming strategies on school attitude and adjustment, self-concept, and academic achievement. Although these research areas are complex, they are amenable to fruitful investigation, given some ingenuity and commitment.

Concluding Remarks

As long as people continue to strive toward the fulfillment of their aspirations, they are vulnerable to frustration and hurt. We have presented a psychoeducational management approach to overcoming adolescent failure, one that is based on a developmental sequence involving (a) remotivation, (b) pride in accomplishment, and (c) mastery and self-control. The key to the success of this approach resides in the adult's courage to care and to risk. Teenagers do not require miracle workers or bionic teachers to help them go forward. They need skilled educators who care about a student's thoughts, feelings, and behavior. Hopefully, this chapter will encourage more teachers to approach unsuccessful adolescents with more realistic expectations and confidence. Failure need not continue to breed failure; not if the teacher accepts the probability of some setbacks in the course of mastery and transmits this persisting optimism to the learner. Ultimately, the measure of self-control depends upon our capacity to cope effectively under adverse or difficult circumstances.

Educational Alternatives for Adolescents Labeled Emotionally Disturbed 10

Peter Knoblock

Right from the start I found myself in an alternative environment. I didn't really focus on it at the time, mostly because it was my first job-like experience. I was a senior in college at the University of Michigan and as one of the students in William Morse's seminar, I was assigned to work with a group of children all of whom had Down's syndrome. The class was located in the Salvation Army building in downtown Ann Arbor. My consciousness at the time only permitted me to look at the children as persons I grew fond of and to gain a beginning understanding of the daily complexities teachers face. Then the teacher became ill and with another college student I became the "teacher." Faced with new responsibilities, I began seeing the situation differently. What I saw was a learning environment with very eager learners who were so far out of the system that it was unlikely they were even visible. Over the years I have tended to think of an educational alternative as one that was either outside of the public school system or represented such different values and practices that it would need to be seen in counterbalance to the existing system—even if it was within the system.

But in 1955 there was no system for trainable retarded children to be out of; it was unheard of (maybe even unthought of) to

273

imagine them in the schools. I became aware of the fact that we were not part of anything. We didn't fit as part of any group or system, but I suppose we were an alternative for these children in the sense that they had nothing else.

How peculiar are the cycles and trends; now it is an accepted fact that such children and youth are part of the school system. On the other hand, many of us are still alarmed at the creation of learning environments or experiences because there is nothing else for them. I'll talk a great deal more about this later because it is truly one of the major issues underlying the alternative educational movement. The issue is, just how do we create educational environments and opportunities for special children that move them toward something and not out of and away from the kinds of experiences and opportunities their nonhandicapped peers experience.

It was more than a decade later, in 1968, that I turned my energy once again to learning environments of a different nature— both inside and outside of the system. In the interim I functioned with hospitals, schools, and a university trying in my own way to acquire my own clinical and educational skills and respond in human ways to the clients, patients, and students who inhabited these environments.

After beginning at Syracuse University in 1962, I settled into a new kind of social system, one in which direct service was not a priority. All of my training and experience up to that point had been of an active nature in schools and clinical settings. As a college professor, I panicked when I asked myself how long it would be before I would have my own ideas and approaches as opposed to presenting ideas from individuals like William Morse, Fritz Redl, and Ralph Rabinovitch, all of whom had been important influences in my professional and personal development. I realized that each of these men managed to combine a level of direct activity with children and schools and at the same time found the time and energy to conceptualize what and how they were doing. I, too, needed to stay involved in some form of direct service. Shortly after arriving in Syracuse I developed relationships with school personnel, and together we developed the first special class program for children labeled *emotionally disturbed*. So here I was again involved in an alternative programming approach, but this time *within the system*. If there is a trend now toward the creation of alternatives, it is directed toward options within the existing structures familiar to schools.

I imported the first clinical teacher, Charles Heuchert, now on the faculty of the University of Virginia, and we began with great enthusiasm. By our standards we were truly an alternative program —we used a treatment team approach, dealt with the behavior of children as opposed to blocking or suppressing it and began developing and documenting a psychoeducational model of teaching. However, even though we were in the public school system, we faced what my class of young children at the Salvation Army building faced: no one really wanted them in the mainstream—at least not until they were fixed, and the problem with that is the price special children frequently pay for attending a separate program. That is, they are expected to come out of it in even better shape than most of the regular class children. There is frequently little tolerance for *any* misbehavior.

I began turning my attention to our college students, specifically the preparation of teachers of emotionally disturbed children. With increasing alarm I saw how great the distance was between the theory we taught them and the practice they experienced with children. In 1968, John L. Johnson and I reconceptualized our teacher preparation program to encompass a field-based training model. With resources provided from the Bureau of Education for the Handicapped, we literally moved our graduate program out of the University and into the schools (Knoblock, Barnes, & Taylor, 1974). For the next 4 years we rode an emotional and intellectual roller coaster. We developed programs for children and teachers in the schools and for the last 2 years outside of the system using community facilities. One thing we found was how difficult it is to share children with other adults in schools. This struck us as rather paradoxical in that we didn't necessarily search out other adults, but they did have expectations of how children should be treated and controlled even if worked with by others.

In order to cultivate a more responsive training environment for our trainees and to generate interventions for troubled children, we developed out-of-school programs during the last two years of the project. In effect we searched for an unserved population that nobody else wanted in order to have a measure of freedom to create facilitative programs. We can all see the trap: Just give us our kids and leave us alone. It is tempting to search out children and youth who are "clinically homeless," but the problem is, who will want them when we're done? We did just that—we found junior high aged people who had been excluded from school and created needed learning environments.

In a sense we had been psychologically burned, just like the young people with whom we had chosen to work. We needed each other, but care must be taken in such situations to avoid acting out one's needs through the population with whom you are working. Our intent was not to run off and hide; rather, we obtained space in a neighborhood boys' club near the schools and encouraged school representatives to visit. They came and reacted negatively. Our differences were not the differences of good versus bad people, but rather basic discrepancies in the goals toward which schools are directed and the means toward which these goals can be attained. In essence, our program looked much too discrepant from what is normally thought of as schooling. Behind such obvious differences, of course, were our similar attempts: to act upon a set of goals, responding to the emotional and cognitive needs of youngsters, and to seek out a variety of instructional and institutional solutions to the children's needs and interests.

My interests in the development of smaller, organizationally more manageable environments remained strong through all of this and in 1970, with a group of parents, we developed a small alternative school, then thought of as a "free school." In the process of studying the life and history of the Onondaga Indian Nation our students named the school *Jowonio*, which in that language means "to set free." As with other alternative schools, we experienced the full range of dilemmas: finding teachers who were comfortable in their role and who could involve children in making some decisions about their own learning; fending off local fire and safety restrictions as well as complying with local and state regulations governing the establishment of "nonpublic" schools; and meeting an incredibly diverse range of parental expectations for what and how their children should learn. But unlike the majority of such schools, we survived and have developed into a very different structure with a focus on the integration of severely emotionally disturbed children and typical children. Our exciting evolution began as a small school responding to children and parents who had moved *away* from the public schools. Over 8 years we began to move *toward* a set of beliefs and instructional practices that included typical children and children labeled *autistic* and *autistic-like*. Now we are attempting to demonstrate and document how a more alternative educational program can be designed for such a complex and diverse population of learners. Our project is part of a national effort by the Bureau of Education for the Handicapped to find out how integrated programs can work.[1]

---

[1] For further information on the project, write to Jowonio, The Learning Place, 601 S. Crouse Avenue, Syracuse, NY 13210.

In looking back at my connection with the alternative movement, I can recognize my own changes. Those educators within any movement who remain dogmatic soon find their constituency passing them by, as indeed happened with the free school movement. I remain committed not to the development of alternatives as an end product, but rather with the hope that if there are options created, then others will raise their expectations and hopes for the learning and futures of all children and for the adults who work with them.

Alternative Education

What Are the Alternative Education Possibilities?

This is not the time to fool ourselves about educational alternatives for adolescents viewed as emotionally disturbed. A recent textbook publicity flyer describes them as "chronic disruptive, norm-violating, and learning disabled." This is a harsh description but undoubtedly reflects how they are viewed. In reality many school programs that are called *alternative programs* are mostly segregated situations designed to remove disruptive students from regular programs. If one thinks about the meaning of an alternative educational approach in terms of exploring alternative educational means and goals, then we can see that today's approaches do not qualify as alternative. The trend is more toward removing disruptive learners from the mainstream and applying the same goals and means they failed at previously.

Some of us become encouraged with the development of several alternative education networks focused primarily on programs within the public schools. The National Alternative Schools Program (NASP) at the University of Massachusetts has as their working definition of *alternative,* "an educational program which provides learning experiences not available in the conventional school, and which is available by choice at no extra cost to every family within its community" (NASP, 1974, p. 3). This definition tends to exclude referral programs for young people thought of as the "special education" population; these youths were obviously not eligible for many of the programs included in the above definition. And as we know, many young people in conflict with school, the law, and adults do not enter such programs by choice. Another network, The National Consortium for Options in Public Education, at Indiana University, has been quite active in sponsoring conferences, encouraging research activities to study alternative programs and processes, and publishing materials and a newsletter (*Changing Schools*).

Alternative education is a difficult concept to define and operationalize. Basically, the concept has remained elusive because alternative educators each bring their own past experiences and beliefs about learning and education. The heterogeneous mix of teachers and students involved in the alternative education movement has fostered a varied range of programs and schools: some developed within the system, while others worked outside the educational system; some evolved radical educational goals, while others reflected a "back to basics" model; some excluded atypical children and youth, whereas others searched for handicapped students.

Published during the short-lived ascendency of the free school movement, Dennison's *The Lives of Children* (1969) describes in fluent detail the daily joys and upsets of a small group of learners and teachers at the First Street School. Among believers, the book attracted great interest. It is one of those rare books that combines theory and practice. Written clearly and at times eloquently, Dennison's insights into the lives of learners with special needs reinforced many of our beliefs at the time that educational alternatives, if viable, would need to be developed outside the system. Dennison delineates three essential points for those who set up alternatives outside the educational system:

1. The proper concern of a school is the present lives of children, not education in a narrow sense or preparation for the future.
2. When the rigid schedules of a school are dismantled, what occurs is not chaos, but rather a new order; one that emphasizes relationships, one that integrates emotional and cognitive feelings, and one that fosters expression of knowledge.
3. Running an alternative school is a simple endeavor, provided the school is small and staffed by competent personnel.

At the same time there were equally impressive accounts written by teachers working within the system, usually designing their own classrooms as more responsive environments and advocating change more in terms of guerrilla warfare than all-out assaults on the system (Herndon, 1971; Kohl, 1967).

Since alternative education can function either within or outside the educational system, its range of possible configurations is comprehensive. Regarding potential educational alternatives, Goodlad, Fenstermacher, LaBelle, Rust, Skager, and Weinberg (1975) point out,

> Recently, much of the rhetoric equates "alternatives in education" with open classrooms, alternative schools, and free schools. But the canvas is much broader. It includes movement toward a variety of options with more traditional concepts of schooling; programs or schools essentially freed from many traditional conceptions and restraints; and a variety of formal and informal educational enterprises having little or nothing to do with schools. Some schools that describe their programs as a return to the three R's also label themselves as an alternative to modern "soft" pedagogy. It is clear that alternatives in education mean and include many different things. (p. 1)

As Goodlad et al. (1975) note, it is necessary to view alternative approaches from a variety of perspectives, including the back-to-basics views that a true return to the three R's would in itself constitute an alternative. By conceiving alternatives this broadly, we allow ourselves to grasp just how educational alternatives are viewed for young people with special needs.

Many of the early alternative programs tended to focus mostly on the need to program for young students thought of as troubled, troubling, or reluctant learners. There does seem to be a growing awareness on the part of educators of secondary school aged pupils that some alternatives need to be forthcoming (Hoover, 1978; National Commission on Resources for Youth, 1974). Recently, a number of junior and senior high school programs have been developed. For example, a comprehensive alternative program has been created that restructures the Berkeley California High School. A number of units were developed and students could choose one of them. Some units imposed relatively less structure on the students and focused on basic learning skills. One unit of 400 students, grades 10–12, also focused on basic skills but each grade developed its own emphasis. Other units focused on ethnic and community awareness along with skill development; promoted arts and sciences; prepared for college; combined emphases. In another instance, Quincy Senior High School in Illinois developed seven alternatives for its 1,500 students in grades 11 and 12: a *traditional* school, emphasizing conventional structure and educational approaches; a *flexible* school, providing a structured flexibility with 20-minute modules and the total amount of class time for each subject varying; a *work-study* school, designed primarily for dropout prone students; a *PIE* school (Project to Individualize Education); a *fine arts* school; a *career* school; and a *special education* school.

Thus we observe the incredible range of possibilities, but we continue to discern the exclusion of children with special needs. Specifically, the definition of an alternative program or school for special children and youth is generally mandated as separate from the regular school program. If there is indeed a trend toward the development of alternative educational approaches, then a large aspect of this movement is toward removing difficult children and youth from the mainstream. Very often, the use of the term *alternative program* or *alternative school* is identified with special-needs learners. This practice is highlighted in a survey by the Council for American Private Education (1978)[2] that lists types of schools as elementary, middle, secondary, combined elementary-secondary, special education, vocational, technical, and alternative. "Alternative schools" they note are not an adjunct to or part of a regular school, but are nontraditional programs established to meet the individual needs of pupils that generally are not met in the regular school. This mostly exclusionary definition is supported by figures provided by the National Alternative Schools Program in its 1975 Directory of Public Alternative Schools and reported by Nelson (1977). He estimates that of 251 alternatives analyzed, 120 were "enrichment" programs and 131 were referral programs for a wide variety of labeled children. It is more than likely that the goals and child population served by alternative programs in suburban districts tend toward the enrichment type and in urban centers are mostly referral in nature.

The paradox facing alternative education is that unless we conceptualize, describe, and implement more of a complex understanding of alternatives, then we perpetuate the already developing trend toward using alternative education as a "cool-out" for children and their families and at the same time satisfy ourselves that we are responding to learner needs. Alternative education can be more accurately understood by reviewing the central theme of this heterogeneous alignment and the goals available to alternative educators. Central to any understanding of alternatives in education

---

[2] For more information, write the Council for American Private Education, 1625 I Street, N.W., Washington, D.C.   20006.

is the notion of *options*. Fantini (1973) specifies a number of ground rules for what he terms *public schools of choice;* that is, an acceptable alternative

1. demonstrates adherence to a COMPREHENSIVE SET OF EDUCATIONAL OBJECTIVES—not particular ones. Proposals cannot, for example, emphasize only emotional growth at the expense of intellectual development. The converse is also true. Comprehensive educational objectives deal with work careers, citizenship, talent development, intellectual and emotional growth, problem solving, critical thinking, and the like.

2. does not SUBSTANTIALLY INCREASE THE PER STUDENT EXPENDITURE over that of established programs. To advance an idea which doubles or triples the budget will at best place the proposal in the category of ideal but not practical. An important factor for reformers to bear in mind is that the new arena will make wiser use of OLD money, not set up quests for add-on money.

3. does not ADVOCATE ANY FORM OF EXCLUSIVITY— racial, religious, or economic. Alternatives offered cannot deny equal access to any particular individual or group.

4. is not SUPERIMPOSED but a matter of choice for all participants—teachers, parents, and students.

5. is viewed as ANOTHER WAY of providing education alongside the existing pattern, which continues to be legitimate. Alternatives are different from special programs for dropouts, unwed mothers, and the like.

6. includes a plan for EVALUATION. (pp. 44–45)

Goodlad and associates (1975) present a typology of educational alternatives (see Table 10–1) that delineates the educational goals and means available to educators. According to Goodlad et al. (1975), the kinds of alternatives we tend to define as *common ends–common means* forms of education are either-or approaches, such as passing or failing (instructional), out or in (institutional), and vocational, college-bound, or other forms of sorting (societal). Goodlad et al. make the point that most educational reform in this century had been of the common ends–alternative means type. That is, we all agree on the goals to be reached, but can we find alternative ways of reaching the aims considered crucial for all to

281

TABLE 10–1 A Typological Grid of Educational Alternatives

Alternative Groupings of Alternatives in Education	Instructional	Institutional	Societal
Common Ends, Common Means	Intraclass ability and achievement grouping; promotion or nonpromotion; marking systems	Interclass ability and achievement grouping; suspension and expulsion criteria and procedures	Ages for entering and leaving; matriculation requirements
Common Ends, Alternative Means	Individualized and small group instruction; variety of learning modes; programmed instruction, mastery learning	Team teaching, nongrading; multiage grouping; modular scheduling; variable patterns of curriculum organization	Decentralization of decision making; out-of-school options; performance contracts; alternative schools; curriculum guides suggesting varied approaches
Alternative Ends, Alternative Means	Organization of learning groups around expressed interests; selection from an array of individualized stimuli (for example, programmed instruction in literature rather than math)	Phases approach, successive emphases, geared first to one set of goals and then another; schools within a school; partial voucher plans	Free schools; voucher plans; some alternative schools' easing up of requirements for entering tertiary education or economic participation in society; public E.T.V.
Self-Selected, Open Ends and Means	No required instructional program; choice of teachers and areas of emphasis (the instructional program now becomes entirely personal)	No institutional requirements; learner does or does not take advantage of it with no fear of punishment or retribution other than personal consequences	Vast variety of formal and informal institutions committed fully or partially to education; school as a place might or might not be one of these; a learning society

Source. From *The Conventional and the Alternative in Education*, p. 24, by J. I. Goodlad, G. D. Fenstermacher, T. J. LaBelle, V. D. Rust, R. Skager, & C. Weinberg. Berkeley, Calif.: McCutchan, 1975. Copyright © 1975 by McCutchan Publishing Corporation. Reprinted by permission of the Publisher.

reach? The list of innovations is truly staggering, many of them shining brightly in the educational firmament and then falling just as quickly. Witness what has happened to programmed instruction, teaching machines, computer-assisted instruction (instructional); modular scheduling, nongraded groupings (institutional); and performance contracting with educational consulting firms, decentralizing authority (societal). Goodlad and associates' reaction to reforms is that in essence the majority of these innovations have involved only minor tinkering with long-established school procedures: variances in time available for learning, place, pupil mix, teachers, external restraints, and approach or style of learning (and teaching).

As soon as educators bring up the possibility of alternative ends and alternative means to achieve these ends, panic rises. We saw panic in the almost immediate hardening of positions against open education when the public and many professional educators agreed that children would be deprived of their learning to read and do other basics. In thinking about alternative ends one must consider a rethinking and reconceptualizing of not only the priorities, but a balance between them. Certainly many radical and alternative educators have been asking no more than the school's responding to the whole child, meaning the child's emotional as well as cognitive life (Jones, 1968; Maslow, 1968; Rogers, 1969); more recently people espousing the ecological point of view argue for including all of the forces impinging upon an individual's functioning as necessary curriculum ingredients (Apter, 1977; Rhodes, 1970; Swap, 1974).

Why Alternatives for Youth with Special Needs?

As with most questions in education, this one is value laden. For many educators and private citizens, the youth of America are getting what they deserve. If they are out of school and not learning, it is their fault for not responding to the existing structure. This blaming the victim approach is a popular one (Ryan, 1971). It assumes that the problem resides within the person and whatever must be done to remedy the situation is dependent upon what the *person* does. The more educators come to believe this line of reasoning, the more punitive and uncaring they and the community will act toward the young people involved. And the longer this perception of who is to blame remains fixed on the individual, the less we will look to contributing factors within the environment. By looking beyond the individual we can search out alternatives, although the mere existence of alternatives will not be a panacea.

It was hoped that with an increased focus on the creation of alternative approaches we could bring about an easing of tensions between school personnel and young people. This hope has only been partly realized, and it is important to try to understand why. One answer may reside in the conditions under which many alternative programs were and are now established. Very often a school system will develop an alternative educational program in response to a crisis situation. The problem begins to represent itself in a kind of figure-ground perceptual experience in which a school building, system, or group of people within a school system come to view a number of young people as not responding to the existing structures. The situation is not unlike the discussion by Rhodes (1970) of the threat-recoil cycle, in which illicit behavior is met with concern by the community and steps are taken to meet this perceived threat. The solutions, of course, may have more to do with meeting the needs and anxiety levels of community members than of the recipients of the help; this is precisely what is happening with the development of alternative school programs for troubled youths. Nonetheless, there are some cogent realities demanding that educators continue the search for alternative environments.

It is inconceivable that the topic of youth in school and learning environments can be looked at from only one viewpoint; it seems much more realistic to view the problem as interactional, between the individual and the school and its representatives. If we are willing to see the problem as interactional, we are more likely to seek out solutions. What is the magnitude of the problem? First, we are faced with huge numbers of young people out of school (Children's Defense Fund, 1974). Conservative estimates indicate that 2 million children and young people are not in school; undoubtedly many of these are labeled *handicapped*. In our large urban centers the drop-out rate (or "push-out" rate, as some refer to it) is masked because many young people, while still officially enrolled, attend school intermittently. For example, in a recent visit to four New York City schools for seriously disturbed children, it was revealed that the absenteeism ranged between 25% to 50% on a daily basis.

Second, the media have long publicized the national drop-out rate. The number of high school dropouts is staggering and we tend to lose track of the young people involved once they leave school. There is no societal structure for responding to young people once they work their way through or out of the schools. Of course, they show up again in statistics on young people not assimilated into the labor force. Predictably, these reports are published at the beginning of summer when the public's fear is aroused about just what it is going to be like to have all those kids on the street for the summer. Third, the common failure to deal with young people directly and honestly has widened the gap between how they see the schools and how people in schools see them. There has been a hardening of positions between young people and school representatives, which has led to some very complicated dynamics regarding the whole topic of alternatives for youth.

There is every reason to believe that we are in the midst of attempts to cool down the issue of disturbed youth in the schools by creating alternatives that are really out of the mainstream. The programming options that are commonly thought of as applicable for younger children are not used as readily for adolescents. Specifically, the use of special class programs, resource teacher models, or itinerant teachers seem to be less prevalent in junior and senior high buildings. Part of the reason may have to do with the concern educators have for grouping youngsters with potentially disruptive behavior together.

Open Learning Environments

For the past several years we have grown alarmed at the intensity of the criticism being leveled at open education. During 1974 and 1975 the major news magazines carried rather strong articles indicating that since open educators had not done their job, the pendulum was swinging back to basics. The October 21, 1974 issue of *Newsweek* carries a feature education story entitled "Back to Basics in the Schools." The article begins by contrasting two alternative schools in Pasadena. One is described as a 2-year-old experiment in open education in which "students are given a maximum of individual freedom, a minimum of teacher supervision" (p. 87). The other is said to be "a bastion of tradition-oriented education. Letter grades, regular examinations, strict dress codes, and detention for delinquents are integral parts of the school's conservative program" (p. 87). And, as if to summarize the effectiveness of these two programs, the article stated enrollment figures: at the open education school, 550 pupils and a waiting list of 515; at the other school, 1700 pupils and a waiting list of more than 1,000. It goes on to ask:

>What is the significance of this astonishing contrast? To many it suggests that U.S. education's so-called wave of the future has crested. The result is that all across the nation, parents, school boards, and often the pupils themselves are demanding that the schools stop experimenting and get back to basics—reading, writing, arithmetic and standards of behavior to boot. (p. 87)

Thus, there appears to be a widespread assumption that open education, widely adopted and implemented, is now failing as critics had anticipated all along.

Articles such as this one prompted a conference of 500 educators, brought together to form a counteroffensive of the back-to-basics movement. And so the battle rages; proponents of open approaches are obligated to conceptualize, articulate, and research such approaches, then communicate the findings to other interested individuals. The next section will explicate the ways in which teachers can make their environments more responsive to the needs of young people, and how in turn the pupils and the adults working with them can feel part of what is happening.

The early proponents of open learning environments, such as Kohl (1967, 1977), Holt (1964), Herndon (1971), and Kozol (1972) greatly influenced those of us who were attempting to conceptualize the applicability of such settings for children and youth with special needs (Knoblock, 1973; Knoblock & Barnes, forthcoming; Meisels, forthcoming). My involvement in the free school movement began when I, along with a small group of concerned parents, began planning for an alternative school in the spring of 1969. At that time we were in the process of moving away from the public schools; as our school developed we realized that it was possible to create an alternative environment, one that approached a set of beliefs and practices that represented a different (not necessarily better) point of view. Now that our school has entered its 9th year of operation, we are established as a community school with both public and private funds, responding to both labeled and unlabeled children.

From our experiences there became evident a number of advantages to those students and teachers who worked in open and humanistic alternative environments.

1. Given what we know of the variability in learning needs and styles, there is a demand for environments that provide greater individualized approaches.

286

2. The teaching profession via many colleges of education has been attempting to attract a more diverse group of persons who would be in a position to demonstrate their skills and share their resources. Such individuals need a wider variety of classroom environments in order to maximize their own competence.

3. If one of our goals is to educate children to value differences, we need environments that integrate handicapped and non-handicapped children. In environments we consider humanistic, a premium is placed on responding to the whole child.

4. Traditional classrooms comprise social systems, and researchers have many different ways of conceptualizing such environments. In one such analysis (Jackson, 1968) there are three aspects of classroom life: crowds, evaluation, and an unequal distribution of power. Humanistic and open learning environments respond to these three aspects in unique ways. For example, much of the large-group instruction in most traditional classrooms is broken down into smaller units. Children are worked with either individually or in small groups. On a different dimension, many alternative programs, such as the mini school (a school within a school) are smaller organizational units within larger school buildings (Kohl, 1977).

   In addition, evaluation in the open school tends to be ongoing and nonjudgmental. Standards that allow, even encourage, some children to fail, be held back, compare themselves against others, and feel negatively about themselves as learners and persons are avoided. In open learning environments no one fails, because goals and programs are measured on an individual basis and defined in small, measurable steps.

   Finally, in open learning environments every attempt is made to foster a partnership between the child and teacher. This is not to say that adult influence is diminished, but rather that it is less oppressive. There is less need to control all of the school day because children's interests and their abilities to learn are trusted. Efforts are made to decide which things children can make decisions about and which are the domain of the adults. Ideally, we strive for a collaborative process that channels many decisions into some format that involves those directly affected by that particular decision.

Within the context of what we are calling *open learning environments,* there is a place for each learner and a commitment to include rather than exclude young people. The definition and intent of open learning environments promote greater *access* to a broader range of children and youth and their concerns. Such environments offer youths ways to see adults as authentic, fully functioning people. This advocacy augurs well for all children. For minority children and youth who are labeled *handicapped,* we talk of equal-access environments that enable them to participate as fully in the life of school and classroom as they are able. For so-called "typical" children and youth, we talk of individualizing instruction so as to guarantee that we and they are responding as specifically and helpfully as possible to their functioning level. While there are many philosophical underpinnings to what is meant by an *open learning environment,* I would prefer to illustrate this approach, beginning with a challenge to the assumptions behind the concept of a regular classroom. I will then discuss several major components that highlight both the why and how of open learning environments.

Regular classrooms? There is absolutely nothing regular about a regular classroom. The fact is that such classrooms have been exclusionary and not necessarily for typical children at all. They are molded learning environments into which certain children have an easier time fitting than others. We believe that such classrooms can be opened up and expanded so that each child has a place in school. The range and variability existing in any classroom group are truly staggering. No matter how we group, re-group, exclude, or slice up the classroom, we are left with a heterogeneous collection of individuals in need of particular responses; this includes the classroom teacher as another person in search of a response.

One could argue that we need to remove the extremes; that is, there are some students so physically handicapped, so retarded, or so distraught or withdrawn that they need to be separated from the group. But is this another assumption in need of challenging? How separated out do these students need to be? Several programs now exist for autistic children within regular school buildings; they operate as more or less separate programs, but at least they are physically situated within typical school buildings. While we have many attitudinal barriers to overcome, at a more basic level many school adults lack contact with and information about atypical children. By responding with inschool programs for the entire range of children, we can push ahead in our goal of enhancing each child's education by equipping teachers and others with a frame of reference for the needs of all.

Everyone, then, needs a response. Our job as teachers, administrators, and support personnel needs to be one of including, not excluding. To be sure, there are management and instructional problems that arise when we truly respond to all learners; but if we are doing our job with "typical" children, we should be facing those issues anyway. In our view, to be an effective facilitator of children's growth, one needs to accept and act on the belief that each child is worthy of an individualized response. We must also rid ourselves of the rather prevalent missionary message: that by taking children with special needs into our school programs, we are doing them a favor. This viewpoint is doubly questionable: Are the handicapped less valued as individuals and contributors to schools and society? Is the environment we are taking them into superior? We must open ourselves up to the realization that each human being is worthy of our time, energy, and respect. In work with all kinds of children, I have never encountered a child who has not developed and changed. I recognize how profoundly impaired some youngsters are, but I feel that maintaining a set of expectations and beliefs about change and growth is one of the most powerful interventions a teacher can have. As we come to believe in the dignity of each person, the teacher-pupil relationship becomes more mutual and we begin to see how much we learn from the pupil. Accepting a wide range of children into our classrooms is not merely a matter of helping them, but includes our own learning, growing, and becoming enriched by virtue of opening ourselves to new persons and new ways of being.

What is regular about regular education has already been questioned. It follows that teachers should normalize their class environments by considering putting together all kinds of children; by thinking in terms of a learning community in which differences are valued and capitalized upon, and in which children and young people are thought of as more alike than different; and in which everyone learns from and is a resource for each other.

Beginning in the late 1960s and continuing up to the present, there have been a number of school and community programs that represented applied examples of more open learning environments. It is important to recognize that the essential aspects of open learning environments relate primarily to (a) a set of beliefs regarding the design of relevant curricula for a specific group of learners, (b) the involvement of learners in the educative process, and (c) the framing of alternative means to accomplish specific goals, rather than the adherence to a particular technology of teaching. The programs described in this section are examples of open learning environments, but each is unique and defies neat categorization. One of the advantages of thinking about opening up the classroom or designing options within a school building is that it can be done in so many ways that surely one tempo will be found that fits any teacher's style and beliefs. The same is true for communities: they can design total and more radical programs or they can initiate alternative approaches on a more careful and systematic basis over time.

In general, the majority of alternative programs have been designed for youths in urban centers. Chicago's Metro High School is an excellent example of an alternative high school program that not only functions on a daily basis but attempts to conceptualize its efforts (Center for New Schools, 1972). Within their school there were many students with special needs; the structures were designed in response to the various subgroups in the school. Based on their experience, a desirable learning community was described as having the following characteristics:

1. A close relationship based on mutual trust and understanding exists between students and staff.

2. Community decision-making is shared through active participation by students, parents, and staff.

3. The human and physical resources of the entire city become a major resource for learning.

4. The characteristics of the traditional curriculum and educational program are completely reconsidered. Irrelevant subject matter designations, grading procedures, and age divisions are either fundamentally changed or eliminated so that learning becomes a more natural and coherent activity related to individual needs and concerns.

5. Students assume a major role in determining the nature and direction of their own learning.

6. Students from diverse cultural backgrounds work together effectively and respect each other. (Center for New Schools, 1972, pp. 334–335)

Alternative schools, like all schools, have met with great difficulties in their efforts to achieve these outcomes. Certainly, some of the reasons center on the difficult nature of some of the learners, particularly those young people in conflict with schools and the adults within them. Grossman (1972) writes of his "nine rotten lousy kids" in an experimental school designed to foster outcomes similar to those listed. Written in collaboration with his teachers, Grossman's book is a collection of anecdotes and accounts of how teachers and young people thought of as alienated, acting-out, and delinquent came to learn together and respect each other. Recently, Hoover (1978) describes a rural program for high school students labeled *emotionally handicapped,* characterizing the program as "democracy in action." This open classroom program involved the student in taking responsibility, self-governance, self-regulation, group decisions, group discussions of individual problems, and acquiring knowledge and skills.

These descriptions of programs and approaches highlight the many complexities and aspects involved in open programs. They reveal how much planning and care goes into the development of such a program. Our experience has been that an enormous amount of planning and development must precede the actual implementation and that once started, a great deal of tender loving care goes into the day-by-day operation. This care needs to be systematic, planful, thoughtful, and often, tough-minded. As an indication of the preparation involved, three of the more important aspects of open environments will be discussed: student participation in decision making, development of a relevant curriculum for youth, and the needs of teachers.

Student Participation in Decision Making

There is an extensive range of decisions young people can make within an environment. One classification scheme assigns decisions into three levels, although these three levels are not mutually exclusive (Center for New Schools, 1972):

1. *Individual Level:* The student can make decisions ranging from initiating actions regarding where to eat lunch to developing an individual work placement.
2. *Group Level:* Students and teachers can work together on a project and assign responsibilities.
3. *Institutional Level:* Students can be part of selecting teachers, planning curriculum offerings, and setting rules governing student behaviors.

These are just examples of possible areas in which students can be involved. Many factors have been found to foster the development of decision-making ability in young people and create a climate supportive of such involvement. For instance, teachers and administrators need to believe that youth are both capable and to be trusted in the environment. Of course, teachers need to be seen the same way by the students. Also, smaller-sized organizational units such as mini schools or schools within schools tend to make decision making more feasible, because communication is more manageable within smaller units.

The kinds of young people who are being labeled and thought of as emotionally disturbed and troubled are often alienated and angry youth for whom school, its adults, and curriculum seem unresponsive at best. If we are to therapeutically respond to this alienation and anger, one step in the right direction is to include students in making classroom and school decisions. In Simpson's *Democracy's Stepchildren* (1971), efforts to teach democratic values are described and the point is made that schools must provide the conditions if such values are to be fostered. Specifically, schools must provide for the gratification of basic needs and must support the acting out of democratic ideals. There are growing numbers of statements supporting the involvement and opening up of school environments to students, parents, community members, and teachers (Newmark, 1976; Ryan, 1976).

Developing a Relevant Curriculum.

Alienation such as that described in the previous section leads to emotional isolation perpetuated by curricula that are irrelevant to needs. In many ways current curricula *(a)* foster an emphasis on facts rather than fantasy and feelings, *(b)* foster a future and past orientation rather than acknowledging the learner's present responses and values, *(c)* foster the presentation of materials, ideas, and concepts that are alien even to the teacher who, just like the children, may be there in body only, and *(d)* foster the continued submergence of the human curriculum—the needs, concerns, relationships, and values that are truly at the heart of the teaching-learning process.

To some, the notion of developing curricula that would respond to the emotional as well as cognitive needs of learners and teachers is still a radical one. Here are some thoughts about what we might do:

1. Make both students and adults feel more able to solve problems. More active learning experiences would be of help, for it is then possible to try out solutions. We would encourage teacher preparation programs to "practice what they teach," in other words, to allow prospective teachers to experience the

values and practices they are being taught. If implemented, this would mean abolishing our practice of lecturing to classes of 200 students on individualizing instruction or creative teaching. Instead, a process needs to be developed in which college students could experience more individualized and creative teaching approaches.

2. Foster the importance of interdependence when functioning in groups, in order to minimize a preoccupation with individual achievement at the expense of group consciousness.

3. Increase the value placed on developing interpersonal skills, both verbal and nonverbal. It is time we recognized that communicating with others is legitimate content!

4. Find ways for children and adults to incorporate more of their life interests into the school experience.

5. Include in school a greater variety of adults and children to maximize everyone's chances of finding someone. It is essential, then, that we be ready for each other in terms of our willingness and ability to respond. It is too risky to expect a given teacher and all of the students in that class to stand ready to interact meaningfully with each other. In order to enhance the opportunities for relationships, we need a variety of persons and opportunities during the school day for people to come together and to find one another.

6. Allow ourselves to respond to the adults' developmental needs as well as the children's. It is time we began to think in dynamic terms of just what it is that a new and inexperienced teacher needs and how such needs might be responded to by other adults—and even children! Similarly, the tensions and pressures on experienced and tenured teachers may be high. We must not assume that people give up their drives toward renewal and change. It is vital that we build on opportunities for such ongoing growth to take place.

7. Discourage the prevalent need for certainty and the ever-elusive "right answer." We need to instill a more experimental attitude in each other that allows for experiencing joy at the process and not just the product.

We can quickly see how these suggestions for minimizing feelings of isolation are related. For as long as each of us can remember, we have been rewarded for isolative behavior: we must not talk to the children sitting near us; we dare not let anyone else see our work lest they steal our answers.

One of the most consistent programming interventions used by educators to respond to young people who either present problems to themselves or to the school is to place them into a vocational training program. We are witnessing a virtual explosion of money and effort into career education. Radical critiques of work training by schools have challenged the motivation of educators for making this such an emphasis. Illich (1971), Reimer (1971), and particularly Berg (1971) observed that merely pointing young people toward the world of work is rarely helpful, because many areas of work and job training are controlled by trade unions whose apprentice programs are highly selective. Furthermore, these critics point to the implicit lowering of expectations for students placed into work education programs. For young people coming through special education programs, these two problem areas are compounded by another issue: the all-too-common practice of viewing job training programs as the one safety-valve programming approach the school can use.

Even though career education has become a major part of the educational scene, the development of a curriculum for experiencing the world of work remains a perplexing task, especially regarding exceptional adolescents. Many of them have experienced failure for so long that they see themselves as unskillful; they are frequently unclear about what they wish to do and can do, having little or no practice or experience in planning or problem solving. All of these skills are essential to the development of job-related abilities and interests.

The following material illustrates the application of open education precepts to the development of a career education program for disturbing youths. William Eyman, one of my very good friends and colleagues, helped develop our alternative school approach for junior and senior high young people; more recently he directed an alternative high school program in New Jersey for acting-out youths. I asked him about the vocational programs he has been involved with and in this section I will include excerpts of his letter and intersperse some of my own comments.

Dear Peter,

During the past summer I had the chance to run a three-week vocational orientation program for fifteen students for our community. Faced with what promised to become an impossible situation, i.e., keeping them occupied for three hours a day with curriculum materials from the local Vocational Resource Center, I decided to ask the kids what they'd like the program to be. . . . "Name three vocations (jobs) you'd be interested in learning about" —a question on the preliminary questionnaire I had distributed. Fifteen young men and women—forty-five possibilities. Yet, the complete list follows:

Army	Racing Driver
Beautician	Secretary
Cop	T.V. repairman
Own store	Nursery Teacher

"List three job goals you would like to have achieved in ten years."

Have a lot of money.	Own more stores.
Make money.	Be working for a rich man.
Be rich.	Not being hassled by the law.

"What are your three greatest strengths?"

I don't know.	None.
Baseball pitcher.	Muscles.
Don't have any.	Don't know.
Good talker.	Dancing.
Nice.	No one told me. . . .

Reviewing this information I realized what I could have known had I stopped to think—that is, how could I expect these young people to have any clear vision of their futures when they had little insight into their present and into their options?

This observation of Bill's, that education has taken on such a future-oriented posture, may be the key to our restructuring vocational approaches. It may not be realistic or even productive to ask young people to "solve" their futures when their immediate needs frequently relate to survival concerns. To build a future one must be in touch with the present and there are examples of schools and individuals who are designing ways in which young people are experiencing themselves, their community, and other people in a more systematic and guided manner (Bremer & van Moschzisker, 1971; Cole & Black, 1971).

The letter continues:

Robert had been, by far, the most disruptive, least engaged "participant" in our first session. He was there only under the threat of losing part of his summer wages. When I ran into him on the street that day as I struggled to create the plan that was going to help Robert and his peers plan the future, I was immediately struck by the ease and enthusiasm with which he handled his present "vocation"—a kid on the street with his friends. . . . It may sound overly simplified, but it was in that moment that the idea for the summer "vocational orientation" program took shape. Forget for the moment the future, what you're going to be. Let's look deeply for a while at what you already are. . . . Well, enough of the background. Here's the program. . . . I wrote the following list of perceptions which formed the foundation of an operating philosophy.

1. All students I had known had expressed some interest in learning.
2. Each had a wide variety of personal experiences.
3. Few expressed a valuing of their own experience as "learning."
4. Most eventually benefitted from a learning program that focused on *personal* experience.
5. Action and, particularly, *inter*action was often a positive motivation in a new learning situation.
6. Most students had lacked many basic skills, particularly those we define as problem-solving skills and expressed a desire to gain them.
7. Most had not clarified a process for learning new skills on their own.
8. Most responded positively to a program that was based partially on their suggestions and in which I had clearly defined the expectations.

I then outlined a program as I envisioned it, to include twelve 2½-hour sessions. At the time I saw a flow of activities as follows:

1. Lesson on documentation of experience (recording what you do).

2. Lesson on the identification of major themes in your life.
3. Lesson on question construction.
4. Lesson on the use of basic reference and resource materials.
5. Lesson on interviewing techniques.
6. Lesson on construction of interviews.

As I often do, I had a handle on *what* I was going to do before I could articulate *why* I was doing it, but, as I planned, the rationale began to emerge. It would help the students, I hypothesized, to know more clearly (a) what they do now; (b) what patterns their behaviors form; (c) how to question what they do; (d) what other people (a wide variety of them) do; (e) the comparison of their own to other people's behaviors and life patterns; (f) the present and future options they have; and (g) how to obtain more information.

The future? Too abstract. Get a clear picture of where you are and lots of comparisons and you'll have a much better chance of knowing where *you* might go.

What a revolutionary thought! Start with what you know about the people involved and then design a program or approach that is responsive. Bill's intention was clear: for this group of essentially turned-off youngsters who feel badly about themselves and who are seen as being bad by school authorities, to dramatically highlight precisely what it is they *can do*. The fact is that the individuals in this group were already making decisions and even acting on some of them. The task was to help them recognize their decision-making abilities and how they could approach new ones.

Also of importance is Bill's listing of the ingredients of an operating philosophy. For the most part, these are beliefs, insights, and practices that are central to the designing of more open learning environments and are applicable to many curricular approaches. Bill reminds us again that actual curriculum materials must be used judiciously in the context of a set of beliefs and practices. Career education has been literally taken over by commercially prepared materials that tell young people what they can do with their futures. Bill and his young people make a case for planning the future in the context of consolidating one's skills in the here and now.

297

Bill's letter goes on to describe a process for eliciting documentation of activities by young people. In effect, he had them keep track of everything they did in a day, and as you might expect, they were into many things. As a group they developed themes such as eating, exercise, health, money, relationships, communication, style, animals, humor, secrets. They went from the general to the more specific, each one selecting an area of interest for more thorough research.

Bill's students then combined steps 3 and 4 (see page 297) by conducting interviews in the community.

We had had a lot of contact with many people in the community, and, when students called those [people] on a list I provided to ask if they'd like to be interviewed, most agreed. In introduction they explained that they were documenting various phenomena in their lives and that they wanted to speak to several people to compare their findings. Again the group met as a whole and we helped each other construct statements and questions that seemed appropriate. Thus prepared, on the fifth day of our program the students (except for three who *were* reluctant to talk to "strangers") left the school to begin their interviews.

Bill and his group were only at the very beginning stages of understanding the complex task of preparing young people for the world of work. Contrast his active approach to the technique currently in vogue—namely, let's find out which occupations are projected to be in demand and funnel people into those fields. Instead, he makes the individual become more conscious of his or her skills, interests, and needs, hopeful that there will be a match to available opportunities. Even more central is the possibility that alive and growing young people will help create some of their own opportunities.

Personal Growth of Children and Teachers

Without commitment to personal goals, any skills a person learns may not be useful to himself, or if useful, may not be used in service to others. Thus a truly complete curriculum approach should place a premium on the needs, concerns, and feelings of all those participating in the school, both adults and youngsters. This strategy is especially important when alternative approaches are used, because most often it is the teacher who must be the child's advocate. Such a teacher must personally view himself as an advocate. He must feel positive about his life and be in touch with his values.

Today some people working with children do not feel positive about teaching. Because they spend long hours working with disturbed children, they become isolated socially and emotionally. They may come to identify with their children's loneliness.

A Poem
By Ira, age 13

It feels awful to be me.
I don't know why it just does.
Because I don't seem to be able
to make any friends.
I don't even know if this is a good story.
Because it's not such a good story to be me.

What is wrong here? Why do so many of our teachers and children feel alienated in school? As Wasserman (1970) points out, "The persistence and prevalence of our schools' antieducational, antihuman, and antibiological ways suggest that not merely chance or teachers' perversity of children's nastiness is the source" (p. xi). Some critics (Kozol, 1972) say that schools train us to be politically impotent, citing the obligatory letter asking for action to an elected official in Washington.

> One of the ways in which schools teach children the idea of their own futility is by a preplanned exercise of effort denial. In school we learn to ask for things we secretly know we won't receive in order to be pardoned by refusal from responsible pursuit of the thing we ask for: "We did our best, put out the most we had, and we failed despite this." The experience challenges, then fails, then gradually grows weary. Technological intelligence and ethical capitulation are twin products of this course of preparation. (p. 16)

In addition to the political level of devastation, the nature of the social system in school encourages loneliness. Teachers feel a type of separateness, a distance between what they are actually doing and what they aspire to do under ideal conditions (emotional isolation). These feelings lead to teachers becoming distant among each other and from the children (social isolation).

Emotional isolation.   Teachers are harangued to respond to children's needs. However teachers also grow and change. They, too, are vulnerable to depression and require support for their concerns. The personal growth needs of teachers are so varied and complex that generalizations are difficult to make. What is clear, however, is that such needs exist and by continuing to avoid them as legitimate areas of a teacher's job we perpetuate deep feelings of loneliness in the form of emotional isolation.

For some individuals, teaching is the substance of their definition. It is easy to lose sight of the many dedicated individuals whose lives have taken on meaning mostly through their time with children; to a very large extent they have become defined by this role. But their behavior with children shows that they are not playing a role—they live it, deeply. We all know of teachers whose personal lives are difficult, but who function well or at least adequately within school. We need to find ways to bring a teacher's life outside of school into closer harmony with the life inside of school. Sometimes a teacher holds himself together in school so he can respond to the enormity of what awaits him after school. Sometimes what awaits him is a creative life—real and fantasied— that he can never find during school. Teachers are artists, poets, musicians, gardeners, collectors, mechanics, readers, thinkers, and feelers; why do they so frequently leave these roles behind while they are teaching?

Social isolation.   A school is a complex social system in which people live together for extended periods. It is easy to find ways in which people become isolated from the system.

For example, the process and content of schooling frequently are in conflict. While most class activities occur in groups, few teachers use the group as a socializing influence. Children are crowded together in a room, sitting practically on top of each other, but they're not allowed to talk to each other.

In another example, most teachers have separate rooms over which they exercise total control. Even if they do not want to function as overlords, they quickly come under pressure to keep "their" children in line. No matter how enthusiastic a teacher may be at the start, it becomes safest to retreat back into one's classroom. In addition, schools have separate rooms for separate functions: the choir only practices in the music room, only teachers in the teachers' room, and so on. This effectively keeps those people involved in those activities in those rooms and keeps other not "central" to other activities out of those rooms.

In special education, it has become a standard joke that programs for special children are located in basement areas. What is not funny about this form of social isolation is the number of special educators who see this as a way of avoiding the rest of the hassles in school; that is, in the basement they can keep a low profile. How sad it is that so many of us who weigh the risks involved in being visible and assertive within a school decide to voluntarily isolate ourselves and our children so that we might function with greater freedom. Such freedom is frequently gained at the cost of feeling more isolated and ultimately, lonely.

Becoming an advocate. Hopefully this analysis of the needs of teachers (and other school adults) suggests some of the interventions that need to occur if young people are going to have advocates representing them in the schools. If teachers are to be in a position to respond to the complex needs of their students, then they too must be getting their "strokes."

Becoming an advocate is a long and complicated process, but there are several useful guidelines for responding to young people and developing alternative programs. First, be aware that any time you refer a student for a psychological or educational evaluation there is the definite possibility that the youth will "fail" the evaluation, be removed from your sphere of influence, and perhaps most damaging of all, be placed into an exclusionary track from which there will be no return. In short, well-intentioned teachers may believe that referrals will help the pupil, but one should always ask, "Is help helpful?" Second, try to create a climate in your school that supports alternative evaluation systems designed to determine what students know as opposed to punishing them for what they do not know ("New Approaches," 1977). Third, make the commitment to relate to the other adults in your school. Children's behavior will not always speak positively for itself, and just because we spend much of our waking hours and energy attempting to understand the needs of our students, we cannot assume this is true of others. If attitudes are to change, each of us has much work to do with other school staff. In practice this may mean finding other potential allies in a school, spending time with them in and out of school, and offering yourself as a resource to them.

Conclusion

This chapter focuses on the development of educational alternatives, an approach to responding to the learning and behavioral problems of secondary school pupils. Accumulating evidence testifies to the magnitude of these problems. If we seriously wish to respond to young people whom we think of as behavior problems, we must begin to plan environments that are more helpful. One advantage of open learning environments as a facilitative, alternative programmatic approach is that they involve teachers and young people in more of a partnership relationship. It is time to recognize that merely patching up what we are already doing hasn't worked. For too long we have assumed that the problem resided within the youngster; that if any changing was to be done he would do it; and that it is not the school's responsibility to modify its programs. Open learning environments hold the promise of including a number of significant persons in the planning and delivery of an education for a young person. Such environments permit us to reconceptualize what is meant by a *relevant curriculum,* which must include an emphasis on affective as well as cognitive experiences. This chapter touched briefly on such issues as student decision making, preparation for work, personal growth needs of teachers, and how open environments can respond to these issues and needs.

The alternative school movement must not provide additional ways of segregating the troubled and troubling. Open learning environments can be designed for all learners, those with special needs and those thought of as typical. We must design environments to which all children and adults have equal access. We need to clarify what is meant by finding alternative ends and alternative means, so that our learning environments can truly be thought of as alternatives.

It is risky to speculate about future developments in alternative programs and schools because there are so many varieties of these and because the results of alternative programs are inconclusive. Some recent developments are encouraging; for example, Public Law 94–142 mandates that every handicapped individual aged 3 through 21 is entitled to an education in the least restrictive setting. As a result of this development, alternative schools and programs that have been designed to maintain troubled and troubling youth away from the mainstream will need to be realigned to include nonhandicapped students as well.

Alternative approaches may come to be seen as not only programmatically feasible, but economically desirable. Within-school options may, in the near future, be seen as less costly than certain present arrangements, especially the placement of difficult children in out-of-state private residential settings. For example, New York State spends millions of dollars to place approximately 12,000 students out of state. Pressure brought about by Public Law 94–142 may compel districts to educate these youth at home, thus providing more normalized settings and cutting costs at the same time.

If there is to be a future for alternative approaches, particularly open learning environments, a number of conditions need to be responded to. In the first place, we need to make a commitment to research and evaluation activities that would clarify the process and outcomes of alternative schooling. This task will necessitate consideration of a variety of outcomes other than scholastic achievement as important and worthy of both study and acceptance. Our research efforts will need to include documentation of specific alternative practices employed and demonstration of their effects on the growth of learners and teachers.

Second, since many secondary school pupils are concerned about coming into frequent contact and conflict with the larger community and its representatives, it would be advantageous to involve those agencies and people with the schools. In many ways this could foster a better climate for alternatives, because many alternative approaches call for resources and time in the community.

Third, the concept and practice of alternatives need to be demystified. To many educators, an alternative approach connotes lack of structure and chaos. This certainly should not be the case, because the implementation of any program, open or otherwise, should be done with great care and planning. To individualize instruction, to respond to emotional as well as cognitive needs of students, and to involve a range of adults and community services are goals that require major planning efforts. One of the old and unfortunately persistent myths is that all one needs to do is set up a program, place the children and adults together, and "it" grows. This organic theory of alternative school development has not proven correct nor should one expect it to work that way. If we are seriously committed to working with upset youth then our task is a complex one and it will require a great deal of orchestration to guarantee a sound educational and behavioral treatment program. Programs and students do not necessarily grow on their own, but in concert with a meaningful relationship with teachers and materials. If alternatives are to be developed, survive, and flourish, they will require great scrutiny and will need to be held accountable to the highest standards.

Legal Issues in Special Education

11

Reed Martin

Let me begin with an explanation of how a lawyer became so deeply involved in special education. My interest in law has always been in civil rights/civil liberties issues; it is easy to find many Constitutional questions in public education. To me, the provision of special education services is largely a civil rights issue, and one of my earliest experiences in education certainly influences that belief.

Civil Rights Struggle

I grew up a Southerner in a segregated school system. In 1961, as president of my college student body, I led a fight to integrate my school. During that time I faced many of the same arguments that I face today on behalf of the handicapped, and I recognize a parallel in the progression of the five similar arguments.

1. Persons in positions of authority who had clearly profited from having our social systems run the way they had been run blindly opposed change. Rather than examining the merits of our requests, administrators attacked the motives of those demanding change.

However, what I was called in the 1960s for advocating desegregation was mild compared to what I am called today.

2. When the issue clearly would not go away, administrators argued that no one really wanted the proposed change. In the 1960s we were told that whites did not want black fellow students and that blacks preferred to be with their own kind. Now I am often told the nonhandicapped do not want special education children in their midst and the handicapped would be less embarrassed about their condition if they were segregated. The fallacy to this argument is that when one asks the children, one finds out that the opposite is true.

3. The argument used to be that no one, black or white, would benefit from integration, because the educational product for all would be lessened. That does not have to be true, although administrators could cause it to happen. Today I see in some school district administrators fanning the flames of a public backlash by telling the parents of the majority nonhandicapped that their children will get a less than adequate education if services must be increased for the handicapped. The spectre of the disruptive influence of one handicapped child in a regular classroom is used in some school districts to keep teachers and unions on the administrators' side in this conflict. You would think we would have learned from the bitter harvest from those seeds sown in the sixties.

4. After all those arguments had been discredited, schools then claimed that they would love to accomodate blacks, but simply could not afford to. Today even schools with increased expenditures for football claim they cannot afford increased services to the handicapped. Clearly it is a matter of budgeting priorities. Left to their own choice, many administrators would put the taxpayers' money into new stadiums. But the choice is no longer left up to them; just as they had to pay for busing and other desegregation aids, they now will have to pay for the extra resources needed in special education programs.

5. Schools claim that whatever decision is made, it should not be forced on them. In the 1960s we heard the argument that it would be more democratic if these decisions were left up to localities and not imposed by Washington. I hear that same argument today in several states trying to avoid new federal regulations. But we cannot leave it up to the individual localities whether or not to pro-

vide equal treatment to all citizens, because in doing so we would be ignoring the Constitution.

Federal Experience

After law school I worked for U.S. Senator Ralph Yarborough. Senator Yarborough served as head of the health and education subcommittees in the Senate and authored many educational initiatives. While working for him I began to realize the need for a vastly increased federal role. By that I do not mean a bigger federal government or a concentration of power in Washington; what is needed is adherence at every level of government activity to Constitutional rights. The crazy quilt of programs across the country—some great, some intolerable—has to be smoothed out to at least an acceptable federal minimum.

Since leaving the Senator's office I have been a consultant on special education matters with schools in about 25 states. I have seen that schools can provide marvelous services to the handicapped. I recently visited one school district in which all facilities have been free of architectural barriers for over 20 years. After seeing that kind of progress, I cannot tolerate schools that say it can't be done, and I want a nationside minimum requirement for services.

Who Are the Advocates?

My experiences around the country have led to another conclusion that has shaped my behavior as an advocate. Those pushing for change are not necessarily the handicapped. Equally important, not all school people oppose change. Most of my work is *with* school systems, and I am always *invited* by someone wanting change. I have discovered that some of the most vigorous advocates for handicapped youngsters are the teachers and special education consultants. So as national standards are developed and schools are forced to upgrade services, one must look for and expect to find advocates for change inside and outside the schools.

Family Experience

I have been strongly influenced by the crisis surrounding my sister, who needed special help. I remember my sister's frustration as her

307

school problems became noticeable, but were blamed on everything except a learning disability; the school problem then became an emotional disturbance. I remember my parents' frustration as they were ignored by the school and were led to believe that they were the real problem. As the school socially promoted her to graduation and washed its hands of her, I saw my parents' renewed frustration as they realized they now had no public agency to turn to and no way to repair the damage.

I learned then that schools must be made accountable for their actions, not in a vindictive assessment of blame but in a constructive requirement that they produce results. The federal laws explained on the next few pages are a blueprint for accountability. With the implementation of today's special education laws, public education in America will never be the same.

Legal Impetus to Educational Rights for the Handicapped

Judicial Decisions

Until the seventies, children with handicapping conditions were accorded few basic rights. Handicapped students were commonly excluded from public schools on the grounds that they could not benefit from education or were too disruptive.

Reversing this trend required both a court statement that children must be educated, and a redefinition of education. One of the best restatements of education came in a recent case, *In the Matter of Tracy Ann Cox,* No. H–4721–75 (N.Y. Fam. Ct., Queens Co., April 8, 1976).

> Not all children can be educated as we usually think of the term "education,"—grade school, junior high school, et cetera. The diagnosis of Tracy Ann's condition is "psychomotor, growth and developmental retardation with seizure disorder." Such a child required another kind of "education,"—how to hold a spoon, feed herself, dress herself, toilet training, et cetera, in addition to speech therapy, psychiatric and psychological treatment, et cetera, —all these and more add up to the education of this and

---

Portions of the descriptions of cases and legislations from the workshop material "Educational Rights of Handicapped Children" by Reed Martin. Champaign, Ill.: Research Press Co., 1977. Copyright 1977 by Research Press. Used by permission.

other mentally retarded children, and they are entitled to be so educated.

Clearly any child could benefit from education under such a standard. State laws that allowed exclusion began to be challenged in federal courts. The United States Supreme Court had ruled in 1954 in *Brown* v. *Board of Education*, 347 U.S. 483:

> Today, education is perhaps the most important function of state and local governments. Compulsory school attendance laws and the great expenditures for education both demonstrate our recognition of the importance of education to our democratic society. It is required in the performance of our most basic public responsibilities, even service in the armed forces. It is the very foundation of good citizenship. Today it is a principal instrument in awakening the child to cultural values, in preparing him for later professional training, and in helping him to adjust normally to his environment. In these days, it is doubtful that any child may reasonably be expected to succeed in life if he is denied the opportunity of an education. *Such an opportunity, where the state has undertaken to provide it, is a right which must be made available to all on equal terms.*

That basic constitutional assumption—that handicapped children also are entitled to the equal protection of the laws and may not be treated differently without due process of law—was used successfully to challenge the exclusion of the handicapped in two landmark federal cases. In *Pennsylvania Association for Retarded Children (P.A.R.C.)* v. *Commonwealth of Pennsylvania*, 334 F. Supp. 1257 (E.D. Pa. 1971), it was determined that states owe retarded children an appropriate program of education and training:

> Expert testimony in this action indicates that all mentally retarded persons are capable of benefiting from a program of education and training; that the greatest number of retarded persons, given such education and training, are capable of achieving self-sufficiency, and the remaining few, with such education and training, are capable of achieving some degree of self-care; that the earlier such education and training begins, the more thoroughly and the more efficiently a mentally retarded person can benefit at

any point in his life and development from a program of education and training.

It is the Commonwealth's obligation to place each mentally retarded child in a free, public program of education and training appropriate to the child's capacity, within the context of a presumption that, among the alternative programs of education and training required by statute to be available, placement in a regular public school class is preferable to placement in any other type of program of education and training.

The following year the same guarantees were applied to children with all types of handicaps in the District of Columbia, in *Mills* v. *Board of Education*, 348 F. Supp. 866 (D.D.C. 1972).

With the successful conclusions in the *P.A.R.C.* and *Mills* cases, 36 right-to-education decisions soon followed in 27 states. It was clearly time to establish a federal standard.

Statutory Action

In 1966, Congress created the Bureau of Education for the Handicapped; in 1970, the first Education of the Handicapped Act was enacted. Following the 1971 decision in *P.A.R.C.* and the 1972 decision in *Mills*, a bill, S. 3614, was introduced in the United States Senate in 1972 to expand the federal role. Many of its provisions were reflected in the Education of the Handicapped Act (Public Law 93–380), passed in 1974, but S. 3614 was reintroduced in the next two legislative sessions, becoming S. 6 and emerging as the Education for All Handicapped Children Act (Public Law 94–142).

The problems addressed are immense, for as Section 3 of P. L. 94–142 declares:

There are more than eight million handicapped children in the United States; one million are excluded entirely from education; more than half of the handicapped children are receiving inappropriate services; families are forced to find services at great distance from their homes and at great expense.

Correcting those problems means schools must offer services to all, as close to home as possible, and at no expense to parents. Regulations explaining how that is to be done are in the *Federal Register*, August 23, 1977 (P.L. 94–142).

In 1971 the United States began an effort that would have even greater consequences for services to the handicapped. An attempt was made to amend the Civil Rights Act to recognize that handicapped citizens have civil rights and thus to prohibit discrimination on the basis of handicap. The spirit of that amendment was included in a final section, Section 504, of the Rehabilitation Act of 1973 (P.L. 93–112). It provided simply that:

> No otherwise qualified handicapped individual . . . shall, solely by reason of his handicap, be excluded from the participation in, be denied the benefits of, or be subjected to discrimination under any program or activity receiving federal financial assistance.

Initial regulations from the Department of Health, Education, and Welfare (H.E.W.) did not emphasize what this meant for education services to handicapped children, and it took further Congressional statement of intent and even a federal court decision before full regulations were promulgated.

On signing those federal regulations, H.E.W. Secretary Joseph Califano signaled the impact of Section 504, stating that it called for dramatic changes in the action and attitudes of institutions and individuals who were recipients of HEW funds. When P.L. 94–142 was enacted, some school systems confidently asserted that they were virtually in compliance already. But no school could claim they were in compliance with Section 504.

Final regulations for Section 504 were published in the *Federal Register*, May 4, 1977. One of the first cases that has relied on Section 504 (29 U.S.C. 794) is *Hairston* v. *Drosick*, 423 F. Supp. 180 (S.D.W.Va. 1976), which states very simply what that law requires:

> The exclusion of a minimally handicapped child from a regular public classroom situation without a bona fide edutional reason is in violation of Title V of Public Law 93–112, "The Rehabilitation Act of 1973." 29 U.S.C. 794. The federal statute proscribes discrimination against handicapped individuals in any program receiving federal financial assistance. To deny to a handicapped child access to a regular public school classroom in receipt of federal financial assistance without compelling educational justification constitutes discrimination and a denial of the benefits of such program in violation of the statute. School

officials must make every effort to include such children within the regular public classroom situation, even at great expense to the school system.

Many other cases now filed are relying on Section 504.

Equally important changes have been occurring in regard to the provision of residential services to developmentally disabled individuals (mentally retarded, autistic, cerebral palsied, or epileptic). In the early seventies, federal courts began to recognize that many of the developmentally disabled were inappropriately placed in residential institutions and, once there, nothing was done that would return them to a more normal setting.

Thus, the Developmentally Disabled Act (P.L. 94–103) was amended in 1975 to include a "Bill of Rights" section. As stated in the proposed regulations, a purpose of that act was to specify the rights of the developmentally disabled:

> That developmentally disabled persons have the right to appropriate treatment, services, and habilitation; that programs should be designed to maximize the developmental potential of the person; and that the Federal Government and States have an obligation to assure that public funds are not provided in programs which do not deliver appropriate treatment, services, and habilitation or do not meet appropriate minimum standards as specified in the Act.

Public Law 94–103, the Developmentally Disabled Assistance and Bill of Rights Act, had final regulations published in the *Federal Register*, January 27, 1977.

Enforcement Machinery

Compliance with these new federal laws is enforced in three important new ways. First, the U.S. Office of Education now has a compliance section that reviews the provision of educational services to the handicapped. They not only examine and approve state plans but also audit the states' performance in the field. Each state is audited every other year to see that the state agency is assuring that local school districts are meeting federal requirements. Between audits, this office also responds to complaints from the handicapped and attempts to secure voluntary compliance from the offending school district.

Section 504 (P.L. 93–112) establishes that educational rights of the handicapped are federal civil rights; thus it will be enforced by the Office of Civil Rights (OCR). OCR responds to complaints from the handicapped and seeks to negotiate compliance. A penalty for noncompliance could be loss of federal funding.

P.L. 94–103 creates in each state an organization for the protection and advocacy of individual rights. As regulations provide:

> . . . not later than October 1, 1977, (1) the State will have in effect a system to protect and advocate the rights of persons with developmental disabilities, (2) such system will have the authority to pursue legal, administrative, and other appropriate remedies to insure the protection of the rights of such persons who are receiving treatment, services, or habilitation within the State, and (3) such system will be independent of any State agency which provides treatment, services, or habilitation to persons with developmental disabilities.

Thus the rights of the handicapped are enforced by the investigations and efforts toward compliance of the Office of Education, the Office for Civil Rights, and each state's Advocacy and Protective Service.

Identifying Handicapped Children

Criteria under which children are eligible for service to the handicapped are defined in federal regulations. The categories are deaf, deaf-blind, hard of hearing, mentally retarded, multihandicapped, orthopedically impaired, other health impaired, seriously emotionally disturbed, specifically learning disabled, speech impaired, and visually handicapped. Federal law requires that children who fit those criteria must be found through an aggressive program to locate, identify, and evaluate the handicapped. The responsibility is clearly the school's.

This identification process is vital to the Congressional goal of reaching all 8 million handicapped school-aged children. But unfortunately some schools do not attempt to identify students in need. In the case of *Pierce* v. *Board of Education*, 358 N.E. 2d 67 (111. App. 1976), it was being alleged that:

> . . . [F]rom 1971 to February, 1974 the plaintiff attended the F. W. Riley School in the City of Chicago. During that

time the minor-plaintiff was discovered to be suffering from a specific learning disability, ... [T]he defendant was advised of this fact by the minor plaintiff's parents and various of the plaintiff's privately retained physicians, who recommended that the boy be transferred from the regular or normal classes of instruction to classes known as special education classes or learning disability classes. Nevertheless, the defendant failed and refused to either transfer the minor to these classes or undertake their own testing and evaluation of the boy. As a result of the defendant's failure to comply with their statutory duties, the plaintiff remained in regular classes at the F. W. Riley School from 1971 to 1974, where he was required to compete with students not suffering from a learning disability and as a result sustained severe and permanent emotional and psychic injury requiring hospitalization and medical treatment.

The Illinois Appellate Court found that the school does have a duty to identify those in need of special services. Doing nothing would be an intentional breach of its duty, which could make school board members liable for any damages shown.

Some schools insist that new due-process procedures place the burden on the parent to push the child forward as a candidate for services and demand a hearing if they are not delivered. In the recent case of *Frederick L. v. Thomas*, 408 F. Supp. 832 (E.D. Pa. 1976), the federal court described the difficulty if parents were to bear the responsibility for identification.

It is disputed whether parent referrals through parent-initiated due process hearings are an effective method for identifying LD's. There is not enough experience with the due process procedures to make definitive findings on this question. To utilize the procedure the parent has to (a) recognize her child is not functioning academically, (b) recognize that the cause of the child's underachievement may be something that requires special education instruction, (c) know that due process hearings are available, (d) believe that through a due process hearing her child—though not a severe behavior problem— may receive special help, (e) properly carry out the procedures for initiating the hearing which includes obtaining an expert psychiatric opinion.

Some schools maintain that if children are receiving some service, that is, if they are in the regular classroom, then identification is not needed because services are already being provided. That argument was flatly rejected in *Frederick L.:*

> . . . [T]here is ample expert testimony in the record to support the conclusion that some learning disabled students would be afforded appropriate educational opportunities if they were placed in regular classes with "supporting services" consisting of instruction in remedial programs not designated special education. For that matter, appropriate supporting services for some LD's may be nothing more than monitoring their academic performance in regular classrooms so that new learning problems that arise because of their disabilities do not go undetected. Placing exceptional children in regular classes in this manner is called "mainstreaming." Under the regulations, it is a preferred strategy.
>
> We cannot find, however, that learning disabled students whose disabilities have *not* been identified and who are in regular classes, or in general remedial programs, or some combination of the two, are properly "mainstreamed." . . . There must first be a diagnosis of the child's exceptionality, and then a determination that mainstreaming under prescribed conditions will be an appropriate placement.

In sum, the child must be identified, evaluated, and properly placed, even if that placement is back where he was found in the first place. Obviously nothing less than a vigorous effort will meet Congressional intent. The recent case of *Mattie T. v. Holladay,* Civil No. DC–75–31–5 (N.D.Miss.Aug. 4, 1977) found that Mississippi was not attempting to identify all eligible students and the federal court ordered changes.

Assessment

Once children are identified as potentially eligible, an equally serious responsibility must be discharged by the agency. Children must be assessed fully and without discrimination.

The common practice of school districts in the past, and the accompanying abuse to children, is explained by affidavits of expert witnesses included in the plaintiff's memorandum in *Mattie T.*

315

In enacting section 613(a)(13)(c), Congress recognized that a great many poor and minority children were being mistakenly classified as mentally retarded on the basis of racially and culturally biased intelligence tests.

Congress was concerned that minority children who are misclassified as mentally retarded would suffer the social stigma of being called retarded, be inappropriately placed in segregated classes for mentally retarded children and denied contacts with non-handicapped children, and receive substantially limited curriculum opportunities.

Congress recognized the problems with discriminatory testing in Senate Report No. 94–168:

The Committee is alarmed about the abuses which occur in the testing and evaluation of children, and is concerned that expertise in the proper use of testing and evaluation procedures falls far short of the prolific use and development of testing and evaluation tools. The usefulness and mechanistic ease of testing should not become so paramount in the educational process that the negative effects of such testing are overlooked.

Those problems have been addressed in the Federal regulations at 45 Code of Federal Regulations 84.35:

1. Tests and other evaluation materials must be validated for the specific purpose for which they are used and administered by trained personnel.
2. Tests and other evaluation materials must include assessment of specific areas and not just a single intelligence quotient.
3. Tests and other evaluation materials must be selected and administered to ensure that what is purported to be measured is measured, rather than reflecting impaired sensory, manual, or speaking skills.
4. Interpretation of evaluation data must draw on a variety of sources, including aptitude and achievement tests, teacher recommendations, and adaptive behavior.
5. Evaluators must have procedures to assure information from all such sources is documented and considered.
6. The placement decision resulting from the evaluation must be

made by a group of persons including those knowledgeable about the specific child and the evaluation data.

Independent Evaluation

To provide an additional safeguard against inadequate assessment of discriminatory assessment, the regulations under P.L. 94–142 allow for an *independent educational evaluation at public expense.* The parent must obtain the evaluation from a qualified examiner not employed by the school system and send the bill to the school. The school must pay or challenge it in an impartial hearing. If at the hearing the school proves its original assessment was "appropriate," the school does not have to pay. But the independent evaluation must become part of the record and be considered in any educational decision about the child.

Individual Education Plan

Once the child is assessed he must be placed on an individual education plan. Unique contributions of P.L. 94–142 are the requirement of an individual education plan for every child receiving special education services, and a specification of exactly what must go into the plan.

Much of the Congressional discussion during passage of P.L. 94–142 focused on the need to include parents in making decisions about the child. Thus they required a joint conference at least once a year. The planning conference should include the parent(s), who should be notified sufficiently in advance so that they can make a contribution at the meeting. If no parent is known, a parent surrogate must be appointed to assume that role. If the parent does not attend the planning conference, the school must document the efforts they made to contact the parents and convince them of the worth of attending. At the meeting, the school must furnish a teacher to provide service to the child and a person qualified to provide or supervise the provision of special education. The child should attend, if that is appropriate, and others may attend at the discretion of the school or the parents.

Present functioning. The individual education plan must begin with a statement of the child's present levels of educational performance. The term *educational performance* is misleading because it suggests only academic problems. But P.L. 94–142 requires that the child be assessed:

. . . in all areas related to the suspected disability, including, where appropriate, health, vision, hearing, social and emotional status, general intelligence, academic performance, communicative status, and motor abilities.

P.L. 94–142 also takes into account that the individual education plan may require the provision of several needed related services. Thus the statement of present level of education performance must include the full range of problems that might need to be addressed by special education and related services.

Goals. The plan must state annual goals in each area of need and the short-term instructional goals to take the child from the present level of educational performance to the annual goal.

The Senate Committee on Labor and Public Welfare recognized in Senate Report No. 94–168 that:

In many instances the process of providing special education and related services to handicapped children is not guaranteed to produce any particular outcome.

P.L. 94–142 requires a goal statement not as a guarantee and not as a contract but as "a written record of reasonable expectations" that may be monitored and cause the program to be constantly revised in order to produce some outcome.

Related services. The plan must state the specific special education and related services to be provided to the child.

Regular education participation. Further, the plan must indicate the extent to which the child will be able to participate in regular educational programs. Every conceivable part of the day should be examined, including classwork, meals, recess periods, physical education, counseling services, and recreational activities, to determine those activities in which the handicapped student may participate with the nonhandicapped. In fact, the handicapped pupil should be in all activities with the nonhandicapped unless the individual education plan requires some other arrangement.

Time constraints. The plan must state the projected dates for initiating services and the anticipated duration of services.

Accountability criteria. The plan must state appropriate objective criteria and evaluation procedures and schedules for determining, at least once a year, whether the short-term objectives are being achieved.

Least Restrictive Alternative

Services to the handicapped child must always be offered in the setting that offers the least deviation from a regular program with the nonhandicapped. To avoid placing the child in a setting that is too restrictive, the school must offer at least a minimum range of alternatives. The range required by P.L. 94–142 includes:

1. The regular classroom. Placement in the regular classroom must be legitimately considered for each child.
2. The regular classroom with itinerant instruction. "Supplemental aids and services" in the regular classroom should be attempted before a more restrictive setting can be justified.
3. Regular classroom for all academic and nonacademic programs possible and resource room for the remainder of the activities.
4. Full time in a special class at the neighborhood school.
5. Assignment to a special school as close to the child's home as possible.
6. Educational services provided in a nonschool setting, such as at home, in a hospital, or in an institution.

The decision about where to place a child must be based on educational needs. The decision cannot reflect solely administrative convenience or the absence of one of the required alternatives. The educational justification must be traceable directly to the individual educational plan. A placement setting cannot be chosen unless it is required by the plan.

In considering alternatives, architectural barriers must not be allowed to interfere. Physical obstacles often limit the accessibility of some programs. Schools have often denied children in wheelchairs and blind children access to regular classes because of curbs, narrow doors, lack of elevators in multistory buildings, transportation problems, inaccessible rest rooms, and fear about evacuation in case of emergencies. Those are real problems, but they must no longer be allowed to bar admission of a child who otherwise could participate with the nonhandicapped. The school should make any and all possible alterations, such as ramps, handrails, and automatic doors, use aides where that would help, reassign classes and therapy facilities to the first floor, and anything else that would help.

Where more substantial structural changes are needed for there to be full program accessibility, the agency has until June, 1980 to complete the change. But funded agencies, in consultation with handicapped persons, must have developed a transition plan by December, 1977. This plan was to have included an identification of physical obstacles that limit accessibility, a description of the methods to be used to make the facility accessible, a specified schedule for doing this, and an indication of the person responsible for implementation.

A final problem in implementing the concept of the least restrictive alternative lies in defining *restrictive*. It certainly applies to the physical setting: the regular class is preferable to the special class. It applies also to distance: the child must attend the school he would attend if nonhandicapped unless the individual plan "requires some other arrangement." Duration should also be considered. One year in a resource room half-days might be more restrictive than one month in a special class. Restraints must also be examined. A short and intensive behavior management program in a special class might be less restrictive than including a child in the regular classroom on medication. Any environment that uses corporal punishment could well be considered more restrictive than one that does not.

A "Free, Appropriate Public Education"

Once an individual education plan is developed for a child, a free, appropriate public education must be offered. The defendant school board in *Mills* maintained that they could not afford to provide a public education to all handicapped children. The federal court answered clearly:

> The defendants are required by the Constitution of the United States, the District of Columbia Code, and their own regulations to provide a publicly-supported education for these exceptional children. Their failure to fulfill this clear duty to include and retain these children in the public school system, or otherwise provide them with publicly-supported education, and their failure to afford them due process hearing and periodic review, cannot be excused by the claim that there are insufficient funds. . . . The inadequacies of the District of Columbia Public School System whether occasioned by insufficient funding or administrative inefficiency, certainly cannot be permitted to bear more heavily on the exceptional or handicapped child than on the normal child.

Many schools that do not offer any appropriate program place the handicapped child in a private school and pay a portion of the cost. A typical result is illustrated in the case of Daniel Kruse. As explained in the complaint *Kruse* v. *Campbell*, No. C.A. 75–0622–R (E.D.Va. March 23, 1977):

> Daniel J. Kruse . . . is a learning disabled child. . . . [F]or great numbers of handicapped children . . . the School Boards fail to operate appropriate programs of special education. Where no appropriate public program is available, the parents of the handicapped children are eligible for a state tuition assistance grant to place the child in a private, special education program. . . . [T]he great majority of "approved" private schools charge more for tuition than the maximum reimbursement grant allows. . . . Because of this scheme, the parents of "certified" handicapped children are forced to subsidize the tuition charged for private placements. All such parents are forced to pay a minimum of one quarter of the tuition and in most cases, considerably more. For those parents who lack the financial resources to meet these costs, this usually means that the child cannot be enrolled in private school or that he or she is later dismissed from the private school when the parents default on their obligation to meet their share of the cost. Thus, the children of poor parents are totally denied the opportunity to obtain an appropriate education under this statutory scheme.

The federal court agreed and a decision was rendered for the plaintiff.

Clearly under the U.S. Constitution, P.L. 94–142, and Section 504, schools must provide education at no cost to the parent.

P.L. 94–142 offers little help in defining *appropriate* and suggests merely that the program offered must meet state education agency standards and conform to an individual educational plan. The appropriateness of the program is a subject for an impartial due-process hearing, and several court cases have given some indication of its meaning. In *Fialkowski* v. *Shapp*, 405 F. Supp. 946 (E.D.Pa. 1975), the plaintiffs were clearly offered an inappropriate program:

> . . . [P]laintiffs bring this action for damages claiming that defendant state and city officials have violated their rights to an appropriate education under the equal protection

> and the due process clauses of the Fourteenth Amendment of the Constitution. Plaintiffs contend that, as multiple-handicapped children, they are denied equal protection under the Constitution because unlike the programs offered to normal and less severely retarded children, the nature of the educational programs offered them is such that no chance exists that the programs will benefit.
>
> An educational program must be assessed in terms of its capacity to equip a child with the tools needed in life. . . . Placement of children with the intelligence of two year olds in a program which emphasizes skills such as reading and writing would seem inadequate for their needs. The harmful consequences of denying plaintiffs an adequate education is underscored by the fact that mentally retarded children have greater need for formal education since they are less likely than ordinary children to learn and develop informally.

Thus where the school offers a program that clearly does not produce results, or has no chance for success, it is inappropriate.

The appropriateness of the program can also be affected by inadequate staff, so P.L. 94–142 specifies steps to be taken in personnel development. A needs assessment must be conducted to determine if there are sufficient qualified personnel available, both teaching and related services, to carry out programs. It should specify whether needs can be met by retraining or if new personnel are needed. Inservice training must be initiated for special education and regular education personnel to meet needs exposed in the needs assessment. Development or modification of instructional materials should be considered and educational research and demonstration projects should be attempted to upgrade personnel skills.

Access to Services

Even though the school might have a good program to offer, a free, appropriate public education may not exist because access to that program is interrupted. One common source of interrupted access is bureaucratic delay in getting around to providing services, including placing children on waiting lists. P.L. 94–142 and Section 504 clearly specify that no eligible child may be excluded, and once included, each must receive appropriate services. Additionally, some children are denied access because their programs are interrupted by summer vacation. Where the nature or severity of the handicap is such that the program must continue, then an appropriate education would presumably include a 12-month schedule. This issue was considered in *In the Matter of Richard G.,* 383 N.Y.Supp. 2d 403 (1976). The appeals court sent the matter for determination "... whether his education would have regressed had he not participated in the summer program." If regression would take place, the school would have to either provide, or pay for, a summer program.

A final way that schools might mistakenly interrupt access to education is through the use of disciplinary procedures that result in suspension or expulsion. The *Mills* case recognized this problem and placed strict limits on the practice:

> Defendants shall not, on grounds of discipline, cause the exclusion, suspension, expulsion, postponement, interschool transfer, or any other denial of access to regular instruction in the public schools to any child for more than two days without first notifying the child's parent or guardian of such proposed action, the reasons therefore, and of a hearing before a Hearing Officer. . . .

Mills added that a suspension cannot occur "without providing for his education during the period of any such suspension."

Full Service

Free, appropriate public education means special education and related services. The absence of any related service may mean the special education offering is ineffective and thus result in a denial of an appropriate program. Related services under P.L. 94–142 means developmental, corrective, and other supportive services, including audiology, counseling services, early identification, medical services (diagnostic only), occupational therapy, parent counseling and training, physical therapy, psychological services, recreation, school health services, social work services in schools, speech pathology, and transportation. No one child may need all these services, but where a service is needed and not made available there might be a denial of access to an appropriate program. Similarly, where the service offered is wholly inadequate (e.g., physical therapy 15 minutes twice a week for a cerebral-palsied child when 1 hour per day is recommended by the evaluation staff) there may still be a denial of an appropriate program.

Procedural Safeguards

Testimony to Congress and in several recent court cases has indicated that the parents are generally left out of the provision of special services to their children. P.L. 94–142 and Section 504 require substantial procedural safeguards to get parents involved. Notice of what the school proposed must be given to parents, according to P.L. 94–142 "[in] a reasonable time before the public agency proposes to initiate or change (or refuses to initiate or change) the identification, evaluation, or placement of the child or the provision of a free appropriate public education to the child." Notice must be written in "language understandable to the general public," and in the native language of the parent. If the school knows the parent cannot read the notice, it must be communicated orally and the school must document that the parent understood the content of the notice.

In addition to a full explanation of procedural safeguards, the specific action proposed at the time of notification must be detailed to include the proposed action, an explanation of why the school proposed the action, a description of the alternatives considered before deciding on the proposed action, the reasons why those alternatives were rejected, each evaluation procedure, test, record, or report the agency will rely on as a basis for the proposed action, and any other factors relevant to the proposed action.

When the parent disagrees with services being provided to the child, he may ask for an impartial due-process hearing. At that hearing they have the following rights:

1. Right to full notice of procedures and rights.
2. Right to have the hearing chaired by an impartial due-process hearing officer (someone not an employee of the state or local agency providing services to the child).
3. Right to a timely proceeding, with a decision in writing within 45 days of the request for a hearing, and within 30 days of an appeal.
4. Right to appear and be accompanied by the child, by counsel, and by persons with special knowledge.
5. Right to present evidence and to prohibit introduction of evidence not disclosed to them 5 days before the hearing.
6. Right to compel attendance of witnesses and to cross-examine them.
7. Right to receive a verbatim copy of the proceedings.

8. Right to a written decision with findings of fact relied upon.
9. Right to appeal to the state education agency and from the state agency to state or federal court.
10. Right to have the child remain in his present educational placement until the proceedings are completed.

Issues Specific to the Handicapped Adolescent

The preceding description of rights of the handicapped applies equally to all ages of school children. But the problems of special education fall particularly hard on adolescents. Many initial fights to assert new rights for the handicapped child will predictably involve older children.

Older children are more easily excluded from school altogether. Students eligible for special education services should be aided up to the age of 18 prior to September of 1980 and up to 21 after this date. Nonhandicapped schoolchildren, however, might be allowed to drop out (or be pushed out) around the age of 16. Thus when faced with a troublesome teen-ager who might need special services, the tendency will be great in schools to create a dropout situation. Similarly, as a teen-ager already receiving services for the handicapped nears the legally permissible age to drop out, some schools might become less responsive and convince the child to seek services elsewhere. For adolescents, the threat of exclusion will be a constant one.

It will be harder for handicapped adolescents to receive a fair initial assessment of handicapping conditions. Younger children, new to the educational environment, might be evaluated with less prejudice. But a teen-ager, with a cumulative record taller than he is, will face many arguments that he is not entitled to anything special. He will probably be perceived by teachers as "slow," "uninterested," "doesn't want to learn," "from a bad family," and so forth. The process of referring that child, who is nobody's favorite, to special education has some real disincentives. A finding of handicaps would reflect badly on the child's teachers and others who had been missing the point up until now. And such a finding would cause the creation of a new program for the child, instead of just holding on for another semester or two until the child drops out. That means that an adolescent with a long educational history would have less of a chance to be referred for special education assessment than a first grader.

Another factor that might get in the way is discipline. Not all handicapped children are physically aggressive, but older (and bigger) aggressive children are likely to be referred for disciplinary sanctions. Certain school administrators who would consider some type of educational readjustment for younger children just will not tolerate aggressive behavior in adolescents. Those administrators want to "teach them a lesson" and the result is that the handicapped and aggressive adolescent is more likely a candidate for corporal punishment (probably illegally administered) than for educational assessment. The failure of this approach typically leads to more corporal punishment and seems to let teachers and others, who ought to be pushing for referral, off the hook.

If assessment can be accomplished for the adolescent, services must be described in an individual education plan (IEP). For the young child, such plans are optimistic statements of how the child might progress year after year. But for the older child, who has seen nothing but academic failure and who now has only a few more years or even months left, those IEPs are likely to be highly limited. Personnel writing the plans must be challenged to increase their efforts, to try to make up for lost time, and not be allowed to formulate a baby-sitting scheme.

Once an IEP is written, services must be carried out in the least restrictive alternative appropriate to the child's educational objectives. The handicapped adolescent raises two kinds of problems. Some teen-agers will never have been served in a public school program, yet they are now to be considered candidates for one under the doctrine of the least restrictive alternatives. The older a child is, and the longer he has not been in a public education atmosphere, the more difficult it will be to convince the school to really consider him.

A similar pressure will be on the handicapped adolescent who *is* in a public school program. Regular education has been failing him and now he is discovered to be eligible for special services. The tendency will be to put him in a one-way program from which he will never return. A younger child might be kept near the mainstream and might eventually return there. But an older adolescent, whom everyone assumes will not have enough time left to remediate his problem and return, will likely be a candidate for an unduly restrictive separate program away from the mainstream. Many adolescents, finally diagnosed as handicapped, could well be served exactly where they were. But the diagnosis will seem to many regular education personnel a good chance to get rid of the problem and refuse the child any chance to remain in the mainstream.

The older an unsuccessful student is, the more likely he is to be considered a candidate for vocational training rather than continued education. The excuse might be that there is too little time left to waste on academic pursuits and the student should learn a saleable skill. The problems with work placement will be exacerbated by such an attitude. Using work programs as a place to deposit unwanted students will increase the chances that they will be dead-end assignments.

Adolescents may face problems with medication. Certain kinds of medication are used with pre-adolescents because of the hypothesis that they have educationally productive side-effects. Thus, in some schools, special education becomes almost a drug subculture. For adolescents, however, the purpose of medication would almost always be institutional convenience (as one administrator told me, "These kids are easier to deal with when we slow them down") and adolescents must be protected against that abuse.

A final complicating factor for adolescents involves consent. Several federal judges have ruled recently [*Bartley* v. *Kremens*, 402 F. Supp. 1039 (E.D.Pa. 1975) and *J.L. & J.R.* v. *Parham*, 412 F. Supp. 112 (M.D.Ga. 1976)] that the adolescent plaintiffs could not be placed in a restrictive facility against their will without due process. The U.S. Supreme Court has not yet ruled directly on this point. Few persons would suggest that a 5-year-old severely retarded child should play a large role in determining an educational program. But as the child gets older and the handicaps are less mentally disabling, where does one draw the line? Should not a 16-year-old learning disabled child play a part in the decision making? Provisions for the IEP meeting and for the impartial hearing both contemplate having the child in attendance. If he is in attendance, must he give his consent? Equally important, if he protests, must there be some due process before placement in a restrictive program? This problem will arise, for now, only with the adolescent special education child; every school district should begin to plan a constructive response.

The Future

I am very optimistic about the future of special education services. Some people look to the difficult and often unsatisfactory 25-year history of desegregation and suggest civil rights for the handicapped will follow a similar path. I disagree. Many persons in positions of power are handicapped or have family members who are handicapped. Now that these issues are finally being raised, I do not think that these people in authority will be insensitive. There will undoubtedly be a difficult period of arguments that our public schools, already doing poorly, will be further handicapped by this additional burden. Coupled with the argument that scarce tax dollars will be diverted away from normal children already in need of additional resources, there will be a backlash; but I know we will survive it.

And we will benefit in three important ways. As handicapped adolescents are found and evaluated, many schools will tend to contract those adolescents out. In the past the school paid a token share, but now they will get the full bill. It will not take many trips to the school board for approval of another $30,000 expenditure for one youth before the board orders development of in-house programs. For a period, the school might try to skip by with an inadequate in-house offering. But eventually, through impartial hearings and lawsuits, the school will be forced to commit the needed resources and upgrade the staff. The entire special education effort will benefit.

A second predictable occurrence will be training of regular classroom teachers to deal with a single handicapped adolescent placed in their class. For several years education has used the catchwords of individual education, *self-paced instruction* and *educational objectives*. There is often little substance beyond the jargon. But with that one handicapped adolescent, the regular classroom teacher is going to have to learn what objectives really are and how to amass data for periodic evaluation. That teacher will also have to be taught classroom management techniques to manage the youth's individual education plan. Once exposed to those techniques, the teacher will undoubtedly use them to the benefit of all adolescents in the classroom. As a result, all adolescents may finally get the individual instructional management that schools have been talking about.

A third benefit should come as parents of both handicapped and nonhandicapped adolescents attend the individual planning meeting for the handicapped adolescent. The youth's weaknesses will be outlined, a plan for the year will be detailed, and the way progress is to be measured will be explained to the parents. Parents will compare that to the treatment they get when they contact the school about their nonhandicapped child and demand annual program plans for all. Schools that have been claiming that they have individual education plans for every child will find that their bluff has been called. Today's special education laws should eventually bring truly individual planning and instruction for everyone.

Obstacles to Educating Handicapped Adolescents

12

David A. Sabatino

I don't really know why I am a special educator. I suspect that it has something to do with my childhood desires; at one time or another I wanted to be almost everything, especially where there was action and interaction with a variety of people. I do remember that an educator was the last thing I desired to be, for three reasons: the male teacher I knew looked so terribly bored, I always disliked school, and most importantly, school never liked me very much either. The rural school I attended was on a hill, and I remember that even as a senior, walking up that hill, looking at that awesome two-story building, I knew exactly how David of the Old Testament felt when he looked upon Goliath. I have always wondered how unique such a feeling is.

The double-barreled anxiety I experienced as a new college student was to earn a living and pass my courses. To reduce that anxiety, I needed a full-time job that precluded the opportunity to schedule a full load of classes. I was able to find such a position as a cottage parent on the evening shift at a juvenile diagnostic center, a state-administered short-term facility for determining appropriate placement of adjudicated youthful offenders. That position met all my requirements and more. It provided me with an interest in a group of people—an interest, I am afraid, much more fascinating than my textbooks or courses, and one that has prompted most of my research and professional interests. However, at that time in my life, a problem was created: I had to pick a career goal for the sake of completing my education. You know how universities are in isolating majors for accounting purposes.

The question simply was, How does one prepare to work with youth in the structures in which they are found? The shock was the firmness in the lines drawn between disciplines, institutions, and community agencies. The pecking order of psychiatrist, psychologist, social worker, and the unholy trinity of institutional population management is only one example of institutional lines of authority I experienced. The tragic gaps in interdisciplinary relationships were evidenced in staff meetings, and the reports to follow on one of my cottage youngsters described a shadow as in Plato's cave, not the person I knew as a cottage attendant. An Oedipus Rex might explain why a youth hated all male authority figures, but it didn't explain to me why he cut his wrists over the sink. And, why did that behavior start after he received a severe concussion which required over 100 stitches to close the wound on his forehead? The frustration of attempting to work and learn was overwhelming. Why did he roll his eyes back in his head for a split second, stop in the middle of sentences, catch himself as from falling, and then stutter for the next five minutes? And, when the observed behaviors were reported, why was the response the common pronouncement, "schizoid personality, dark and depressive"?

All I really knew as a cottage parent on a ward for adjudicated kids was a sick sense that someone must have answers and I needed the information. I wanted the skills of each of those professionals, so that some day I could do what needed to be done, be all things to a tremendous array of human suffering that seemed to have a common element: education. All these kids, at some point, were in the public schools and ran into difficulty in either conduct, attendance, or academic performance.

It wasn't even clear to me how I could best reach across disciplines. I had no plan. Through fate and two professors I admired, I obtained a bachelor's degree in speech and hearing disorders. Though I didn't plan to become a speech clinician, that curriculum offered me the opportunity to include many courses in psychology, social work, and special education. One thing that did make sense to me was the training I received in two applied settings, one the speech clinic, the other a psychoeducational clinic.

My master's program was not planned either. I had thought of going into a 60-hour program in school psychology. But, instead, I was awarded a fellowship in audiology that would take me into every clinical setting imaginable. I was fascinated with the children at the state school for the retarded and extended it into a job after graduation. While there, I attempted to start a class for so-called autistic children who were in residence, a group who were in need of differential diagnosis for possible deafness, emotional disorders, brain injury, and/or mental retardation. I wanted so badly to provide those people communication and social stimulation, but everything went wrong. The absence of preparation, consultation, materials—I felt that the Maytag repairman's life was a continuous communal spree compared to mine. I felt the need for help, but didn't even know what questions to ask. I must admit, my first teaching experience with the handicapped was bigger than I was, an absolute frustrating experience. To avoid the classroom in the future, I applied for a school psychology internship based on doctoral admission to the Department of Psychology.

What I learned, working three years as a school psychologist, was that to help children was to facilitate for teachers while communicating with parents. And, as early as 1963, the school system in which I worked developed a continuum of special education services, using resource teachers, special education teacher consultants, and an educationally oriented medical-social diagnostic clinic in the schools. The result was a simplistic view of special education based on the fact that humans spend their lives attempting to adjust to their environment. Depending on the degree to which a person does not adjust, we label him this or that. To facilitate for children or youth in an educational plant, someone must provide for teachers, social workers, speech clinics, psychologists, and others. The major mission is to service teachers in response to their questions: What adaption of educational environment or curriculum is needed? How do I accomplish it? And then there is the all important looking-glass question, Is what I am doing the most appropriate thing I could do? It was from these experiences that I became interested in administration and completed a doctorate by combining educational administration and special education.

The sadness in being unable to be all things to all people has been somewhat fulfilled by being able to advocate administratively for those who do work directly with kids. Most rewarding has been the search for special educational delivery structures that are accountable, and the enrichment of professionals who work in close relationship, focusing on the achievement of instructional objectives.

My research interest continues to be the search for a systematic structure through which learner characteristics can be viewed, measured, and/or observed. The result of ascertaining learner characteristics in a descriptive manner is to avoid the use of worn-out labels and the placement of children or youth by so-called diagnostic categories. Rather, the search for interaction between learner trait and curriculum interaction, which would promote the development of rules for preparing and implementing the most appropriate short- and long-term objectives, is what I see as the work of special education. My other writing interests include the search for administrative structures that may provide unserved and underserved children or youth needed programs and services. The most recent effort is two volumes in specialized secondary education. One of the major themes in these volumes is an examination of the gaps that exist in the current service-delivery models for adolescent youth. It is in that vein that I will attempt to analyze the issues and pitfalls in delivering specialized educational services to adolescents. The first issue involves recent action to expand educational services to some unserved and underserved children and youth, and some reservations about whether the present levels of commitment are sufficient to insure effective delivery of those services. Next, I will examine special education not as a noble service to all handicapped youth in the name of human kindness, but as a component ideology in the American way of life. Finally, a number of the roadblocks to adequate special education for adolescents will be discussed.

Special Education and the Underserved

Special education has developed rapidly in recent years. Initial litigation (*Pennsylvania Association of Retarded Children* v. *Commonwealth of Pennsylvania,* 1972) requiring a free, appropriate education for all children for a 5½-hour school day was the hallmark of the early 1970s. Subsequent legislation (P.L. 93–112, Section 504, 1973), authorized accessibility to all physical facilities, insuring equal employment opportunities for the handicapped by including them in Title IX for nondiscriminatory hiring purposes. The now-mandated education for all handicapped children under Public Law 94–142

(1975) certainly supports serious progress across many sectors of our society in a vitalized effort to provide a standard, monitored format for special education services. There has been a rapid increase in the last 20 years in the numbers of special education personnel prepared and employed, and in the numbers of children and youth served. Despite all these favorable developments, the question still remains: Will all handicapped children eventually be served? The answer may be that this society will remain unwilling to provide fully developed programs for selected unserved and underserved groups of handicapped persons. We must then consider which handicapped populations are likely to remain underserved or unserved, and why. I suggest that secondary special education has not had a champion and is viewed by most as expendable.

It is instructive to consider recent events related to a traditionally underserved group of handicapped children and youth, the severely and profoundly mentally retarded. In a scant 5 years it has become obvious that institutionalized programs, even those directed at restoring these people to successful community reentry, inhibit community living success (Brown, Nietupski, & Hamre-Nietupski, 1976). Recent data conclusively indicate that if normalization is to be achieved, it must begin in the interaction of children with community environments. Therefore, training becomes realistic when it takes place in community-based facilities—a thought that presents a radical change to the beliefs of the last 50 years, requiring a vital new role for special educators.

Service delivery to trainable and subtrainable persons is a community-based cradle-to-the-grave proposition, not just for those aged 3–21, a legal mandate to be achieved by 1980. However, will the public and private sectors of the community be willing to provide the life-long support severely and profoundly mentally retarded persons need? If not, the initial efforts to deliver services to this traditionally underserved group may falter.

Edgerton, Eyman, and Silverstein (1975) report a trend toward smaller community treatment centers as alternatives to large residential facilities. However, the larger institutions have not gone out of business and in fact serve a significant number of retarded persons. There are 200,000 persons, approximately 10% of the mentally retarded, residing in institutions (U.S. Department of Health, Education, and Welfare, 1972). They live in 150 large institutions, 500 private institutions, and a variety of smaller hospitals, foster care homes, convalescent hospitals, and the like.

335

Hobbs (1975) found that approximately 30% of the residents are children and 81% of these had IQs below 50. The quality of life within these institutions varies tremendously.

The policy toward normalization is a current trend, meaning that placement in smaller, community-based facilities for the severely and profoundly mentally retarded is based on reasons other than the generalization that deplorable conditions exist in all institutions. Perhaps society will develop resources to deinstitutionalize severely handicapped children and youth because this is a humane goal, and because cost-reduced means of obtaining that end will result. But it might also be that widespread community acceptance and participation is at least a generation away, because the current generation of adults has not been prepared to take part in a shared community experience with trainable and subtrainable retarded citizens. At any rate, there is little reason to believe that most citizens are ready to share a hymnal with a subtrainable mentally retarded person.

Pupils showing severe behavioral disturbances constitute another low incidence group that has been traditionally underserved by the public schools. Treatment typologies for the seriously behaviorally disturbed have evolved to sophisticated levels, but most current interventions are dependent upon nonpublic education settings for meaningful service delivery. The question is, To what degree should the public schools provide for this population?

It certainly doesn't require a Philadelphia lawyer to note that the field has yet to develop even a remote level of consistency in defining emotional disabilities (Kanner, 1962; Kauffman, 1977). An operational assessment and, in turn, service delivery cannot occur when disagreement on the characteristics that constitute behavioral disorders remains so profound (Achenbach, 1974). Epstein, Cullinan, and Sabatino (1977) have discriminated two generic definitions of behavioral disturbance: those that are prepared by authorities in the field and those that are operationalized to deliver services. Most state definitions are unclear, providing just enough leeway so that street-level bureaucrats in local educational agencies can operationalize policy at the local level; thus it is the local people who determine who is to receive service and what that service shall be. Could the inconsistency across states and the ambiguity within state definitions be, in fact, a planned occurrence? While the federal government has a master plan that addresses services for all handicapped children, and the state educational agency has standards to provide funding at the local level, the local director of special education may actually determine the real regulations.

The degree, type, and amount of services are the prerogative of the local administrators, who may depend upon social organizational pressures, as described later in this chapter, to define the extent of those services. In general, public school officials have been conditioned to exclude norm-violating pupils from their buildings. Other state and private agencies (i.e., corrections or welfare) have absorbed troublesome youth, relieving education. Therefore, public education has not developed the means nor the will to program for obstreperous youth.

Perhaps the most populous category of underserved and frequently unserved handicapped pupil is the mildly handicapped adolescent. According to Metz (1973), the national projected incidence of handicapped in elementary schools is 12%, of which 75% are reached by special education programs and services. But while 5.9% of junior and senior high school students are thought to be handicapped, only 20% of the secondary school age group that qualifies for special education services receives such services. Thus, while more than three times as many children are served in elementary schools than are served in secondary schools, the incidence of handicapped elementary pupils is assumed to be only twice that of secondary pupils. Why is this true? First, it is estimated that 55% of the U.S. school population consists of enrolled elementary students, with secondary pupils comprising 40%. Five percent of secondary students in the United States are not enrolled in public schools. Second, as indicated previously, the projected incidence of the handicapped at the secondary level is only one-half that at the elementary level. I would suggest that of the 5% of "lost" secondary pupils, the majority are "stopped" from attending public school (Burke & Simons, 1965; Children's Defense Fund, 1974); and a large share of these may be rightly considered handicapped. The result is that fewer handicapped pupils remain in secondary schools (thus the lower incidence figure of 5.9).

In addition to pupils who are encouraged not to attend school, the large number of school dropouts undoubtedly includes many youths who need specialized services because they are unequipped to compete in school due to high-incidence handicapping conditions (mental retardation, emotional disturbance, learning disability). Since the advent of industrialization and urbanization, dropout rate has remained constant at about 12% (Schreiber, 1968), rang-

337

ing up to over 17% among the disadvantaged (Dauw, 1970). When these percentages are converted to numbers, it is apparent that nationally 700,000 students fail to complete 8 years of formal education annually.

Former U.S. Commissioner of Education Howe has stated emphatically, "Attempts to coax and persuade potential dropouts to stay in school, when the school continues to fail them, accomplishes absolutely nothing" (Schreiber, 1968, p. 1). There exists a "catch-22" problem confronting secondary school aged youth who run into difficulty within the secondary schools. On the one hand, if they get into trouble, the most frequent form of correction is suspension from school. The dilemma the student faces is that if he gets into trouble, he can expect to be denied the privilege of going to school. When he returns to school, the expectation is that he will be able to reenter the same old social and academic environment and achieve (self-provided amelioration in the absence of any assistance from the school). If he should get into trouble again, the same corrective measures will apply—expulsion. Apparently, secondary school officials reason that school is a privilege for those who, by either natural gift and/or appropriate guidance, find success therein. If a youth succeeds in school, his chances are higher for success in society (Bower & Lambert, 1961). If the youth experiences difficulty in the school society, how can he be expected to perform in society? Those educators who practice suspension as an intervention do not consider this question. Schreiber spoke of the unwanted and unemployable school aged youth on the streets when he wrote, "We must reconstruct our educational system to provide relevant, successful experiences for all children so that they will become and remain an integral part of our society" (1968, p. 6). Instead of pursuing this goal, the secondary schools have assumed a role of differentiating the good from the bad, and marking them as such for society.

Various lines of evidence indicate that many secondary youth who have records of nonattendance are properly considered handicapped. For example, Burke and Simons (1965) report that in their study, 76% of nonattenders were reading below grade level, 73% had been retained in school 2 or more years, and only 59% had normal IQs (90–110 range). Of those that did function in the normal IQ range, the majority experienced failure in at least one academic subject area, and over two-thirds failed at least one grade. Douglass (1969, p. 34) defines the following nine characteristics of dropouts:

1. An academic record of low school achievement.

2. A family background of low economic and cultural status, with parents who did little, if anything, to give the students a good attitude toward school.

3. Poor reading ability despite continued promotion, grade after grade, year after year. The majority of such students do not learn to read well enough to complete materials of junior high school level and some materials of intermediate level.

4. Markedly lower ability to learn verbal materials.

5. Lack of membership in interest clubs or other types of extra-curricular activities. The dropout doesn't belong. He is not a part of the school.

6. A record of antisocial behavior.

7. Associates with other underachieving students, and with children from culturally disadvantaged homes with inferior morals and morale, including some juvenile delinquents.

8. An unfavorable attitude towards school and teachers.

9. A record of absenteeism, which may be resultant of factors 2, 3, 4, 7, and 8.

Perhaps the only options for students with these problems are either to drop out or to become angry and express aggression toward the school.

The U.S. Office of Education conservatively estimates that 1.8% of the population in the secondary schools, or approximately 314,000 youths, are learning disabled. The prevalence of behavioral disorders varies according to the definition, diagnostic procedures, and socio-cultural environmental conditions, but estimates range from about 1% to 10% (Clarizio & McCoy, 1976). A national survey of special education, directed by Schultz, Hirshoren, Manton, and Henderson (1971), produced prevalence estimates ranging from 0.5% to 15%.

The incidence of mildly mentally retarded high school students is estimated at 0.75%. However, most states provide excessive IQ leeway above the so-called upper limit of mental retardation (IQ 70), permitting at least a mid-70 IQ or even low 80 IQ score for special education placement or services. Therefore, the prevalence of secondary youth with borderline IQs who may qualify for special education may well exceed 10%, assuming that their vocabulary development and usable language comprehension is assessed on intelligence tests as functionally retarded.

Secondary special education programs exist for 85% of the mentally retarded, 54.8% of the learning disabled, and 44.1% of the behaviorally disordered (Metz, 1973). In short, there are roughly just half enough special education programs for the most conservative estimates of the number of "high-incidence handicapped" pupils (mentally retarded, learning disabled, behaviorally disordered) in the secondary schools. What, then, for those pupils not included in the 5.9% handicapped estimate; those who just never caught on or caught up, or didn't like school, or the school didn't like them—that large group of undifferentiated, undiagnosed youth who fail to attend or fail to achieve? Barone (1977) presents the following dismal predictions regarding the approximate 2.5 million handicapped youth who will leave school over the next 4 years.

525,000—21%—will be either fully employed or enrolled in college

1,000,000—40%—will be underemployed and at the poverty level

200,000— 8%—will be in their home community and idle much of the time

650,000—26%—will be unemployed and on welfare

75,000— 3%—will be totally dependent and institutionalized

Special Education as an Institutional Structure

The ineffectual efforts of education in general, and particularly secondary education and special education, to respond suitably to the needs of adolescents, and of society with respect to adolescents, can be better understood by viewing education as an institution and examining secondary education and special education as social systems operating within the process of organizational socialization. As human society moved towards civilization and organization on a large scale, various institutions arose to serve various functions. Thus, there are now institutions related to industry, military, and government, as well as education. As an institution, education has one special characteristic: it is a reactive interpreter, conveying the values, rules, skills, and artistry of other institutions. Like other institutions, education can be interpreted in terms of social systems and organizational socialization.

Social systems are organizational units contained within some identifiable boundary (i.e., economic, geographic, political, professional), where the functions are interdependent and interact with regularity. Social systems are characterized by interaction and interdependency among units and organization of units into recognizable wholes (see Carr, 1955; Getzels, Lipham, & Campbell, 1968; Homans, 1959; Parsons, 1951).

Organizational socialization is the process by which participants in a particular social structure, especially new members, are provided information and rules so as to eventually be shaped to fit the social structure. That is, organizational socialization is a learning process in which members are made aware of the formal and informal social structure of the group (Etzioni, 1964; Hoy, 1968; Parsons, 1951; Willower, 1969).

Education, as a social system, exists in the context of the broader institutional picture. Education must relate to other community, state, private, and governmental agencies, each of which may be viewed as social systems with organizational socialization patterns of their own. Education is itself an institution of complex social system structure, comprised of many substructures, each having its own mission.

Social systems have both formal and informal communication processes that are critical to the shaping of membership roles and decision making. The formal communication process may require a member to function in a specific way; the informal communication process may suggest certain expectations. When these two communication processes are not providing congruent information, role discrepancies may result, active coalitions may form, and unfortunate effects on organizational morale and missions may come about.

Furthermore, just as people inside an organization seek compatibility, most institutional social systems discourage stepping too far outside the realm of compatibility with other institutions. These three characteristics of education as a social system—the complex organization of subsystems, the potential incompatibility of formal and informal communication processes, and the unwillingness to cross the boundaries of another agency's jurisdiction, have combined to inhibit the growth of special education at the secondary level.

First, the three major curriculum delivery areas, vocational, regular, and special education, comprise one set of institutional substructures; another set relates to the delivery of education according to student age groups and grade levels, another to the substructures of special education, such as special classes and resource rooms for hearing and vision impaired, physically handicapped, emotionally disturbed, learning disabled, and so on. As various levels of these substructures interact within the social system of a particular school, various barriers related to communication, role responsibilities, and the like arise. Additionally, in the case of the social system of secondary education, the informal communication process frequently suggests that deviant or handicapped youth are not the same as the "innocent little handicapped children" who can be controlled in the elementary school, and appropriate educational opportunities may not be offered. This is particularly so if the informal communication process suggests that role expectancies for its members are protected by a rationalization and denial of responsibilities for the population of adolescent handicapped. Certainly, many secondary educators believe that adolescents are better served by juvenile authorities, courts, drug centers, and other public and private agencies, not the schools.

Although the major mission of special education as a social system is the delivery of educational services to the handicapped, special education at the secondary level has received relatively little emphasis. Special education is a discipline that has relied on many other basic and applied fields of study. Special educational interventions overlap those used in psychiatry, orthopedic and physical medicine, neurology, traditional clinical and behavioral psychology, and adaptive techniques used by occupational and physical therapists. Many of the organizational socializational influences that promote special education for the young handicapped child deny it for the mildly handicapped adolescent. Special education literature is filled with the term *child;* references rarely are made to youth, and then only in the last few years. Thus, not only has special education not developed as a subsystem within the social system of secondary education, but there is not even a strong tradition emphasizing service to adolescents within the special education social system. This latter phenomenon can be better understood by examining special education as an ideology.

Special education is an ideology in the very real sense that an ideology is the collective unconscious of certain groups. An ideology obscures the real conditions of society, both to itself and to others, and thereby stabilizes itself (Mannheim, 1960). Even for such a noble undertaking as educating the handicapped, society's conscience is rarely stable. Special education as a social system is interdependent with philosophic, political, and especially economic societal considerations. In a time of plenty, humane interest for the handicapped may be observable to all and appropriately portrayed as a community problem, but in times of cultural, economic, military, or political crisis, the community's ability to observe the needs of the handicapped may be repressed and denied. It was not that pre-industrial societies were unwilling to support the handicapped; there simply were not enough resources to support those who could not or would not provide for themselves or society. The present situation with regard to secondary level special education departs from this idea by only a few degrees; society will support small handicapped children, but large, mildly (not visibly) handicapped youth are still subject to the older view.

As has been mentioned, one special feature of education as an institution is that it is a reactive institution. It is significant that major legislative and other initiatives to provide educational services for the handicapped have come primarily from outside the educational social system. Historically, educators have not been advocates for the handicapped; this is especially true regarding secondary educators, whose organizational socialization is academically and vocationally oriented.

This ideology of special education did not result from Christianity or the Renaissance, which freed humanity from ignorance; the philosophic revolution, which freed humanity from beliefs; the social revolution, which freed humanity from birthright; the political revolution, which freed humanity from the law; nor the scientific revolution, which established medicine. Special education is a natural phenomenon, a result of our increasing control over nature, especially since the industrial revolution. When the society is no longer predominantly concerned with basic survival issues, attention can be focused on other concerns in the social order. Additionally, there are at least three benefits to society currently provided by special education.

First, the handicapped may be viewed as an act of nature, and in confronting the problems of the disabled, humanity continues its war against nature. Second, in our industrial society, heavy emphasis is placed on productivity. Appropriate effort and resources provided for the handicapped may succeed in increasing the number of productive persons in society. The third value of special education has to do with our industrial society's continuing search for its conscience or soul. The American theme embodied in the words "land of the free and the home of the brave" must be continually tested and renewed in new frontiers. The latest test of this American ideal may be in the nation's willingness to serve its weakest members. Americans do not wish that history remember this nation as an industrial giant that revolutionized technology through assembly line production; rather, that history record that the contribution of this country is a spirit of freedom from whatever enslaves, including handicapped conditions.

Roadblocks to Special Education for Adolescents

The following section describes 10 impediments to the development of the proper secondary level education for the high-incidence handicapped. These impediments are processes described earlier as organizational socialization.

Economics

Most state governments are not ready to absorb the excess cost of educating additional handicapped secondary students. Formulas provide for financial reimbursement for the education of the handicapped, at a rate several times that of educating regular students. Most state governments keep a watchful eye on expenditures in all areas of finance, but particularly education. Generally, the portion of a state's financial pie going to education exceeds 50%, and in many states exceeds 75%. Inflation, soaring utility costs, and increased salaries have all raised the cost of public education. Projections of a 30% reduction in secondary students by 1981 are encouraging to state governments, but special education is an open-ended cost factor that continues to skyrocket. Many states now require their departments of education to use percentage limits to control special education funding. States may adopt low-incidence figures, controlling the number of handicapped students eligible for secondary special education but ignoring the realistic need.

Teacher-Pupil Relationship

Historically, elementary school educators have been child-centered, while secondary teachers have been subject-centered. Secondary teachers traditionally have taught departmentalized subjects in which classes change throughout the day. A secondary teacher may lecture to a class and require limited individual participation. Generally it is expected that students will distribute themselves over a range of letter grades, including failing grades. Rarely does a secondary teacher know how a student is performing in another class. Secondary classes are larger to begin with, and secondary teachers are forced to make some assumptions about achievement levels, motivation, and interest of their students. Therefore, secondary teachers seldom have the type of student contact that permits the judgment that a mild handicap may exist. The result is that few students are referred or even suspected of having high-incidence handicaps.

Lack of "Basic Skills" Focus

Theories and efforts in the field regarding academic skill acquisition have focused largely on pupils in the elementary grades, despite the fact that many pupils make it into secondary schools without satisfactory academic achievement. Popular older theories to explain academic underachievement in normal learners (Robinson, 1946), the mildly mentally retarded (Ingram, 1935), or brain-injured (Strauss & Lehtinen, 1947) convey the notion that children outgrow the reason for the disability, and, if remediation is provided, they will gain the skills necessary for a normal high school experience. Unfortunately, data on handicapped students entering high school indicate that they have neither outgrown the contributing deficit nor obtained grade level academic achievement (Bhaerman, 1977).

Supportive Personnel Lacking

Because most specialized services are located in elementary schools, the referral emphasis and resulting support services (primarily school psychologists) also remain in the elementary schools. Nicholson (1971) reports that more than 75% of all school psychological services are concentrated in the elementary school. Teacher contact with the psychologist stimulates referrals, and follow-up contact with the psychologist generates further referrals. Conversely, when psychologists are not seen regularly in the secondary schools, there is set into practice a classical example of Homans's (1959) postulate on creating dissonance among people in an institutional organization: The less educators communicate with fellow educators who have different roles, the greater the dissonance. In turn, the greater the dissonance, the less informal communication, which results in a further reduction of formal communication. Or as one high school counselor put it, "There is no reason for me to refer a student to a school psychologist regardless of the amount of difficulty the student is experiencing. We don't see much of the school psychologist here."

Lack of Alternative Education

Youths who experience school failure and those who are stopped or dropped from attendance require specialized assistance if they are to profit from returning to school. Frequently, they require an alternative to that of the regular academic program (Hoyt, 1976). But there are not enough alternative programs and specialized services, and funding to create those needed services is short. Even with the advent of P.L. 94–142, the cost reimbursement made available to local educational agencies is insufficient to initiate the expensive specialist-to-student ratio required by most alternative or specialized programs. The financial situation is untenable now and will worsen by 1980 when services are required for youth to age 21. Most states cannot afford to provide secondary specialized programs for all "dropped or stopped" youth and will probably not have the dollar capability until additional federal revenue earmarked for secondary program development is appropriated by Congress.

Shortage of Vocational Counselors

There is a critical shortage of vocational counselors who have been properly trained to use assessment in prevocational and vocational programming for the mildly handicapped adolescent. Traditionally, vocational counselors have employed psychometric or work-analysis procedures to specify desired programs to promote employability of their clients. Unfortunately, standard assessment devices, such as aptitude, interest, intelligence, or work sampling tests do not provide valid data for handicapped clients (Kolstoe, 1960; Kolstoe & Shafter, 1961; Olshansky, 1973). The reason is that their disabilities alter the results of standardized assessment procedures not adapted to the handicap; thus the counselor measures the handicap and not the person or the person's potential.

Present Focus of Vocational Education

Vocational education achieved status in educational circles by competing for the academically successful student who was vocationally, not college, oriented. The original charge of vocational educators was to continue the ancient apprenticeship system. Vocational training was kept distinctly separate from academic education until the late 1800s and consisted of on-the-job training by day, classes by night. Although most vocational educators are sympathetic toward the handicapped, they do not sense the contribution their training can make to these people's lives. The problem is that no one has clearly differentiated the goals of vocational training for handicapped and nonhandicapped persons; thus, vocational educators may actually avoid the handicapped. Massive retraining of vocational educators in special education, and mutual planning between the two disciplines are necessary.

Federal Support and Local Cooperation

The role relationships between vocational rehabilitation agencies and public education remain unclear and incongruent. This situation results in "cracks" in service delivery, through which youths tend to fall. In 1943, via the Barden-LaFollette Act, Congress provided state rehabilitation agencies the capability to offer their services to the mentally retarded, broadening the concept of rehabilitation to persons with sensory and physical handicaps. Progress was slow: In 1943, only 10 workshops for the mentally retarded were identified in the United States. The 1954 Vocational Rehabilitation Amendment did promote the development of 39 new workshops. Obviously, there were limited services beyond the high schools for known handicapped groups through programs provided by rehabilitation monies. Thus, many mildly mentally retarded youth who found themselves running out of suitable programs in the public schools had virtually no alternatives. To remedy this, the President's Panel on Mental Retardation (1962) called for vocational training for handicapped persons through entry into appropriate vocational areas, cooperative work-study-experience programs, well-organized on-the-job training programs, and vocational guidance throughout the person's school career. Still, the various institutions and agencies failed to work together (Cohen, 1963).

In 1965, President Johnson signed Public Law 89–333 (Vocational Rehabilitation Amendments of 1965), which included provisions for the economically disadvantaged and mentally handicapped individuals. The act provided grants to states and nonprofit organizations to develop or expand comprehensive vocational programs, to build, equip, and staff workshops and other facilities; it also made funds available for the training of individuals whose progress in a rehabilitation program was not assured. Until this point, vocational rehabilitation services were limited to those handicapped individuals who displayed a reasonable chance of successfully completing a program and obtaining employment. The 1968 amendments to P.L. 89–333 placed emphasis on developing

347

programs for minority and disadvantaged individuals. Thirty-five million dollars were provided to develop work-study programs for vocational education clients, but stringent qualifications were established. In essence, the 1968 amendments indicated growing concern for employment and underemployment, but conversely tightened the reins of funding for vocational education. Rehabilitation programs came under pressure to justify their expenditures on an input-output basis, and the policy of providing rehabilitation services to severely disabled individuals underwent close scrutiny by government officials. This trend continued into the 1970s, with a commitment to big business at the expense of social programs. A systems analysis approach to vocational rehabilitation became predominant, and many of the programs for the handicapped were lost in the shuffle. There simply have not been well-coordinated, federal-state long-term vocational rehabilitation efforts for mildly handicapped youth.

Uncoordinated Helping Efforts

High school-aged youths on the street are often the responsibility of several agencies, but rarely do these organizations coordinate their efforts. Any list of public or private agencies that administer programs for adolescents would be lengthy: welfare, juvenile court, mental health, vocational centers, drug and alcoholism centers, family planning, health care, youth activities, church groups or projects, mentioning only a few. Frequently, more than one agency may be working with a youth, even focusing on the same problem at the same time. Coordination of these efforts rarely occurs; typically the schools are not informed that a youth in attendance is being seen by another public or private agency. The confusion resulting from poor communication among agencies may be an especially serious problem for the adolescent who is not attending school.

The absence of coordination is rooted in territorial boundaries thought to exist between agencies. A particular social system may attempt to exclude other agencies claiming responsibility, or members may exert pressure on the organization structure to exclude youth from membership because services are being offered by other agencies. In this all too common situation, the young person is caught in the middle.

Professional Training

There is a vicious circle of (a) few professional positions in the secondary special education, (b) limited openings for a person with the appropriate training, and (c) a relative lack of appropriate university preparation programs. A recent national survey of 150 universities indicated that only 17% have secondary special education training programs (Miller, Lotsof, & Miller, 1976). Clark and Oliverson (1973) found that only 9 of 47 states had any secondary special education certification distinct from elementary. Basically, higher education has failed to anticipate the need for trained secondary special educators, and many states are using an elementary-oriented special education curriculum as the vehicle to achieve certification; in most states certification is K–12. When special educators have been employed in secondary schools, directors of special education have had to respond by employing elementary-trained special educators who generally attempt to employ elementary-level remedial instruction and curricula with a student audience that has "had it" with such nonsense. It is little wonder that most evaluations of secondary special education have indicated that the programs are inadequate and inappropriate (Clark & Evans, 1976; Sabatino, 1974; Schlichter & Ratcliff, 1971).

Such a state of affairs is due largely to two situations. First, most special education professional preparation programs are not designed to initiate secondary programs because they lack faculty strength in those areas of development important to secondary youth. Second, the vast majority of special education teacher trainees are women, who have historically gravitated toward work with younger children. It is my belief that unless fully prepared for the much harder to handle older student, they might have difficulty controlling the class while trying to teach. Indeed, a genuine fear of secondary youth is justified: Over 60% of all secondary special education students were initially referred because of serious disciplinary problems (Miller, 1975). In addition to these two main factors, other problems for special education at the secondary level are that few teaching materials exist and progress is compounded by many variables far beyond the teacher's control.

Future Perspectives

It is not the author's intent to demean regular, special, or vocational educators, or schools in general. The main criticism is that, particularly regarding mildly handicapped adolescents, the ideology of special education has failed to evolve. Although no master plan can be suggested, there are certain developments that would help special education programs for adolescents to emerge.

349

A Data Base

Special education must work toward a base of data on secondary handicapped students, including incidence information, what happened to them during the course of high school, and follow-up assessment after school departure. Now different agencies have different figures for the same groups of students. The adolescent special education literature is practically devoid of a sound data base. The Bureau of Education for the Handicapped has sought and received very few requests for funds to support the development of useful data bases regarding secondary school special education pupils. In short, the problem statements must be identified and data brought to bear on those statements if the parameters of secondary special education are to be clarified.

The identification of first-priority children and youth, those who have traditionally been unserved, has been mandated by P.L. 94–142. Together with the intended impact of the Rehabilitation Act of 1973, this should insure that handicapped adolescents out of school who are not receiving services for handicapped will be identified. We must be careful in this identification process; the data bases can only reflect the data contributed. If screening or identification procedures are not instituted properly, the resulting data will not reflect potentially unrecognized handicapped populations in secondary schools. By 1980, this data base must include information on those up to age 21. One suspects that to produce the appropriate data bases, a national clearinghouse or other consolidated effort will be needed.

Professional Preparation

Secondary special education is not yet a top priority of teacher training programs or the federal agencies that support them. There is an overwhelming need for universities to develop secondary special education programs articulated among career education, secondary education, vocational education, and special education (Miller et al., 1976). Secondary special education programs, however, must not simply become a replica of elementary training efforts. There are two major issues that should be addressed in developing a professional preparation program at the secondary level.

First, the basis for preparing persons to work with secondary students must be vocational-career education skills. The remedial-clinical model used historically in the preparation of special education personnel should not be the major emphasis. The professional special educator must have the communication skills to work in harmony with vocational counselors, work-study coordinators, regular high school teachers, and administrators. Perhaps more than any other training program, those programs for preparing secondary special educators demand interdisciplinary training.

Second, professionals currently working with adolescents must recognize and concentrate effectively on the handicapped. Special educators have much to offer counselor- and teacher-preparation programs. For example, vocational programmers could profit from exposure to current assessment and training procedures advocated by special educators, such as task analysis of the skills needed for an actual work assignment and the identification of social correlates and contingencies associated with work assignment (Rotatori & Switzky, 1977). Such techniques must become available to those who work with mildly handicapped adolescents and will probably become known only when preparation programs are developed that cut across traditional departmental boundaries.

Cooperation

State agencies, specifically state educational departments, must assume leadership in developing teaching credentials that require (a) distinct preparation in special education for all secondary school personnel, and (b) licensure for special educators that specifies a 7–12 emphasis instead of the current K–12 certificate provided in most states. Cooperative interagency planning is needed, emphasizing role relationships among agencies, with attention to means of communication among those involved. Cooperative planning among vocational, special, and regular educators is of paramount importance. State educational agencies will have the opportunity, through the monitoring process of the Individualized Education Program required by P.L. 94–142, to determine the types and amount of specialized instruction delivered to high school students.

There are no longer enough resources available to state and local education agencies to permit a continuation of role duplication and other varieties of overlap among educational and other human service agencies. Interagency communication will permit those working with the adolescent handicapped to coordinate vocational-career efforts, alternative program offerings, and other services in a more efficient manner.

351

Information Sharing

There is a tremendous need for local educational agencies to share instructional procedures for educating handicapped secondary students through cooperative inservice training arrangements. Joint action by local special education administrators and school principals could accomplish several desirable objectives: (a) creating among regular educators an awareness of the need to teach special populations; (b) explaining how handicapping conditions contribute to the educational problems of troubled youths in the secondary schools, with an emphasis on developing workable referral processes; (c) encouraging counselors and department heads to develop an active advocacy with teacher audiences; (d) providing high school principals, department heads, and central office administrators with basic information on education of the handicapped.

Development of a Secondary Special Education Ideology

Special educators have generally failed to view their professional practice against a social-political backdrop. To believe that special education will continue to flourish because it is necessary to society, and that society will keep on paying the bill because of all the good that is demonstrated through the yearly restoration of the handicapped, is not merely naïve thinking; it is woefully neglectful of fact and dangerous to the development of our profession.

The ideology of special education can be revitalized, but not by ignoring its basic place within social-political forces. Neither educators nor special educators have initiated any call for educational services to the handicapped; the early history of extracting special education services for the visually and hearing impaired at the turn of the century was the direct result of parent and community lobbies, not educator advocacy. The Pennsylvania decision and other litigation that triggered much-needed legislation, such as P.L. 94–142, resulted from individual parents and parental organizations, not professionals. And yet, special educators continue to assume a distant attitude, to the effect that the professional person must not become involved with the mechanics of the process.

Pirsig (1974), in the popular novel, *Zen and the Art of Motorcycle Maintenance,* has something to offer all practicing special educators. His message is that we all truly enjoy the products of technology but rarely appreciate the mechanical mastery under the skin of that product. If special educators continue to be just drivers and not mechanics, the profession will have to passively accept the decisions made by the engineers of our technological world, be it the courts, the Congress, or the parent organizations. To engineer our own ideology of secondary special education, we must be willing to work with the tradesman; understand labor's protective unionism; become sensitive to management and marketing needs; exert pressures on nonschool agencies to relate to school agencies; have state agencies and departments begin cooperation; and help universities develop appropriate, relevant secondary special education programs, producing effective advocates for needed changes. I personally doubt that everyone will be willing to accomplish these tasks in my lifetime.

REFERENCES

Abelson, H. I., & Fishburne, P. M. *Nonmedical use of psychoactive substances, 1975/76: A nationwide study among youth and adults.* Princeton, N.J.: Response Analyses Corporation, 1976.

Abeson, A., & Blacklow, J. *Environmental design: New relevance for special education.* Arlington, Va.: Council for Exceptional Children, 1971.

Abeson, A., & Zettel, J. The end of the quiet revolution: The Education for all Handicapped Children Act of 1975. *Exceptional Children,* 1977, *44,* 114–128.

Abidin, R. R. *Parenting skills.* New York: Human Sciences Press, 1976.

Achenbach, T. M. *Developmental psychopathology.* New York: Ronald Press, 1974.

Adult functional competency: A summary. Austin, Tex.: Division of Extension, University of Texas, 1975.

Allen, V. L. *Children as teachers: Theory and research on tutoring.* New York: Academic Press, 1976.

Alschuler, A., Tabor, D., & McIntyre, J. *Teaching achievement motivation.* Middletown, Conn.: Education Ventures, 1970.

American Institute for Research. *Impact of educational innovation on student performance: Project methods and findings for three cohorts* (Project LONGSTEP Final Report, Vol. 1). Palo Alto, Calif.: American Institute for Research, 1976.

Angoff, W. H. (Ed.). *The College Board Admissions Testing Program: A technical report on research and development. Activities relating to the Scholastic Aptitude Test and achievement tests.* Princeton, N.J.: Educational Testing Service, 1971. (ERIC Document Reproduction Service No. ED 050 181)

Angoff, W. H. Viewpoint: Why the SAT scores are going down. *English Journal,* 1975, *64,* 10–11.

Anthony, J. *On drug education.* Unpublished manuscript, Drug Information and Education Program, University of Minnesota, 1974.

Apter, S. J. Applications of ecological theory toward a community special education model. *Exceptional Children,* 1977, *43,* 366–373.

Armstrong, D. G. Alternative schools: Implications for secondary school curriculum workers. *The High School Journal,* 1973, *56,* 267–275.

Arter, J. A., & Jenkins, J. R. Examining the benefits and prevalence of modality considerations in special education. *Journal of Special Education*, 1977, *11*, 281–298.

Ausubel, D. P., Montemayor, R., & Srajian, P. *Theory and problems of adolescent development*. New York: Grune & Stratton, 1977.

Ayllon, T., & Azrin, N. *The token economy*. New York: Appleton-Century-Crofts, 1968.

Back to the basics in the schools. *Newsweek*, October 21, 1974, pp. 87–94; 95–96.

Baer, D. M., Wolf, M. M., & Risley, T. R. Some current dimensions of applied behavior analysis. *Journal of Applied Behavior Analysis*, 1968, *1*, 91–97.

Bailey, J. S., Wolf, M. M., & Phillips, E. L. Home-based reinforcement and the modification of pre-delinquents' classroom behavior. *Journal of Applied Behavior Analysis*, 1970, *3*, 223–233.

Bailey, L. J., & Stadt, R. W. *Career education: New approaches to human development*. Bloomington, Ill.: McNight Publishing, 1973.

Balow, B., & Blomquist, M. Young adults 10–15 years after severe reading disability. *Elementary School Journal*, 1965, *66*, 44–45.

Bandura, A. The stormy decade: Fact or fiction? *Psychology in the Schools*, 1964, *1*, 224–231.

Bandura, A. *Principles of behavior modification*. New York: Holt, Rinehart & Winston, 1969.

Barone, S. *General issues in elementary and secondary education* (Committee on Education and Labor, 95th Congress). Washington, D.C.: U.S. Government Printing Office, 1977.

Barsch, R. *The parent teacher partnership*. Arlington, Va.: Council for Exceptional Children, 1969.

Bartley v. Kremens, 402 F.Supp. 1039 (E.D.Pa. 1975).

Bateman, B. D. Educational implications of minimal brain dysfunction. *Reading Teacher*, 1974, *27*, 662–668.

Bauer, D. What research says about interest in learning. *Educational Leadership*, 1975, *33*, 100–104.

Bayh, B. *Our nation's schools—A report card: "A" in school violence and vandalism*. Preliminary report of the subcommittee to investigate juvenile delinquency. Washington, D.C.: U.S. Government Printing Office, 1975.

Beck, M. Childhood chemotherapy and later drug abuse. *American Journal of Psychiatry*, 1975, *132*, 436–438.

Berg, I. *Education and jobs: The great training robbery*. Boston, Mass.: Beacon Press, 1971.

Berman, A., & Siegel, A. *Delinquents are disabled: An innovative approach to the prevention and treatment of juvenile delinquency.* Final report of The Neuropsychology Diagnostic Laboratory at the Rhode Island Training Schools, 1974.

Bernard, L. L. *Instinct: A study in social psychology.* New York: Henry Holt, 1924.

Bhaerman, R. D. *Career education and basic academic achievement: A descriptive analysis of the research.* Washington, D.C.: U.S. Office of Education, U.S. Government Printing Office, 1977.

Bibace, R., & Hancock, K. Relationship between perceptual and conceptual cognitive process. *Journal of Learning Disabilities,* 1969, *2,* 17–29.

Birnbrauer, J., Wolf, M., Kidder, J., & Tague, C. Classroom behavior of retarded pupils with token reinforcement. *Journal of Experimental Child Psychology,* 1965, *2,* 119–135.

Blackburn, G. M. (Ed.). *Colloquium series on career education for handicapped adolescents.* West Lafayette, In.: Purdue University, 1976.

Blauat, H., & Flocco, W. A survey of a workable drug abuse program. *Phi Delta Kappan,* 1971, *52,* 532–533.

Block, J. H. (Ed.). *Mastery learning: Theory and practice.* New York: Holt, Rinehart & Winston, 1971.

Bloom, B. S. Individual differences in school achievement: A vanishing point. In L. J. Rubin (Ed.), *Facts and feelings in the classroom.* New York: Viking, 1973.

Bloomer, R., & Ducharme, R. A model instructional program for the emotionally disturbed, learning disabled child. In B. T. Saunders (Ed.), *Approaches with emotionally disturbed children.* Hicksville, N.Y.: Exposition Press, 1974.

Blum, R. H. *Horatio Alger's children.* London: Jossey-Bass, 1972.

Borland, B., & Heckman, A. Hyperactive boys and their brothers: A 25 year follow-up study. *Archives of General Psychiatry,* 1976, *33,* 669–675.

Bowe, A. *Special education curriculum for junior and senior high school.* Syracuse, New York: Syracuse City School District, 1970.

Bower, E. M. The modification, mediation, and utilization of stress during the school years. *American Journal of Orthopsychiatry,* 1964, *34,* 667–674.

Bower, E. M. Primary prevention of mental and emotional disorders: A frame of reference. In H. F. Clarizio (Ed.), *Mental health and the educative process.* Chicago: Rand McNally, 1969.

Bower, E. M. Mental health. In R. Ebel (Ed.), *Encyclopedia of educational research* (4th ed.). New York: Macmillan, 1970, 811–828.

Bower, E. M., & Lambert, N. M. *Bower's two-step process for identifying emotionally handicapped pupils.* Princeton, N.J.: Educational Testing Services, 1961.

Brantner, J. A. *Videotape on drug use and abuse.* Minneapolis: University of Minnesota, 1974.

Braucht, G. H., Brakarsh, D., Follingstad, D., & Berry, K. L. Deviant drug use in adolescence. *Psychological Bulletin*, 1973, *79*, 92–106.

Brecher, E. M. *Licit and illicit drugs.* Boston: Little, Brown, 1972.

Bremer, J., & van Moschzisker, M. *The school without walls.* New York: Holt, Rinehart & Winston, 1971.

Briskin, A. *Rosemount Drug Education Program.* Unpublished manuscript, Department of Counseling and Student Personnel Psychology, University of Minnesota, 1974.

Broden, M., Hall, R. V., & Mitts, B. The effect of self-recording on the classroom behavior of two eighth-grade students. *Journal of Applied Behavior Analysis*, 1971, *2*, 191–199.

Brolin, D. Programming retarded in career education. In J. Girard (Ed.), *Perspectives: Career education.* Lawrence, Kans.: Department of Special Education, University of Kansas, 1975.

Brolin, D. *Vocational preparation of retarded citizens.* Columbus, Ohio: Charles E. Merrill, 1976.

Brolin, D. E. Career development: A national priority. *Education and Training of the Mentally Retarded*, 1977, *12*, 154–155.

Brolin, D. (Ed.). *Life centered career education: A competency based approach.* Reston, Va.: Council for Exceptional Children, 1978.

Brolin, D., Cegelka, P., Jackson, S., & Wrobel, C. *Official policy of The Council for Exceptional Children as legislated by the 1978 CEC Delegate Assembly.* Reston, Va.: Council for Exceptional Children, 1977.

Brolin, D., & Thomas, B. *Preparing teachers of secondary level educable mentally retarded: A new model.* Department of Rehabilitation and Manpower Services: University of Wisconsin-Stout, 1972.

Bronfenbrenner, U. The origins of alienation. *Scientific American*, 1974, *231*, 51–53.

Brown v. Board of Education, 347 U.S. 483 (1954).

Brown, G. Personal communication, 1978.

Brown, L. L., & Hammill, D. D. *Behavior Rating Profile: An ecological approach.* Austin, Tex.: Pro-Ed, 1978.

Brown, L., Nietupski, J., & Hamre-Nietupski, S. The criterion of ultimate functioning and public school services for severely handicapped students. In M. A. Thomas (Ed.), *Hey, don't forget about me! New directions for screening the severely handicapped.* Reston, Va.: Council for Exceptional Children, 1976.

Brown, R. I. Cognitive changes in the adolescent slow learner. *Journal of Child Psychology and Psychiatry*, 1972, *13*, 183–193.

Brown, V. L. Curriculum development resources. In L. Mann, L. Goodman,

& J. L. Wiederholt (Eds.), *Teaching the learning-disabled adolescent* Boston: Houghton Mifflin, 1978.

Brown, V., Hammill, D. D., & Wiederholt, J. L. *Test of Applied Reading Comprehension.* Austin, Tex.: Pro-Ed, 1978.

Brownstone, J. E., & Dye, C. J. *Communication workshop for parents of adolescents.* Champaign, Ill.: Research Press, 1973.

Brutten, M., Richardson, S. O., & Mangel, C. *Something's wrong with my child.* New York: Harcourt Brace Jovanovich, 1973.

Bryan, T. H. Learning disabled children's comprehension of nonverbal communication. *Journal of Learning Disabilities,* 1977, *10,* 501–506.

Bryan, T. H., & Bryan, J. H. *Understanding learning disabilities.* Port Washington, N.Y.: Alfred Publishing, 1975.

Bryant, N. D., & McLoughlin, J. A. Subject variables: Definition, incidence, characteristics, and correlates. In N. D. Bryant & C. E. Kass (Eds.), *Final report: Leadership training institute in learning disabilities* (Vol. 1). Tucson, Ariz.: University of Arizona, Department of Special Education, 1972.

Bullock, L. J., & Brown, R. K. *Research bulletin: Educational provisions for emotionally disturbed children: A status report.* Florida Educational Research and Development Council, 1972, *8,* 1.

Bullock, L. M., & Whelan, R. J. Competencies needed by teachers of the emotionally disturbed and socially maladjusted. *Exceptional Children,* 1971, *37,* 485–489.

Bureau of Education for the Handicapped. *Selected career education programs for the handicapped.* Washington, D.C.: U.S. Government Printing Office, 1973.

Burke, N. S., & Simons, A. Factors which precipitate dropouts and delinquency. *Federal Probation,* 1965, *29,* 28–32.

Bursuk, L. Z. *Sensory mode of lesson presentation as a factor in the reading comprehension improvement of adolescent retarded readers.* Paper presented at the annual convention of the American Educational Research Association, New York, New York, February 1971. (ERIC Document Reproduction Service No. ED 047 435)

Campbell, S. B. Mother-child interaction: A comparison of hyperactive, learning disabled, and normal boys. *American Journal of Orthopsychiatry,* 1975, *45,* 51–74.

Cantrell, R. P., & Cantrell, M. L. *A taxonomic investigation of children's problems and correlated intervention strategies: An empirical approach to classification.* Unpublished manuscript, 1974. (Available from Prevention-Intervention Project, Metro-Davidson County Public Schools Nashville, TN).

Carkhuff, R. R. *Helping and human relations* (Volumes 1 & 2). New York: Holt, Rinehart & Winston, 1969.

Carkhuff, R. R. Helping and human relations: A brief guide for training lay helpers. *Journal of Research and Development in Education*, 1971, *4*, 17–27.

Carman, R. S. Internal-external locus of control, alcohol use and adjustment among high school students in rural communities. *Journal of Community Psychiatry*, 1974, *2*, 120–133.

Carnegie Corporation's Council on Children. *All our children*. New York: Harcourt Brace Jovanovich, 1977.

Carney, R. E. *Coronado California drug abuse prevention program: Risk taking and drug abuse* (ESEA Title III Project No. 68.5380). Coronado, Calif.: Coronado Unified School District, June 1971.

Carr, R. J. *Analytical sociology*. New York: Harper & Row, 1955.

Cautela, J. R. Covert sensitization. *Psychological Reports*, 1967, *20*, 459–468.

Cawley, J. F. An instructional design in mathematics. In L. Mann, L. Goodman, & J. L. Wiederholt (Eds.), *Teaching the learning-disabled adolescent*. Boston: Houghton Mifflin, 1978.

Cegelka, P. T. Exemplary projects and programs for the career development of retarded individuals. *Education and Training of the Mentally Retarded*, 1977, *12*, 161–162.

Cegelka, P. T., & Phillips, M. W. Individualized education programming at the secondary level. *Teaching Exceptional Children*, 1978, *10*, 84–87.

Center for New Schools. Strengthening alternative high schools. *Harvard Educational Review*, 1972, *42*, 313–350.

Chaffin, J., Davison, R., Regan, C., & Spellman, C. Two follow-up studies of former mentally retarded students from a Kansas work-study project. *Exceptional Children*, 1971, *37*, 733–738.

Charles, C. M. *Individualizing instruction*. St. Louis, Mo.: Mosby, 1976.

Chelser, M., & Fox, R. *Role playing in the classroom*. Ann Arbor, Mich.: University of Michigan, 1964.

Cheney, C., & Morse, W. C. Psychodynamic interventions in emotional disturbance. In W. C. Rhodes & M. L. Tracy (Eds.), *A study of child variance: Volume 2: Interventions*. Ann Arbor, Mich.: University of Michigan, 1972.

Children's Defense Fund. *Children out of school in America*. Cambridge, Mass.: Washington Research Project, 1974.

Clarizio, H., & McCoy, G. F. *Behavior disorders in children*. New York: Thomas Y. Crowell, 1976.

Clark, G., & Oliverson, B. Education of secondary personnel: Assumptions and preliminary data. *Exceptional Children*, 1973, *39*, 41–46.

Clark, G. M. Mainstreaming for the secondary educable retarded. Is it defensible? *Focus on Exceptional Children*, 1975, *7*, 1–5.

Clark, G. M., & Evans, R. N. *Preparing vocational and special education personnel to work with special needs students: A state of the art.* Paper presented at the National Workshop on Special Needs Vocational Teacher Education, University of Illinois, Champaign, Ill., January 1976.

Clark, L. H., Klein, R. L., & Burks, J. B. *The American secondary school curriculum* (2nd ed.). New York: Macmillan, 1972.

Clark, R. E., & Sieber, J. *Warranted uncertainty and drug use: A follow-up study.* Paper presented at the annual meeting of the American Educational Research Association, New York, 1977.

Clements, J. E., & Alexander, R. N. Parent training: Bringing it all back home. *Focus on Exceptional Children,* 1975, *7* (5), 1–12.

Clements, S. D. *Minimal brain dysfunction in children* (NINDS Monograph No. 3, U. S. Public Health Service Publication No. 1415). Washington, D.C.: U.S. Government Printing Office, 1966.

Cofer, C. N., & Appley, M. H. *Motivation: Theory and research.* New York: John Wiley, 1964.

Cohen, A. Y. The journey beyond trips: Alternatives to drugs. *Journal of Psychedelic Drugs,* 1971, *3,* 2.

Cohen, H. L., Filipczak, J. A. & Bis, J. S. CASE project. In J. Schlien (Ed.), *Research in Psychotherapy* (Vol. 3). Washington, D.C.: American Psychological Association, 1968, 34–41.

Cohen, J. S. Employer attitudes toward hiring mentally retarded individuals. *American Journal of Mental Deficiency,* 1963, *67,* 705–712.

Cohen, S. A. Studies of visual perception and reading in disadvantaged children. *Journal of Learning Disabilities,* 1969, *2,* 498–507.

Cohen, S. I., Keyworth, J. M., Kleiner, R. I., & Brown, W. L. Effective behavior change at the Anne Arundel Learning Center through three different minimum contact interventions. In R. Ulrich, T. Stacknik, & Mabry (Eds.), *Control of Human Behavior* (Vol. III). New York: Scott Foresman, 1974.

Cole, M., & Black, S. *Checking it out: Some lower east side kids discover the rest of America.* New York: Dial Press, 1971.

Colella, H. V. Career development center: A modified high school for the handicapped. *Teaching Exceptional Children,* 1973, *5,* 110–118.

Coleman, J. C. *Abnormal psychology and modern life* (5th ed.). Glenview, Ill.: Scott, Foresman, 1976.

Coleman, J. S., et al. *Equality of educational opportunity.* Washington, D.C.: U.S. Government Printing Office, 1966.

Coleman, J. S. *Youth: Transition to adulthood.* Chicago: University of Chicago Press, 1974.

Coles, R., & Piers, M. *Wages of neglect: New solutions for children of the poor.* Chicago: Quadrangle, 1969.

Comptroller General's Report to Congress. *Training educators for the handicapped: A need to redirect federal programs.* (HRD–76–77). Office of Education, Department of Health, Education, and Welfare, 1976.

Congressional Budget Office. *The teenage unemployment problem: What are the options?* Washington, D.C.: U.S. Government Printing Office, 1976.

Connolly, C. Social and emotional factors in learning disabilities. In H. R. Myklebust (Ed.), *Progress in learning disabilities* (Vol. 2). New York: Grune & Stratton, 1971.

Council for Exceptional Children. *Teacher idea exchange: A potpourri of helpful hints.* Reston, Va.: Council for Exceptional Children, 1977.

Covington, M. V., Crutchfield, R., Davies, L., & Olton, R. *The productive thinking program.* Columbus, Ohio: Charles E. Merrill, 1972.

Cox, In the matter of, No. H–4721–75 (N.Y.Fam. Ct., Queens Co., April 8, 1976).

Cox, S. The learning disabled adult. *Academic Therapy,* 1977, *13,* 79–86.

Cronbach, L. J. Beyond the two disciplines of scientific psychology. *American Psychologist,* 1975, *30,* 116–127.

Curti, M. *The social ideas of American educators.* Paterson, N.J.: Littlefield, Adams, 1959.

D'Alonzo, B. J. Trends and issues in career education for the mentally retarded. *Education and Training of the Mentally Retarded,* 1977, *12,* 156–158.

Dauw, E. G. Individual instruction for potential dropouts. *NASSP Bulletin,* 1970, *54,* 9–21.

Davidson, W. *Kentfields rehabilitation program: An alternative to institutionalization.* Kentsfield, Mich.: Kentsfield Institution, 1970.

Davis, E. D. *Focus on secondary education: An introduction to principles and practices.* Glenview, Ill.: Scott, Foresman, 1966.

DeCharms, R. *Personal causation.* New York: Academic Press, 1969.

DeCharms, R. *Enhancing motivation.* New York: Halstead Press, 1976.

deHirsch, K. Two categories of learning difficulties in adolescents. *American Journal of Orthopsychiatry,* 1963, *33,* 87–91.

Dellefield, C. Wanted: A *working* definition of career education. *Educational Leadership,* 1974, *31,* 11.

Dennison, G. *The lives of children: The story of the First Street School.* New York: Random House, 1969.

Deshler, D. D. & Alley, G. R. Assessment of learning disabled adolescents. Unpublished manuscript, University of Kansas, 1975.

Deshler, D. D. New research institutes for the study of learning disabilities. *Learning Disability Quarterly,* 1978, *1,* 68. (a)

Deshler, D. D. Psychoeducational aspects of learning disabled adolescents.

In L. Mann, L. Goodman, & J. L. Wiederholt (Eds.), *Teaching the learning-disabled adolescent.* Boston: Houghton Mifflin, 1978. (b)

DeWitt, F. B. Tear off the label: The older student and SLD. *Academic Therapy,* 1977, *13,* 69–78.

Diggory, J. C. *Self-evaluation: Concepts and studies.* New York: Wiley, 1966.

Dinkmeyer, D., & McKay, G. D. *STEP: Systematic training in effective parenting.* Circle Pines, Minn.: American Guidance Service, 1976.

DiTullio, W. M. Program planning for children with emotional disturbance and multiple disabilities. In B. T. Saunders (Ed.), *Approaches with emotionally disturbed children.* Hicksville, N.Y.: Exposition Press, 1974.

Division on Career Development. *Newsletter.* 1977, *1* (1), cover page.

Divoky, D. (Ed.). *How old will you be in 1984?* New York: Avon, 1969.

Dohner, V. A. Alternatives to drugs—A new approach to drug education. *Journal of Drug Education,* 1972, *2,* 3–22.

Douglass, H. R. An effective junior high school program for reducing the number of dropouts. *Contemporary Education,* 1969, *41,* 34–37.

Douvan, E., & Adelson, J. *The adolescent experience.* New York: Wiley, 1966.

Dreikurs, R. *Children: The challenge.* New York: Hawthorn, 1964.

Dreikurs, R., Grunwald, B., & Pepper, F. *Maintaining sanity in the classroom: Illustrated teaching techniques.* New York: Harper & Row, 1971.

Dunn, L. M. Special education for the mildly retarded: Is much of it justifiable? *Exceptional Children,* 1968, *35,* 5–22.

Dunn, L. M. An overview. In L. M. Dunn (Ed.), *Exceptional children in the schools: Special education in transition* (2nd ed.). New York: Holt, Rinehart & Winston, 1973.

Durkin, D. Some questions about questionable instructional materials. *The Reading Teacher,* 1974, *8,* 13–21.

Edgerton, R. B., Eyman, R. K., & Silverstein, A. B. Mental retardation system. In N. Hobbs (Ed.), *Issues in the classification of children* (Vol. 2). San Francisco: Jossey-Bass, 1975, pp. 62–87.

The education of adolescents: The final report & recommendations of the national panel on high school & adolescent education. (HEW Publication No. [OE] 76-00004). Washington, D.C.: U.S. Dept. of Health, Education & Welfare, 1976.

Eisenberg, L. The clinical use of stimulant drugs in children. *Pediatrics,* 1972, *49,* 709–715.

Ellis, A. *Emotional education.* New York: Julian, 1972.

Engelmann, S. *Preventing failure in the primary grades.* Chicago: Science Research Associates, 1969.

Epstein, M., Cullinan, D., & Sabatino, D.A. State definitions of behavior disorders. *Journal of Special Education,* 1977, *11,* 417–425.

Epstein, M. H., Hallahan, D. P., & Kauffman, J. M. Implications of the reflectivity-impulsivity dimension for special education. *Journal of Special Education,* 1975, *9,* 11–25.

Erikson, E. H. *Identity and the life cycle: Psychological issues.* New York: International Universities Press, 1959.

Erikson, E. H. *Childhood and society.* New York: W. W. Norton, 1950, (2nd ed.) 1963.

Erikson, E. H. *The challenge of youth.* New York: Doubleday, 1965.

Etzioni, H. *Modern organization.* Englewood Cliffs, N.J.: Prentice-Hall, 1964.

Evans, R., Hoyt, K., & Mangum, G. *Career education in the middle/junior high school.* Salt Lake City, Utah: Olympus Publishing, 1973.

Fagan, S. A. *Organizational manual for a school-based teacher internship program in supplementary education.* Rockville, Md.: Montgomery County Public Schools, 1977. (a)

Fagen, S. A. Minimizing emotional wear and tear through adaptive frustration management. *Proceedings of a Conference on Preparing Teachers to Foster Personal Growth in Emotionally Disturbed Students, Advanced Institute for Trainers of Teachers for Seriously Emotionally Disturbed Children.* University of Minnesota, May 29–31, 1977, 67–78. (b)

Fagen, S. A., & Guedalia, L. J. *Individual and group counseling: A compentency-based manual for in-service training.* Washington, D.C.: Psychoeducational Resources, 1977.

Fagan, S. A., & Hill, J. M. *Behavior management: A compentency-based manual for in-service training.* Washington, D.C.: Psychoeducational Resources, 1977.

Fagen, S. A., & Long, N. J. A psychoeducational curriculum for the prevention of behavioral and learning problems: Teaching self-control. In N. J. Long, W. C. Morse, & R. G. Newman (Eds.), *Conflict in the classroom: The education of children with problems* (3rd ed.). Belmont, Calif.: Wadsworth, 1976. (a)

Fagen, S. A., & Long, N. J. Teaching children self-control: A new responsibility for teachers. *Focus on Exceptional Children,* 1976, *7* (8), 1–12. (b)

Fagen, S. A., Long, N. J., & Stevens, D. J. *Teaching children self-control.* Columbus, Ohio: Charles E. Merrill, 1975.

Fantini, M. D. *Public schools of choice.* New York: Simon & Schuster, 1973.

Fedder, R. *Guidance in the homeroom.* New York: Teachers College Press, 1967.

Felixbrod, J. J., & O'Leary, K. D. Effects of reinforcement on children's academic behavior as a function of self-determined and externally imposed contingencies. *Journal of Applied Behavior Analysis*, 1973, *6*, 241–250.

Felker, D. W. *Building positive self-concepts*. Minneapolis, Minn.: Burgess, 1974.

Fernald, G. *Remedial techniques in basic school subjects*. New York: McGraw-Hill, 1943.

Ferreira, A. *Prenatal environment*. Springfield, Ill.: Charles C Thomas, 1970.

Fialkowski v. *Shapp*, 405 F.Supp. 946 (E.D.Pa. 1975).

Frederick L. v. *Thomas*, 408 F.Supp. 832 (E.D.Pa. 1976).

Frederiksen, L. W., & Frederiksen, C. B. Teacher-determined and self-determined token reinforcement in a special education classroom. *Behavior Therapy*, 1975, *6*, 310–314.

Freud, A. Adolescence as a developmental disturbance. In G. Caplan & S. Lebovici (Eds.), *Adolescence: Psychosocial perspectives*. New York: Basic Books, 1969.

Friedenberg, E. Is the pigeon always right? *Ramparts*, December 1974/ January 1975, *13* (5), 55–60.

Friedman, R., Archer, M., & Lordeman, A. *Five years in the public schools: A summary of PREP findings*. Paper presented at the annual meeting of the American Psychological Association, Washington, D.C., September 1976.

Gallagher, P. A. A synthesis of classroom scheduling techniques for emotionally disturbed children. In E. L. Meyen, G. A. Vergason, & R. J. Whelan (Eds.), *Strategies for teaching exceptional children*. Denver, Col.: Love, 1972.

Gartner, A., Kohler, M., & Riessman, F. *Children teach children: Learning by teaching*. New York: Harper & Row, 1971.

Gaudry, E., & Spielberger, C. *Anxiety and educational achievement*. New York: Wiley, 1971.

Gearheart, B. R. *Teaching the learning disabled: A combined task-process approach*. St. Louis, Mo.: Mosby, 1976.

Gearheart, B. R., & Weishahn, M. W. *The handicapped child in the regular classroom*. St. Louis, Mo.: Mosby, 1976.

Geis, G., Morgan, E. L., Schor, M., Bullington, B., & Munns, J. G. *Addicts in the classroom: The impact of an experimental narcotics program on junior high school students*. Los Angeles: California State College, Economic Youth Research Institute, March 1969.

Gersten, J., Langher, T., Eisenberg, J., Simcha-Fagen, O., & McCarthy, E. Stability and change in types of behavior disturbance of children and adolescents. *Journal of Abnormal Child Psychology*, 1976, *4*, 111–127.

Gesell, A., Ilg, F. L., & Ames, L. B. *Youth: The years from ten to sixteen*. New York: Harper, 1956.

Getman, G. M. The visualmotor complex in the acquisition of learning skills. In J. Hellmuth (Ed.), *Learning disorders* (Vol. 1). Seattle, Wash.: Special Child Publications, 1965.

Getzels, J. W., Lipham, J. M., & Campbell, R. F. *Educational administration as a social process.* New York: Harper & Row, 1968.

Giffin, M. How does he feel? In E. Schloss (Ed.), *The educator's enigma: The adolescent with learning disabilities.* San Rafael, Calif.: Academic Therapy Publications, 1971.

Gillespie, P. H., & Sitko, M. C. Reading problems. In L. Mann, L. Goodman, & J. L. Wiederholt (Eds.), *Teaching the learning disabled adolescent.* Boston: Houghton Mifflin, 1978.

Ginott, H. G. *Between parent and teenager.* New York: Macmillan, 1969.

Girardeau, F. L., & Spradlin, J. E. Token rewards in cottage program. *Mental Retardation,* 1964, *2,* 345–351.

Glasser, W. *Schools without failure.* New York: Harper & Row, 1969.

Glasser, W. *Reality therapy.* New York: Harper & Row, 1965.

Glasser, W. A new look at discipline. *Learning,* 1974, *3,* 6–11.

Goffman, E. *Asylums.* New York: Anchor Books, 1961.

Gold, M. W. Task analysis of a complex assembly task by the retarded blind. *Exceptional Children,* 1976, *43,* 78–84.

Goldhammer, K., & Taylor, R. E. *Career education: Perspective and promise.* Columbus, Ohio: Charles E. Merrill, 1972.

Goldiamond, I. Toward a constitutional approach to social problems: Ethical and constitutional issues raised by applied behavior analysis. *Behaviorism,* 1974, *2,* 1–79.

Goodlad, J. *Behind the classroom door.* Belmont, Calif.: Wadsworth, 1970.

Goodlad, J. I., Fenstermacher, G. D., LaBelle, T. J., Rust, V. D., Skager, R., & Weinberg, C. *The conventional and the alternative in education.* Berkeley, Calif.: McCutchan, 1975.

Goodman, J. K. Preventing the causes of drug abuses. *Journal of Drug Education,* 1972, *2,* 263–268.

Goodman, K. Effective teachers of reading know language and children. *Elementary English,* 1974, *51,* 823–828.

Goodman, K. S., & Goodman, Y. M. *Learning to read is natural.* Paper presented at the Conference on Theory and Practice of Beginning Reading Instruction, Pittsburgh, April 1976.

Goodman, L. The efficacy of perceptual-motor training for orthopedically handicapped children. *Rehabilitation Literature,* 1973, *34,* 299–304.

Goodman, L. Educational programming: A survey of current practice. In L. Mann, L. Goodman, & J. L. Wiederholt (Eds.), *Teaching the learning-disabled adolescent.* Boston: Houghton Mifflin, 1978.

Goodman, L., & Mann, L. *Learning disabilities in the secondary school: Issues and practices.* New York: Grune & Stratton, 1976.

Goodman, L., Mann, L., & Proger, B. *Alternative methods for the assessment of modality strengths and weaknesses in kindergarten and first grade children: Implications for aptitude-treatment-interaction research.* Montgomery County, Pa.: Unpublished manuscript, 1978.

Goodman, L., & Wiederholt, J. L. Predicting reading achievement in disadvantaged children. *Psychology in the Schools,* 1973, *4,* 181–184.

Goodman, Y. M., & Burke, C. L. *Reading miscue inventory manual: Procedure for diagnosis and evaluation.* New York: Macmillan, 1972.

Gordon, S. Reversing a negative self-image. In L. E. Anderson (Ed.), *Helping the adolescent with the hidden handicap.* Belmont, Calif.: Fearon Publishers/Lear Siegler, 1970.

Gordon, T. *Parent effectiveness training.* New York: Wyden, 1971.

Gorham, K. A lost generation of parents. *Exceptional Children,* 1975, *42,* 521–525.

Gorman, A. H. *Teachers and learners: The interactive process in education.* Boston: Allyn & Bacon, 1974.

Gottman, J., & McFall, R. Self-monitoring effects in a program for potential high school dropouts. *Journal of Consulting and Clinical Psychology,* 1972, *39,* 273–281.

Gray, J. *The teacher's survival guide.* Belmont, Calif.: Fearon, 1974.

Green, M., Blake, B. F., & Zenhausern, R. Some implications of a survey of middle class adolescent marijuana users. *Proceedings of the 81st Annual Convention of the American Psychological Association,* 1973, *8,* 681–682.

Greene, M. F., & Ryan, O. *The school children: Growing up in the slums.* New York: Pantheon, 1965.

Gronlund, N. E. *Stating behavioral objectives for classroom instruction.* New York: Macmillan, 1970.

Grossman, H. *Nine rotten lousy kids.* New York: Holt, Rinehart & Winston, 1972.

Hairston v. Drosick, 423 F.Supp. 180 (S.D.W.Va. 1976).

Hall, G. S. *Adolescence: Its psychology and relations to physiology, anthropology, sociology, sex, crime, religion, and education.* New York: Appleton, 1904.

Hallahan, D. P., & Cruickshank, W. M. *Psychoeducational foundations of learning disabilities.* Englewood, N.J.: Prentice-Hall, 1973.

Hammill, D. D., & Bartel, N. R. *Teaching children with learning and behavior problems.* Boston, Mass.: Allyn & Bacon, 1975.

Hammill, D. D., Colarusso, R. P., & Wiederholt, J. L. Diagnostic value of the Frostig test: A factor analytic approach. *Journal of Special Education,* 1970, *4,* 279–282.

Hammill, D. D., Goodman, L., & Wiederholt, J. L. Visual-motor processes: Can we train them? *The Reading Teacher*, 1974, *27*, 469–481.

Hammill, D. D., Goodman, L., & Wiederholt, J. L. Use of the Frostig DTVP with economically disadvantaged children. *Journal of School Psychology*, 1971, *9*, 430–435.

Hammill, D. D., & Larsen, S. C. The effectiveness of psycholinguistic training. *Exceptional Children*, 1974, *41*, 5–15. (a)

Hammill, D. D., & Larsen, S. C. The relationship of selected auditory perceptual skills and reading ability. *Journal of Learning Disabilities*, 1974, *7*, 429–435. (b)

Hammill, D. D., & Wiederholt, J. L. Review of the Frostig visual perception test and the related training program. In L. Mann & D. A. Sabatino (Eds.), *The first review of special education* (Vol. 1). Philadelphia: Journal of Special Education Press, 1973.

Hansen, L. S. *An examination of the definition and concepts of career education.* Washington, D.C.: National Advisory Council for Career Education, 1977.

Haring, N. G., & Bateman, B. *Teaching the learning disabled child.* Englewood Cliffs, N.J.: Prentice-Hall, 1977.

Harman, D. Illiteracy: An overview. *Harvard Educational Review*, 1970, *40*, 226–243.

Harris, R. *I'm OK, you're OK.* New York: Harper & Row, 1967.

Harvey, J. Future trends in personnel preparation. *Exceptional Children*, 1976, *43*, 148–151.

Havighurst, R. J. *Human development and education.* New York: Longman, Green, 1953.

Havighurst, R. J. Social deviancy among youth: Types and significances. In W. W. Wattenberg (Ed.), *Social deviancy among youth* (Yearbook of the National Society for the Study of Education, Part 1). Chicago: University of Chicago Press, 1966.

Havighurst, R. J. *Developmental tasks and education.* New York: McKay, 1972.

Hawley, R., & Hawley, I. *A handbook of personal growth activities for classroom use.* Amherst, Mass.: Education Research Associates, 1972.

Hechinger, F. M. SAT scores: What happened to the best and the brightest? *Saturday Review/World*, February 9, 1974, p. 5.

Herndon, J. *How to survive in your native land.* New York: Simon & Schuster, 1971.

Herr, E. L. *Review and synthesis of foundations of career education.* (HEW Publication No. Inf–Ser–61). Columbus, Ohio: Center for Vocational and Technical Education, Ohio State University, 1972.

Herr, E. L. *The emerging history of career education: A summary view.* Washington, D.C.: National Advisory Council on Career Education, 1977.

Hewett, F. *The emotionally disturbed child in the classroom.* Boston, Mass.: Allyn & Bacon, 1968.

Hewett, F. M., & Forness, S. R. *Education of exceptional learners.* Boston: Allyn & Bacon, 1974.

Heyneman, S. P., Mintz, P. C., & Mann, A. J. *Toward interagency coordination: FY 76 federal research and development on adolescence, fourth annual report.* Washington, D.C.: Social Research Group, George Washington University, 1977.

Hobbs, N. Helping disturbed children: Psychological and ecological strategies. *American Psychologist,* 1966, *21,* 1105–1115.

Hobbs, N. The re-education of emotionally disturbed children. In E. M. Bower & W. G. Hollister (Eds.), *Behavioral science frontiers in education.* New York: Wiley, 1967.

Hobbs, N. Helping disturbed children: Psychological and ecological strategies. In H. Dupont (Ed.), *Educating emotionally disturbed children.* New York: Holt, Rinehart & Winston, 1969.

Hobbs, N. Nicholas Hobbs. In J. M. Kauffman & C. D. Lewis (Eds.), *Teaching children with behavior disorders: Personal perspectives.* Columbus, Ohio: Charles E. Merrill, 1974.

Hobbs, N. (Ed.). Issues in the classification of children (Vols. 1 & 2). San Francisco: Jossey-Bass, 1975. (a)

Hobbs, N. *The futures of children.* San Francisco: Jossey-Bass, 1975. (b)

Hogenson, D. L. Reading failure and juvenile delinquency. *Bulletin of the Orton Society,* 1974, *24,* 164–169.

Hollister, W. G. The concept of 'strens' in preventive interventions and ego-strength building in the schools. In N. Lambert (Ed.), The protection and promotion of mental health in schools. *Monographs of the U.S. Department of Health, Education, and Welfare,* 1965, No. 5.

Holt, J. *How children fail.* New York: Dell, 1964.

Holt, J. *The underachieving school.* New York: Dell, 1969.

Homans, G. C. *The human group.* New York: Harcourt, Brace, & World, 1959.

Homme, L. *How to use contingency contracting in the classroom.* Champaign, Ill.: Research Press, 1970.

Hoover, J. A rural program for emotionally handicapped students: Democracy in action. *Teaching Exceptional Children,* 1978, *10,* 30–33.

Horrocks, J. E. *The psychology of adolescence: Behavior and development* (3rd ed.). Boston: Houghton Mifflin, 1969.

Hosford, R. E., & Brown, S. D. Innovations in behavioral approaches to counseling. *Focus on Guidance,* 1975, *8* (2), 1–11.

Hoy, W. K. Pupil control ideology and organizational socialization: A further examination of the influence of experience on the beginning teacher. *The School Review*, 1968, *76*, 312–323.

Hoyt, K. B. *Career education and the business-labor industry community.* Paper presented at the National Apprenticeship and Training Directors Conference, Washington, D.C., June 10, 1975. (a)

Hoyt, K. B. Speech presented at the Conference on Research Needs Related to Career Education of the Handicapped, Princeton, N.J., January 17–19, 1975. (b)

Hoyt, K. B. *Career education for special populations. Monographs on career education.* Washington, D.C.: U.S. Office of Education, U.S. Government Printing Office, 1976.

Hoyt, K. B. According to Hoyt. *American Education*, 1977, *13*, 10–13. (a)

Hoyt, K. B. Refining the career education concept (Part II). *Monographs on Career Education.* Washington, D.C.: U.S. Government Printing Office, 1977. (b)

Hoyt, K. B. To look at education, work, life in a more personal way. In National School Boards Association, *Research Report: Career Education*, 1977. (c)

Hoyt, K. B., Evans, R. N., Mackin, E. F., & Mangum, G. L. *Career education: What it is & how to do it* (2nd ed.). Salt Lake City, Utah: Olympus Publishing, 1974.

Hungerford, R. H. DeProposo, C. J., & Rosenzweig, L. E. The nonacademic pupil. *A Philosophy of Occupational Education.* New York: Association for the New York City Teachers of Special Education, 1948.

Hutt, M. L., & Gibby, R. G. *The mentally retarded child: Development, education, and treatment* (3rd ed.). Boston: Allyn & Bacon, 1976.

Illich, I. *Deschooling society.* New York: Harper & Row, 1971.

Ingram, C. P. *Education of the slow-learning child.* Yonkers, N.Y.: World Book, 1935.

Ivey, A. *Microcounseling: Innovations in interviewing training.* Springfield, Ill.: Charles C Thomas, 1971.

Ivey, A., & Alschuler, A. (Eds.). Psychological education: A prime function of the counselor. *Personnel and Guidance Journal*, 1973, *51* (9).

Jackson, P. W. *Life in classrooms.* New York: Holt, Rinehart & Winston, 1968.

James, W. *Principles of psychology.* New York: Holt, 1890.

James, M., & Jongeward, D. *Born to win: Transactional analysis with Gestalt experiences.* Reading, Mass.: Addison-Wesley, 1973.

Jersild, A. T., Brook, J. S., & Brook, D. W. *The psychology of adolescence.* New York: MacMillan, 1978.

Jessor, R., Young, H. B., Young, E. B., & Tesi, G. Perceived opportunity, alienation, and drinking behavior among Italian and American youth. *Journal of Personality and Social Psychology*, 1970, *15*, 215–222.

J.L. & J.R. v. Parham, 412 F.Supp. 112 (M.D.Ga. 1976).

Johnson, D. W. *A theory of social effectiveness.* Unpublished paper, Psychological Foundations Department, University of Minnesota, 1974.

Johnson, D., & Myklebust, H. R. *Learning disabilities: Educational principles and practices.* New York: Grune & Stratton, 1967.

Johnson, L. V., & Bany, M. A. *Classroom management: Theory and skill training.* New York: Macmillan, 1970.

Johnson, D., & Johnson, F. *Joining together: Group therapy and group skills.* Englewood Cliffs, N.J.: Prentice-Hall, 1975.

Johnson, D. O., & Pearson, P. O. Skills management systems: A critique. *The Reading Teacher*, 1975, *28*, 757–764.

Johnston, L., & Bachman, J. Drug use has risen among young people. *Institute for Social Research Newsletter*, Summer 1976, *4*, 8.

Joint Commission on the Mental Health of Children. *Mental health: From infancy through adolescence.* New York: Harper & Row, 1973.

Jones, R. *Fantasy and feeling in education.* New York: New York University Press, 1968.

Josselyn, I. M. The adolescent today. In W. C. Sze (Ed.), *Human life cycle.* New York: Aronson, 1975.

Kanfer, F. H. The many facets of self-control. In R. B. Stuart (Ed.), *Behavioral self-management: Strategies, techniques and outcome.* New York: Bruner/Mazel, 1977.

Kanfer, F. H., & Goldstein, A. P. (Eds.). *Helping people change: A textbook of methods.* New York: Pergamon Press, 1975.

Kanner, L. Emotionally disturbed children: A historical review. *Child Development*, 1962, *33*, 97–102.

Kapfer, P. G., & Kapfer, M. B. (Eds.). *Learning packages in American education.* Englewood Cliffs, N.J.: Educational Technology Publications, 1973.

Kaplan, H. B., & Mergerowitz, J. H. Social and psychological correlates of drug abuse: A comparison of addict and non-addict populations from the perspective of self theory. *Social Science and Medicine*, 1970, *4*, 203–275.

Karoly, P. Behavioral self-management in children: Concepts, methods, issues and directions. In M. Hersen, R. M. Eisler, & P. M. Miller (Eds.), *Progress in behavior modification* (Vol. 5). New York: Academic Press, 1977.

Kauffman, J. M. *Characteristics of children's behavior disorders.* Columbus, Ohio: Charles E. Merrill, 1977.

Kaufman, L. M., & Wagner, B. R. Barb: A systematic treatment technology for temper control disorders. *Behavior Therapy*, 1972, *3*, 84–90.

Kaufman, M. J., Gottlieb, J., Agard, J. A., & Kukic, M. B. Mainstreaming: Toward an explication of the construct. *Focus on Exceptional Children,* 1975, *7*(3), 1–12.

Kazdin, A. E., & Bootzin, R. R. The token economy: An evaluative review. *Journal of Applied Behavior Analysis,* 1972, *5,* 343–372.

Kelly, E. W. School phobia: A review of theory and treatment. *Psychology in the Schools,* 1973, *10,* 33–41.

Kennedy, E. *Implementing career education: Procedures and techniques.* Unpublished manuscript, University of Kentucky, n.d.

Keogh, B. Hyperactivity and learning disorders: Review and speculation. *Exceptional Children,* 1971, 38, 101–110.

Keogh, B., & Sitko, M. (Eds.). From the editors. *Behavioral Disorders,* 1977, 2, 130–131.

Kiesler, C. A. *The psychology of commitment.* New York: Academic Press, 1971.

Kirk, S. A. *Educating exceptional children.* Geneva, Ill.: Houghton Mifflin, 1972.

Kirk, S. A., & Johnson, G. O. *Educating the retarded child.* Boston, Mass.: Houghton Mifflin, 1951.

Kline, C. L. The adolescents with learning problems: How long must they wait? *Journal of Learning Disabilities,* 1972, *5,* 262–284.

Kline, J. A. Evaluation of a multimedia drug education program. *Journal of Drug Education,* 1972, *2,* 229–239.

Knoblock, P. Open education for emotionally disturbed children. *Exceptional Children,* 1973, *39,* 358–365.

Knoblock, P., & Barnes, E. A model for an integrated program for disturbed and typical children. In W. M. S. Miesels (Ed.), *Open education and young children with special needs.* University Park Press, forthcoming.

Knoblock, P., Barnes, E., Apter, S., & Taylor, S. *Preparing humanistic teachers for troubled children.* Syracuse, N.Y.: Syracuse University, 1974.

Kohl, H. *36 children.* New York: World Publications, 1967.

Kohl, H. *On teaching.* New York: Shocken, 1976.

Kokaska, C., & Kolstoe, O. P. Special education's role in career education. *Journal of Career Education,* 1977, *3,* 4–18.

Kolstoe, O. P. The employment evaluation and training program. *American Journal of Mental Deficiency,* 1960, *65,* 17–31.

Kolstoe, O. P., & Shafter, A. J. Employability prediction for mentally retarded adults: A methodological note. *American Journal of Mental Deficiency,* 1961, *66,* 287.

Koppitz, E. M. *Children with learning disabilities.* New York: Grune & Stratton, 1971.

Kounin, J. S. *Discipline and group management in classrooms.* New York: Holt, Rinehart & Winston, 1970.

Kozol, J. How schools train children for political impotence. *Social Policy,* 1972, *3,* 16–22.

Krasner, L. *Assessment of token economy programs in psychiatric hospitals.* Paper presented at the Symposium on the Role of Learning in Psychotherapy, London, 1968.

Kronick, D. *What about me? The LD adolescent.* San Rafael, Calif.: Academic Therapy Publications, 1975.

Kronick, D. Learning from living: The pros and cons of labeling. *Academic Therapy,* 1977, *13,* 101–104.

Kroth, R. L. *Communicating with parents of exceptional children: Improving parent-teacher relationships.* Denver, Col.: Love, 1975.

Krumboltz, J. D., & Krumboltz, H. B. *Changing children's behavior.* Englewood Cliffs, N.J.: Prentice-Hall, 1972.

Kruse v. *Campbell,* No. C.A. 75–0622–R (E.D.Va. March 23, 1977).

Kunzelman, H. P. (Ed.). *Precision teaching.* Seattle, Wash.: Special Child, 1970.

Kvaraceus, W. C. Problems of early identification and prevention of delinquency. In W. W. Wattenberg (Ed.), *Social deviancy among youth* (Yearbook of the National Society for the Study of Education, Part 1). Chicago: University of Chicago Press, 1966.

Lake, T. (Ed.). *Career education: Exemplary programs for the handicapped.* Reston, Va.: The Council for Exceptional Children, 1974.

Lange, A. J., & Jakubowski, P. *Responsible assertive behavior: Cognitive/ behavioral procedures for trainers.* Champaign, Ill.: Research Press, 1976.

Larsen, S. The influence of teacher expectations on the school performance of handicapped children. *Focus on Exceptional Children,* 1975, *6* (8), 1–14.

Larsen, S., & Hammill, D. The relationship of selected visual perceptual abilities to school learning. *Journal of Special Education,* 1975, *7,* 281–291.

Laten, S., & Katz, G. *A theoretical model for assessment of adolescents: The ecological/behavioral approach.* Madison, Wisc.: Specialized Educational Services, Madison Public Schools, 1975.

Law center outlines legal issues in competency testing for the handicapped. *Education Daily,* February, 1978, pp. 3–4.

Law Enforcement Assistance Administration. *First comprehensive plan for federal juvenile delinquency programs.* Washington, D.C.: U.S. Government Printing Office, 1976.

Lawrence, T. M. (Ed.). Precision teaching. *Teaching Exceptional Children,* 1971, *3,* 106–160.

373

Lazarus, A., & Fay, A. *I can if I want to.* New York: Morrow, 1975.

Lefcourt, H. M. *Locus of control: Current trends in theory and research.* Hillsdale, N.J.: Lawrence Erlbaum Associates, 1976.

Lerner, J. W. *Children with learning disabilities: Theories, diagnosis, and teaching strategies* (2nd ed.). Boston: Houghton Mifflin, 1976.

Lerner, J. W. Instructional strategies: A classification schema. In L. Mann, L. Goodman, & J. L. Wiederholt (Eds.), *Teaching the learning-disabled adolescent.* Boston: Houghton Mifflin, 1978.

Lerner, J. W., & Evans, M. A. LD programs at the secondary level: A survey. *Academic Therapy,* 1977, *13,* 7–19.

Leshan, E. *Conspiracy against childhood.* New York: Atheneum, 1967.

Lipe, D., & Jung, S. Manipulating incentives to enhance school learning. *Review of Educational Research,* 1971, *41,* 249–280.

Long, N. J. Helping children cope with feelings. *Childhood Education,* 1969, *45,* 367–372.

Long, N. J., Morse, W. C., & Newman, R. G. (Eds.). *Conflict in the classroom* (3rd ed.). Belmont, Calif.: Wadsworth, 1976.

Long, N. J., & Newman, R. G. Managing surface behavior of children in school. In N. J. Long, W. C. Morse, & R. G. Newman (Eds.), *Conflict in the classroom* (2nd ed.). Belmont, Calif.: Wadsworth, 1971. (a)

Long, N. J., & Newman, R. G. The teacher and his mental health. In N. J. Long, W. C. Morse, & R. G. Newman (Eds.), *Conflict in the classroom* (2nd ed.). Belmont, Calif.: Wadsworth, 1971. (b)

Loufer, M. W. Long-term management and some follow-up findings on the use of drugs with minimal cerebral syndromes. *Journal of Learning Disabilities,* 1971, *4,* 519–522.

Lovitt, T. C. Applied behavior analysis and learning disabilities, Part I: Characteristics of ABA, general recommendations, and methodological limitations. *Journal of Learning Disabilities,* 1975, *8,* 432–443. (a)

Lovitt, T. C. Applied behavior analysis and learning disabilities, Part II: Specific research recommendations and suggestions for practitioners. *Journal of Learning Disabilities,* 1975, *8,* 504–518. (b)

Lovitt, T. C., & Smith, J. O. Effects of instructions on an individual's verbal behavior. *Exceptional Children,* 1972, *38,* 685–693.

Lyon, H. C. *Learning to feel—Feeling to learn.* Columbus, Ohio: Charles E. Merrill, 1971.

Lyman, H. H. *Library materials in service to the adult new reader.* Chicago: American Library Association, 1973.

MacCulloch, M. J., Williams, C., & Birtles, C. J. The successful application of aversion therapy to an adolescent exhibitionist. *Journal of Behavior Therapy and Experimental Psychiatry,* 1971, *2,* 61–66.

MacDonald, W. S. *Battle in the classroom: Innovations in classroom techniques.* Scranton, Pa.: Intext Educational, 1971.

MacLeod, A. *Growing up in America: A background to contemporary drug abuse.* (HEW Publication No. [OE]73–1004). Washington, D.C.: National Institute of Mental Health, 1973.

MacMillan, D. L. *Mental retardation in school and society.* Boston: Little, Brown, 1977.

MacMillan, D. L., & Semmel, M. I. Evaluation of mainstream programs. *Focus on Exceptional Children,* 1977, *9,* 1–14.

Madsen, C. H., & Madsen, C. K. *Teaching discipline: A positive approach for education development.* Boston: Allyn & Bacon, 1974.

Mahler, C. A framework for group counseling. In G. Gazda (Ed.), *Theories and methods of group counseling in the schools.* Springfield, Ill.: Charles C Thomas, 1969.

Mahoney, M. J., & Thoresen, C. E. (Eds.). *Self-control: Power to the person.* Monterey, Calif.: Brooks-Cole, 1974.

Mann, L. Perceptual training: Misdirections and redirections. *American Journal of Orthopsychiatry,* 1970, *40,* 30–38.

Mann, L., & Phillips, W. Fractional practices in special education. *Exceptional Children,* 1967, *33,* 311–317.

Mann, P., & Suiter, P. *Handbook in diagnostic teaching: A learning approach.* Boston: Allyn & Bacon, 1974.

Mannheim, K. *Ideology and utopia.* Chicago: Harcourt, Brace, 1960.

Marland, S. *Career education now.* Speech presented before the annual convention of The National Association of Secondary School Principals, Houston, Texas, 1971.

Marland, S. P. *Career education: A proposal for return.* New York: McGraw-Hill, 1974.

Marland, S. P. *Career education update.* Washington, D.C.: National Advisory Council for Career Education, 1976.

Martin, E. W. Individualism and behaviorism as future trends in educating handicapped children. *Exceptional Children,* 1972, *38,* 517–525.

Martin, E. W. New public priorities: Education of handicapped children. *Compact,* August, 1971, pp. 523–524.

Martin, R., & Lauridsen, D. *Developing student discipline and motivation* Champaign, Ill.: Research Press, 1974.

Maslow, A. H. Some educational implications of the humanistic psychologies. *Harvard Educational Review,* 1968, *38,* 385–396.

Maslow, A. *Motivation and personality.* New York: Harper & Row, 1954, (2nd ed.), 1970.

Masters, R., & Houston, J. *Mind games.* New York: Dell, 1972.

Masterson, J. F. The symptomatic adolescent five years later: He didn't grow out of it. *American Journal of Psychiatry,* 1967, *123,* 1338–1345.

Mattie T. v. Holladay, Civil No. DC–75–31–5 (N.D.Miss. Aug. 4, 1977).

Mauser, A. J. Learning disabilities and delinquent youth. *Academic Therapy,* 1974, *9,* 389–402.

McCandless, B. R. *Adolescents: Behavior and development.* Hinsdale, Ill.: Dryden Press, 1970.

McIntosh, D., & Dunn, L. Children with specific learning disabilities. In L. Dunn (Ed.), *Exceptional children in the schools.* New York: Holt, Rinehart & Winston, 1973.

McKee, J. M. *Experimental manpower laboratory for corrections: Phase III final report.* Montgomery, Alabama: Rehabilitation Research Foundation, 1973.

McPartland, J., & McDill, E. *Research on crime in the schools.* Paper presented at the annual meeting of the American Educational Research Association, San Francisco, 1976.

Meacham, M. L., & Wiesen, A. E. *Changing classroom behavior: A manual for precision teaching.* Scranton, Pa.: International Textbook, 1969.

Meichenbaum, D. H., Bowers, K. S., & Ross, R. R. Modification of classroom behavior of institutionalized female adolescent offenders. *Behavior Research and Therapy,* 1968, *6,* 343–353.

Meisels, S. J. Open education and the integration of children with special needs. In Guralnick, J. J. (Ed), *Early intervention and the integration of handicapped and non-handicapped children.* Baltimore: University Park Press, forthcoming.

Metz, A. S. *Number of pupils with handicaps in local public schools, Spring, 1970.* (HEW Publication No. [OE] 11107). Washington, D.C.: U.S. Government Printing Office, 1973. (a)

Metz, A. S. *Statistics on education of the handicapped in local public school.* Washington, D.C.: U.S. Government Printing Office, 1973. (b)

Meyen, E. L., & Deshler, D. D. The Kansas Research Institute in Learning Disabilities. *Learning Disability Quarterly,* 1978, *1,* 73–74.

Miller, L., Barrett, C., & Hampe, E. Phobias of childhood in a prescientific era. In A. Davis (Ed.), *Child personality and psychopathology.* New York: Wiley, 1974.

Miller, S. R. *Secondary assessment and programming.* Unpublished paper, Northern Illinois University, 1975.

Miller, S. R., Lotsof, A., & Miller, T. A. *Survey of needs and direction in secondary programs.* Unpublished paper, Northern Illinois University, 1976.

Miller, T. L., & Switzky, H. N. The least restrictive alternative: Implications for service providers. *Journal of Special Education,* 1978, *12,* 123–131.

Millon, T., & Millon, R. *Abnormal behavior and personality.* Philadelphia: W. B. Saunders, 1974.

Mills v. Board of Education of the District of Columbia, 348 F. Supp. 866 (D.D.C., 1972).

Minskoff, E. H. Creating and evaluating remediation for the learning disabled. In E. L. Meyen, G. A. Vergason, & R. J. Whelan (Eds.), *Alternatives for teaching exceptional children.* Denver, Col.: Love, 1975.

Montgomery County Public Schools. *Student rights/responsibilities with staff implementation guidelines.* Rockville, Md.: Montgomery County Public Schools, 1977.

Moran, M. R. Nine steps to the diagnostic prescriptive process in the classroom. *Focus on Exceptional Children,* 1975, 6 (9), 1–14.

Morse, W. C. Worksheet on life space interviewing for teachers. In N. J. Long, W. C. Morse, & R. G. Newman (Eds.), *Conflict in the classroom* (2nd ed.). Belmont Calif.: Wadsworth, 1971.

Morse, W. C. The helping teacher/crisis teacher concept. *Focus on Exceptional Children,* 1976, 8 (4), 1–11.

Mosher, R., & Sprinthall, M. Psychological education: A means to promote personal development during adolescence. *Counseling Psychologist,* 1971, 2, 3–82.

Mulligan, W. A study of dyslexia and delinquency. *Academic Therapy,* 1969, 4, 177–187.

Murray, H. A., Barrett, W. G., & Homburger, E. *Explorations in personality.* New York: Oxford University Press, 1938.

Myers, P., & Hammill, D. *Methods for learning disorders.* New York: Wiley, 1976.

Myklebust, H. R. *Development and disorders of written language: Studies of normal and exceptional children.* New York: Grune & Stratton, 1973.

National Advisory Committee on Dyslexia and Related Reading Disorders. *Reading disorders in the United States.* Washington, D.C.: U.S. Department of Health, Education, & Welfare, U.S. Government Printing Office, August 1969.

National Alternative Schools Program. *A national directory of public alternative schools.* Amherst, Mass.: University of Massachusetts, 1974.

National Assessment of Educational Progress. *What students know and can do: Profiles of three age groups.* Denver: Education Commission of the States, 1975.

National Association of Vocational Education Special Needs Personnel. *Program of work.* 1976-77.

National Center for Health Statistics. *Monthly vital statistics report, 25 N–10.* Washington, D.C.: U.S. Government Printing Office, 1976.

National Commission on Marijuana and Drug Abuse. *Drug use in America: Problem in prespective.* Washington, D.C.: U.S. Government Printing Office, 1973.

National Commission on Resources for Youth. *New roles for youth in the school and the community.* New York: Citation, 1974.

NEA again says: Get rid of standardized tests. *NEA Reporter,* 1977, *16* (7), 3.

NEA resolution 77–33: Education for all handicapped children. *Today's Education,* 1977, *66* (4), 52.

New law requires free public education for all disabled children. *NEA Reporter,* 1977, *16* (7), 4–5.

National Panel of High School and Adolescent Education. *The education of adolescents* (HEW Publication No. [OE] 76–00004). Washington, D.C.: U.S. Government Printing Office, 1976.

National School Public Relations Association. *Discipline crisis in schools: The problems, causes and search for solutions.* Arlington, Va.: National School Public Relations Association, 1973.

National School Public Relations Association. *Suspensions and expulsions: Current trends in school policies and programs.* Arlington, Va.: National School Public Relations Association, 1976.

Neff, W. S. *Work and human behavior.* Chicago: Aldine Publishing, 1968.

Neill, S. B. Violence and vandalism: Dimensions and corrections. *Phi Delta Kappan,* 1978, *59,* 302–306.

Nelson, C. M. Alternative education for the mildly and moderately handicapped. In R. D. Kneedler & S. G. Tarver (Eds.), *Changing perspectives in special education.* Columbus, Ohio: Charles E. Merrill, 1977.

Nelson, C. M., & Kauffman, J. M. Educational programming for secondary school age delinquent and maladjusted pupils. *Behavioral Disorders,* 1977, *2,* 102–113.

Nelson, R. T. Helpful hints for your high school's alternative program. In R. Eiben & A. Milliren (Eds.), *Educational change: A humanistic approach.* La Jolla, Calif.: University Associates, 1976.

New approaches to assessing learning. *Social Policy,* September/October, 1977.

Newcomer, P. L., & Hammill, D. D. *Psycholinguistics in the schools.* Columbus, Ohio: Charles E. Merrill, 1976.

Newman, R. *Groups in schools: A book about teachers, parents and children.* New York: Simon & Schuster, 1974.

Newmark, G. *This school belongs to you and me.* New York: Hart, 1976.

Nicholson, B. A survey of referral problems in 59 Ohio school districts. In F. P. Holt & R. Kichlighter (Eds.), *Psychological services in the schools.* Dubuque, Iowa: William C. Brown, 1971.

Noar, G. *Individualized instruction: Every child a winner.* New York: Wiley, 1972.

Nolen, P. A., Kunzelmann, H. P., & Haring, N. G. Behavioral modification in a junior high learning disabilities classroom. *Exceptional Children,* 1967, *34,* 163–168.

Norem-Hebeisen, A. A. *Differentiated aspects of the self-esteeming process among suburban adolescents and dysfunctional youth.* Unpublished doctoral dissertation, University of Minnesota, 1976.

Northcutt, N. *The adult performance level competency-based high school diploma pilot project.* Austin, Tex.: The University of Texas, 1976.

Offer, D. *The psychological world of the teenager: A study of normal adolescent boys.* New York: Basic Books, 1969.

Ohio State Department of Education. *Dealing with aggressive behavior: A curriculum for middle school and junior high.* Cleveland, Ohio: Educational Research Council of America, Lakewood City Board of Education, and the State of Ohio Department of Education, 1971.

O'Leary, K. D., & Drabman, R. Token reinforcement programs in the classroom: A review. *Psychological Bulletin,* 1971, *75,* 379–398.

O'Leary, K. D., & O'Leary, S. G. *Classroom management: The successful use of behavior modification.* New York: Pergamon, 1972; (2nd ed.), 1977.

O'Leary, K. D., Poulos, R. W., & Devine, V. T. Tangible reinforcers: Bonuses or bribes? In A. M. Graziano (Ed.), *Behavior therapy with children* (Volume II). Chicago: Aldine, 1975.

O'Leary, S. G., & O'Leary, K. D. Behavior modification in the school. In H. Leitenberg (Ed.), *Handbook of behavior modification and behavior therapy.* Englewood Cliffs, N.J.: Prentice-Hall, 1976.

Olshansky, S. Evaluating workshop evaluations. *Rehabilitation Record,* 1973, *14,* 22.

Oliver, L. I. *Behavior patterns in school of youth 12–17 years.* (National Health Survey, Series 11, No. 139, U.S. Department of Health, Education, & Welfare). Washington, D.C.: U.S. Government Printing Office, 1974.

O'Toole, J. *Work in America.* Cambridge, Mass.: The MIT Press, 1973.

Otto, W., McMenemy, R. A., & Smith, R. J. *Corrective and remedial teaching* (2nd ed.). Boston: Houghton Mifflin, 1973.

Palomares, U., & Logan, B. *A curriculum on conflict management: Practical methods for helping children explore creative alternatives in dealing with conflict.* La Mesa, Calif.: Human Development Institute, 1975.

Parsons, T. *The social system.* New York: The Free Press, 1951.

Payne, B. *Getting there without drugs.* New York: Viking Press, 1973.

Pennsylvania Association for Retarded Children v. Commonwealth of Pennsylvania, 334 F.Supp. 1257 (E.D.Pa. 1971).

Pennsylvania Association for Retarded Children v. *Commonwealth of Pennsylvania,* 343 F. Supp. 279 (E.D.Pa. 1972).

Pierce v. *Board of Education,* 358 N.E.2d 67 (111.App. 1976).

Pfeiffer, J. W., & Jones, J. E. *A handbook of structured experiences for human relations training* (Volumes 1, 2). Iowa City, Iowa: University Associates, 1969, 1970.

USOE gets money for training teams in how to deal with school crime, violence. *Phi Delta Kappan,* 1978, *59,* 367.

Phillips, E. L. Problems in educating emotionally disturbed children. In N. G. Haring & R. L. Schiefelbusch (Eds.), *Methods in special education.* New York: McGraw-Hill, 1967.

Phillips, E. L. Achievement Place: Token reinforcement procedures in a home-style rehabilitation setting for "pre-delinquent" boys. *Journal of Applied Behavior Analysis,* 1968, *1,* 213–223.

Phillips, E. L., Phillips, E. A., Fixsen, D. L., & Wolf, M. M. *The Teaching-Family handbook.* Lawrence, Kans.: University of Kansas Printing Service, 1972.

Phillips, E. L. Phillips, E. A., Fixsen, D. L., & Wolf, M. M. Behavior shaping works with delinquents. *Psychology Today,* June 1973, pp. 74–79.

Phillips, L. *Human adaptation and its failures.* New York: Academic Press, 1968.

Pirsig, R. M. *Zen and the art of motorcycle maintenance.* New York: William Morrow, 1974.

Pittel, S. M., Gryla, L., & Hoffer, R. Developmental factors in adolescent drug use. *Journal of the American Academy of Child Psychiatry,* 1971, *10,* 640–660.

Polsgrove, L. Self-control: An overview of concepts and methods for child training. *Proceedings of a Conference on Preparing Teachers to Foster Personal Growth in Emotionally Disturbed Students, Advanced Institute for Trainers of Teachers for Seriously Emotionally Disturbed Children.* University of Minnesota, May 29–31, 1977, 29–55.

Premack, D. A. Toward empirical behavior laws. I: Positive reinforcement. *Psychological Review,* 1959, *6,* 219–233.

President's Committee on Employment of the Handicapped. *Pathways to employment.* Washington, D.C.: U.S. Government Printing Office, 1976.

President's Panel on Mental Retardation, President's Committee on Mental Retardation. *Report to the President: A proposed program for national action to combat mental retardation.* Washington, D.C.: U.S. Government Printing Office, 1962.

Price, M., & Goodman, L., & Mann, L. *Learning disabilities in the secondary school: Student progress and characteristics.* Montgomery County, Pa.: Unpublished report, Montgomery County Intermediate Unit, 1976.

Public Health Service. *Approaches to adolescent health care in the 1970's.* Washington, D.C.: U.S. Government Printing Office, 1975.

Public Law 88–201. Vocational Act of 1963, 88th Congress, 1963.

Public Law 93–112. Vocational Rehabilitation Act of 1973. Section 504, July 26, 1973. Regulations published in Federal Register, May 4, 1977.

Public Law 93–380. Education of the Handicapped Act, 1974. Regulations published in *Federal Register,* August 21, 1974.

Public Law 94–103. Developmentally Disabled Assistance and Bill of Rights Act, 1975. Regulations published in the *Federal Register,* January 27, 1977.

Public Law 94–142. Education for All Handicapped Children Act of 1975, 94th Congress, November 29, 1975. Regulations published in *Federal Register,* August 23, 1977.

Randall, D., & Wong, M. R. Drug education: A review. *Journal of Drug Education,* 1976, *6,* 1–21.

Randolph, N., & Howe, W. *Self-enhancing education: A program to motivate learners.* Palo Alto, Calif.: Educational Progress, 1966.

Raths, L. E., Harmin, M., & Simon, S. B. *Values and teaching.* Columbus, Ohio: Charles E. Merrill, 1966.

Redl, F. The concept of the life space interview. *American Journal of Orthopsychiatry,* 1959, *29,* 1–18.

Redl, F., & Wineman, D. *Controls from within: Techniques for the treatment of the aggressive child.* Glencoe, Ill.: The Free Press, 1952.

Reimer, E. *School is dead: Alternatives in education.* Garden City, N.Y.: Doubleday, 1971.

Reinert, H. R. *Children in conflict: Educational strategies for the emotionally disturbed and behaviorally disordered.* St. Louis, Mo.: Mosby, 1976.

Reynolds, M. C. Saying out of jail. *Teaching Exceptional Children,* 1978, *10,* 60–62.

Rhodes, W. C. The disturbing child: A problem of ecological management. *Exceptional Children,* 1967, *33,* 449–455.

Rhodes, W. C. A community participation analysis of emotional disturbance. *Exceptional Children,* 1970, *36,* 309–314.

Rhodes, W. C., & Tracy, M. L. (Eds.). *A study of child variance.* (Vol. 2) *Interventions.* Ann Arbor: University of Michigan Press, 1974.

Richard G., In the matter of, 383 N.Y. Supp. 2d 403 (1976).

Ricks, D. Supershrink. In D. Ricks, A. Thomas, & M. Roff (Eds.), *Life history research in psychopathology* (Vol. 3). Minneapolis: The University of Minnesota Press, 1974.

Robbins, L., Robbins, E. S., & Stern, M. Psychological and environmental factors associated with drug abuse. *Drug Dependence,* 1970, *5,* 1–6.

Robbins, M. P., & Glass, G. V. The Doman-Delacato rationale: A critical analysis. In J. Hellmuth (Ed.), *Educational therapy* (Vol. II). Seattle, Wash.: Special Child, 1968.

Robins, L. N. *Deviant children grown up.* Baltimore: Williams & Wilkins, 1966.

Robinson, H. H. Libraries: Active agents in adult reading improvement. *ALA Bulletin*, 1963, *57*, 416–420.

Robinson, H. *Why pupils fail in reading.* Chicago, Ill.: University of Chicago Press, 1946.

Rogers, C. R. *Client-centered therapy.* Boston: Houghton Mifflin, 1951.

Rogers, C. R. *On becoming a person.* Boston: Houghton Mifflin, 1961.

Rogers, C. R. *Freedom to learn.* Columbus, Ohio: Charles E. Merrill, 1969.

Rohwer, W. Prime time for education: Early childhood or adolescence. *Harvard Educational Review*, 1971, *41*, 316–341.

Rollins, S. P. Youth education: Problems. In R. H. Muessig (Ed.), *Youth education: Problems/perspectives/promises.* Washington, D.C.: Association for Supervision and Curriculum Development, National Education Association, 1968.

Rose, S. D., Flanagan, J., & Brierton, D. *Counseling in a correctional institution: A social learning approach.* Paper presented at the Authors' Forum National Conference on Social Welfare, Dallas, Texas, 1971.

Rosenberg, H., & Graubard, P. Peer use of behavior modification. *Focus on Exceptional Children*, 1975, *7* (6), 1–12.

Rosenberg, M. B. *Mutual education: Toward autonomy and independence.* Seattle, Wash.: Special Child, 1972.

Rosenthal, J. H. Self-esteem in dyslexic children. *Academic Therapy*, 1973, *9*, 27–39.

Rosenthal, R., & Jacobson, L. *Pygmalion in the classroom.* New York: Holt, Rinehart & Winston, 1968.

Ross, A. O. The application of behavior principles in therapeutic education. *Journal of Special Education*, 1967, *1*, 275–286.

Ross, D., & Ross, S. *Hyperactivity: Research, theory, and action.* New York: Wiley, 1976.

Rotatori, A. F., & Switzky, H. *An alternative to vocational assessment of the severely handicapped adult client.* Unpublished manuscript, Northern Illinois University, 1977.

Rothman, E. P. *The angel inside went sour.* New York: David McKay, 1970.

Ryan, C. *The open partnership.* New York: McGraw-Hill, 1976.

Ryan, W. *Blaming the victim.* New York: Vintage, 1971.

Sabatino, D. A. *Neglected and delinquent children.* Educational Development Center, Wilkes-Barre, Pa.: Wilkes College, 1974.

Sabine, G. *When you listen, this is what you can hear . . . Teen-agers tell about their parents, schools, teachers, and student protest.* Iowa City, Iowa: American College Testing Program, 1971.

Saettler, H. Current priorities in personnel preparation. *Exceptional Children,* 1976, *43,* 147–148.

Saltus, R. Teen suicides linked to weakening family ties. *Detroit Free Press,* October 4, 1976.

Samuels, M. S., & Moriarty, P. H. *The concept of classroom crisis control.* Schiller Park, Ill.: Motorola Teleprograms, 1975.

Sarason, I. G. Verbal learning, modeling, and juvenile delinquency. *American Psychologist,* 1968, *23,* 254–266.

Sarason, I. G., & Ganzer, V. J. Modeling and group discussion in the rehabilitation of juvenile delinquents. *Journal of Counseling Psychology,* 1973, *20,* 442–449.

Sarason, I.G., & Sarason, B. *Constructive classroom behavior: A teacher's guide to modelling and role-playing techniques.* New York: Behavioral Publications, 1974.

Schafer, W. E., & Polk, K. Delinquency and the schools. In Task Force on Juvenile Delinquency, *Juvenile delinquency and youth crime.* Washington, D.C.: U.S. Government Printing Office, 1967.

Schlichter, K. J., & Ratcliff, R. G. Discrimination learning in juvenile delinquents. *Journal of Abnormal Psychology,* 1971, *77,* 46–48.

Schrank, J. *Media in value education: A critical guide.* Chicago, Ill.: Argus, 1970.

Schreiber, D. 700,000 dropouts. *American Education,* 1968, *4,* 1; 5–7.

Schultz, E. W., Hirshoren, A., Manton, A. B., & Henderson, R. A. Special education for the emotionally disturbed. *Exceptional Children,* 1971, *38,* 313–319.

Schwartz, L. A. Clinical teacher model for interrelated areas of special education. *Exceptional Children,* 1971, *37,* 565–571.

Schwitzgebel, R. K. Limitations on the coercive treatment of offenders. *Criminal Law Bulletin,* 1972, *8,* 269–319.

Scranton, T. R., & Downs, M. C. Elementary and secondary learning disabilities programs in the United States: A survey. *Journal of Learning Disabilities,* 1975, *8,* 394–399.

Senate Report No. 94–168 (Report of Senate Committee on Public Law 94–142, 1975).

Serwer, B. L., Shapiro, B. J., & Shapiro, P. P. The comparative effectiveness of four methods of instruction on the achievement of children with specific learning disabilities. *Journal of Special Education,* 1973, *7,* 241–250.

Shaftel, F., & Shaftel, G. *Role-playing for social values: Decision-making in the social studies.* Englewood Cliffs, N.J.: Prentice-Hall, 1967.

Shah, S. A. *A behavioral conceptualization of the development of criminal behavior, therapeutic principles, and applications.* A Report to the President's Commission on Law Enforcement and the Administration of Justice. Washington, D.C.: U.S. Government Printing Office, 1966.

Shah, S. A. Preparation for release and community follow-up. In H. L. Cohen, A. L. Cohen, I. Goldiamond, J. Filipczak, & R. Pooley (Eds.), *Training professionals in procedures for the establishment of educational environments.* Silver Springs, Md.: Institute for Behavioral Research, Educational Facility Press, 1968.

Shah, S. A. A behavioral approach to out-patient treatment of offenders. In H. C. Richard (Ed.), *Unique programs in behavior readjustment.* Elmsford, N.Y.: Pergamon, 1970.

Sharp, B. B. *Learning: The rhythm of risk.* Rosemont, Ill.: Combined Motivation Education Systems, 1971.

Sherry, M., & Franzen, M. Zapped by ZING: Students and teachers develop successful problem solving strategies. *Teaching Exceptional Children,* 1977, *9,* 46–47.

Shostrom, E. L. From abnormality to actualization. *Psychotherapy: Theory, research and practice,* 1973, *10,* 36–40.

Siegel, E. *The exceptional child grows up.* New York: E. P. Dutton, 1974.

Silberberg, N. E. & Silberberg, M. C. School achievement and delinquency. *Review of Educational Research,* 1971, *41,* 17–34.

Silberberg, N. E., Iverson, I. A., & Goins, J. T. Which remedial reading method works best? *Journal of Learning Disabilities,* 1973, *6,* 547–555.

Silberberg, N., & Silberberg, M. Myths in remedial education. *Journal of Learning Disabilities,* 1969, *2,* 209–217.

Silberman, C. E. *Crisis in the classroom: The remaking of American education.* New York: Random House, 1970.

Simpson, E. L. *Democracy's stepchildren.* San Francisco: Jossey-Bass, 1971.

Simon, S., Howe, L., & Kirschenbaum, H. *Values clarification: A practical handbook of strategies for teachers and students.* New York: Hart, 1972.

Silver, L. B. Emotional and social problems of children with developmental disabilities. In R. E. Weber (Ed.), *Handbook on learning disabilities.* Englewood Cliffs, N.J.: Prentice-Hall, 1974.

Sitko, M. C., & Gillespie, P. H. Language and speech difficulties. In L. Mann, L. Goodman, & J. L. Wiederholt (Eds.), *Teaching the learning-disabled adolescent.* Boston: Houghton Mifflin, 1978.

Skinner, B. F. *Science and human behavior.* New York: Free Press, 1953.

Sklansky, M. A., Silverman, S. W., & Rabichow, H. G. *The high school adolescent: Understanding and treating his emotional problems.* New York: Association Press, 1969.

Smith, F. *Understanding reading.* New York: Holt, Rinehart & Winston, 1971.

Smith, F. Twelve easy ways to make learning to read difficult and one difficult way to make it easy. In F. Smith (Ed.), *Psycholinguistics and reading.* New York: Holt, Rinehart & Winston, 1973.

Smith F. *Comprehension and learning: A conceptual framework for teachers.* New York: Holt, Rinehart & Winston, 1975.

Social Research Group. *The status of children—1975.* Washington, D.C.: George Washington University, 1975.

Solomon, R. W., & Wahler, R. G. Peer reinforcement control of classroom problem behavior. *Journal of Applied Behavior Analysis,* 1973, *6,* 49–56.

Stalford, C. *Historical perspectives on disruption and violence in schools.* Paper presented at the annual meeting of the American Educational Research Association, New York, April 1977.

Stanford Research Institute. *Compensatory education and early adolescence: Reviewing our national strategy.* Menlo Park, Calif.: Stanford Research Institute, 1975.

Stanford, G., & Stanford, B. D. *Learning discussion skills through games.* New York: Citation, 1969.

Stellern, J., Vasa, S. F., & Little, J. *Introduction to diagnostic-prescriptive teaching and programming.* Glen Ridge, N.J.: Exceptional Press, 1976.

Stephens, T. M. *Implementing behavioral approaches in elementary and secondary schools.* Columbus, Ohio: Charles E. Merrill, 1975.

Stevenson, H. W. *Children's learning.* New York: Appleton-Century-Crofts, 1972.

Stewart, M. Is hyperactivity abnormal? And other unanswered questions. *School Review,* 1976, *84,* 31–42.

Stewart, M., Palkes, H., Miller, R., Young, C., & Welner, Z. Intellectual ability and school achievement of hyperactive children, their classmates, and their siblings. In D. Ricks & M. Roff (Eds.), *Life history research in psychopathology* (Vol. 3). Minneapolis: University of Minnesota Press, 1974.

Strauss, A. A., & Lehtinen, L. E. *Psychopathology and education of the brain-injured child.* New York: Grune & Stratton, 1947.

Stotland, E. *The psychology of hope.* San Francisco, Calif.: Jossey-Bass, 1969.

Stuart, R. B. Behavioral contracting within the families of delinquents. *Proceedings of the American Psychological Association,* Miami, Fla., 1970.

Stuart, R. B. Behavioral contracting within the families of delinquents. *Journal of Behavior Therapy and Experimental Psychiatry,* 1971, *2,* 1–11.

Stuart, R. B. Teaching facts about drugs: Pushing or preventing? *Journal of Educational Psychology,* 1973, *66,* 189–201.

Stuart, R. B. (Ed.). *Behavioral self-management: Strategies, techniques, and outcome*. New York: Brunner/Mazel, 1977.

Stuart, R. B., & Tripodi, T. Experimental evaluation of three time-constrained behavioral treatments for pre-delinquents and delinquents. In R. D. Rubin, J. P. Brady, & J. D. Henderson (Eds.), *Advances in Behavior Therapy* (Vol. 4.). New York: Academic Press, 1973.

Stuart, R. B., Tripodi, T., & Jayaratne, S. Changing adolescent behavior through reprogramming behavior of parents and teachers: Experimental evaluation. *Canadian Journal of Behavioral Sciences*, 1972, 8(2), 132–144.

Stumphauzer, J. S. *Behavior therapy with delinquents*. Springfield, Ill.: Charles C Thomas, 1973.

Subcommittee to Investigate Juvenile Delinquency. *Our nation's schools —A report card: "A" in school violence and vandalism*. Washington, D.C.: U.S. Government Printing Office, 1975.

Sullivan, H. S. *Conceptions of modern psychiatry*. Washington, D.C.: William Alanson White Foundation, 1947. (Paperback edition, Norton, 1953.)

Super, D. E. *Career education and the meanings of work*. Monographs on Career Education, U.S. Department of Health, Education, & Welfare. Washington, D.C.: U.S. Government Printing Office, 1976.

Swap, S. M. Disturbing classroom behaviors: A developmental and ecological view. *Exceptional Children*, 1974, *41*, 163–172.

Swift, M. S., & Spivack, G. Therapeutic teaching: A review of teaching methods for behaviorally troubled children. *Journal of Special Education*, 1974, *8*, 259–289.

Swift, M. S., & Spivack, G. *Alternative teaching strategies: Helping behaviorally troubled children achieve*. Champaign, Ill.: Research Press, 1975.

Swisher, J. D., & Crawford, J. L. An evaluation of a short term drug education program. *School Counselor*, 1971, *18*, 265–272.

Swisher, J. D., & Horan, R. E. Drug abuse prevention (or evaluation of Temple University's drug education program). *The Journal of College Student Personnel*, 1970, *11*, 337–341.

Swisher, J. D., & Horan, R. E. Effecting drug attitude change in college students via induced cognitive dissonance. *Journal of Student Personnel and Teacher Education*, 1972, *11*, 26–31.

Swisher, J. D., & Warner, R. W., Jr. A study of four approaches to drug abuse prevention. (Final Report). Washington, D.C.: U.S. Office of Education, Bureau of Research, 1971.

Swisher, J. D., Warner, R. W., & Herr, M. Experimental comparison of four approaches to drug abuse prevention among 9th and 11th graders. *Journal of Counseling Psychology*, 1972, *19*, 328–332.

Tarver, S. G., & Hallahan, D. P. Attention deficits in children with learning disabilities: A review. *Journal of Learning Disabilities*, 1974, *7*, 560–568.

Tawney, J. W., Kruse, C. G., Cegelka, P. T., & Kelly, D. L. A teacher's guide to instructional programming. *Teaching Exceptional Children*, 1977, *10*, 2–6.

Taylor, F. D., Artuso, A. A., Stillwell, R. J., Soloway, M. M., Hewett, F. M., & Quay, H. C. A learning center plan for special education. *Focus on Exceptional Children*, 1972, *4*(3), 1–7.

Tharp, R., & Wetzel, R. *Behavior modification in the natural environment.* New York: Academic Press, 1969.

Thoresen, C. E., & Mahoney, M. J. *Behavioral self-control.* New York: Holt, Rinehart & Winston, 1974.

Thorne, G. L., Tharp, R. G., & Wetzel, R. J. Behavior modification techniques: New tools for probation officers. *Federal Probation*, 1967, *31*, 21–27.

Tolor, A. An evaluation of a new approach in dealing with high school underachievement. *Journal of Learning Disabilities*, 1970, *3*, 520–529.

Torrance, E. P., & Myers, R. E. *Creative learning and teaching.* New York: Dodd, Mead, 1970.

Uhlman, W. F., & Shook, G. L. A method for maintaining high rates of performance in an open classroom setting. In T. A. Brigham, R. Hawkings, J. W. Scott, & T. F. McLaughlin (Eds.), *Behavior analysis in education.* Dubuque, Iowa: Kendall/Hunt, 1976.

U. S. Bureau of the Census. *1970 Census of the population: Detailed characteristics.* Washington, D.C.: U.S. Government Printing Office, 1972.

U. S. Bureau of the Census. *Characteristics of American youth.* Washington, D.C.: U.S. Government Printing Office, 1973.

U.S. Commission on Civil Rights. *Racial isolation in the public schools.* Washington, D.C.: U.S. Government Printing Office, 1967.

U.S. Department of Health, Education, and Welfare. *Mental retardation source.* Washington, D.C.: U.S. Government Printing Office, 1972.

U. S. Employment and Training Administration. *Sheltered workshop study.* Washington, D.C.: Department of Labor and Employment Standards Administration, Employment and Training Administration, June 1977.

U.S. Office of Education. *Career education: A handbook for implementation.* Washington, D.C.: U.S. Government Printing Office, 1972.

Valett, R. E. *The remediation of learning disabilities.* Belmont, Calif.: Fearon, 1967.

Virgilio, C. L. A comparison of the effects of the school health education study (SHES) approach and the lecture-discussion approach upon drug knowledge and attitudes of high school students. Ann Arbor Microfilms, 1971.

Vinton, D. A., Pantzer, B. D., Farley, E. M., & Thompson, W. A. *Planning and implementing career education for the special student with emphasis on the leisure occupations.* Lexington, Ky.: University of Kentucky, 1976.

Volkmor, C. B., Langstaff, A. L., & Higgins, M. *Structuring the classroom for success.* Columbus, Ohio: Charles E. Merrill, 1974.

Walker, D. F. The hard lot of the professional in a reform movement (editorial). *Educational Leadership,* 1978, *35,* 83–85.

Wallace, G., & Larsen, S. C. *Educational assessment of learning problems: Testing for teaching.* Boston: Allyn & Bacon, 1978.

Walton, J. *Toward better teaching in the secondary school.* Boston: Allyn & Bacon, 1966.

Warner, R. W., & Swisher, J. D. Alienation and drug abuse: Synonymous. *NASSP Bulletin,* 1971, *55,* 55–62.

Warner, R. W., Swisher, J. D., & Horan, R. E. Drug abuse prevention: A behavioral approach. *NASSP Bulletin,* 1973, *57,* 49–54.

Wasserman, M. *The school fix, NYC, USA.* New York: Simon & Schuster, 1970.

Wennberg, H., & Hare, B. Services for learning disabled students in elementary and secondary schools. *Academic Therapy,* 1977, *13,* 57–62.

Weil, A. T. *The natural mind.* New York: Houghton Mifflin, 1973.

Weiner, I. *Psychological disturbance in adolescence.* New York: Wiley, 1970.

Weiss, H. G., & Weiss, M. S. *A survival manual: Case studies and suggestions for the learning disabled teenager.* Great Barrington, Mass.: Treehouse Associates, 1974.

Wender, P. *Minimal brain dysfunction in children.* New York: Wiley, 1971.

Werry, J., & Sprague, R. Hyperactivity. In C. Costello (Ed.), *Symptoms of psychopathology.* New York: Wiley, 1969.

White House Conference on Youth. *Report of the White House Conference on Youth.* Washington, D.C.: U.S. Government Printing Office, 1971.

White, R. W. Motivation reconsidered: The concept of competence. *Psychological Review,* 1959, *66,* 297–333.

Wiederholt, J. L. Adolescents with learning disabilities: The problem in perspective. In L. Mann, L. Goodman, & J. Wiederholt (Eds.), *Teaching the learning-disabled adolescent.* Boston: Houghton Mifflin, 1978.

Wiederholt, J. L., & Hammill, D. D. Use of the Frostig-Horne visual perception program with kindergarten and first grade economically disadvantaged children. *Psychology in the Schools,* 1971, *8,* 268–274.

Wiederholt, J. L., Hammill, D. D., & Brown, V. *The resource teacher: A guide to effective practices.* Boston: Allyn & Bacon, 1978.

Wiggins, X. R. *Doing drug education*. Atlanta: Southern Regional Education Board, 1972.

Wiggins, X. R. *Beyond the three R's*. Atlanta: Southern Regional Education Board, 1974.

Wiig, E. H., & Harris, S. P. Perception and interpretation of nonverbally expressed emotions by adolescents with learning disabilities. *Perceptual and Motor Skills*, 1974, *38*, 239–245.

Wiig, E. H., & Semel, E. M. *Language disabilities in children and adolescents*. Columbus, Ohio: Charles E. Merrill, 1976.

Willower, D. J. The teacher subculture and rites of passage. *Urban Education*, 1969, *2*, 103–114.

Wilson, J. W., & Armstrong, T. Techniques for initiating independent study. In R. Eiben & A. Milliren (Eds.), *Educational change: A humanistic approach*. La Jolla, Calif.: University Associates, 1976.

Wolf, M. M., Phillips, E. L., & Fixsen, D. L. The Teaching-Family: A new model for the treatment of deviant child behavior in the community. In S. W. Bijou & E. L. Ribes-Inesta (Eds.), *Behavior modification*. New York: Academic Press, 1972.

Wolpe, J. *Psychotherapy by reciprocal inhibition*. Stanford, Calif.: Stanford University Press, 1958.

Wong, M. R. Different strokes: Models of drug abuse prevention education. *Contemporary Educational Psychology*, 1976, *1*, 285–303.

Wood, L. O., Meyer, B. D., & Grady, S. C. Exceptional adults learn in Browand Community College's Continuing Education Program. *Teaching Exceptional Children*, 1977, *10*, 7–9.

Wood, M. M. (Ed.). *Developmental therapy: A textbook for teachers as therapists for emotionally disturbed young children*. Baltimore, Md.: University Park, 1975.

Worrell, J., & Nelson, C. M. *Managing instructional problems: A case study workbook*. New York: McGraw-Hill, 1974.

Wren, G. C. *Coping with series*. Circle Pines, Minn.: American Guidance Service, 1971.

Wylie, R. C. *The self concept: A review of methodological considerations and measuring instruments*. Lincoln, Nebr.: University of Nebraska Press, 1974.

Wynne, E. A. Behind the discipline problem: Youth suicide as a measure of alienation. *Phi Delta Kappan*, 1978, 307–315.

Younie, W. & Clark, G. Personnel training needs for cooperative secondary school programs for mentally retarded. *Education and Training of the Mentally Retarded*, December, 1969, *4* (4), 186–194.

Ysseldyke, J. E. Diagnostic-prescriptive teaching: The search for aptitude–treatment–interactions. In L. Mann & D. Sabatino (Eds.), *The first review of special education* (Vol. 1). Philadelphia: Buttonwood Farms, 1973.

About
the Authors

Donn E. Brolin received a B.S. degree from Bradley University in 1958, a M.S. degree from the University of Wisconsin at Madison in 1963, and a Ph.D. degree from the University of Wisconsin at Madison in 1969. He is currently professor of education in the Department of Counseling and Personnel Services at the University of Missouri at Columbia.

Dr. Brolin has had extensive practical experience as a psychologist, counselor, and administrator in programs for the handicapped, particularly the mentally retarded. He has established two undergraduate programs in rehabilitation services and one in secondary special education and has directed two U.S. Office of Education projects relative to career education for handicapped persons. He is active in many professional organizations and was the first president of the Council for Exceptional Children's Division on Career Development (1976–78).

Brolin, D. Value of rehabilitation services and correlates of vocational success with the mentally retarded. *American Journal of Mental Deficiency,* 1972, *76,* 644–651.

Brolin, D. Career education needs of secondary educable students. *Exceptional Children,* 1973, *39,* 619–624.

Brolin, D. *Vocational preparation of retarded citizens.* Columbus, Ohio: Charles E. Merrill, 1976.

Brolin, D. Career development: A national priority. *Education and Training of the Mentally Retarded,* 1977, *12,* 154–156.

Brolin, D. (Ed.). Life-centered career education: A competency based approach. Reston, Va.: The Council for Exception Children, 1978.

Brolin, D., & Kokaska, C. Critical issues in successful job placement of the educable mentally retarded. *Rehabilitation Literature,* 1974, *10,* 16–18.

Brolin, D., & Kokaska, C. *Career education for handicapped children and youth.* Columbus, Ohio: Charles E. Merrill, forthcoming.

Brolin, D., McKay, D., & West. L. Trainer's manual for life-centered career education. Reston, Va.: The Council for Exceptional Children, 1978.

James C. Brolin received his B.S. degree from Northern Illinois University in 1962, a M.S. degree from the University of Wisconsin at Madison in 1969 and is presently completing requirements for his doctorate at Auburn University. He is currently an extension associate for Rehabilitation Services Education, Auburn University, traveling extensively throughout the southeastern states conducting training programs in vocational education.

Mr. Brolin has served as a teacher, school counselor, rehabilitation counselor, rehabilitation facility administrator, and college instructor.

Brolin, J., & Lesnik, M. To be or not to be: Avoiding language traps in the rehabilitation process. *Journal of Rehabilitation,* 1977, *43,* 27–29.

Sankovsky, R., & Brolin, J. New directions for training vocational evaluators. *Vocational Evaluation and Work Adjustment Bulletin,* 1977, *10* (2), 39–43.

Sankovsky, R., Brolin, J., & Coffey, D. Vocational evaluators identify training needs: Report of a national survey. *Vocational Evaluation and Work Adjustment Bulletin,* 1977, *10* (1), 15–19.

Patricia T. Cegelka received a B.S. degree in history in 1964, a M.S. degree in special education in 1968, and a Ed.D. degree in special education in 1970, all from the University of Kansas. She is currently an associate professor of special education at the University of Kentucky.

Prior to her position at Kentucky, Dr. Cegelka served as a teacher, materials consultant, and evaluator in public school programs for mentally retarded children and youth. Dr. Cegelka holds editorships with several leading professional journals and has served as project director for numerous U.S. Office of Education training and development grants. She has also written articles on career and vocational education for mildly handicapped individuals.

Cegelka, P. T. Incidental learning in nonretarded and retarded children. *American Journal of Mental Deficiency,* 1972, *76,* 581–586.

Cegelka, P. T. Sex-role stereotyping in secondary work study programs. *Exceptional Children,* 1976, *42,* 323–328.

Cegelka, P. T. Exemplary projects and programs for the career development of retarded individuals. *Education and Training of the Mentally Retarded,* 1977, *12,* 161–163.

Cegelka, P. T., & Cegelka, W. J. A review of research: Reading and the educable mentally handicapped. *Exceptional Children,* 1970, *37,* 187–200.

Cegelka, P. T., Berdine, W. M., & Cleaver, B. A learning center quadrant approach utilizing contingency management for adolescent TMRs. In A. Thomas (Ed.), *Developing skills in severely and profoundly handicapped children.* Reston, Va.: Council for Exceptional Children, 1977.

Cegelka, P. T., & Phillips, M. W. Individualized education programming at the secondary level. *Teaching Exceptional Children,* 1978, *10,* 84–87.

Harvey F. Clarizio is a professor of school psychology in the College of Education, Michigan State University. He has worked in numerous mental health clinics in Illinois, Minnesota, and Michigan, and prepared teachers to work with emotionally disturbed children at Illinois State University.

Dr. Clarizio received a B.A. degree in psychology from St. Thomas College in 1956, a M.A. degree in child psychology from the University of Minnesota in 1958, and an Ed.D. degree in educational psychology from the University of Illinois in 1966.

Clarizio, H. F. (Ed.). *Mental health and the educative process: Selected readings.* Chicago: Rand McNally, 1969.

Clarizio, H. F. *Toward positive classroom discipline.* New York: Wiley, 1971.

Clarizio, H. F., Craig, R. C., & Mehrens, W. A. (Eds.). *Contemporary issues in educational psychology.* Boston: Allyn & Bacon, 1970.

Clarizio, H. F., & McCoy, G. F. *Behavior disorders in children* (2nd ed.). New York: Thomas Y. Crowell, 1976.

Douglas Cullinan is an assistant professor in the Department of Learning and Development at Northern Illinois University. He has taught emotionally disturbed and mentally retarded pupils in public schools, and educationally handicapped delinquents in a state detention facility. He has published on various topics related to special education for children and adolescents. Dr. Cullinan is associated with Project ExCEL, a Child Service Demonstration Center in learning disabilities, and serves as associate editor of *Exceptional Children*.

Dr. Cullinan received a B.A. in psychology (1966), and an M.A. (1968) and Ed.D. (1974) in special education from the University of Virginia.

Cullinan, D. Verbalization in educable mentally retarded children's observational learning. *American Journal of Mental Deficiency*, 1976, *81*, 65–72.

Cullinan, D. Behavior modification with adolescent problems. In D. A. Sabatino & A. J. Mauser (Eds.), *Intervention strategies for specialized secondary education*. Boston: Allyn & Bacon, 1978.

Cullinan, D., Epstein, M. H., & Silver, L. Modification of impulsive tempo in learning disabled pupils. *Journal of Abnormal Child Psychology*, 1977, *5*, 437–444.

Cullinan, D., Kauffman, J. M., & LaFleur, M. K. Modeling: Research with implications for special education. *Journal of Special Education*, 1975, *9*, 202–221.

Lloyd, J., Cullinan, D., & Epstein, M. H. Behavior disorders of children. In B. Bateman & A. Archer (Eds.), *Introduction to special education*. New York: McGraw-Hill, forthcoming.

Michael H. Epstein is an assistant professor in the Department of Learning and Development, Northern Illinois University. He is also currently project director of Project ExCEL, a Child Service Demonstrating Center in learning disabilities. Dr. Epstein has taught learning and behaviorally handicapped pupils and has authored numerous journal articles and books dealing with handicapped children and adolescents, particularly in the areas of cognitive tempo, behavior disorders, and applied behavior analysis.

Dr. Epstein received a B.S. degree in business (1969) and an M.S. Ed. degree in special education (1971) from American University, and an Ed.D. in special education from the University of Virginia (1975).

Epstein, M. H., Hallahan, D. P., & Kauffman, J. M. Implications of the reflectivity-impulsivity dimension for special education. *Journal of Special Education,* 1975, *9,* 11–25.

Epstein, M. H., Cullinan, D., & Sternberg, L. Impulsive cognitive tempo in severe and mild learning disabled children. *Psychology in the Schools,* 1977, *14,* 290–294.

Epstein, M. H., Cullinan, D., & Sabatino, S. A. State definitions of behavior disorders. *Journal of Special Education,* 1977 *11,* 417–425.

Epstein, M. H., Rothman, S. G., & Sabatino, D. A. Programs for youth in trouble in the secondary school. In D. Sabatino & A. Mauser (Eds.), *Intervention strategies for specialized secondary education.* Boston: Allyn & Bacon, 1978.

Payne, J. S., Mercer, C. D., & Epstein, M. H. *Education and rehabilitation techniques.* New York: Behavioral Publications, 1974.

Stanley A. Fagen is presently staff development consultant for Montgomery County Public Schools, Maryland. His previous professional positions include that of chief child clinical psychologist at Walter Reed Hospital in Washington, D.C., director of psychology training at Children's Hospital. of Washington, D.C., school psychologist at Hillcrest Children's Center in Washington, D.C., and faculty appointments at George Washington University, American University, and the Washington School of Psychiatry. Dr. Fagen has written extensively in the areas of psychoeducational management, teacher training, and behavioral self-control.

Dr. Fagen received a B.S. degree from Brooklyn College in 1957, a M.A. degree from the University of Pennsylvania in 1959, and a Ph.D. degree from the University of Pennsylvania in 1963.

Fagen, S. A. The Mark Twain teacher internship program. In T. Lake (Ed.), *Manpower development: Exemplary programs for the handicapped.* Reston, Va.: Council for Exceptional Children, 1973.

Fagen, S. A., & Guedalia, L. G. *Individual and group counseling: A competency-based manual for in-service training.* Washington, D.C.: Psychoeducational Resources, 1977.

Fagen, S. A., & Hill, J. M. *Behavior management: A competency-based manual for in-service training.* Washington, D.C.: Psychoeducational Resources, 1977.

Fagen, S. A., & Long, N. J. Before it happens: Prevent discipline problems by teaching self-control. *Instructor,* 1976, *85,* 42–47.

Fagen, S. A., & Long, N. J. Teaching children self-control: A new responsibility for teachers. *Focus on Exceptional Children,* 1976, *7*(8), 1–12.

Fagen, S. A., Long, N. J., & Stevens, D. J. *Teaching children self-control: Preventing emotional and learning problems in the elementary school.* Columbus, Ohio: Charles E. Merrill, 1975.

Fagen, S. A., Long, N. J., & Stevens, D. J. A psychoeducational curriculum for the prevention of behavioral and learning problems: Teaching self-control. In N. J. Long, W. C. Morse, & R. G. Newman (Eds.), *Conflict in the classroom* (3rd ed.). Belmont Calif.: Wadsworth, 1976.

Dean L. Fixsen received the A.B. degree in psychology in 1968 from Kansas State College, the M.A. degree in psychology in 1968 from the University of Kansas, and the Ph.D. degree in psychology in 1970 from the University of Kansas. Dr. Fixsen has held positions as a research assistant, Parsons State Hospital; research associate, Bureau of Child Research, University of Kansas; co-director of Achievement Place; and is presently director of evaluation, Father Flanagan's Boys' Home in Nebraska. He is on the board of directors of the Society for the Experimental Analysis of Behavior, and an associate editor of the *Journal of Applied Behavior Analysis.*

Fixsen, D. L., Wolf, M. M., & Phillips, E. L. Achievement Place: The reliability of self-reporting and peer reporting and their effects on behavior. *Journal of Applied Behavior Analysis,* 1972, *5,* 19–36.

Fixsen, D. L., Phillips, E. L., & Wolf, M. M. Achievement Place: Experiments in self-government with pre-delinquents. *Journal of Applied Behavior Analysis,* 1973, *6,* 31–47.

Fixsen, D. L., Wolf, M. M., & Phillips, E. L. Achievement Place: A teaching-family model of community based group homes for youths in trouble. In L. A. Hammerlynck, L. C. Handy, & E. J. Mash (Eds.), *Behavior change: Methodology, concepts, and practice.* Champaign, Ill.: Research Press, 1973.

Fixsen, D. L., Phillips, E. L., & Wolf, M. M. The Teaching-Family model of group home treatment. In E. Craighead, A. Kazdin, & M. Mahoney (Eds.), *An introduction to behavior modification.* New York: Houghton Mifflin, 1976.

Fixsen, D. L. Phillips, E. L., & Wolf, M. M. The Teaching-Family Model: An example of mission-oriented. In T. A. Brigham & A. C. Catania (Eds.), *The handbook of applied behavior research: Social and instructional processes.* New York: Irvington/Halstead, 1977.

Libby Goodman is now director of special education for administrative services of the Philadelphia, Pennsylvania public schools. Her previous professional positions include that of coordinator of learning disabilities programs at Montgomery County Pennsylvania, teacher of mildly handicapped children, and instructor at Temple University. Dr. Goodman has also served as the project director of numerous U.S. Office of Education grants.

Dr. Goodman received a B.A. degree in education from Douglas College in 1968, a M.Ed. in special education from Temple University in 1969, and an Ed.D. in special education from Temple University in 1973.

Goodman, L. Montessori education for the handicapped: The method—the research. In D. Sabatino & L. Mann (Eds.), *The second review of special education*. Philadelphia: Buttonwood Farms, 1974.

Goodman, L. Meeting children's needs through materials modification. *Teaching Exceptional Children*, 1978, *10*, 92–95.

Goodman, L., & Mann, L. *Learning disabilities in the secondary school: Issues and practices*. New York: Grune & Stratton, 1976.

Goodman, L., & Wiederholt, J. L. Predicting reading achievement in disadvantaged children. *Psychology in the Schools*, 1973, *10*, 181–185.

Mann, L., Goodman, L., & Wiederholt, J. L. (Eds.). *The learning disabled adolescent*. New York: Houghton Mifflin, 1978.

Mann, L., & Goodman, L. Perceptual training: A critical retrospect. In E. Schopler & R. J. Reichler (Eds.), *Psychopathology and child development: Research and treatment*. New York: Plenum Press, 1976.

Peter Knoblock received a B.A. degree in education in 1956, a M.S. degree in school psychology in 1957, and a Ph.D. in psychology and education in 1962, all from the University of Michigan. He is currently a professor of special education and coordinator of programs for teachers of emotionally disturbed children at Syracuse University at Syracuse, New York.

Prior to his present position at Syracuse, Dr. Knoblock served as a school psychologist, cabin counselor, and teacher of emotionally disturbed children. Dr. Knoblock is a past president, Council for Children with Behavioral Disorders, Council for Exceptional Children. Dr. Knoblock has written numerous papers on alternative and open education for handicapped children.

Knoblock, P. The needs of teachers for specialized information regarding their role in interdisciplinary teams. In W. M. Cruickshank (Ed.), *Preparation of teachers of brain-injured children.* Syracuse, N.Y.: Syracuse University Press, 1966.

Knoblock, P. (Ed.). *Intervention approaches in education of emotionally disturbed children.* Syracuse, N.Y.: Syracuse University Press, 1966.

Knoblock, P., & Goldstein, A. P. *The lonely teacher.* Boston: Allyn & Bacon, 1971.

Knoblock, P. Open education for emotionally disturbed children. *Exceptional Children,* 1973, *39,* 358–365.

Knoblock, P. A model for an integrated program for disturbed and typical children. In S. Meisels (Ed.), *Open education and young children with special needs.* Baltimore: University Park Press, forthcoming.

Knoblock, P. Psychological considerations of emotionally disturbed children. In W. M. Cruickshank (Ed.), *Psychology of exceptional children and youth* (4th ed.). Englewood Cliffs, N.J.: Prentice-Hall, forthcoming.

Knoblock, P., & Garcia, R. A. Toward a broader concept of the role of the special class for emotionally disturbed children. *Exceptional Children,* 1965, *31,* 329–335.

Reed Martin received the B.A. degree in philosophy from Rice University in 1962 and the J.D. degree in 1965 from the University of Texas School of Law, where he was an associate editor of the *Texas Law Review* and a member of the moot court board of directors. He spent 10 years in Washington, D.C., where he provided legal services to four federal agencies and served for a year on the staff of Senator Ralph Yarborough. Now living in Houston, he has taught courses on law and psychology at the graduate school of psychology at the University of Houston.

Reed Martin created and directs the public law division of Research Press Publishing Company. He has provided services to over 50 educational agencies and facilities for the handicapped in 30 states and has conducted conferences on educational rights in 15 states. He serves as a consultant to the Texas Advocacy Agency and on the boards of the Houston Association for Retarded Citizens and the Children's Resource and Information Service.

Martin, R. *Performance contracting in education.* Champaign, Ill.: Research Press, 1970.

Martin, R. Performance contracting: Did we learn? *American School Board Journal,* 1972, *159* (11), 30–32.

Martin, R. *Developing student discipline and motivation.* Champaign, Ill.: Research Press, 1974.

Martin, R. *Legal challenges to behavior modification.* Champaign, Ill.: Research Press, 1975.

Martin, R. *Educating handicapped children: The legal mandate.* Champaign, Ill.: Research Press, forthcoming.

Martin, R., & Blaschke, C. Contracting for educational reform. *Phi Delta Kappan,* 1971, *52* (7), 403–406.

Gaye *McNutt* is area coordinator of special education at the University of Oklahoma. Her previous experiences include 7 years of teaching both regular and special education students as well as assisting in the development of a curriculum for moderately to severely retarded adults.

Dr. McNutt received a B.S. degree in elementary education and mathematics in 1968. Graduate study in special education led to an M.Ed. degree in 1974 and Ph.D. in 1977 from the University of Texas at Austin. Dr. McNutt's current interests focus on identification of and serving the learning disabled, the improvement of current teaching practices, and effective methods for teaching reading to the learning disabled.

Hammill, D. D., Larsen, S., & McNutt, G. The effects of spelling instruction: A preliminary survey. *Elementary School Journal,* 1977, *78,* 67–72.

Wiederholt, J. L., & McNutt, G. *Secondary school programming for handicapped children. First year report.* Austin, Tex: Texas Education Agency, 1976.

Wiederholt, J. L., & McNutt, G. Evaluating materials for handicapped adolescents. *Journal of Learning Disabilities,* 1977, *10,* 132–140.

Elaine A. Phillips received the B.S. degree in education in 1966 from Kansas State College and the M.A. degree in human development in 1971 from the University of Kansas. She has held professional positions as a teacher, special education teacher, research assistant, and teaching-parent in various public and private school facilities. Ms. Phillips has presented at national and state conferences and has published papers on behavior therapy with adolescents.

Phillips, E. L., Phillips, E. A., Fixsen, D. L., & Wolf, M. M. *The Teaching-Family handbook*. Lawrence, Kans.: University of Kansas Printing Service, 1972.

Phillips, E. L., Phillips, E. A., Wolf, M. M., & Fixsen, D. L. Achievement Place: Development of elected manager system. *Journal of Applied Behavior Analysis*, 1973, *6*, 541–561.

Elery L. Phillips received the B.S. degree in psychology in 1966 from Kansas State College, the M.A. degree in human development in 1968 from the University of Kansas, and the Ph.D. degree in human development in 1971 from the University of Kansas. Dr. Phillips is deputy director for Youth Care at Father Flanagan's Boys' Home in Nebraska. He began his professional experiences as a research assistant at Achievement Place and then as teaching parent and director of Achievement Place. Dr. Phillips has also served as co-principal investigator and/or as director for numerous federal grants and as a presenter at many regional and national professional meetings. He is on the board of editors of the *Journal of Applied Behavior Analysis* and serves as a reviewer to other professional journals.

Phillips, E. L. Achievement Place: Application of token reinforcement procedures in a home-style rehabilitation setting for pre-delinquent boys. *Journal of Applied Behavior Analysis,* 1968, *1,* 213–224.

Phillips, E. L., Phillips, E. A., Fixsen, D. L., & Wolf, M. M. Achievement Place: The modification of pre-delinquent behaviors with token reinforcement. *Journal of Applied Behavior Analysis,* 1971, *4,* 45–59.

Phillips, E. L., Fixsen, D. L., Phillips, E. A., & Wolf, M. M. Behavior shaping works with delinquents. *Psychology Today,* June 1973, 74–79.

Phillips, E. L., Wolf, M. M., Fixsen, D. L., & Phillips, E. A. Achievement Place: A community alternative to institutionalization. In A. Sandowsky (Ed.), *Child and adolescent development.* New York: The Free Press, 1973.

Phillips, E. L., Wolf, M. M., Fixsen, D. L., & Bailey, J. S. The Achievement Place Model: A community based, family-style, behavior modification program for pre-delinquent youth. In Ribes-Inesta & A. Bandura (Eds.), *Analysis of Delinquency and Aggression.* New York: Wiley, 1976.

David A. Sabatino is professor and chairman of learning and development at Northern Illinois University. Prior to his present appointment, he was associate professor of school psychology at Pennsylvania State University. Dr. Sabatino's earlier experiences include teacher of deaf and autistic children, audiologist, school psychologist, and director of pupil personnel services. He has also served as principal investigator and/or consultant on numerous U.S. Office of Education and state grants. Dr. Sabatino holds editorships with several major special education and school psychology journals and has written extensively in the areas of special education programming, special learner aptitudes, and secondary school services.

Dr. Sabatino received the B.S. degree in education in 1960, the M.A. degree in school psychology in 1961, and the Ph.D. in special education administration in 1966, all from the Ohio State University.

Mann, L., & Sabatino, D. A. (Eds.). *The first review of special education* (Vols. 1 & 2). Philadelphia, Pa.: Buttonwood Farms, 1973.

Sabatino, D. A. Evaluation of resource rooms for children with learning disabilities. *Journal of Learning Disabilities,* 1971, *4,* 26–35.

Sabatino, D. A. A scientific approach towards a discipline of education. *Journal of Special Education,* 1971, *5,* 15–22.

Sabatino, D. A. School psychology–special education: To acknowledge a relationship. *Journal of School Psychology,* 1972, *10,* 99–105.

Sabatino, D. A. Resource rooms: The renaissance in special education. *Journal of Special Education,* 1972, *6,* 335–347.

Sabatino, D. A., & Mauser, A. J. (Eds.). *Specialized education in today's secondary schools.* Boston: Allyn & Bacon, 1978.

Sabatino, D. A., & Mauser, A. J. (Eds.). *Intervention strategies for specialized secondary education.* Boston: Allyn & Bacon, 1978.

J. Lee Wiederholt is associate professor and coordinator of general special education programs at the University of Texas at Austin. He received his B.S. degree from Rockhurst College in Kansas City and both his M.Ed. and Ed.D. degrees from Temple University in Philadelphia.

Dr. Wiederholt has taught the mild to moderately handicapped at both the secondary and elementary level. In addition, he was a supervisor of resource programs in the Philadelphia Public Schools and an assistant professor/research associate with the Leadership Training Institute in Learning Disabilities at the University of Arizona.

Dr. Wiederholt has served on several editorial boards, professional committees, and in elected offices. He is also the author of numerous articles, books, chapters, government reports, and editorials.

Hammill, D. D., Colarusso, R. P., & Wiederholt, J. L. Diagnostic value of the Frostig test: A factor analytic approach. *Journal of Special Education,* 1971, *4,* 279–282.

Hammill, D. D., & Wiederholt, J. L. *The resource room: Rationale and implementation.* New York: Grune & Stratton, 1972.

Hammill, D. D., & Wiederholt, J. L. Review of the Frostig test and training program. In L. Mann & D. A. Sabatino (Eds.), *The first review of special education.* New York: Grune & Stratton, 1973.

Wiederholt, J. L. Planning resource rooms for the mildly handicapped. *Focus on Exceptional Children,* 1974, *5,* 1–10.

Wiederholt, J. L. Historical perspectives on the education of the learning disabled. In L. Mann & D. A. Sabatino (Eds.), *The second review of special education.* New York: Grune & Stratton, 1974.

Wiederholt, J. L., & McNutt, G. Evaluating materials for handicapped adolescents. *Journal of Learning Disabilities,* 1977, *10,* 132–140.

Wiederholt, J. L., Hammill, D. D., & Brown, V. *The resource teacher: A guide to effective practice.* Boston: Allyn & Bacon, 1978.

Montrose M. Wolf received the B.S. degree in psychology in 1959 from the University of Houston, the M.A. degree in psychology in 1961 from Arizona State University, and the Ph.D. degree in psychology in 1963 from Arizona State University. Dr. Wolf began his professional experience as a research assistant-professor at the University of Washington, later served as an assistant professor of psychology at the University of Arizona, then as a research associate, Bureau of Child Research, University of Kansas. Currently he is professor of human development there. Dr. Wolfe collaborated on some of the earliest, classic studies using applied behavior analysis with severe emotionally disturbed children. He holds editorships and consultantships with several professional journals and organizations; he is a past president of the Society for the Experimental Analysis of Behavior and was the first editor for the *Journal of Applied Behavior Analysis*. Dr. Wolf has also served as co-principal investigator and/or director on numerous federal and state research and demonstration projects. He has also published extensively in the areas of child and adolescent development and behavior modification.

Baer, D. M., Wolf, M. M., & Risley, T. R. Some current dimensions of applied behavior analysis. *Journal of Applied Behavior Analysis*, 1968, *1*, 91–97.

Birnbrauer, J. S., Wolf, M. M., Kidder, J. B., & Tague, C. E. Classroom behavior of retarded pupils with token reinforcement. *Journal of Experimental Child Psychology*, 1965, *2*, 219–235.

Wolf, M. M., Risley, T. R., & Mees, H. L. Application of operant conditioning procedures to the behavior problems of an autistic child. *Behavior Research and Therapy*, 1965, *1*, 302–312.

Wolf, M. M., Giles, D., & Hall, R. V. Experiments with token reinforcement in a remedial classroom. *Behavior Research and Therapy*, 1968, *6*, 51–64.

Wolf, M. M., Phillips, E. L., & Fixsen, D. L. The teaching family: A new model for the treatment of deviant child behavior in the community. In S. W. Bijou & E. L. Ribes (Eds.), *First symposium on behavior modification in Mexico*. New York: Academic Press, 1972.

Martin R. Wong is associate professor of educational psychology at George Peabody College for Teachers. Prior to his present position, he was associate professor of educational psychology at the University of Nebraska and assistant professor in the Drug Information and Education Program at the University of Minnesota. Dr. Wong has written numerous articles in the areas of drug education and classroom management.

Dr. Wong received the B.A. degree in journalism from San Jose State College in 1960, the M.A. degree in educational psychology from Michigan State University in 1967, and the Ph.D. degree in educational psychology from Michigan State University in 1969.

Heistad, G., Zimmerman, R., & Wong, M. Measuring changes in attitude toward drug abuse. *Journal of Drug Education,* 1975, *5,* 41–54.

Randall, D., & Wong, M. Drug education: A review. *Journal of Drug Education,* 1976, 6, 1–21.

Wong, M. A three dimensional structure of drug attitudes. *Journal of Drug Education,* 1976, 6, 181–191.

Wong, M. Theories and models in drug education. *Contemporary Educational Psychology,* 1976, *1,* 285–303.

Wong, M., & Zimmerman, R. Changes in teachers' attitudes toward drugs associated with a social seminar course. *Journal of Drug Education,* 1975, *4,* 361–367.

Indices

Name Index

Name Index

Cohen, H. L., 207
Cohen, J. S., 96, 347
Cohen, S. A., 64
Cohen, S. I., 208
Colarusso, R. P., 64, 408
Cole, M., 295
Colella, H. V., 266
Coleman, J. C., 71–72
Coleman, J. S., 10, 16, 22, 41
Coles, R., 243
Connolly, C., 243
Cook, I. D., 149
Covington, M. V., 263
Cox, S., 103, 104
Craig, R. C., 396
Crawford, J. L., 190
Cronbach, L. J., 101
Crouse, W. H., 151
Cruickshank, W. M., 51
Crutchfield, R., 263
Cullinan, D., 1, 336, 397, 398
Curti, M., 162

D'Alonzo, B. J., 169
Dauw, E. G., 338
Davidson, W., 207
Davies, L., 263
Davis, E. D., 69
Davis, K. E., 154
Davison, R., 168
DeBusk, C. W., 153
DeCharms, R., 198
deHirsch, K., 105
Dellefield, C., 158
Deshler, D. D., 23, 104, 105
Devine, V. T., 258
DeWitt, F. B., 105
Diggory, J. C., 236, 245
Dinkmeyer, D., 263
DiTullio, W. M., 266
Divoky, D., 243
Dohner, V. A., 200
Douglass, H. R., 338
Douvan, E., 36
Downs, M. C., 20, 91
Drabman, R., 207
Dreikurs, R., 261, 266
Ducharme, R., 257
Dunn, L., 48, 246
Dunn, L. M., 20
Durkin, D., 99
Dye, C. J., 268

Edgerton, R. B., 335
Eisenberg, J., 42
Eisenberg, L., 187
Ellis, A., 263
Engelmann, S., 257
Epstein, M. H., 1, 261, 336, 397, 398
Erikson, E. H., 4, 37, 39, 197, 239, 253
Etzioni, H., 341
Evans, M. A., 104
Evans, R., 85
Evans, R. N., 76, 349
Eyman, R. K., 335

Fagen, S. A., 27, 235, 237, 238, 245, 247,
    248, 249, 250, 258, 260, 261, 262, 263,
    264, 266, 267, 399
Fantini, M. D., 281
Farley, E. M., 165, 180
Fay, A., 268
Fedder, R., 238
Felixbrod, J. J., 266

Felker, D. W., 245, 250
Fenstermacher, G. D., 279, 282
Fernald, G., 65, 84
Ferreira, A., 15
Filipczak, J. A., 207
Fishburne, P. M., 187
Fixsen, D. L., 203, 206, 209, 210, 266, 400,
    405, 406, 409
Flanagan, J., 209
Flocco, W., 190
Follingstad, D., 196
Forness, S. R., 243, 252, 260
Fox, R., 267
Fraenkel, W.A., 152
Franklin, B., 162
Franzen, M., 266
Frederiksen, C. B., 262
Frederiksen, L. W., 262
Freud, A., 239
Friedenberg, E., 101
Friedman, R., 59

Gallagher, P. A., 261
Ganzer, V. J., 209
Gartner, A., 262, 267
Gaudry, E., 243
Gearheart, B. R., 243, 257, 260
Geis, G., 194
Gersten, J., 42
Gesell, A., 3
Getman, G. M., 98
Getzels, J. W., 341
Gibby, R. G., 20
Giffin, M., 103, 105
Giles, D., 409
Gillespie, P. H., 107, 108
Ginott, H. G., 268
Girardeau, F. L., 207
Glass, G. V., 64
Glasser, W., 241, 250, 261, 262, 263
Goffman, E., 205
Goins, J. T., 52
Gold, M. W., 257
Goldhammer, K., 166
Goldiamond, I., 246
Goldstein, A.P., 247, 249, 257, 267
Goodlad, J. I., 256, 279, 281, 282, 283
Goodman, J. K., 197
Goodman, K., 101
Goodman, K. S., 65
Goodman, L., 20, 22, 25, 49, 52, 64, 89, 91,
    93, 96, 97, 98, 100, 110, 401
Goodman, Y. M., 65, 83
Gordon, S., 103, 241
Gordon, T., 262, 266, 268
Gorham, K., 263
Gorman, A. H., 259
Gottlieb, J., 170
Gottman, J., 261, 265
Goulding, P.M., 149
Grady, S. C., 167
Graubard, p., 262
Gray, J., 261
Green, G.J., 153
Green, M., 197
Greene, M. F., 243
Gronlund, N. E., 266
Grossman, H., 290, 291
Grunwald, B., 261
Gryla, L., 198
Guedalia, L. J., 237, 250, 258, 262, 266, 267,
    399

Hall, G. Stanley, 2–3

Name Index

Little, J., 257
Lloyd, J., 397
Logan, B., 249, 263, 264, 266, 268
Long, N. J., 237, 249, 250, 257, 261, 266, 267, 399
Lordeman, A., 59
Lotsof, A., 349
Loufer, M. W., 187
Lovitt, T. C., 65, 257
Lyman, H. H., 91–92
Lyon, H. C., 259

McCandless, B. R., 5
McCarthy, E., 42
McCoy, G. F., 43, 50, 339, 396
MacCulloch, M. J., 206
McDill, E., 54
MacDonald, E., 154
MacDonald, W. S., 262
McFall, R., 261, 265
McIntosh, D., 48
McIntyre, J., 259
McKay, G. D., 263, 393
McKee, J. M., 207
MacLeod, A., 252
McLoughlin, J. A., 107
McMenemy, R. A., 108
MacMillan, D. L., 43, 59–60, 109, 111, 112
McNutt, G., 24, 63, 404, 408
McPartland, J., 54
Mackin, E. F., 76
Madsen, C. H., 257
Madsen, C. K., 257
Mahler, C., 268
Mahoney, M. J., 247, 249, 262
Mangel, C., 107
Mangum, G. L., 76, 85
Mann, A. J., 23
Mann, L., 20, 22, 49, 52, 64, 91, 93, 96, 98, 100, 110, 401, 407
Mann, P., 249, 257
Manneheim, K., 342
Manton, A. B., 339
Margules, M., 151
Marland, S. P., 157, 159
Martin, E. W., 13, 126
Martin, R., 27, 258, 305, 308, 403
Maslow, A. H., 33–34, 196, 200, 240, 283
Masters, R., 200
Masterson, J. F. 32, 42
Mauser, A. J., 407
Meacham, M. L., 256
Mees, H. L., 409
Mehrens, W. A., 396
Meichenbaum, D. H., 207, 249
Meisels, S. J., 286
Mercer, C. D., 398
Mergerowitz, J. H., 197
Metz, A. S., 18, 20, 337, 340
Meyen, Edward L., 23
Meyer, B. D., 167
Miller, L., 42, 44
Miller, R., 42
Miller, S. R., 349, 350
Miller, T. A., 349
Miller, T. L., 112
Millon, R., 71–72, 82
Millon, T., 71–72, 82
Minskoff, E. H., 261
Mintz, P. C., 23
Mitts, B., 261
Montemayor, R., 5
Moran, M. R., 257
Morgan, E. L., 194

Moriarty, P. H., 257
Morse, W. C., 250, 257, 258, 261, 267, 274
Mosher, R., 263
Mulligan, W., 104
Munns, J. G., 194
Murray, H. A., 196
Myers, P., 51
Myers, R. E., 265
Myklebust, H. R., 98, 105, 108, 260

Neff, W. S., 128
Neill, S. B., 11
Nelson, C. M., 18, 20, 21, 262, 280
Nelson, R. T., 262
Newcomer, P. L., 52, 96, 97
Newman, R., 268
Newman, R. G., 250, 257, 261, 266
Newmark, G., 292
Nicholson, B., 345
Nietupski, J., 335
Noar, G., 260
Nolen, P. A., 258
Norem-Hebeisen, A. A., 197
Northcutt, N., 92

Offer, D., 239
O'Leary, K. D., 101, 207, 247, 249, 258, 261, 266, 267
O'Leary, S. G., 101, 247, 249, 258, 261, 267
Oliver, L. I., 9
Oliverson, B., 349
Olshansky, S., 346
Olton, R., 263
O'Neal, L., 154
O'Toole, J., 12
Otto, W., 108

Palkes, H., 42
Palomares, U., 249, 263, 264, 266, 268
Pantzer, B. D., 165, 180
Parsons, T., 341
Payne, B., 200
Payne, J. S., 398
Pearson, P. O., 74
Pepper, F., 261
Pfeiffer, J. W., 259
Phillips, E. A., 203, 209, 210, 266, 405, 406
Phillips, E. L., 26, 203, 206, 207, 208, 209, 210, 211, 257, 266, 400, 405, 406, 409
Phillips, L., 239, 261
Phillips, M. W., 172, 395
Phillips, W., 64
Piers, M., 243
Pirsig, R. M., 352
Pittel, S. M., 198
Polk, K., 56
Polsgrove, L., 247, 249, 265
Poulos, R. W., 258
Premack, D. H., 261
Price, M., 100
Proger, B., 96

Quay, H. C., 265

Rabichow, H. G., 258
Randall, D., 189, 190, 195, 410
Randall, F., 152
Randolph, N., 260
Ratcliff, R. G., 349
Raths, L. E., 192
Redl, F., 257, 258, 262, 267, 274
Regan, C., 168
Reimer, E., 294
Reinert, H. R., 258

416

Name Index

Subject Index

Subject Index

Subject Index

Stanford Research Institute, 107, 108, 109
State employment office, and vocational education, 136
State rehabilitation agencies, 137
Statutory actions. See Public Laws (P.L.)
Storm and stress period, 35–36, 239
Stress, minimized, 257, 261, 266
Students
    analysis of mildly handicapped, 95–98
    characteristics, entry, 255, 259, 263
    goals, 256, 259, 263
    personal growth of, 298–301
Subcommittee to Investigate Juvenile Delinquency, 11
Subcultural differences, and delinquency, 55
Suicidal behaviors, 47–48
Symbols, used in society, 36
Symptomatic Adolescent Research Project, 42

Tasks, 257, 261, 265
Teachers
    as advocates, 301
    personal growth of, 298–301
    role as special educators, 133–35
    team of, in vocational education, 131–33, 135–38
    training of, 22–23
    and unsuccessful adolescents, 243–46
Teacher-pupil relationship, 344
Teaching-family model, 26, 210
    curriculum, 218
    individualized counseling component, 212
    interaction, 219
    motivation system, 211, 219–22
    professional consultants, 216
    programming for natural home, 224–28
    programming for school behavior, 223
    realistic environment, 216–18
    research and evaluation, 231–32
    self-government, 212–22
    token economy, 211
    youth characteristics, 228–31
Teaching parents, 212
    responsibility of, 213–15
    training, 215
Teaching techniques, specialized, 98, 100
Testing, psychometric, 128–29 (see also Assessment)
Test-related approaches, for mildly handicapped, 97
Token economies. 207, 208, 211
Traditional school, 279
Trust, and psychological functioning, 197–98

Underachievers, 93, 106
U.S. Bureau of the Census, 8, 18
U.S. Department of Health, Education, and Welfare, 9, 69, 311, 335
    Comptroller General's Report to Congress, 133, 136

U.S. Labor Department, 138
    Employment and Training Administration, 137
U.S. Office for Civil Rights, 313
U.S. Office of Education (USOE), 23, 49, 77, 178, 312, 313, 339
    Office of Career Education, 157, 158, 180
U.S. Senate Report 94–168, 316, 318
University of Kansas, Department of Human Development and Family Life, 203, 204, 212, 231

Values-clarification program, for drug education, 191–92
Venereal disease, 14, 15
Violence and vandalism, in schools, 10–12
Visual difficulties, 50
Vocation, defined, 158
Vocational assessment, 128–29, 142
Vocational counselors, shortage of, 346
Vocational education, 25, 68, 82
    arguments against, 124–25
    arguments for, 126
    competencies, six, 130–33
    components of, five, 128–30
    defined, 122–124
    differs from general education, 124
    and the employer, 138
    the future of, 144–48
    introduction to, 121
    materials for students, 149–52
    materials for teachers, 153–54
    model program, nine steps, 140–44
    the need for, 127
    and open education, 294–98
    present focus on, 346
    role with public education, 347
    special educator's role, 133–35
    team of teachers, 135–38
    training, 129
Vocational Education Act of 1963, 163, 169
    (see also P.L. Public Laws)
Vocational Information and Evaluation Work Sample (VIEWS), 173
Vocational problems, 12
Vocational Rehabilitation Act of 1973, 91, 137
Vocational Rehabilitation Amendment of 1954, 347
Vocational Rehabilitation Service, 137
Vocational rehabilitation/special education work-study programs, 168–69

White House Conference on Youth, 22
White House Conference on Handicapped Individuals (1977), 178
Work format, 260, 265
Work-sample methods
    in career education, 172–73
    and vocational assessment, 129
Work-study programs, 168–69
Work-study school, 280